Early Childhood Special Education:

Birth to Three

Edited by
June B. Jordan
James J. Gallagher
Patricia L. Hutinger
Merle B. Karnes

CEC

ERIC

A Product of the ERIC Clearinghouse on Handicapped and Gifted Children
Published by The Council for Exceptional Children

Library of Congress Cataloging-in-Publication Data

Early childhood special education: birth to three / edited by June B. Jordan ... [et al.].

"A product of the ERIC Clearinghouse on Handicapped and Gifted Children."
Bibliography: p.
1. Handicapped children--Services for--United States. 2. Infants--Services for--United States
3. Toddlers--Services for--United States. 4. Special education--United States. I. Jordan,
June B. II. Council for Exceptional Children. III. ERIC Clearinghouse on Handicapped and
Gifted Children.
HV888.5.E24 1988
362.4'0880542--dc19
87-36529 CIP
ISBN 0-86586-179-X

A product of the ERIC Clearinghouse on Handicapped and Gifted Children.

Published in 1988 jointly by The Council for Exceptional Children and its Division for Early
Childhood (DEC), 1920 Association Drive, Reston, Virginia 22091-1589.

Second Printing 1990.
Stock No. P325 Price $27.00

This publication was prepared with funding from the U.S. Department of Education, Office
of Educational Research and Improvement, contract No. 400-84-0010. Contractors
undertaking such projects under government sponsorship are encouraged to express freely
their judgment in professional and technical matters. Prior to publication the manuscript was
submitted to The Council for Exceptional Children for critical review and determination of
professional competence. This publication has met such standards. Points of view, however,
do not necessarily represent the official view or opinions of either The Council for Exceptional
Children or the Department of Education.

Printed in the United States of America.

Book cover and design by Angeline V. Culfogienis.

Update on Early Childhood Special Education: Birth to Three

❏ Since the printing of this text 2 years ago, the nation has experienced a flurry of activity related to providing early intervention services to young children with handicaps and their families. The impetus for this momentum, to a large extent, has been states' efforts to implement P.L. 99-457, the Education of the Handicapped Act Amendments of 1986. As discussed in Chapter 10, P.L. 99-457 requires that in order for states to receive funding, they must have policies that assure a free and appropriate education is available to all eligible children from their third birthdays by 1991; and also by 1991, states must have in place a statewide system of early intervention services for eligible children from birth through age 2. These timelines and the increased federal funding have resulted in extensive state planning activities, increases in state early intervention funding, efforts to coordinate existing interagency resources, and efforts to identify and implement effective and appropriate personnel standards and family-focused methods of service delivery.

One of the most evident arenas of change and activity has been the public policy arena. In order to meet the impending 1991 timelines of policies for preschool full service and statewide early intervention systems, states have focused on four major policy areas: coordination, eligibility determinations, funding, and state legislation.

States have been involved in many coordination efforts over the past 2 to 4 years. First of all, all states established Interagency Coordinating Councils as required under P.L. 99-457. Secondly, states have been attempting to identify and coordinate all existing resources in order to assess their ability to serve all eligible children and families, and what additional resources are necessary. Finally, states have to varying degrees been attempting to coordinate the birth-to-3 planning efforts with their efforts to plan services for 3- to 5-year-olds and with efforts to plan services for nonhandicapped children.

Determining who will be eligible for early intervention services has also been a focus of recent attention. P.L. 99-457 gives states great discretion in determining who will be considered handicapped or developmentally delayed, and whether to serve any or all children considered to be "at risk" of developing a delay or handicapping condition. States have paid early attention to this policy area largely due to the impact on the number of children subsequently entitled to services and the resources, therefore, that will be needed to provide those services. Thus, state and federal funding levels have been a necessary initial concern to parents, advocates, service providers, and policy makers. While every state governor chose to participate in the early stages of P.L. 99-457 and in developing early intervention services, they and other groups have cautioned that without sufficient levels of federal and state dollars, the goal of providing services to all eligible children is an impossible one for states to meet. Many states have increased their state funding. Federal funds have increased from no appropriation in 1986 for such a program for infants and toddlers to $79 million in 1989-90; and from $28.7 million in 1986 for the preschool program to $251 million in 1989-90.

In order to meet the 1991 requirements, states have concentrated their legislative efforts on the above funding issues and on meeting the requirement that there be a state policy that entitles preschool services. Therefore, most state-level service mandates passed since 1986 have been for the 3- to 5-year-old population--and have been dramatic indeed. Since 1986, 14 states have passed legislation mandating that services be provided to children from age 3 or below by 1991-92 (National Association of State Directors of Special Education, [NASDSE], 1989). NASDSE reports that:

- The mandates of two of the states, Minnesota and Utah, were effective as of 1988-89.
- The mandates of three of the states (Idaho, Wyoming, and New York) were effective as of 1989-90.
- Six states (Arkansas, California, Florida, Ohio, Tennessee, and Vermont) passed mandates to become effective in 1991-92.
- Five remaining states (Delaware, Kentucky, Missouri, South Carolina, and Pennsylvania) reported that they anticipate changes in their legislation mandates by 1990; two states (Oregon and West Virginia) expect changes by 1991.

Since 1988, the date of the first printing of this text, nearly all of this legislative activity has taken place. While only Minnesota has passed new legislation since 1988 enacting a mandate from birth, several states report that such legislative action is anticipated (Pennsylvania, Oregon, West Virginia). As noted in Chapter 10, early intervention legislative mandates have typically followed a "trickle-down" pattern; that is, states enact mandates for the 3- to 5-year-old population and then eventually lower the entitlement to children from birth. If this pattern holds true, legislative activities will be focusing on providing entitlements to eligible children from birth in the years to come.

Barbara J. Smith
University of Pittsburgh
Pittsburgh, Pennsylvania
January 1990

REFERENCES

National Association of State Directors of Special Education. (October 18, 1989). *Memorandum to all State Directors of Special Education regarding 1989 NASDSE survey results*, pp. 1-5.

Contents

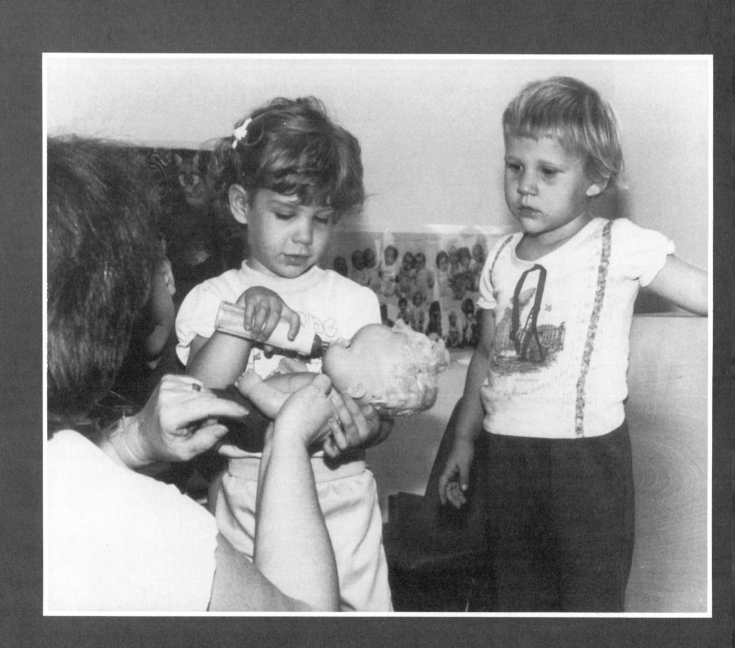

1.
Introduction

James J. Gallagher

It is important to realize how the current legislative mandate differs from P.L. 94-142.

❏ This volume represents a comprehensive effort on the part of a group of well-qualified professionals to describe the nature of a new territory, infants and toddlers with handicapping conditions, that Public Law 99-457, the Education of the Handicapped Act Amendments of 1986, propels us into, whether we are ready or not. For many years we have discussed the importance of the early years to the development of children with handicapping conditions, but it took a legislative mandate to energize entire professions into considering the consequences of a total mandate for service. It is important to realize just how thoroughly the current legislative mandate for service to children from birth on differs from the earlier comprehensive legislation, Public Law 94-142, the Education for All Handicapped Children Act of 1976. Of course, the title of that earlier legislation was a misnomer since it did not provide for *all* handicapped children, particularly children from ages 0 through 2, and that is precisely what the new legislation is about—to close the circle, finally to make a federal commitment to provide resources so that every handicapped child receives appropriate services.

Fundamental changes in work patterns can cause difficulty.

The implementation of P.L. 94-142 was, and remains in many areas, a difficult task, mainly because its provisions contain much more than a commitment of federal resources. It also contains provisions that require changes in the professional's approach to these children and in their relationship with parents. Anything that requires fundamental changes in the work patterns of a group of well-established professionals can be counted upon to cause some difficulty. The introduction of an individualized education program, the concept of the least restrictive environment, the due process provisions, plus other provisions all have the potential for major implementation hassles.

P.L. 99-457 has its share of policy issues.

With P.L. 94-142 there was at least a stable base, the established public school system, to deal with. Even those of us who wished to depart from established practice, at least knew where our starting point was. With children from 0 to 3 years of age, however, we are more on our own. The legislation for this age group, P.L. 99-457, also has its share of policy issues that guarantee a difficult implementation, including the provision for an individualized family service plan, the requirements for cross-disciplinary cooperation, and the defining of an "at-risk" group.

We have the responsibility of devising a service world of our own.

Planning for a complex service delivery process to a diverse clientele, without having a model already in place, is both anxiety producing and opportunity producing. Instead of complaining about having to live with a "world we never made," the public school system, we have the responsibility of devising a service world of our own and making the rules for its operation, for good or ill.

Questions addressed represent a good primer in pursuing this field.

The chapters in this volume all try to grapple with the reality of these issues and seek some plausible answers to them given our current knowledge and practice. The questions addressed in these chapters represent a good primer for anyone interested in pursuing this field. Some of these questions are as follows:

1. **Who will provide leadership for this program at the state and local level?** (Garland & Linder: Chapter 2, Administrative Challenges in Early Intervention). The lack of established administrative channels for this program is best reflected in the fact that at least five different state agencies have been identified by governors as the lead agency for their state in planning for implementation of P.L. 99-457. Whoever is determined to be the lead agency, the other agencies will have to

participate in a significant way for the program to work at all. How will all of this play out at the state level? The local level?

2. ***How do we find the infants and toddlers with handicaps who need services?*** (Hutinger: Chapter 3, Linking Screening, Identification, and Assessment with Curriculum). If we cannot find them, we cannot serve them, and we have no established organization like the public school system to help us by gathering practically all children in an accessible place; nor do we have the tools, the measuring instruments, in which we can place confidence.

3. ***Are there programs currently existing that can provide effective models for the new program?*** (Karnes & Stayton: Chapter 4, Model Programs for Infants and Toddlers with Handicaps). We have a number of existing programs whose experience can be drawn upon as these new programs grow and mature. Not the least of these earlier models is the Handicapped Children's Early Education Program (HCEEP), established in 1968 for the purpose of providing models of excellence in the provision of services for young handicapped children. This demonstration program was designed so that other programs would be encouraged to begin services to preschool handicapped children. The hope was that we would have some guidelines or proven practices to follow when major state or federal action occurred. There have been several hundred such programs funded, and the question now is, How helpful will they prove to be in the design of this much broader service delivery mandate?

4. ***How shall we maximize the parent involvement in early childhood special education?*** (Robinson, Rosenberg, & Beckman: Chapter 5, Parent Involvement in Early Childhood Special Education). There has been, in the 1980s, a major emphasis in early childhood programs on parent involvement. Yet this trend has been a recent one, and many professionals already in the field have had little training or experience in designing such programs. How do we follow the mandate of P.L. 99-457 for an individualized family service plan in a way that will allow us to take advantage of the parental resources, provide for parental empowerment, and protect family privacy?

5. ***Who are the professionals or paraprofessionals who will be called upon to provide service in this program?*** (McCollum & Hughes: Chapter 6, Staffing Patterns and Team Models in Infancy Programs). How will we use the existing service models to define our appropriate roles? The interests of the client and family are matched in this instance with the interests of a variety of professional fields concerned with continuing or expanding their current influence. In a community of equals, who decides who will do what?

6. ***Will we have some new professional roles created by this new program?*** (Thorp & McCollum: Chapter 7, Defining the Infancy Specialization in Early Childhood Special Education). There is a clear likelihood that we will modify existing professionals' roles by requiring them to work in transdisciplinary teams, but there is also a genuinely new role to be created here. Whether we call it the *infant interventionist* or *developmental specialist* or *case manager*, there is a new set of skills and a much broader professional orientation than we have been accustomed to in the past. What are the duties inherent in the new role? Who will prepare professionals for their new roles, and where will such training take place?

7. ***How will we work across disciplines, each with its own differing languages and traditions, to form an effective service team?*** (Woodruff & McGonigel: Chapter 8, Early Intervention Team Approaches: The Transdisciplinary Model). This is not merely a version of the second question but really goes to the heart of what has always been a difficult issue for those providing services for handicapped children, namely, how do we work together, who will lead the team, how will we compromise our own discipline's approach in order to work with others? Even with the child guidance clinic model, which stressed interdisciplinary coordination, we have no clear path to a solution.

8. ***How do we know that what we are doing is helping anyone?*** (Johnson: Chapter 9, Program Evaluation: The Key to Quality Programming). As difficult as evaluation has been as a concept and as an operation in standard educational settings, the problems become even more difficult with this young target population. We face the problem of assessing not just the particular child involved but also the child's family. It is entirely possible that the gains from service delivery will be more manifest in the other members of the family than in the target child. Unless we have a clear portrait of the changes in all members of the family unit, we may well underestimate our own impact.

9. ***In what way can public policy help families with young children with handicaps?*** (Smith: Chapter 10, Early Intervention Public Policy: Past, Present, and Future). For decades we have made statements about how important it is to identify and provide treatment for handicapped children early in their life spans, but it took federal legislation to put this principle into full-scale action. What are the potential uses of the policy route that can facilitate the goals of high-quality service? We have not completed the policy statements about infants and toddlers and their families with P.L. 99-457. That law gives great leeway to states and local communities to devise their own policies in the process of implementing the federal law, so policy will continue to be set for several years at various levels of government.

10. ***How can this legislation be implemented more effectively?*** (Trohanis: Chapter 11, Preparing for Change: The Implementation of Public Law 99-457). We are well aware that good legislation, or well-meaning efforts at state or federal levels, can come to naught at the local level unless the program is implemented with intelligence and due concern for the input of everyone, but particularly those at the local level. The implementation of a law such as this may well be one of the most delicate conditions of statecraft, all the more so for not being recognized as such. The success of this law in providing services to children with handicaps will depend heavily on how the law is translated at state and local levels.

As all of the authors take pains to state, in one way or another, we are feeling our way in this new wilderness. We have profited immensely from earlier developments and demonstration programs in special education. There are major research and personnel training efforts that clearly are a major resource as well. We need, above all, a good supply of patience and willingness to discuss mutual problems so that we can all do what we wish to do—provide high-quality services for children and families who are much in need of those services.

We need a good supply of patience and willingness to discuss mutual problems.

2.
Administrative Challenges in Early Intervention

Corinne W. Garland and Toni W. Linder

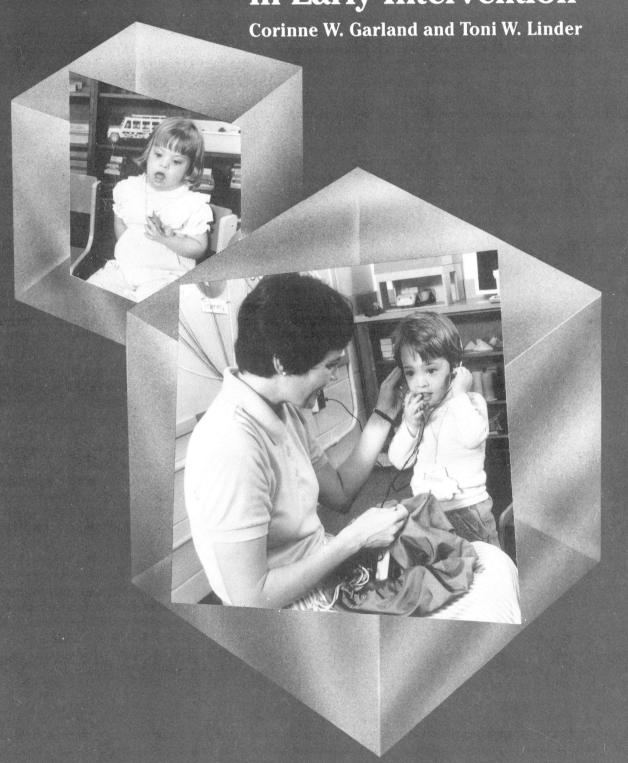

❑ Early intervention programs, like all educational and human service programs, exist within the context of some form of governance or administration. Typically, they do not suffer for lack of management—defined by Webster, oddly enough, as "handling, controlling; making and keeping submissive; altering by manipulation"; and finally, "succeeding in accomplishing; directing or carrying on business or affairs." They may, however, suffer from lack of leadership. Webster defines lead as "to lead or guide on a way; to direct on a course; to direct the performance of, as in an orchestra" (a particularly apt analogy for our purposes); "to go at the head of or to be first among; to tend toward a definite result."

Good management should be the minimum performance expectation.

Good management, to be sure, is necessary for the efficient program operations that funders and consumers expect. However, good management should be the minimum performance expectation of administrators. The field of early intervention, challenged anew by the opportunity of the Education of the Handicapped Act Amendments of 1986 (P.L. 99-457), needs administrators who are able to go beyond management and are willing to make a commitment to leadership. Bennis (1984) made the distinction clear. "Leaders are people who do the right thing; managers are people who do things right." Early intervention needs administrators who can guide the course of service and program development, conduct the collaborative work of multiple disciplines and agencies as an orchestra, and direct the agency toward expected results for children and families. This chapter explores the tasks critical to leadership in early intervention.

MODELS FOR ADMINISTRATION

❑ Several models for leadership and administration can be applied to early intervention. Wimpelberg, Abroms, and Catardi (1985) examined four such models presented by Bolman and Deal (1984):

1. The technical model.
2. The human relations model.
3. The political model.
4. The symbolic model.

The technical model is a structural one.

The *technical model* is a structural one, typical of many educational institutions. It is based on the assumption that organizations "exist primarily to accomplish established goals" (Wimpelberg et al., 1985, p. 3) and that a linear and specialized organizational structure designed to coordinate and control, typically from the top down, is the most appropriate structure for meeting established goals. We have had ample opportunity to observe this model at work.

The human relations model is based on organizations existing in order to serve human needs.

The *human relations model* is based on the assumption that "organizations exist to serve human needs" (Wimpelberg et al., 1985). The success of the organization rests not on the structure, but on the degree to which personnel participate in the work of the organization and the degree to which organizational and personal goals are in synchrony.

The political model is based on the power to succeed in competition for resources.

The *political model*, emerging in the literature in the austere financial climate of the 1980s, is based on the power of the organization to succeed in the competition for dwindling resources through strategies of bargaining, negotiating, and successful conflict resolution.

Finally, the *symbolic model* rests not on structure, participation, or power, but on meaning (Wimpelberg et al., 1985), or the perception of an organization by its constituents. The success of this model, which emphasizes marketing strategies of image building and messages of feeling rather than fact, is typified by the funds generated by entertainer Jerry Lewis for multiple sclerosis research through "Jerry's Kids." As we examine the tasks of leadership in early intervention, we will want to reexamine the array of models at our disposal to determine which ones will serve us best.

The symbolic model rests on the perception of an organization by its constitutents.

Basic Leadership Tasks

❏ Organizational literature not only gives us models for administration, but defines basic leadership tasks and skills. Ends and Page (1977) suggested 10 basic leadership functions:

1. Establish, communicate, and clarify goals.
2. Secure commitment to goals.
3. Define and negotiate roles.
4. Secure commitment to assigned roles.
5. Develop clear plans for activities.
6. Set and communicate performance standards.
7. Provide feedback to individuals and to the group.
8. Provide coaching and supervision.
9. Provide a model of enthusiasm and a sense of purpose.
10. Control the group process.

Bennis (1984) identified four sets of leadership skills which might be seen as encompassing all 10 functions. The 90 successful leaders in his study shared a clear sense of goals or mission; the ability to communicate those goals; the ability to inspire and maintain the trust of others; and a clear understanding and effective use of their own skills.

A picture emerges from these studies and others (Lay-Dopyera & Dopyera, 1985) of the leader as one who is committed to a mission that is clearly communicated to others, and who creates an organizational environment in which the responsibility for both goal setting and goal accomplishment is shared with a team. Clear goal setting, discussed earlier as the basis for the technical model of administration, is widely cited in the literature as the first step in effective management. However, in a departure from the technical model in which administration hands down goals to be accomplished by subordinates, organizational researchers (Bennis, 1984; Dyer, 1987; Ends & Page, 1977) are clear that in organizations that perform well, leadership tasks are shared with team members. This seems especially important for early intervention programs.

Clear goal setting...first step in effective management.

Leadership tasks are shared with team members.

Drawing from the organizational literature, we can conclude that there are at least four tasks specific to administration of early intervention programs which imply the need for an alternative to the technical model:

- Building an early intervention team.
- Creating an environment which supports families as members of the team.
- Setting goals in collaboration with that team.
- Communicating goals to those who can effect their accomplishment.

The following section addresses the administrative aspects of building a team; Chapter 8 by Woodruff and McGonigel deals with programmatic considerations related to the team approach.

BUILDING AN EARLY INTERVENTION TEAM

Team Building: A Historical View

The team concept derives from the human relations model.

❑ The team approach is not original to early intervention. The team concept derives from the human relations model of management, emphasizing the importance of the group and the use of group methods to build effective work relationships. Beginning with the now famous Hawthorne study carried out by Harvard faculty at an Illinois plant of the Western Electric Company, researchers in the field of organizational development have examined group dynamics and the process of team building (Bennis, 1984; Dyer, 1987; Ends & Page, 1977). Their work provides the field of early intervention with both the theoretical and methodological support for what now carries the weight of legislation—a team approach.

Prior to the passage of Public Law 94-142, (the Education for All Handicapped Children Act of 1975), handicapped children were typically served by a single discipline, most frequently a classroom teacher, while other specialty services were recommended based on a child's "primary presenting problem." Specialists in the fields of speech and language and physical and occupational therapy treated children in clinical settings that were isolated from classroom programs.

Children were "pulled" out to receive therapies.

The multidisciplinary team evaluation and the related services mandated in P.L. 94-142 were products of a growing understanding by parents and professionals of the compound effects of developmental delays. However, the multidisciplinary team was based on the assumption that while a variety of disciplines were needed, they could function independently of one another. Children were "pulled out" of their classrooms in order to receive the speech, physical, and occupational therapies prescribed in their IEPs.

Problems in the multidisciplinary model were apparent. Agencies and professionals delivered services that frequently overlapped, and parents were frequently left to choose between conflicting priorities and service strategies which they only rarely had been involved in selecting. It was the harsh economic reality of the 1970s that forced professionals to reexamine an approach that resulted in wasteful and duplicative efforts, and to develop new, collaborative, "interdisciplinary" strategies in which communication increased and therapists were invited into the classroom to integrate their activities with a child's educational program.

Team members began to view children from a broad developmental perspective.

Finally, as teachers, therapists, and representatives of other disciplines worked together, discussing child needs and planning activities, they developed programs that integrated efforts across developmental domains and disciplinary boundaries. Team members began to view children from a broad developmental perspective and began to share information and expertise with one another. A decade ago, the United Cerebral Palsy 0-3 Project (Patterson & Hutchinson, 1976) developed a model for interaction of disciplines that offered teams the opportunity to enhance the quality of information sharing and to minimize intrusiveness on the family. This is the service delivery approach we call *transdisciplinary*. (The evolution of the transdisciplinary team approach is treated in greater detail in Chapter 8 by Woodruff and McGonigel.)

Extending Team Membership

❑ The role of the family on the team has undergone a similar evolutionary process. Prior to P.L. 94-142, institutional procedures isolated parents from decision making and even from information about their own children. However, P.L. 94-142 required schools to secure at least a token level of parent participation through the IEP process. Since then, research supporting the importance of family involvement has heightened the level of acceptance and acknowledgment of the family as full team members. The gradual evolution of family involvement will be accelerated considerably by the impact of P.L. 99-457, which will move early intervention programs further and faster toward services in which families are fully participating members.

Evolution of family involvement will be accelerated by P.L. 99-457.

Organizational and Multiagency Teams

❑ The early intervention leader must continue to expand his or her view of team membership, crossing the boundary of the early intervention program, even the walls of one agency, and ensuring team development at several levels (Figure 1). The administrator must ensure that the early intervention team exists as part of a larger "organizational team" which brings working groups together to develop shared goals and expectations that both complement and exceed their individual tasks or missions. While each team's work may be highly differentiated, it is important to have a mechanism of integration to tie the group together for goal setting (Lawrence & Lorsch, 1967). When this organizational team works well, it is more easily incorporated into the larger community or interagency team.

The political model of administration, that is, the building of constituencies and securing of resources, supports the bargaining for and pooling of resources among agencies. *Networking*, a key word in business and organizational politics, is necessary among agencies to meet the complex service needs of children and families and to build stronger bases of advocacy. New models for multiagency teams are being developed and implemented based on the recognition that no one agency has all the services required to meet the "diverse and complex needs of young children and their families" (Woodruff, McGonigel, Garland, Zeitlin, Shanahan, Chazkel-Hochman, Toole, & Vincent, 1985). By joining forces on a multiagency team, creative skills and resources are joined to carry out problem solving that exceeds the capacity of any one agency.

Networking is necessary among agencies.

Goals of the multiagency team may include (a) assessing needs and planning services to meet the needs of individual children and families; (b) assessing availability of community services for handicapped children; (c) developing new services or modifying existing services to meet community needs; (d) advocating on behalf of children and families on state and local levels with regard to fiscal, legislative and programmatic issues; and (e) coordinating funding for more effective use of community resources.

The administrator can increase the likelihood of success by making a firm commitment of staff time to attend team meetings. The scope of the team's task should determine whether the appropriate participant is an early intervention service provider, a transportation coordinator, an

Figure 1. Team-Building Levels.

LEVEL I	**UNIT TEAMS** • Unidisciplinary • Multidisciplinary • Interdisciplinary • Transdisciplinary
LEVEL II	**ORGANIZATIONAL TEAMS** • Intra-agency • Unit Leaders • Subcommittees • Parent Groups • Advisory Boards
LEVEL III	**INTERAGENCY TEAMS** • Related Local Agencies • Local Support Agencies • Advocacy Groups • State Agency Representatives

executive director, or a board chairman. Regardless of who fills the role, each representative on a multiagency team must be empowered to lend his or her agency's commitment to the decisions of the team.

Individual agency priorities occasionally must be subordinated.

Individual agency priorities and needs occasionally must be subordinated to the needs of the multiagency team. Therefore, administrators must encourage their representatives to take on a new role in a multiagency context. Multiagency team members must suspend, temporarily, their role identification as members of one particular agency's staff in favor of their team membership role. This will allow them to act, while mindful of their agency responsibilities, for the good of the total team. Team representatives must be free to carry out their team goals in a supportive climate in which they do not fear administrative reprisal for team actions.

Creating a Climate for the Team

❑ Team building is a method for helping the team engage in a continuing process of self-examination, gathering information about themselves as individuals and as a group, and using those data to make decisions. Team building, viewed in this way, is a change strategy, and can take place only in an organization in which the leader encourages self-examination and creates a climate that supports change.

Team building is a change strategy.

The climate of a group refers to how the team members feel about one another, how much they enjoy working together, and how they feel about their joint endeavor. It is a mix of attitudes, emotions, and interpersonal behavior. The leader can control the climate first by example and second by dealing directly with inappropriate attitudes, feelings and behaviors...before (they) poison the whole team. (Ends & Page, 1977, p. 52)

Change grows from a perception that an alteration in structure or function is needed (Zaltman & Duncan, 1977). Problems arise when staff and administration do not share similar perceptions. Thus, when the change is suggested by an administrator, staff may react as if disapproval of individual or group performance is implied. However, in a climate in which staff and program evaluation for the purpose of improvement is routine and continuing, change is no stranger, nor is it to be feared. In a climate in which the team participates in self-evaluation and program evaluation, data suggesting the need for change will have been generated by the team or its members. When the climate supports training as a necessary and desirable allocation of program resources, team members are confident that they will have the time, materials, and coaching needed to incorporate change into their repertoire of behaviors.

Problems arise when staff and administration do not share similar perceptions.

In a climate in which the team plays an active role in goal setting, the process of change is a collaborative one. This collaborative process must, of course, include families as members of the team. O'Donnell and Childman (1969) found that consumer participation in change lessens consumers' alienation and enhances their feelings of being in control.

When the team plays an active role in goal setting, the process of change is a collaborative one.

In creating a climate for change, the human resource model of administration serves well, bringing organizational and human needs into synchrony. Maslow (1954) provided a theoretical base for placing a high priority on human needs for continuing self-development, true for organizations as well as individuals. An agency in a dynamic state of growth and change is like Maslow's "self-actualizing" adult or Allport's (1955) "becoming" personality.

The collection of personalities that comprise a team cannot be overlooked (Garland, 1982). Openness and a willingness to take risks are personal characteristics that enhance an individual's ability to make changes. The administrator committed to change as a continuing strategy for organizational development should look for these qualities as program staff are hired. When it is the administrator who lacks those qualities, then the door to the office closes on leadership and change, leaving only management, if that.

Openness and willingness to take risks enhance an individual's ability to make changes.

Dyer (1987) offers a checklist to determine whether the organization is ready for team building. Several items on this checklist (Figure 2) are most appropriate to early intervention programs, making it an excellent instrument for determining the extent to which program leadership supports team building.

Strategies for Team Building

❑ Teams are made, not born, (Fewell, 1983) and the leadership challenge is clear: to create and support an environment in which professionals and families participate in setting goals, and in which they pool their skills and resources to accomplish those goals. There are many opportunities in the management process for administrators committed to building a strong team to provide guidance in this direction.

If an organization is ready to tackle the job of team building, a systematic approach that includes the following steps is necessary:

A systematic approach is necessary.

Figure 2. Dyer's Team Building Checklist.

Are you (or your manager) prepared to start a team-building program? Consider the following statements. To what extent do they apply to you or your department?

	Low		Medium		High
	1	2	3	4	5
1. You are comfortable in sharing organizational leadership and decision making with subordinates and prefer to work in a participative atmosphere.	1	2	3	4	5
2. You see a high degree of interdependence as necessary among functions and workers in order to achieve your goals.	1	2	3	4	5
3. The external environment is highly variable and/or changing rapidly and you need the best thinking of all your staff to plan against these conditions.	1	2	3	4	5
4. You feel you need the input of your staff to plan major changes or develop new operating policies and procedures.	1	2	3	4	5
5. You feel that broad consultation among your people as a group in goals, decisions, and problems is necessary on a continuing basis.	1	2	3	4	5
6. Members of your management team are (or can become) compatible with each other and are able to create a collaborative rather than a competitive environment.	1	2	3	4	5
7. Members of your team are located close enough to meet together as needed.	1	2	3	4	5
8. You feel you need to rely on the ability and willingness of subordinates to resolve critical operating problems directly and in the best interest of the company or organization.	1	2	3	4	5
9. Formal communication channels are not sufficient for the timely exchange of essential information, views, and decisions among your team members.	1	2	3	4	5
10. Organization adaptation requires the use of such devices as project management, task forces, and/or ad hoc problem-solving groups to augment conventional organization structure.	1	2	3	4	5
11. You feel it is important to surface and deal with critical, albeit sensitive, issues that exist in your team.	1	2	3	4	5
12. You are prepared to look at your own role and performance with your team.	1	2	3	4	5
13. You feel there are operating or interpersonal problems that have remained unsolved too long and need the input from all group members.	1	2	3	4	5
14. You need an opportunity to meet with your people and set goals and develop commitment to these goals.	1	2	3	4	5

Note: From *Team Building: Issues and Alternatives* (2nd ed.) by W. Dyer, 1987. Reading, MA: Addison-Wesley. Reprinted by permission.

Step 1. Examine current levels of team interaction.

Step 2. Assess the need for team development.

Step 3. Select priorities.

Step 4. Plan specific strategies.

Step 5. Implement plans.

Step 6. Evaluate strategies used.

Step 7. Reevaluate the level of team functioning.

This is a planning cycle familiar to early interventionists who bring the same diagnostic, data-gathering approach to the assessment and planning of children's individual developmental programs.

Information about the team can be gathered in a variety of ways, using team-building surveys or individual interviews. Figure 3 provides an example of a team-building instrument used by an early intervention program to assess the strengths of the team and the areas in which the team needs work in group process (Neugebauer, 1983). The instrument helps teams to examine the ways in which they work together in setting goals, carrying out plans, and handling conflict. Team members working either individually, in writing, or together, in discussion, rate their team functioning on each of the items offered. Mean scores are tallied, and low items become the priorities for the team. Together, the team must identify team-building goals, strategies for intervention, and time lines for accomplishment and reevaluation.

The instrument helps teams evaluate.

Another good model for team building is offered by Project Bridge (Handley & Spencer, 1986). Project Bridge offers a process for generating alternative strategies in a way that draws on the group's potential for creative problem solving. While Project Bridge was designed specifically to assist teams in generating strategies for serving children and families, like the diagnostic approach suggested above, it is easily generalizable to the team-building task.

Regardless of instrumentation, the accuracy of the needs assessment process depends on the degree to which team members feel safe enough to respond honestly about team performance and team-building needs. Some teams will feel comfortable enough to carry out a needs assessment in a group setting, each individual indicating the score he or she assigned an item, and the group examining its own diversity or consensus. For others, fear of group response or administrative reprisal will make it necessary for team ratings to be done in writing and submitted to a neutral third party such as a consultant. For the administrator entering a situation in which trust does not already abound, the challenge is doubled. The administrator must determine whether he or she has the skills to create an environment in which team building can occur or whether the more specialized skills of a consultant are needed. In such a case, a consultant offers a safe alternative for the team whose members are reluctant to share openly with one another or their leader (Dyer, 1987). Regardless of the process chosen, data from interviews and surveys should be summarized and shared with the group. In team building, as in all organizational goal setting, the role of the group in determining the priorities for their efforts is crucial to the success of the team-building effort.

Some teams will feel comfortable to carry out a needs assessment in a group setting.

A consultant offers a safe alternative.

Administrative commitment to team building is a key ingredient in its success. This commitment is easily communicated to the team by the administrator's allocation of time for the team-building effort, both in the team's schedule and in his or her own schedule. Conversely, the administrator who drops in for a few minutes on the team-building session between budget committee meetings, or who literally takes a back seat in the process, communicates an aloofness from the process that guarantees failure.

Choosing Team Members: Securing Commitment to Roles

❏ Newspaper advertisements for early intervention positions give clues to priorities in hiring. Qualifications such as discipline specialization, educational degree, years of experience, and licensure in the state in which programs operate all meet management requirements, but fail to

Figure 3. Team Effectiveness Rating Scale.

Rate the effectiveness of your team on a scale of 1 to 7 in terms of each of the variables listed below. Below each variable are descriptions of the worst case (rated 1) and the best case (rated 7) for that variable. You can rate your team very low (1), very high (7), or anywhere in between, depending on how you perceive the situation.

_____ 1. Clarity of Goals
   (1) The team has no set goals.
   (7) The team has challenging yet achievable goals which members well understand.

_____ 2. Level of Cohesion
   (1) Team members have no group loyalty; have no sense of belonging to a team; and tend to exhibit hostility toward each other.
   (7) Team members exhibit a strong sense of loyalty to the team; are highly concerned with the performance of the team; and feel responsible for helping each other improve.

_____ 3. Level of Sensitivity
   (1) Team members are insensitive to the needs and feelings of each other; expressions of feelings are ignored or criticized.
   (7) Team members exhibit outstanding sensitivity to each other; feelings are openly expressed and responded to with empathy.

_____ 4. Openness of Communications
   (1) Team members are guarded and cautious in communicating, listen superfically but inwardly reject what others say, and are afraid to criticize or be criticized.
   (7) Team members are open and frank in communicating, reveal to the team what they would be reluctant to expose to others, and can freely express negative reactions without fear of reprisal.

_____ 5. Handling Conflict
   (1) Conflicts are denied, suppressed, or avoided.
   (7) Team members bring conflicts out into the open and work them through.

_____ 6. Decision Making
   (1) When problems or opportunities arise, decisions are delayed endlessly, and, when made, are never implemented.
   (7) Decisions are made on time and implemented fully.

_____ 7. Participation
   (1) The team leader makes all plans and decisions and orders their implementation.
   (7) All team members participate in shaping the decisions and plans for the team.

_____ 8. Evaluation
   (1) The team does not assess any aspect of its performance.
   (7) The team regularly questions the appropriateness of its goals. It evaluates its progress in achieving its goals, the performance of individual team members, and the functioning of the team. Objective feedback is freely and frequently shared.

_____ 9. Control
   (1) Discipline is imposed totally from above.
   (7) Discipline is totally self-imposed; team members are responsible for controlling their own behavior.

_____ 10. Use of Member Resources
   (1) Team members' knowledge, skills, and experiences are not utilized by the team.
   (7) Team members' resources are fully utilized by the team.

Note: Team Effectiveness Rating Scale, by R. Neugebauer, 1983. Reprinted with permission from the November, 1983 issue of the *Child Care Information Exchange* (a management magazine for center directors), P.O. Box 2890, Redmond, WA 98073.

lead toward team building. New staff members must bring not only all the necessary and obvious professional qualifications, but also a commitment to the team approach. Staff must perceive their roles not simply as members of their disciplines, but also as members of an early intervention team, and as part of the larger organizational team. Personnel interviews must address the candidate's ability to contribute to a team. Job descriptions must delineate not only disciplinary but team expectations and responsibilities.

New staff members must bring a commitment to the team approach.

A team approach demands mutual respect among team members and across disciplinary boundaries. Building a cohesive team requires involving existing staff in selection of new team members. This calls on the administrator to practice a little role release, training staff in interviewing skills and sharing decision-making prerogatives which, in the traditional technical model, reside within administration.

The structure of the interview itself can search out the skills and philosophical biases of a potential team member. Asking concrete questions about how the candidate would schedule a parent-child session provides information about whether and how the applicant implements the team approach. A candidate's description of a session in which motor, language, and cognitive skills are addressed sequentially, and in which parents play only an observer or learner role, belies any philosophical statements about an integrated team approach to development.

Questions regarding the role of individual and group therapy reveal the person's application of team approaches. Questions should be designed to elicit information about the applicant's comfort with role release, role expansion, and exchange. For example, asking how the applicant would resolve team conflict may give insight into interpersonal and problem-solving skills. Information regarding the candidate's professional activities also reveals a level of professional commitment to growth and change, important to team and program development. Figure 4 provides a sample interview format.

Questions regarding individual and group therapy reveal the person's application of team approaches.

Building Teams by Building Skills

❑ As interest in a team approach to early intervention has grown, so has the awareness that early intervention professionals, skilled and experienced in their own disciplines, may lack the skills needed to work as members of an early intervention team. Preservice programs have not traditionally included training in how to develop teams or in the skills needed for role sharing and role release. When INTERACT, an early intervention professional organization, developed a monograph entitled *Basic Competencies for Personnel in Early Intervention Programs* (Zeitlin, 1982), it provided a comprehensive treatment of the subject except for the skills related to team participation. However, the subsequent INTERACT publication (Woodruff et al., 1985) reflected the growing awareness of the need for team skills:

Professionals skilled in their own disciplines may lack skills to work on a team.

Infants and their families require the services of professionals with a wide variety of skills. If a team approach is used, working as part of a team is part of those skills. As the benefits of interdisciplinary and trans-disciplinary service models become widely acknowledged, typical personnel preparation programs which provide training in single disciplines may need to expand to include training across disciplines. (p. 15)

Figure 4. Sample Interview Format.

I. Training and Experience

    A. What training has the candidate had?
        1. Where was the candidate trained?
        2. What was the philosophical orientation of this training program?
        3. What degrees, specialized certificates, or endorsements has the candidate earned?
        4. What additional inservice training has the candidate received?
        5. What familiarity does the candidate have with specific concepts or techniques that may be deemed appropriate to this program's philosophy?
           a. Piagetian approaches
           b. neurodevelopmental treatment
           c. sociolinguistics
           d. pragmatics
           e. social learning theory
           f. behavioral learning theory
           g. attachment theory
        6. What training or experience has the candidate had in counseling skills?
        7. What assessment measures or approaches has the candidate been trained to administer?

    B. What has the candidate's previous work experience included?
        1. What ages, types of handicaps or severity level has the candidate worked with?
        2. In what capacity has the candidate worked with families?
        3. What team members has the candidate worked with? In what capacity? What type of team interaction?
           a. unidisciplinary
           b. multidisciplinary
           c. interdisciplinary
           d. transdisciplinary
        4. In what settings (home-based, center-based)?
           a. How much experience has the candidate had with therapeutic intervention? Educational intervention?
           b. How much experience has the candidate had in working with individuals, small groups, large groups?
        5. What type and level of training has the candidate done before?
           a. with teams on the job
           b. inservice training
           c. at conferences

II. Individual Philosophy

    A. Have the candidate describe the "ideal" program for serving the types of children and families in this target population.
        1. What would be the ideal schedule?
        2. How many children would be on the caseload?
        3. How much individual and group therapy and education time would be allotted?
        4. How would the candidate use team members?
        5. How would the candidate serve families?
           a. What would be the goals?
           b. What options for service delivery would be available?
        6. What should the parent's role in the program be?
        7. What assessment and evaluation measures would the candidate select?
        8. What educational and treatment approaches would be incorporated?

(Continued)

Figure 4. Sample Interview Format. (Continued)

B. What would the candidate describe as ideal team functioning?
   1. How does the candidate see his or her role in relation to other team members?
   2. How does the candidate feel about teachers or therapists implementing his or her treatment or educational intervention?
   3. If asked to teach others these skills, how would the candidate go about this?
   4. At what level would the candidate like to be involved with administrative hiring, supervision, program evaluation?

C. Professionalism
   1. What type of ongoing training does the candidate perceive would be useful to him or her?
   2. To what professional journals does the candidate subscribe?
   3. What was the last conference the candidate attended? Why?
   4. What type of presentations has the candidate made? To whom? Where?
   5. What does the candidate see as current trends and controversies in the field? (Pursue if any are of interest.)
   6. What books (text or others) have influenced their approach to children and families?
   7. What does the candidate describe as his or her strengths?
   8. What does the candidate describe as his or her weaknesses?
   9. What are the candidate's short- and long-term goals for the future?

D. Personal Influences
   What life experiences have influenced the candidate's approach to children and families?

In fact, personnel preparation programs are now moving toward offering training that crosses disciplinary and department boundaries. Federal priorities for Infant Inservice Training Projects within the Handicapped Children's Early Education Program (HCEEP) reflect a commitment to teams that include families and to training "to facilitate team efforts to deliver effective services" (*Federal Register*, Aug. 27, 1986). All of these provide evidence of a new and heightened awareness of the need for early intervention professionals to develop the skills related to serving children and families using a team approach.

It is the administrator's task to complement the existing skills of the early intervention staff through supervision and inservice training in team skills. Staff development, an important component of any program, becomes a priority for team building. Here, as in other areas of team performance, the collaborative approach must extend to allowing team members to be actively involved in planning, developing, and evaluating the staff development efforts.

Staff development becomes a priority for team building.

However, there are few good instruments for assessing the skills of team members, let alone their skills in the team process. In a survey conducted by Buck and Rogers (1987), all HCEEP model demonstration programs that described themselves as using a team approach were asked to describe staff evaluation instrumentation, particularly with regard to team skills. The same survey was sent to early intervention programs in Virginia. A surprisingly small number of programs had any formal instruments at all; even fewer addressed team skills. Even those programs that stressed a team approach frequently limited their examination of team interaction skills to the traditional "works well with others." Interestingly, programs were more likely to be rigorous in examining the ways in which staff worked with and involved families than the ways in which they collaborated with other paid team members.

There are models of needs assessment for staff development and team building.

There are, however, some models of needs assessment for staff development and for team building. Garland (1979), in the *Skills Inventory for Teachers* (SIFT), has addressed some skills specific to team interaction in several sections of the 150-item instrument. Skills addressed include "recognizes need for and obtains consultation from other team members; can describe the roles of all team members including parents; and elicits ideas, questions and concerns from all participants." An instrument for self-evaluation that examines more closely the attitudes affecting team dynamics comes from Project Bridge (Handley & Spencer, 1986). That self-assessment, which uses a 5-point scale, is accompanied by a team assessment. Designed for a team member's own use, it asks searching questions, calling for a rigorous look at one's own attitudes and behaviors:

> To what extent do you think a child's family should be involved in selecting and implementing a service plan for an at-risk child or a child with disabilities? To what extent have you worked to enhance team cohesiveness and mutual understanding? (p. 18)

Administrators are challenged to seek out and use instrumentation that assists them and their staffs in identifying needs for skill development and performance improvement in the area of team performance and to design and implement staff development plans that meet those needs. Staff development plans intended to meet the needs of personnel who have varied team-building skills must offer a range of options in both content and format. Staff development methods which fall along a continuum, ranging from informal, on-the-job observations to more formal training events, will be selected based on need and preferred learning style (see Figure 5).

Administrators are challenged to lead.

Once again, administrators are challenged not just to manage, but to lead, by example and model. An administrator seeking honest self-appraisal and an open responsiveness to performance evaluation from staff must similarly find mechanisms to appraise his or her own skills and performance as a team leader. Skills in planning, organizing, coaching, persuading, and negotiating are all needed by the team leader. A team leader can certainly benefit from the self-evaluation checklist provided by Ends and Page (1977) or from the self-examination used in the Bridge Model. However, a systematic approach for evaluating the performance of an administrator must be provided, with specific attention to team-building skills.

Staff must have mechanisms for providing feedback to their team leader without fear of reprisal, if that leader is to grow more skilled in team building. This is another instance in which instrumentation and methodology are not readily available. However, administrators committed to getting feedback about their own team performance will be rigorous in eliciting information, receiving it without defensiveness, and using it to plan behavior change. Figure 6 is an excerpt from an administrator's evaluation used at Child Development Resources in Lightfoot, Virginia. The survey examines the administrator's performance in the areas identified as priorities by the board. Items include information about the administrator's ability to lead the agency toward its established goals, and

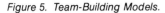

Figure 5. Team-Building Models.

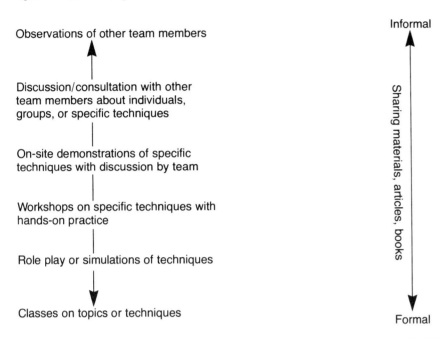

meet required time lines. However, the way in which the administrator works as a member of the team is clearly an important component of performance, and items also address interaction with staff, board, clients, and the community. The survey is mailed to all staff and board, including parents. It is returned to an impartial third party to summarize and present, in confidence, to personnel decision makers and to the administrator. Together, administrator and key board members set targets for performance improvement. The high rate of return indicates the degree to which the staff and board feel that their participation is important and the degree of comfort they feel with the process.

Scheduling

❑ Football teams spend hours practicing together and are coached to improve their game. Orchestras rehearse their performance as a group under the guidance of the conductor. Time to practice is at least as important as time to perform, and practice hours outweigh game or concert time. Administrators must allow time for the team to plan, practice, and critique their work together. Administrators should regard this time as part of a strategy that ensures the quality of direct service and as an opportunity for staff development and program improvement.

Administrators must allow time for the team to plan, practice, and critique their work together.

Administrators will encourage the sharing of information and skills among team members and will expect developmental specialists and therapists to help parents and other team members integrate helpful child care, management, therapeutic, and developmental strategies into the child's day. Administrators will want to examine the best use of time to ensure cross-disciplinary planning and intervention as well as individual treatment time. Early intervention teams must have time to plan the assessment process; communicate concerns, questions, and findings; write integrated assessment reports; and plan and critique their staffings

Administrators will encourage sharing of information and skills.

Figure 6. Excerpt from an Administrator's Evaluation.

The following questions, to be completed by staff and board, deal with the Executive Director's attitudes toward her own performance and need for performance improvement. Please rate how consistently the Executive Director shows the following behaviors from "1" (never) to "5" (consistently) or "N/O" (no opportunity to observe).

34. Assesses own behavior in terms of staff and board feedback and program evaluation results.

    1   2   3   4   5   N/O

35. Elicits and accepts performance feedback and suggestions for performance improvement.

    1   2   3   4   5   N/O

36. Is able to change behavior based on feedback.

    1   2   3   4   5   N/O

37. Recognizes and expresses own need for skill, information, or performance improvement.

    1   2   3   4   5   N/O

38. Seeks professional development through conferences, workshops, staff meetings, or individual study or reading.

    1   2   3   4   5   N/O

to ensure that parents participate in a meaningful, rather than perfunctory, way. This can occur in planning meetings, in classroom or home-based activities, and in individual conferences and consultations. Whatever the setting, specific allocation of time for these activities in the schedule is critical.

Work hours must be set in response to client needs.

The human relations model for administration is an effective one to apply to scheduling, which must be flexible. Work hours must be set in response to client, rather than to organizational, needs. Evenings, Saturdays, and other nontraditional work time must be options for working with families who need to be sufficiently free from conflicting priorities to give their attention to their role as team members. Flexible personnel policies will allow administrators to match client needs with staff preferences for work hours. This approach meets the human needs that staff and clients share to manage their work, study, and family responsibilities in individual patterns that fit individual needs and lifestyles.

BUILDING FAMILY FOCUSED TEAMS

❑ Early intervention professionals have acknowledged that "unique biological, physical, and psychological dependence of the infant on his family" (Woodruff et al., 1985) has made it necessary for early intervention programs to become "family focused" (Dunst, 1985). Administrators must recognize that more than terminology has changed and that family-focused services differ significantly from the last decade's goal of obtaining parent involvement in child focused services. Family focused services are designed viewing the child in the context of the family and the family as the appropriate recipient of services. Administrators must take the lead in developing organizational practices and procedures that allow the team to bring a family focus to early intervention.

Services are designed viewing the child in the context of the family.

Not just administrators, but all team members, need to re-examine their expectations of the family's role in order to bring a family focus to early intervention. Working with parents as partners on the team does not involve making parents into therapists or teachers. It does mean actively involving families in assessing their own and their child's needs. It means planning and securing interagency coordination of the complex web of services needed by the family and helping families obtain those services. It means supporting families in their efforts to cope with problems and stresses associated with raising a handicapped child and helping them to encourage the development of that child. It means accepting families' own expectations and limits on the degree to which they desire to be involved, as parents, not as professionals.

The complex and emotionally demanding task of implementing a family-focused approach to service delivery falls to direct service staff. However, administrators are responsible for providing a structure that encourages a family focus and for creating an organizational climate that not only enables but requires a family-focused approach. Administrators must develop strategies for securing active and meaningful consumer involvement not only in planning their own children's programs, but also in designing service delivery systems. Parent participation in selecting individualized family service plan (IFSP) goals and strategies, required by P.L. 99-457, is not meaningful unless the service delivery system itself is responsive to family needs.

Together with consumer and community representatives, administrators must ensure that there are a range of service options available for parents to choose from, based on parents' needs and interests. The team should be involved in presenting alternatives for families, assisting when needed, and clarifying the consequences of options chosen. Administration must provide alternative ways in which families can be involved in their child's program as well as in other aspects of the program. Fiscal policies and insurance must be examined to make sure that they facilitate rather than block the delivery of services, such as transportation, to families.

Administrators must ensure a range of service options.

Administrators must develop personnel policies that respond to the need for flexible staff hours required to meet varied family needs. Written role or job descriptions should be clearly specified so that each team member understands his or her responsibilities to families, not just to children. Staff development plans should include goals for developing specific skills needed in family-focused intervention and strategies for meeting those goals. If staff are to take this commitment seriously, data collection and personnel and program evaluation must focus on services to families rather than on child progress data alone. Family participation in program evaluation, both in informal and formal ways, must be ensured by administrative openness to families and by use of evaluation strategies that offer opportunity for participation by families of widely varied educational levels. Consumer representation is necessary on governing

Administrators must develop policies for flexible staff hours.

Family participation in program evaluation must be ensured.

boards as well as on advisory boards, providing further evidence of true administrative commitment to families as team members.

GOAL SETTING AND THE PROCESS OF CHANGE

Participants

❑ Looking once more at the definition of leadership, one must be struck by the strong emphasis on having goals and steering a course toward those goals. The reader may wonder why goal setting, typically first chronologically among administrative tasks, was not treated earlier in this chapter. In fact, if the leader is to succeed in reaching goals, the *team* must share his or her commitment. Therefore, building a team that can contribute to goal setting becomes a goal in itself, one that provides a foundation for setting other goals.

If the leader is to succeed, the team must share commitment.

Program goals are not to be confused with the overall mission of the agency or its statement of philosophy. An agency committed to creating conditions that foster mental health among children and families needs to set specific goals each year that are consistent with its overall mission. When stated goals are not specific, it is virtually impossible to develop plans to achieve them, and absolutely impossible to secure genuine commitment from group members (Ends & Page, 1977). Goals should reflect a dissonance between conditions that exist and those that are ideal, and they should challenge the group to make changes needed to move closer to the ideal. Leaders strive for excellence, not perfection. Leaders can help the group set goals that approach the ideal, goals that are challenging, yet realistic.

Goals should reflect a dissonance between conditions that exist and those which are ideal.

The administrator who wishes to bring about a team approach in direct service but who uses a technical, linear management model, in which administration sets goals to be carried out by the team, loses an opportunity to teach team behavior by example, to obtain valuable and needed information, and to garner important political support. What seems clear is that all those who have responsibility for implementation and all those who have a stake in the agency participate in setting goals, whether in an advisory or decision-making role. Both the human relations model and the political model have much to offer to the goal-setting task, providing a framework for goal setting that meets the needs of participants and enlists their commitment to accomplishing goals.

Planning for Planning

❑ Like team building, goal setting requires time, administrative commitment, and clearly defined roles. Administrative time given to planning and administrative participation in the goal-setting process are statements of support and commitment. The planning group must have time to consider and define needs, set goals, identify resources, and plan strategies. Many organizational development specialists recommend that the goal-setting session take place in a location away from the daily workplace to stimulate creative thinking and minimize distraction. Administrative planning should include a clear definition of the process to be used for setting goals, and the expectations for each participant.

Goal setting requires time, administrative commitment, and defined roles.

Role confusion creates conflict and frustration in any work environment. Staff, board, parents, and other participants in the goal-setting process must have clearly defined roles. If goal setting is a policy-making function, residing in an administrative or governing board, staff should have an opportunity to share their knowledge and expertise regarding the program and its needs. The staff needs to understand that, in this context, their role is to serve as consultants to a process essentially controlled by the board.

Role confusion creates conflict and frustration.

Program improvement, unlike policy making, is typically a staff responsibility, and goal setting in this area is typically controlled by staff. However, two-way communication with the governing board is essential if the board is expected to secure the resources and support necessary to allow goals to be reached. The board members need to understand and accept their role as policy makers who consult with and support staff in their program improvement and implementation roles. For parents to be true partners in a program, a system for consumer participation in goal setting should be developed. Parents, too, must be clear about whether their role is an advisory or decision-making one.

Parents must be clear whether their role is advisory or decision-making.

Models for Setting Goals

❑ Administrators planning the goal-setting process need not only to define the roles of participants, but also to provide a model, or method, for the goal-setting process. The data-collecting model used with success in team building is, similarly, effective for setting organizational goals. Goal setting, as discussed earlier, is a process for resolving the dissonance between actual and ideal, whether in performance or in services available. An effective goal-setting process provides information to participants that allows them to identify such discrepancies. For example, demographic data may indicate a lack of success in reaching and serving a minority population. When data are shared with the planning team, a goal of increasing minority participation in program planning and in use of services may be set. Once data are available to the planning team, a variety of methods for setting goals can be used (Delbecq & Vandeven, 1971; Handley & Spencer, 1986).

Administrators need to provide a model.

Whatever the process used for goal setting, it must be viewed as the first step in a planning cycle that involves the following steps:

- Assessing needs.
- Setting goals.
- Generating strategies/alternatives.
- Developing an action plan.
- Identifying and securing resources.
- Implementing the plan.
- Evaluating and continuing the process.

Goal setting and the planning process are treated in numerous sources in early intervention literature (Linder, 1983).

Time Lines for Goal Setting

❑ The administrator is responsible for developing a timetable for the planning cycle. The time line for planning must be designed with several considerations in mind. Primary among these is integrating the goal-setting and fiscal planning processes. Goals set in September for the current school year are meaningless if decisions about fiscal resources, material and equipment purchases, staff available, and training opportunities have been decided months ago in the budget process. Goal setting should take place in advance of budgeting, providing the information needed by financial planners to develop their budgets and providing the philosophy and direction for the budget itself. Goal setting should provide the impetus for securing the resources needed for reaching goals. Seen from the fiscal perspective, a budget is merely the translation of the agency's goals, priorities, and action plan into financial terms.

Goal setting should take place in advance of budgeting.

Leaders in the planning process are concerned with more than immediate priorities. Leaders engage in a continuing cycle of goal setting and planning, addressing immediate priorities, anticipating trends, and incorporating them into long-term planning. A 5-year plan, developed using the participatory process described above and conveyed to the community with clarity and meaning, provides a blueprint for action for those whose work determines whether service needs are met.

A 5-year plan provides a blueprint for action.

Evaluation

❑ Evaluation provides the basis for goal setting and program planning. While it is not the purpose of this chapter to address the merits or methods of evaluation, administrative responsibility for ensuring an evaluation component in both team building and planning is clear. With purposes and audiences in mind, the administrator and teams will want to explore alternative approaches to obtaining data to determine how successful their team-building efforts have been and whether or not program goals set in the planning process have actually been accomplished. The following strategies may be used:

- Case studies.
- Observations.
- Surveys and questionnaires.
- Management information systems.
- Experimental and quasi-experimental methods.
- Cost analysis.
- Informal feedback.

As discussed earlier, the administrator helps the team use evaluation as a data base to identify discrepancies between actual and ideal and to plan for change. Evaluation needs to provide data sufficient in number and quality to lay the foundation for goal setting and the planning process. The evaluation process, like each step in the goal-setting and planning process, will be a collaborative one, with parents and staff involved in selecting and implementing methodology, having an opportunity to contribute valuable data to the process.

Evaluation needs to provide data for goal setting.

FROM PLANS TO REALITY

Image Building: Using the Symbolic Model

❑ Once goals have been set, the administrator needs to communicate the meaning and mission of the agency and the urgency of its goals to a wider, external audience. Leadership does not stop with goal setting, but accepts the challenges of communication and advocacy necessary to

The administrator needs to communicate to a wider external audience.

secure the political and fiscal support that enables plans to be implemented and goals to be reached. Looking once again at models for administrative tasks, the symbolic model serves as a useful prototype.

The work an administrator has done in orchestrating the process of team building and goal setting within his or her own agency provides the tools needed to influence broader constituencies. The same evidence of need, the same clear statement of goals, the well-developed plan of action, and the commitment of one's own team to reaching those goals are the prerequisites to the advocacy process. Legislative, policy, fiscal, and programmatic decision makers look for clear evidence of need before allocating resources, and they will be persuaded by support from a coalition created by building a team that includes consumers and other agencies. Administrative staff and policy-making board leaders who have shared in goal setting will share the task of creating support for the program and its goals within the community at large.

Decision makers will be persuaded by support from a coalition.

The symbolic model provides a framework for creating the desired perception. It is critically important for the administrator to have a clear grasp of the meaning of the agency and an ability to convey that meaning. Moreover, early intervention leaders must know their constituents. Communication with the community and especially with key decision makers should be continuous and not limited to budget hearings.

Communication should be continuous.

From newsletters and brochures to "child checks" in the community, the administrator must have a clear grasp of the meaning of the program and must send consistent messages to its constituents that reinforce their belief in the truth of those messages. Strategies include

- Widely disseminated annual reports.
- Newsletters.
- Mass media.

The administrator must also ensure a system for continuous two-way communication with constituents. Strategies the administrator can use include

- Advisory committees.
- Task forces.
- Orientation meetings.
- Open houses.
- Community coffees.

This two-way communication results in valuable information for the administrator and at the same time enlists constituents in the process of identifying needs and planning change. It is far easier to secure the personnel, material, and fiscal resources needed to implement change when those on whom you rely to provide support have been instrumental in identifying the need for change.

In addition to planned communication, almost everything that happens in a human service program can reach the public, contributing to the image of the program in the local and professional community. This raises a question that is often troublesome for administrators. How does one handle the bad news—the staff reductions, the long hours children spend on the bus, the sprained wrist on the playground, and the herpes in the classroom?

If the agency is committed to a partnership with a broad, public constituency, and to creating in the community a picture of an open and honest system of communication, the mandate is clear. Administrators

Administrators must determine when and how bad news should be shared.

The plan for a better future is the task of leadership.

must determine when and how bad news should be shared. This can be done by determining which audiences share the right and need to know when things go wrong and by knowing which others are likely to learn of a problem regardless of administrative action. An administrator who provides a clear problem statement and a viable plan for improvement is generally perceived by consumers and decision makers not as the cause of disequilibrium, but as the architect of plans for a better future. The plan for a better future is the task of leadership in early intervention, both on a symbolic and literal level. If there is a discrepancy between the ideal and reality, then goal setting and planning must move programs closer to the idea. Early intervention leaders will convey their goals, their plans for a better future, to those whose support is needed to make the plan a reality.

SUMMARY

❑ Administration of early intervention programs should be characterized by good management to ensure that services are delivered safely and efficiently, in keeping with local, state, and federal laws and regulations. Administration must go beyond management, to provide leadership in four important areas:

● Building an early intervention team.

● Creating an environment that supports families as members of the team.

● Setting goals in collaboration with that team.

● Communicating goals to those who can effect their accomplishment.

Four models for administration provide a framework for work in those areas. A multiple-model approach provides a useful structure for administrators of early intervention programs, who can draw on all four models:

● Technical model.

● Human relations model.

● Political model.

● Symbolic model.

In building an early intervention team and supporting families as part of that team, the human relations model provides a structure for selecting organizational goals to meet staff and family needs. The political model provides a framework for extending the team beyond the early intervention program, building multiagency teams and networks on behalf of young children and their families. The technical model is characterized by clearly defined goals and an equally clear understanding of locus of responsibility for reaching goals. However, if the commitment to a team approach is strong, the team will be involved in the goal-setting process, eschewing the linear structure typically supported by the technical model. Finally, the early intervention leader can use the symbolic model to convey to a broad and necessary constituency clear goals and a clear understanding of the mission and meaning of early intervention programs.

REFERENCES

Allport, G. W. (1955). *Becoming.* New Haven, CT: Yale University.

Bennis, W. (1984). The four competencies of leadership. *Training and Development Journal, 38*(8), 15-19.

Bolman, L. G., & Deal, T. E. (1984). *Modern approaches to understanding and managing organizations.* San Francisco: Jossey Bass.

Buck, D., & Rogers, L. (1987). *Staff evaluation for early intervention service providers.* Lightfoot, VA: Child Development Resources (unpublished study).

Delbecq, A., & Vandeven, A. (1971). A group process model for problem identification and program planning. *Journal of Applied Behavior Science, 7.*

Dunst, C. J. (1985). Rethinking early intervention. *Analysis and Intervention in Developmental Disabilities, 5*, 165-201.

Dyer, W. (1987). *Team building: Issues and alternatives.* (2nd ed). Reading, MA: Addison-Wesley.

Ends, E. J., & Page, C. W. (1977). *Organizational team building.* Cambridge, MA: Winthrop.

Federal Register, Vol. 51, 166, Aug. 27, 1986.

Fewell, R. R. (1983). The team approach to infant education. In S. G. Garwood & R. R. Fewell (Eds.), *Educating handicapped infants: Issues in development* (pp. 299-322). Rockville, MD: Aspen.

Garland, C. W. (1979). *Skills inventory for teachers.* Lightfoot, VA: Child Development Resources.

Garland, C. W. (1982). Change at a private nonprofit agency. In Pascal Trohanis (Ed.), *Strategies for change.* Chapel Hill, NC: TADS.

Handley, E. E., & Spencer, P. E. (1986). *Project BRIDGE, decision making for early services: A team approach.* Elk Grove, IL: American Academy of Pediatrics.

Lawrence, P., & Lorsch, J. (1967). *Organization and environment: Managing differentiation and integration.* Cambridge, MA: Harvard University, Division of Research, Graduate School of Business Administration.

Lay-Dopyera, M., & Dopyera, J. (1985). Administrative leadership: Styles, competencies, repertoire. *Topics in Early Childhood Special Education, 5*(1), 15-24.

Linder, T. W. (1983). *Early childhood special education: Program development and administration.* Baltimore, MD: Paul Brookes.

Maslow, A. (1954). *Motivation and personality.* New York: Harper and Row.

Neugebauer, R. (1983). Team effectiveness rating scale. *Child Care Information Exchange*, November, p. 4.

O'Donnell, E. J., & Childman, C. S. (1969, June). Poor people on public welfare boards and committees. *Welfare in Review*, pp.1-10.

Patterson, G., & Hutchinson, D. (1976). *Resource for the transdisciplinary team.* New York: United Cerebral Palsy.

Wimpelberg, R. K., Abroms, K. I., Catardi, C. L. (1985). Multiple models for administrative preparation in early childhood special education. *Topics in Early Childhood Special Education, 5*(1), 1-14.

Woodruff, G., McGonigel, M., Garland, C., Zeitlin, S., Shanahan, K., Chazkel-Hochman, J., Toole, A., & Vincent, E. (1985). *Planning programs for infants* (TADS State Series Paper #2). Chapel Hill, NC: University of North Carolina, Technical Assistance Development System.

Zaltman, G., & Duncan, R. (1977). *Strategies for planned change.* New York: John Wiley and Sons.

Zeitlin, S. (Ed.). (1982). *Basic competencies for personnel in early intervention programs.* Westar Series Paper #14. Monmouth, OR: Western States Technical Assistance Resource.

3.
Linking Screening, Identification, and Assessment with Curriculum

Patricia L. Hutinger

❑ This chapter has two purposes. First, the information gathered about a child and family during the identification processes (screening, diagnosis, and assessment) is examined, relationships among the processes are identified, and the resulting early intervention curriculum and services are explored. Second, some of the issues related to these relationships are discussed. Screening information is a preliminary step in the identification process. It is the initial process for children who are at risk or who seem to demonstrate behavior that is below developmental level; however, it is not necessary for children who have a diagnosed handicapping condition. The information gained in the identification process, which includes diagnosis, and in the subsequent assessment is the information used to plan appropriate activities for the child and family. The term "curriculum" in infant programs is used in a broad sense to cover the entire range of developmental intervention activities and services and does not refer to narrow academic curricula used by the schools for older children. Figure 1 shows a system that incorporates the identification processes into an early intervention framework.

"Curriculum" is used to cover the entire range of developmental intervention activities.

THE IMPACT OF PUBLIC LAW 99-457

❑ The Education of the Handicapped Act Amendments (P.L. 99-457), passed in late 1986, addresses the relationships among screening, assessment, and curriculum. The Act defines the components of a statewide system to provide a free, appropriate public education to handicapped children from birth through age 2. (The terms "birth through 2" and "birth to 3" are used interchangeably here since they both refer to the same period in a child's life.) Minimum components are required for comprehensive, coordinated, multidisciplinary programs of early intervention services for all handicapped infants, toddlers, and their families.

In addition, Section 676 of the Act requires that a timely, comprehensive, and multidisciplinary evaluation of the functioning of each handicapped infant and toddler and the needs of the families must be performed in order to assist appropriately in the development of the children. Individualized family service plans and case management are also required. The new law results in infant personnel no longer writing only individual service or intervention plans for children, but also plans for the entire family. Curriculum then includes activities and services for both children and family members. This chapter focuses primarily on the child portion of the program, indicating points of contact with family roles and participation, while Chapter 5 focuses on families.

The new law results in plans for the entire family.

The Act also includes a comprehensive child find system and a system for referrals to service providers that includes timelines and provides for participation by professionals from primary referral sources such as hospitals, physicians, public health facilities, and related agencies.

Provisions of the law speak directly to linkages between screening, assessment, and curriculum. Those linkages are expected to be made in a timely fashion since a part of Section 676 addresses timelines for child find and referrals. Section 677 indicates that the individualized family service plan must be developed within a reasonable time after the assessment, but notes that with the parents' consent early intervention services may commence prior to the completion of the assessment. The

Figure 1. A System of Identification Processes and Services for Families of Handicapped and At-Risk Children Under 3 Eligible for Early Intervention Services.

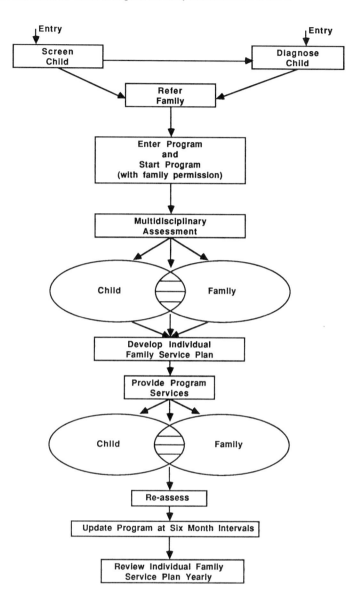

individualized family plan must be reviewed once a year with a documented update of the program provided to the family at least at 6-month intervals.

Public Law 99-457 defines "early intervention services" as developmental services designed to meet a handicapped infant's or toddler's developmental needs (physical development, cognition, language, social, and self-help skills) that are provided in conformity with an individualized family service plan. Services specified in P.L. 99-457 include:

- Family training, counseling, and home visits.

- Special instruction.

- Speech pathology and audiology.

- Occupational therapy and physical therapy.

- Psychological services.

- Case management services.
- Medical services only for diagnostic or evaluation purposes.
- Early identification, screening, and assessment services.
- Health services necessary to enable the infant or toddler to benefit from the other early intervention services.

Services are to be linked together.

If these services are to be provided in a coordinated way, then we must link them together in a comprehensive, thoughtful, and effective manner.

AN EFFECTIVE LINKING SYSTEM

The link is the handicapped child.

❑ What is the link between screening, assessment, and curriculum? The link is the handicapped child, together with the coordinated, accurate, and timely information collected about that child, including strengths and needs. However, the solder, or process that holds the link together is the coordinated interagency system for linking, which must be provided by others—the community, the family, and the team of early intervention service providers—together with a consistent, sound developmental philosophy. The key to the system is a single point of reference, a case manager who can keep all the information about the child and family from a variety of disciplines organized and coordinated so that decisions and activities are consistent with what is known. If the case manager operates effectively, families are more likely to benefit from all the available resources the interagency system can provide.

The solder is the coordinated interagency system.

The key is a case manager.

Both Bricker (1986) and Neisworth, Willoughby-Herb, Bagnato, Cartwright, and Laub (1980) have addressed linking assessment with intervention or curriculum target objectives. Bricker argued convincingly for an approach that links assessment, intervention, and evaluation through the use of assessment measures that are consistent with program philosophy as well as through analysis of progress at three levels: (a) daily/weekly progress; (b) progress toward long-range goals and training objectives; and (c) progress toward program goals. She also argued that since few other useful models exist at the present time, the normal developmental sequences used as a general reference provide a useful framework to build generative response classes that lead to independent functioning and problem-solving skills. Neisworth and his associates (1980) have noted that developmental scales and most preschool curricula are constructed on the normal sequence of developmental tasks, abilities, and behaviors. Most developmental scales and curricula focus on similar developmental areas: motor, language, cognitive, personal, and social. Although "readiness" is included in their listing, it is not an appropriate area for measurement in infant and toddler programs since its connotation is primarily academic and intended for older children.

Scales and curricula focus on similar areas.

Measures are only tools.

Insisting that the processes of assessment, intervention, and subsequent reassessment must be linked and are inseparable (Bricker, 1986; Neisworth et al., 1980) is essential, but not enough. The tools we use to accomplish these processes must be consistent with a sound program philosophy. Bricker (1986) has laid the framework for this clearly; her work should be reviewed by early intervention personnel and planners. Yet the measures are only tools; they do not stand alone, nor are they the rationale for the program. Tools are only instruments to provide more effective services to children and their families. It is because children demonstrate handicaps or delays that families become a part of early intervention services. Without the child, families would have no need for services or individualized family service plans, nor would intervention programs need to exist.

When you solder two pieces of metal together, the timing must be right. If the metal gets too hot, it melts. If it doesn't get hot enough, the solder doesn't "take" and the two pieces do not hold together. In much the same way, the timing of assessment, intervention, and reassessment activities must be reasonable. Bricker's (1986) system provides for three different assessment timing phases: daily/weekly, quarterly, and yearly. Collection of data at these time periods provides data for three levels of progress analysis: daily activities, long-range goals and training objectives, and program goals.

Timing of assessment, intervention, and reassessment must be reasonable.

Information about children and families, together with the appropriate signed release forms, must be collected and updated on a regular basis. P.L. 99-457 uses a 6-month period with an annual review, but Bricker's suggestion for data collection provides more useful information. All the information should be compiled in well-organized file folders, a computer data base, or a combination of the two, together with the appropriate signed release forms and a checklist to ensure that data are collected regularly at appropriate times. Figure 2 shows a sample record-keeping checklist for children used by the Outreach: Macomb 0-3 Rural Project.

Information must be collected and updated on a regular basis.

An effective linking system is integrated, not fragmented. Information about the child's medical diagnosis must be instantly available when decisions are made about activities that parents want to do at home. Activities and services are also integrated, not isolated. The speech and language specialist must consider the physical therapy goals for the child in planning activities that further communication. All service providers must consider information about the child's preferred toys and play activities, as well as the family's wishes for the child. If a child is to use switches to turn on battery-operated toys, the physical therapist's input is necessary for positioning. A computerized electronic communication program such as *Choices* (Whitaker, 1984) or *Peek 'n Speak* (Whitaker, 1985) for a young physically handicapped child must be initiated by a team consisting of the family members, the speech and language therapist, a technology expert, and other related personnel (depending on the nature of the child's handicap).

Activities and services are integrated not isolated.

Many professionals with widely varied backgrounds and training are involved in gathering information and implementing plans for handicapped children and their families. Physicians, public health nurses, social workers, psychologists, physical therapists, occupational therapists, vision specialists, language therapists, child development specialists, and parents are usually involved in gathering data, planning, and implementing the plans. Fewell (1983b) has reviewed the team approach and team roles in depth. Information gathered in screening and diagnosis is used to identify the children and families in need of birth-to-3 services. Assessment information is used both to plan specific activities and to measure progress, although measures for each must be different.

Many professionals are involved.

ESTABLISHING DEFINITIONS: A COMMON TERMINOLOGY

❑ Often there is confusion among professionals about the specific meanings of terms such as "child find," "screening," "identification,"

Figure 2. A Sample Child Record-keeping Form Used in the Macomb 0-3 Model.

CHILD SUMMARY
Macomb 0-3 Rural Project

Child identification number: _____ Child's name: _____

Child entered Project: _____ _____ Child terminated Project: _____ _____
(date)   C.A.   (see termination form)   (date)   C.A.

Evaluation

Test: _____ Alpern-Boll _____

	1st testing score date	2nd testing score date	3rd testing score date	4th testing score date	5th testing score date	6th testing score date
Physical Age						
Self-Help Age						
Social Age						
Academic Age						
Comm. Age						
Chron. Age						

Test: _____ REEL _____

	1st testing score date	2nd testing score date	3rd testing score date	4th testing score date	5th testing score date	6th testing score date
Receptive Quotient						
Expressive Quotient						
Language Quotient						
Chron. Age						

Test: _____ Hunt and Uzgiris _____

Test: _____

Defining terms puts everyone on a similar footing.

"referral," "assessment," "evaluation," and "diagnosis." Sometimes these terms are tossed around as if they all mean the same thing. Sometimes program staff seem to consider the terms synonymous. But they are not! Clarifying what is meant and what is not meant leads to better understanding among professionals from varied disciplines, and makes it much easier for families to understand what is happening, both to them and to their children. Defining terms puts everyone on a similar footing.

Figure 2. A Sample Child Record-keeping Form Used in the Macomb 0-3 Model. (Continued)

Evaluation of Project: <u>Parent Satisfaction Questionnaire:</u>

    Dates administered listed below:

    ——————— ——————— ——————— ——————— ———————

Child or parent videotaped:

    Dates taped listed below:

    ——————— ——————— ——————— ——————— ———————

    ——————— ——————— ——————— ——————— ———————

    ——————— ——————— ——————— ——————— ———————

Areas of Delay Statement:

Based upon initial testing and observation of the child, the following areas have been determined in need of concentrated work:*

_____

_____

_____

                                _____
                                          (CDS)

*For more detailed information, see biyearly goals

                        <u>Supplemental Services</u>
                            (dates)

Medical Diagnosis   ——————— ——————— ——————— ———————

Speech Evaluation   ——————— ——————— ——————— ———————

Hearing Evaluation   ——————— ——————— ——————— ———————

Vision Evaluation   ——————— ——————— ——————— ———————

Occupational Therapy ——————— ——————— ——————— ———————

Physical Therapy   ——————— ——————— ——————— ———————

Psychological Services ——————— ——————— ——————— ———————

Within the State of Illinois alone, it has often been recommended that terms be defined so that early intervention professionals from varying backgrounds use the same language. In 1980, after reviewing survey data, a study of Illinois preschool program staff, administrators, and parents (Hutinger & Swartz, 1980) recommended establishing agreement on the definitions and accompanying clarification of terms. Five years later, a study of Illinois birth-to-3 programs (Hutinger, Mietus, Smith-Dickson, & Rundall, 1985) reviewed responses from service providers, administrators, and parents, and again recommended clarification of terms. The Illinois Advisory Council to the Early Childhood State Planning Grant again addressed the issue of term clarification in 1986. Establishing clear definitions is a problem that has been addressed and acted on, but not resolved.

Defining terms is essential to coordination, cooperation, and trust.

Even though defining terms is sometimes called a philosophical exercise in semantics, it is essential if we are to establish coordination, cooperation, and trust among educators, the medical community, social workers, psychologists, speech and language therapists, and others who must join together to mount an effective birth-to-3 program. Indeed, a review of assessment literature reveals differing definitions for processes and functions for tests. Powell (1981) described a number of appropriate infant tests, but combined screening and assessment. Horowitz (1982) discussed scales used by physicians at birth and during the neonatal period, but did not distinguish between screening and assessment in developmental measures. Fewell (1983a) and others (Bricker, 1986; Neisworth et al., 1980; Peterson, 1987) discriminated between screening, assessment, and evaluation. Perhaps one result of the differences among experts on these issues is reflected in the wide variation in assessment procedures used in infant programs. The results of the recent Illinois study of birth-to-3 programs show widespread misuse of tests (Hutinger et al., 1985). For example, some programs routinely use screening tests for assessment purposes to place children in curricular activities. The terms that follow have been defined in a context that will be used throughout this chapter.

Child Find

Activities include mass media events.

❑ *Child find* includes the entire set of activities involved in attempting to locate children who need services. Activities include mass media events and a number of publicity-seeking processes. Child find activities may be preliminary to screening (which is also a child find activity) and are carried out in order to locate children who need intervention services. Child find activities are designed to notify community members that screening and other comprehensive services are available for children who may need special services for one reason or another. Publicizing the possible reasons why children may benefit from early intervention in newspapers, on radio, and on television is also a part of child find. Effective child find efforts provide the information the public needs to make a strong rationale for birth-to-3 services, in addition to locating those who need services.

Identification

❑ *Identification* refers to the determination that the child displays a clear biological or established risk condition, or that screening results suggest that the child is developmentally delayed or "at risk" for handicapping conditions according to specified criteria. Child find, screening, and assessment are part of the identification process. Identification of children with obvious handicapping conditions such as Down syndrome falls in the realm of the medical profession. Even though education personnel and parents sometimes complain that the doctor told them that "she will grow out of it," the quality of training for new medical professionals and the current awareness and knowledge gained by practicing physicians through training from the Academy of Pediatrics and contact with early intervention specialists have led to earlier identification of children and families in need of early intervention services. As a result of increasing awareness and knowledge and society's current focus on early intervention, many physicians acknowledge the relevance of early intervention and provide valuable assistance to early intervention programs.

Many physicians provide valuable assistance.

Continuing work through the Division of Maternal and Child Health, Department of Public Health, and neonatal intensive care units, together with coordination of early intervention services offered by other agencies such as the Department of Mental Health and Developmental Disabilities, Department of Rehabilitation Services, Division of Crippled Children, State Board of Education, and Department of Public Aid also focus on the importance of early identification of children with special needs. The state-level agencies, which frequently have regional- or local-level counterparts, are those participating in the interagency effort in Illinois (Deppe, 1986). Other states may have different cooperating agencies. Every state has a Governor's Planning Council on Developmental Disabilities. Usually this council has a staff member with experience in early childhood programming, if not specific birth-to-3 programming. These Councils have contacts with medical, educational, and social services as well as funding sources for some aspects of infant programming, such as personnel training, special projects, research studies, and conferences.

Councils have contacts.

Eligibility

❑ The degree of a child's delay or the nature of the handicapping condition that qualifies the child for services is determined in an *eligibility* statement. At the present time, criteria for determining eligibility for entering a birth-to-3 program vary from state to state and among programs within a specific state. Determining criteria is a time-consuming process. In Illinois, members of a State Advisory Council examined eligibility criteria for more than a year in order to recommend a uniform basis for entry into birth-to-3 programs. When Illinois service providers were questioned in 1984, a wide range of eligibility requirements were cited (Hutinger et al., 1985) ranging from "must be toilet trained" to "developmental delay of 2 or more months in two areas of development." These requirements were not uniform and, in some instances, were inappropriate.

Criteria vary from state to state.

Section 672 of P.L. 99-457 defines handicapped infants and toddlers as individuals from birth through age 2 who are in need of early intervention services because they (a) are experiencing developmental delays as measured by appropriate diagnostic instruments and procedures in one or more of the following areas: cognitive development, physical development, language and speech development, psychosocial development, or self-help skills; or (b) have a diagnosed physical or mental condition that has a high probability of resulting in developmental delay. The term may also include, at a state's discretion, infants and toddlers who are "at risk" for substantial developmental delays if early intervention services are not provided. However, each state must define the term "developmentally delayed."

Each state must define "developmentally delayed."

A variety of definitions for infants at risk or high risk are contained in the literature. Tjossem (1976) distinguished three categories of risk factors, although they are not mutually exclusive: established risk, biological risk, and environmental risk. Ramey, Trohanis, and Hostler (1982) suggested viewing risk in terms of onset, identifying three major developmental

Three categories...established risk, biological risk, environmental risk.

periods: prenatal (from conception to birth), perinatal (from onset of labor and delivery to the fourth week of extrauterine life), and postnatal (subsequent time periods).

A number of different terms have also been used to define the criteria for eligibility. The Illinois Advisory Council to the Early Childhood State Plan, composed of professionals from a variety of disciplines, parents, and state agency task force personnel, recently formulated definitions for eligibility according to Tjossem's (1976) three broad categories of risk factors. These three categories and their definitions are included in the draft of the Illinois Early Childhood State Plan (Deppe, 1986).

Established risk was defined as a diagnosed medical disorder.

First, established risk was defined as a diagnosed medical disorder with a known etiology that bears "relatively well-known" expectancies for developmental outcomes within varying ranges of developmental disabilities.

Insults, based on medical history, increase the probability of a disability.

Second, biological risk was defined as it applies to infants and young children with a history of prenatal, perinatal, neonatal, or early developmental events resulting in biological insults to the developing central nervous system. Such insults, based on medical history, either singly or collectively increase the probability that the child will develop a disability.

Third, environmental risk was defined as it applies to families and their infants and toddlers who are considered biologically sound, but whose early life experiences (including maternal and family care, health care, nutrition, opportunities for expression of language, adaptive behavior, and patterns of physical and social stimulation) are so limiting that there is a high probability of delayed development.

Criteria for delayed development include results of appropriate assessment procedures such as a family needs inventory, social history, observation of parenting skills, maternal/infant risk index, and/or child assessment with a standardized tool. The Illinois group also noted that some children begin to show developmental delays or deviations of an unknown etiology some time during the second year of life, while others suffer an illness or an accident that results in a developmental delay.

Referral

Referrals come from community sources.

❏ *Referral* is the process whereby a child's family is directed to specific services by an individual or agency. Referrals to an early intervention program come from a variety of community sources including physicians, public health nurses, hospitals, private agencies, schools, and individual community members. Referrals are also made when screening results show clearly that the child displays delayed development. Some Illinois families reported that they referred themselves (Hutinger et al., 1985), but others indicated that they were referred to infant programs by physicians and other professionals. If good working relationships with the medical community have been established, referrals from physicians become a customary step in the early intervention process.

Screening

Screening should not be used to provide assessment information.

❏ *Screening* is the broad initial individual testing of a child to determine whether or not the child may have a handicap. Screening procedures take a minimum amount of time and should not be used to provide assessment information (although they sometimes are). A list of appropriate screening instruments is provided at the end of this chapter. Screening procedures should *not* be used with a child who has a diagnosed handicapping condition, whether it is biological or an established risk. The child's diagnosed condition is enough to move him or her immediately into the assessment procedures. Part of the screening process also includes checking the age of the child and where the family lives in order to be sure they are eligible for services from a particular agency.

Assessment

❑ *Assessment* involves systematic observation and standardized testing of the child who has been screened and determined to exhibit behaviors below developmental level in the various domains of development (i.e., cognitive, gross motor, fine motor, communication, social, and self-help) or who demonstrates an obvious handicapping condition. Assessment results are used to determine both eligibility for services and specific skills and areas for intervention program planning. Periodic reassessment, at regular intervals, must be conducted for children and families who are already participating in programs. Assessment results are used to begin or to continue planning an intervention program.

Results are used to determine eligibility and for program planning.

Diagnosis

❑ *Diagnosis* is an activity related to the medical condition of the child and is carried out primarily by medical professionals. It involves a synthesis and analysis of both hard signs and soft signs displayed by the child and is often characterized by labels such as "cerebral palsy," "Down syndrome," or a specific syndrome such as "Williams Elfin Facies." Diagnosis, as carried out by physicians, is a rigorous process characterized by a physical examination and a neurological examination, as well as laboratory and radiographic evaluation. For example, an audiologist may conduct tests to determine whether or not a young child has a hearing loss. Diagnostic information must be available during the assessment phase for each child admitted to a program. Diagnostic information is often available prior to assessment, since infants are usually seen by doctors before they are seen by early intervention staff.

Diagnosis is carried out by the medical profession.

Diagnostic information is often available prior to assessment.

The definition of diagnosis as a medical activity is often a point of contention with some professionals in other fields. However, physicians argue, and rightly so, that one of their primary and unique functions is diagnosis. Although Peterson (1987) has argued for a broader definition of diagnosis, our position is that in programs for children under 3 years of age the role of the physician is critical to the success of early intervention efforts. Further, if medical and educational professionals are to cooperate, we must recognize the unique role of medical professionals in diagnosis, although this may mean that educators must give up a term they have long used and held dear.

In the third edition of Gesell and Armatruda's classic *Developmental Diagnosis* (1974), editors Knobloch and Pasamanick, who are both physicians, included a succinct paragraph describing the physician's role in diagnosis.

> The physician is concerned with the maturity and health of an infant or child; he has the responsibility for making a diagnosis, even if it is one of no disease. He is not asked to derive an IQ, or measure

"intelligence" as such. It is his task to assess central nervous system function: to identify the presence of any neuromotor or sensory deficit, to discover the existence of treatable developmental disorders, to detect infants at risk of subsequent deterioration, and to determine pathologic conditions of the brain which preclude normal intellectual function, no matter how optimal the environmental circumstances. He is exercising his responsibility of protecting the total growth of the child under his care. To effect this protection he makes an analytic assessment of behavior. (p. 17)

Evaluation

Evaluation includes analysis of information over time.

❑ The term *evaluation* includes the overall gathering and analysis of information related to a child's and family's program and progress over time. Evaluation information represents several cycles of data collection. Observation and test scores over time, the reports on the child's progress and diagnosis over time, and information gathered from the family and service delivery personnel are part of the evaluation system. Program evaluation includes systematic data collection and analysis for all the components of the early intervention, including staff development and administration.

Evaluation includes data collected to establish the child's progress on a systematic basis (every 6 months is a reasonable schedule), using instruments other than those used for assessment purposes. Although it is beyond the scope of this chapter to discuss the nature of data collected to document the efficacy of early intervention, it is an important part of a birth-to-3 program's evaluation plan. Comprehensive discussions of evaluation may be found in Chapter 9 of this text by Johnson, in Sheehan and Gallagher (1983), and in Suarez (1982).

BEGINNING THE CYCLE: SCREENING

❑ Although infants and toddlers come into birth-to-3 programs from different referral sources, many come because a screening test indicates a need to gather more information about the child. If the birth-to-3 program is new to the community, screening and other child find processes provide a way to establish a caseload of those needing intervention services.

Infant projects do not emerge as full blown programs.

Programs for young handicapped and developmentally delayed infants, toddlers, and their families cannot be compared to Athena of Greek mythology, who emerged full-grown from the head of Zeus. Infant projects do not emerge as full-blown programs, complete with clients and community support, without comprehensive preparatory activities. Rather, new infant programs usually begin with planning and hiring staff, and then attempt to find children and families to serve. During the first months, the caseload may be only a handful of clients. It takes time not only to establish successful program operation and publicity, but also to establish trust in the community, so that members are willing to accept and support

Trust must be established.

a program for infants and families. New programs must establish trust if they are to be successful and effective over time. Established programs must continually maintain activities that promote positive community awareness and interagency collaboration. While this chapter is not designed to detail the steps needed to prepare for community and agency coordination, working together is necessary to establish and maintain a viable birth-to-3 program. Interagency coordination must be recognized and addressed by those beginning or upgrading programs for young handicapped children. Community coordination is a necessary condition in order to establish effective use of limited resources, to maximally organize and manage programs, and to effectively screen, assess, and program.

Community coordination is necessary.

Establishing effective community coordination is an important component that must be demonstrated by each of eight demonstration projects that were funded by the Illinois legislature in 1985 for a 3-year period. The demonstration projects, using Project Nexus (Helmstetter et al., 1985) materials as a guide, have been collecting data on coordination and collaboration in many areas, including screening, assessment, and programming for families. Several of the projects, including the Rural Assist Infant Network (RAIN) at Western Illinois University (Smith-Dickson & Hutinger, 1986), have used mass screenings as a strategy to combine agency resources to accomplish a useful task that benefits families, communities, and the agencies themselves.

A great deal of spadework, including presentations (to ministers' groups, hospital staff, community agencies, school personnel, local service groups); publicity (newspaper stories, radio and television stories, brochures, flyers, and posters); and face-to-face information exchange is needed to let the community know that a program and services are available to work with the very youngest children whose problems make their families feel uneasy and sometimes inadequate. Screening of very young children, whether it is mass screening, screening upon referral, or routine screening done by public health nurses or their counterparts, provides a vehicle to bring the birth-to-3 program to the attention of those who might need its services. The publicity needed to successfully implement mass screening in an urban or rural area is a means of gaining public awareness for a birth-to-3 program. It is also the means for a new program to locate children and families who need services. Mass screenings represent a way for the established program to ensure the broadest possible publicity so that families who need services can find them. However, mass screenings, are not the only way to identify infants and toddlers who may benefit from early intervention services.

Publicity and face-to-face exchange are needed.

Mass screenings are not the only way to identify infants.

In existing birth-to-3 programs, children are often referred for services by physicians, public health nurses, or personnel from other agencies. Sometimes the referring agency or individual has screened the child and found that delays in at least one area of development indicate a potential need for early intervention. If successful interagency cooperation is functioning, results of one agency's screening are accepted by another agency. This does away with the need for rescreening. At other times, no screening has taken place, but someone, perhaps the parent, thinks there is a problem and calls the early intervention staff. In these instances the birth-to-3 program does the screening on an individual basis. It is worth repeating that children with obvious handicaps do *not* need to be screened. However, every child referred either is screened by the referring agency or by the birth-to-3 program and found to meet established criteria of risk or developmental delay or is diagnosed with an identifiable handicapping condition before an assessment is done. Public Law 99-457 requires states to establish their own definitions of developmental delay.

Children with obvious handicaps do not need to be screened.

CONTINUING THE CYCLE: ASSESSMENT

❑ A wide range of tests and procedures are used in early intervention programs. For example, as reported in the Illinois 0-3 Study (Hutinger et al., 1985), in 1984, Illinois birth-to-3 programs reported using over 25 different assessment instruments, ranging from formal standardized tests such as the Bayley Scales of Infant Development (Bayley, 1969) to checklists made by staff members. Appropriate assessment activities include a variety of reliable, valid tests and systematic observation procedures pinpointing behaviors to a fine degree in order to find an appropriate match between the child's existing behaviors and those milestones toward which the child will be moving.

Activities include valid tests and systematic observation.

The purpose of assessment is to determine areas of strengths and weakness of the child and family. Although this section addresses child assessment, it should be kept in mind that parents are members of the assessment team. Parents provide a wealth of information about the child and, in many cases, participate actively in the process. A play situation that allows parents to interact with the child while professionals watch and sometimes give suggestions provides useful information (i.e., arena assessment is a natural and nonthreatening situation for the child). Sometimes it is more beneficial to conduct assessment in the child's home rather than in the agency setting.

Sometimes conduct assessment in the child's home.

The family should receive services as soon as possible after determination of eligibility. Public Law 99-457 indicates that services may begin prior to assessment with the family's permission. In practice, this has been the case in many programs. However, in other instances long periods of time have passed between screening and service delivery for children and families. In Illinois, urban parents and staff reported average waits of 6.85 months, although rural parents and staff indicated that they waited only an average of 2.7 months (Hutinger et al., 1985). The intent of the identification and service provision in the laws is to get needed services to children as soon as possible, thereby eliminating some family stressors.

The intent is to get services to children as soon as possible.

P.L. 99-457 requires a multidisciplinary team of professionals to carry out assessment procedures. Usually, each set of professionals is responsible for collecting a portion of the necessary information. How they collect it is related both to their profession and to the nature of their interaction with other professionals (i.e., transdisciplinary, multidisciplinary, or interdisciplinary), as well as to the customary procedures in their particular agency or unit. Public Law 99-457 requires a multidisciplinary approach.

Bennett (1982) defined multidisciplinary, interdisciplinary, and transdisciplinary functions and roles. Those definitions were also adapted for the Illinois Early Childhood State Plan (Deppe, 1986). Multidisciplinary assessment is done separately by members of various disciplines with each writing separate reports. In an interdisciplinary mode, a member of each discipline assesses the child separately; they then meet to share recommendations and develop a service plan based on collaboration. Transdisciplinary team members work more closely together, with professionals assessing *across* traditional disciplines, thereby developing knowledge and skills in disciplines other than their own.

Transdisciplinary team members work more closely together.

If you ask a physical therapist who routinely uses a transdisciplinary approach about the uniqueness of the data she collects, she may tell you that she observes another professional who is giving the Bayley, or that she may administer the Peabody Developmental Motor Scales (Fewell & Folio, 1974). But you are likely to hear that the physical therapist is more interested in observing the child than in administering standardized tests. A physical therapist who is accustomed to doing her own assessment and then sharing it with the other professionals who work with a specific child in an interdisciplinary mode is interested in her own findings and their implications for comprehensive intervention. In a multidisciplinary mode, the physical therapist's assessment and recommendations are made separately, then combined with others to develop the child's goals.

Whatever the nature of their teaming approach, various professionals have differentiated roles and responsibilities in gathering information. Medical professionals are responsible for initial screening using the APGAR (Apgar, 1953) or neonatal Behavioral Assessment Scale (Brazelton, 1973), in addition to the myriad of tests and observations related to the child's diagnosis and treatment. Physical therapists or occupational therapists may depend on observation or a test such as the Milani-Comparetti Developmental Scale (Milani-Comparetti & Gidoni, 1977). Psychologists may use the Bayley Scales of Infant Development (Bayley, 1969), while child development specialists might use the Battelle Developmental Inventory (Newborg, Stock, Wnek, Guidabaldi, & Svinicki, 1984) or the Evaluation and Programming System for Infants and Young Children (Bricker, Bailey, & Gentry, 1985). Social workers might use the Home Observation for Measurement of the Environment (Caldwell & Bradley, 1978), the Feetham Family Function Survey (Roberts & Feetham, 1982), or another interview instrument.

The information collected needs to be shared with all the professionals involved, after the family's rights are ensured and the appropriate releases secured, so that as much as possible of what is known about the child can be used to make decisions about appropriate goals and objectives. A team effort, with professionals and families sharing their areas of expertise, is most likely to lead to the development of the best plan possible for a particular approach to intervention.

A team effort is most likely to lead to the best plan.

Assessment is carried on at regular 6-month or 3-month intervals, as specified by the individualized program and/or observation of the child's behavior, in order to develop new goals as the child acquires previously targeted skills. Assessment findings are used to decide on appropriate activities for an individual child and family. Throughout this chapter, regular reassessment has been referred to, usually citing 6-month intervals for documented family updates of the program, with a yearly review. Keeping records of assessment results is necessary, as is a summary of assessments and their dates for each child. A simple record-keeping form used by Project ACTT (Activating Children Through Technology) is shown in Figure 3. ACTT, a supplemental component of a birth-to-3 program, involves the use of computer technology in child activities. A record-keeping form for an entire program would include more information.

Although some early childhood professionals believe that there are no appropriate assessment instruments for handicapped and developmentally disabled children, there is a group of instruments that can be used with young handicapped youngsters, even though a great deal of work is still needed in this area. There is a list of instruments used for assessment at the end of this chapter. Instrument selection depends on the age of the

There is a group of instruments that can be used.

child, the nature of the handicapping conditions, and the purpose of testing.

A number of problems do exist related to the nature of test construction and the outcome information obtained for handicapped young children (Bricker, 1986; Fewell, 1983a). There are also useful new directions in the assessment of handicapped infants and toddlers. For example, William Bricker and Campbell (1980) listed a set of 19 dimensions of assessment for children with specialized service needs. These include surviving and thriving, mobility, manipulation, consequence preference, compliance, motor imitation, and verbal imitation. Fewell pointed to the work of Brooks-Gunn and Lewis (1981), which was designed to describe the development of very young handicapped children across various dimensions and skills such as information-processing and mother-infant interaction. Fewell also cited the work of Simeonsson, Huntington, Short, and Ware (1982), which examined domains that traditional instruments did not include. Their Carolina Record of Individual Behavior (CRIB) is an observational instrument that is completed during the administration of a developmental assessment instrument or after a period of observation.

Fewell (1983a) pointed to researchers' dissatisfaction with available assessment measures and their subsequent exploration of new assessment arrangements including the use of natural environments and events and the measurement of child-parent interaction. She then included an observational assessment of infant behavior, the Behavioral Observation Form, which can be used throughout the assessment process. It could be used to analyze videotapes of infant and toddler behavior or in actual situations.

Figure 3. A Sample Record-keeping Form Used in the Technology Component of Birth-to-Three Programs by Project ACTT.

ACTT: Birth to 3 Evaluation Checklist

Early Childhood Specialist: _____ Agency: _____

Child's Name: _____ ID#: _____ Closing Date: _____

Birthdate: _____ Program Entry Date: _____

	Recommended	Date(s) Completed					
Parent Consent Forms	updated yearly						
Uzgiris and Hunt Scales (or selected assessment)	6 month intervals						
Parent Questionnaire	entry date						
Parent Satisfaction Questionnaire	6 month intervals						
Videotaping of Computer Sessions	selected sessions (as needed)						
Computer Interaction Form	each computer session (collect every 6 months)						
Computer Intervention Planning Form	each computer session (collect every 6 months)						

The list of assessment measures included in this chapter contains the Human Interaction Scale used by White and Watts (1973) to code and analyze mother-child, child-child, child-peer, and child-another adult interactions. The Human Interaction Scale includes five dimensions: activities, initiation index, encouragement index, interaction technique, and compliance index. This scale was used in a large study to examine the problem of structuring the experiences of the first 6 years of life in order to encourage maximal development of human competence. Information from the scale is useful in determining the nature of interactions within families.

The Nursing Child Assessment Teaching Scale (Barnard, 1979) was designed to record parent-child behaviors during a teaching task. Interactions between parent and child provide information about the nature of the relationship between the two, pointing to the presence of problems. Fewell (1983a) suggested that the results of a scale such as the Nursing Child Assessment Teaching Scale show how parent responses can be structured to reduce behavior problems and promote learning.

Rosenberg, Robinson, & Beckman (1986) considered several approaches to parent-child interaction, including molar and molecular rating scales. Molar scales condense classes of behaviors presumed to reflect a larger aspect of parent-child behavior. Examples are the Maternal Behavior Rating Scale (Mahoney, Powell, & Finger, 1986) and The Teaching Skills Inventory (Rosenberg, Robinson, & Beckman, 1984; Rosenberg & Robinson, 1985). Molecular Coding Systems include more narrowly defined categories and record specific behavioral events. The Human Interaction Scale (White & Watts, 1973) and the Social Interaction Assessment/Intervention model (McCollum & Stayton, 1985) are examples of molecular instruments.

Molar scales condense classes of behavior.

Observational methods for assessing communication efforts have also been developed in recent years. Analysis of Mean Length Utterance (Miller, 1981) provides a strategy to sample child language at specified times in natural daily activities and provides useful information about the child's use of language to communicate. A pragmatic approach to language focuses more on the child's communication, its intent, and the need to influence people or objects in the environment. Use of a pragmatic approach has moved us away from counting the number of words in a child's vocabulary to looking at the intent of the child's communication, a much more beneficial approach for both child and family. Mean Length Utterance, using a series of language samples, is a more useful way to assess the child's efforts at communication than the Peabody Picture Vocabulary Test (Dunn & Dunn, 1981).

A pragmatic approach focuses on communication.

Videotaping child performance in selected representative situations over time, then analyzing the performance changes using one of the observational scales cited here, or another scale focusing on a specific child behavior (such as social interaction with peers), provides objective information about the child to family members and early intervention team members. Videotapes are also useful in recording the progression of family skills. While videotapes require resources that some programs may not have, systematic collection of tapes is useful for a variety of purposes, including dissemination of information about the program to community decision makers. If a program decides to collect videotapes, it must establish a cataloging system to access information.

Videotaping provides objective information.

Norm-referenced measures have been standardized on representative samples.

A surprising number of tests are used by early intervention program staff. Ideally, the tests depend on the purpose for which they are being administered and, as pointed out earlier, are consistent with program philosophy. Norm-referenced measures such as the Bayley Scales of Infant Development (Bayley, 1969) have been standardized on representative samples of children (most often nonhandicapped children) in order to establish norms. A child's score can be compared with those of other children of the same age. These tests are more likely to be used as general measures of development and as instruments to collect scores that can be analyzed statistically to measure child progress for program evaluation purposes. Criterion-referenced measures such as the Evaluation and Programming System for Infants and Young Children (Bricker & Gentry, 1985) compare a child's score or performance to a specified level of mastery. They are far more likely to be easily translated into intervention programming activities.

Fewell (1983a) discussed curriculum-referenced tests composed of precisely stated items accompanied by a curriculum that specifies instructional strategies. Curriculum-referenced tests include the Peabody Developmental Motor Scales (Fewell & Folio, 1974) and the Skills Inventory from The Oregon Project for Visually Impaired and Blind Pre-school Children (Brown, Simmons, & Methvin, 1979). Dunst's (1981) *Infant Learning: A Cognitive Linguistic Intervention Strategy* is a curriculum guide based on the Piagetian sensorimotor stages designed on the basis of the *Infant Psychological Development Scales.* The *Ordinal Scales of Psychological Development* (Uzgiris & Hunt, 1975) were developed from both a different content than norm-referenced tests and a different test construction model. The sensorimotor period is the content. The scales are based on a Piagetian sequence of behavior achievements and are relatively independent of age (Uzgiris & Hunt, 1975).

The two scales cover a wide range of social and nonsocial developmental skills.

Dunst (1981) developed a curriculum matrix using items from the Griffiths (1954, 1970) and the Uzgiris and Hunt (1975) scales, noting that the two scales have been "found to have general utility for identifying a child's particular intervention needs" (p. 1). He also indicated that the two scales cover a wide range of social and nonsocial developmental skills, assess the child's ability to initiate and respond to different stimuli, tap progressively more complex behaviors, and lead to a "good estimation" of a child's developmental capabilities in specific rather than global terms. This is perhaps the most important criterion for the design of appropriate intervention procedures.

Assessment instruments are used for placement, but once a child is determined eligible for early intervention services, further assessment is essential to determine the most appropriate activities and strategies. A measure of child and parent interaction provides further information about appropriate teaching styles and family functions. Other measures of family needs and strengths are addressed elsewhere in this book.

MAINTAINING THE CYCLE: PLANNING CURRICULUM

❑ Planning individualized programs for handicapped infants, toddlers, and their families begins with gathering a great deal of information from a variety of sources. That information is then paired with goals, objectives, and selected activities appropriate for both the child and the family, with special attention given to the set of unique needs and characteristics of the family unit. Gathering information for, developing, and then implementing a plan for intervention must be done whether the child and family are new clients in a birth-to-3 program or have participated in the program for some time.

The "appropriate activities" constitute what many call "curriculum." Rather than imposing a definition that assumes an "educational" flavor, early intervention curriculum is better thought of as the sum total of activities and services that can be carried out to meet the goals of the whole program plan for the child and family. This means we must consider *who* provides activities and services. Public Law 99-457 requires that qualified professionals, including special educators, speech and language pathologists and audiologists, occupational therapists, physical therapists, social workers, nurses, and nutritionists provide early intervention services. The result of such a team effort is that the early intervention curriculum used to meet individual family plans must necessarily include a wide range of activities.

Curriculum is thought of as the sum total of activities and services.

The broad definition of curriculum takes into account who carries out curricular activities, who is the target of the activities, and the nature and integration of curricular activities across developmental domains. The individualized family service plans include specific plans for the child and the family. Bricker (1986) addressed family assessment, affirming that it should address three areas: the family's needs and concerns, their understanding of the child's problems, and the extent of their instructional skills. Bristol and Gallagher (1982) also addressed individual family plans, noting that assessment, programming, and evaluation should focus on the broader context of family development.

IFSPs include specific plans for the child and family.

When long-term goals and short-term objectives are set for very young children, the activities that lead to the accomplishment of those objectives and goals are part of the "curriculum." If a 15-month-old child has difficulty with head control, and her intervention team has planned a variety of experiences using a mercury head switch and various battery-operated toys and a tape recording of her father's whistle, her family members may need to learn the skills necessary to provide the experiences. The child's activity hinges on the skills the parents develop. If computers are to be used for communication, then family members need to learn to use the software, hardware, and peripherals necessary for the child to communicate (Hutinger, Perry, Robinson, Weaver, & Whitaker, 1986). If the child needs special positioning to sit up, the parents need to learn techniques from the physical therapist and also will probably learn how to make various supports to help the child accomplish the goal. Both the child activity and the skills needed to help the family carry out the activity must be part of the early intervention program.

The child's activity hinges on the skills parents develop.

Although the information contained here is focused more directly on the child component of the curriculum, the family is an integral part of the curricular process and the early intervention team. They make decisions about what they want for their child and they carry out many activities. Just as child programs are different because of individual differences, the level of a family's participation varies because of the family's unique characteristics and interaction with the child. For example, in Project ACTT activities, parents participate on the following levels: obtaining information, assisting in intervention, and conducting intervention (Hutinger, 1987). Parents of more severely handicapped children often move quickly to the third level, actually carrying out activities. Since its inception

The level of a family's participation varies.

in 1975, the Macomb 0-3 Rural Model has been based on the premise that parents are the primary change agents for their children (Hutinger & McKee, 1980), and are therefore integrally involved with all aspects of the child's program. An informal, differential family-needs assessment when a family began in the program, and at 6-month intervals, was also a part of the original Macomb Model. Sharing Centers were designed in the Macomb Model to function like family cooperative nursery schools (Hutinger, 1986; Hutinger, Donsbach, Cunningham, Longanecker, & Sharp, 1981), involving parents in a number of organizational, instructional, and social functions. The parent cooperative nursery school has been a part of the educational environment for young nonhandicapped children for at least 60 years. Parents, siblings, and program children participate in many different Sharing Center activities designed to meet intervention objectives.

Emphasis is on family needs and participation.

Heavy emphasis is now placed on assessment of family needs and participation in their child's intervention program. When the Handicapped Children's Early Education Program (HCEEP) was established 17 years ago, emphasis was on the active role of the family. In 1985, when Project RAIN (Rural Assist Infant Network) and the other Illinois birth-through-2 demonstration programs were funded, emphasis on family needs assessment and participation was, and continues to be, of great importance. Head Start has always focused on family participation in the classroom, in the community, and as advisors. The configuration of the family system (whether members are equal or differentiated, open or closed to outsiders), the nature of the family's communication patterns, and the family's methods of solving problems have a direct impact on the family's response to early intervention for their handicapped infant. Since families have responsibility for their children for many more years than the infant intervention program staff are associated with the children, it makes sense to franchise families, giving them the skills they need to be both advocates for the child and primary change agents as well. Yet it is important to remember that the parent role is one that must involve play, happiness, and pleasant interactions (Satir, 1972). Sometimes when parents assume the role of interventionists, they become so serious about making sure that the child accomplishes an activity they forget to enjoy their children. We must not let this happen.

Head Start has always focused on family participation in the classroom.

The Individualized Family Service Plan

❑ According to P.L. 99-457, the individualized family service plan (IFSP) must contain the following:

1. A statement of the child's present levels of development (cognitive, speech and language, psychosocial, motor, and self-help).
2. A statement of the family's strengths and needs related to enhancing the child's development.
3. A statement of major outcomes expected to be achieved for the child and family.
4. The criteria, procedures, and timelines for determining progress.
5. The specific early intervention services necessary to meet the unique needs of the child and family, including the method, frequency, and intensity of service.

6. The projected dates for the initiation of services and expected duration.

7. The name of the case manager.

8. Procedures for transition from early intervention into the preschool program.

While there are similarities between the IFSP and the individualized educational program (IEP) of P.L. 94-142, the inclusion of the family in P.L. 99-457 marks an important landmark in early intervention programming. The IFSP is developed by a multidisciplinary team after initial assessment information has been gathered.

Inclusion of the family in P.L. 99–457 marks an important landmark.

Child Goals

❑ The process of developing an IFSP is similar to that of the IEP, but the content is different. Results of the child *and* family assessment measures are used to plan the services or activities for each family. Long-range goals are developed by paying attention to the child's strengths and weaknesses, the family's needs, and the interactions between the child and family (Bricker, 1986).

When we are part of an effort to set goals for infants and toddlers, we need to think about what will happen when those children reach adolescence or adulthood. The ultimate goals are for them to be socially adjusted and to have as much autonomy and as many functional skills as possible. This means making use of as many avenues of accessing children's functional modalities as possible, including obtaining new and helpful medical advances, technology applications including microcomputers and their accompanying hardware, and instructional strategies that incorporate play, elements of novelty, and enjoyment. Bricker (1986) noted that play is the work of the young child. This is an important assumption. The Macomb 0-3 Model has been based on this view of play since its beginning in 1975.

Goals are to be socially adjusted, have autonomy, functional skills.

The most effective activities for gaining new skills are part of the child's daily, ongoing, real-life experiences. Picking up cubes of cheese to eat and putting them in your mouth has more relevance to a child who wants a snack than putting buttons in a jar. Operating a tape recorder with a switch to listen to music or mother's voice is a way to affect the environment, gain a sense of self-confidence, and learn to control your hand or knee or head. Activities leading to the attainment of important developmental goals integrate several skills. Activating the randomly appearing stars on a computer screen (Hutinger, Perry, Robinson, Weaver, & Whitaker, 1986) leads to the realization that touching keys has an effect, to sustained visual and auditory attention, to fine motor manipulations, and to a need to communicate with someone about those bright stars and sounds.

Operating a tape recorder is a way to affect environment.

Developing long-range goals is accomplished by listing the behaviors the child demonstrated during the assessment phase. The process used by the Macomb projects (Macomb 0-3 Rural Project and Project ACTT) to determine program goals, objectives, and instructional strategies provides examples for child programs. The Program Planning Guide portion of the Macomb 0-3 Core Curriculum (Hutinger, Marshall, & McCartan, 1983) is a useful form for indicating the behaviors the child displays. A sample page from the Program Planning Guide is shown in Figure 4. A computer version of the Program Planning Guide, the CORE

CORE provides a quick way to record data.

(Hutinger, Marshall, McCartan, Nelson, & Hutinger, 1986) provides a quick way to record data about initial and ongoing child performance in the curriculum. The CORE also provides a listing of suggested new skill areas to target next, after the child has accomplished targeted skills, and it prints out a list of the child's current individualized plan. It provides a useful tool for maintaining child records and for planning new skills.

The Macomb 0-3 Core Curriculum is based on a functional developmental approach to early intervention. It contains goals in six major areas of child development: gross motor, fine motor, cognition, social, communication, and self-care. Each curricular area is divided into a cluster of related behaviors in skill areas. Each skill has a corresponding sequence of skills that leads to the behavior described in the skill area statement. Activity examples reflect the curriculum's functional approach.

Figure 4. An Example of a Core Curriculum Program Planning Guide.

PROGRAM PLANNING GUIDE

1.0.00 Gross Motor

SKILL AREA AND SEQUENCE	AGE	DATE SKILL ACQUIRED
1.1.00 Child moves in a prone (on-stomach) position		
1.1.1 Turns head side to side	1 month	
1.1.2 Lifts head off surface momentarily	1-2 months	
1.1.3 Lifts head 45°	2 months	
1.1.4 Keeps head steady when carried in upright position	2-3 months	
1.1.5 Lifts head 90°	3 months	
1.1.6 Raises chin and shoulders off surface with weight on forearms	3 months	
1.1.7 Sustains head lift at 90°	4 months	
1.1.8 Bears weight on forearms	4-6 months	
1.1.9 Bears weight on one forearm and reaches with other arm	4-6 months	

(Continued)

They focus on child behavior and involve daily routines, life situations, and playtimes. References are included in the curriculum. Adaptations are also included that suggest activities and other ideas for use with children who have visual, auditory, and/or motor impairments. Samples of skill areas in each of the major domains are shown in Figure 5. The curriculum is arranged in a developmental sequence or hierarchy.

Activity examples focus on behavior, daily routines, playtimes.

A relatively new emphasis in programming activities for handicapped infants and toddlers is that of technology. The use of switches and battery-operated toys has been advocated for older handicapped children for some time. However, when switches and toys are viewed as the beginning of cause-and-effect activities, and are used in contingency intervention (Brinker & Lewis, 1982), technology takes on new importance. Infants and toddlers benefit from the use of computers, whether the

Infants and toddlers benefit from use of computers.

Figure 4. An Example of a Core Curriculum Program Planning Guide. (Continued)

PROGRAM PLANNING GUIDE

2.0.00 FINE MOTOR

SKILL AREA AND SEQUENCE	AGE	DATE SKILL ACQUIRED
2.1.00 Child visually focuses on objects		
2.1.1 Focuses both eyes on a nonmoving object held eight inches from eyes	1-2 months	
2.1.2 Follows moving object with coordinated eye movement	1-2 months	
2.1.3 Tracks moving object in horizontal 90° arc	1-2 months	
2.1.4 Tracks moving object in horizontal 180° arc	2-3 months	
2.1.5 Tracks moving object as it moves towards and away from him/her	3 months	
2.1.6 Anticipates a regular pattern of movement	4-6 months	
2.1.7 Visually focuses on and observes hand	3-6 months	

©MACOMB 0-3 REGIONAL PROJECT

Figure 5. Samples of Curriculum Areas and Skills from the Core Curriculum.

1.0.00 GROSS MOTOR

Skill Area: 1.1.00   Child moves in a prone (on-stomach) postition.

Skill Sequence	Activity Examples	References	Adaptions
1.1.1 Turns head side to side	Place child on stomach on firm surface. Adult should lie beside child and entice child to turn head toward adult by talking to child, touching child or using noise making toy. Adult should attempt this on both sides of the child Caregiver or sibling should talk to child, first on one side of the crib at eye level and close bars, then on	General gross motor references: Cohen & Gross ND Vol I, pp.133-142 Finnie N. PH Fredricks TA Vol II, pp. 64-65 Utley, Holvett, Barnes PH pp. 279-288 Macomb 0-3 Core	Motorically Impaired: Child is placed on stomach on roll or wedge with the thickest end of the wedge supporting chest. If child is unable to raise head, adult should stimulate child's vertibral column contractures by pressing firmly along the vertebral

2.0.00 FINE MOTOR

Skill Area: 2.1.00 Child Visually focuses on objects.

Skill Sequence	Activity Examples	References	Adaptions
2.1.1 Focuses both on a non-moving object held 8" from eyes	Place child on patterned sheet. Encourage child to focus by pointing at different colors. -Use brightly colored or patterned towels on shoulders when feeding child. -Place mobile over	Cohen & Gross ND Vol I, pp. 143-151 Fredricks TA Vol II, PP. 50-51, 74-76 Melnechuk BI pp. 214-15 Macomb 0-3	Visually Impaired Use bright colors close to child.

3.0.00 COGNITION

Skill Area: 3.3.00 Child differentiates between objects.

Skill Sequence	Activity Examples	References	Adaptions

3.3.1 Observes objects.	Hang mobile above child's crib, or suspend object in walker or stroller.
	
	Place floating objects in tub when bathing child.
	
	Hold objects in front of child wiggling, squeaking, or activating them to attract child's
		Applies to entire skill sequence:
		
		Melnechuk BI pp. 186-199
		      204-208
		      235-236
		      239
		      289-404
		
		Furano et. al. pp. 1-51 ND,GA
		
		Bailey & Burton
			Visually Impaired It may help to shine flashlight on object for child. When doing this, be aware of the problem of surface glare which could make it harder to see if light is coming from wrong

(Continued)

computer is a record-keeping device for the professional or a tool that responds to the child. This is not to say that all children need computers; however, severely handicapped children are able to respond to the environment in more active ways when they have access to the tools of technology (Hutinger, 1987). Hindrances to the use of technology are related to fears that machines will control children, adult fear of learning to use the technology, the costs of the equipment, and the complexity of using the equipment. Nevertheless, the promise of technology in early intervention curricula lies in its use as a tool and its ability to help very young handicapped children access the environment and develop a sense of control over that environment. The work of project ACTT has been based on this assumption.

Figure 5. Samples of Curriculum Areas and Skills from the Core Curriculum. (Continued)

4.0.00 COMMUNICATIONS

Skill Area: 4.1.00 Child Responds to auditory stimuli.

Skill Sequence	Activity Examples	References	Adaptions
4.1.1 Shows response to animate auditory stimuli	Adult approaches child slowly, with varying degrees of quietness (speaking low to louder). Watch for child's responses to this.	Furano et. al. GA p. 1-2, 7 Macomb 0-3 GA Core Curriculum, 1980	Hearing Impaired: Adult should be in child's visual field. May place lips gently against child's head or on hand to allow child to feel vibrations.
4.1.2 Shows response to inanimate auditory stimuli	Adult should shake rattle, play music box, play quiet music on tape recorder, record player or radio.	Furano et. al.GA pp. 11, 15 Macomb 0-3 GA Core Curriculum, 1980	Hearing Impaired: Use rattles, noisemakers of high or low pitch. Use toys, objects that make noise and also vibrate or make

5.0.00 SOCIAL

Skill Area: 5.2.00 Child initiates social interaction with adults.

Skill Sequence	Activity Examples	References	Adaptions
5.2.1 Observes adult.	Adult can sit child nearby during routine daily living activities. Adult should periodically look at, touch, talk to, and smile at child. Adult may use colored lipstick on own face to draw attention or wear hat.	Furano et. al. GA p. 127 Macomb 0-3 GA Core Curriculum, 1980	Visually Impaired If child is visually impaired "observes" may mean child listens or attends adult rather than watches; looks in adult's direction.

6.0.00 SELF CARE

Skill Area: 6.2.00 Child ingests semi-solids.

Skill Sequence	Activity Examples	References	Adaptions
6.2.1 Swallows semi-solids.	To prevent the child's head from being tipped back during feeding, hold the spoon just in front of the child's mouth to encourage child to come forward, bring child forward toward spoon, placing the food in at the side of the mouth if the child is inclined to push it out with tongue.	Fredricks TA Vol I p. 47 Utley, Hovoet, Barnes P, H pp. 290-7 Furano et al. GA p. 159 Macomb 0-3 GA Core Curriculum 1980	Motorically Impaired: Position the child in an upright position either in the adult's arms or by using a standard high chair which has been adapted to provide the child with increased hip flexion. If using a high

Robinson (1986a,b) described details of the Project ACTT birth-to-3 technology intervention. The Project ACTT birth-to-3 Curriculum (Hutinger, Perry, Robinson, Weaver, & Whitaker, 1986) includes sections on goals and activities for children and families, as well as detailed information on setting up the environment and working closely with families. Switch use is viewed as a way to help children acquire both a sense of autonomy and the skills they need to control various technology devices. A sample ACTT activity curriculum is shown in Figure 6.

A variety of curricula for use with handicapped infants and toddlers is available and reflects different points of view about how very young children learn. A short list of selected curricula is included at the end of this chapter.

A variety of curricula is available.

Figure 6. Sample ACTT (Activating Children Through Technology) Curriculum Activity.

Birth to 3 Curriculum

Activity Name: Controlling a Toy Through Head Movement

Content Area: Cognition–Beginning Development of Causality
Concept Through Head Control Movement

Teaching Objectives:

1. Provide child opportunities for controlling an object by moving his head appropriately.
2. Reinforce cause and effect concepts.

Child Objectives:

1. Activate toy by raising head slightly when placed in on-stomach position.
2. Notice movement of toy when head is raised.
3. Repeat process of raising head to re-activate toy when toy stops.

Materials: Several battery-operated toys containing appropriate sensory stimulus response for the child
Battery Interrupter
Mercury headband switch
Blanket or pad for floor
Towel roll
Wooden blocks to mark off boundary for toy

Procedures:

Introduce the toy to the child by placing the toy close to child's hand so he can physically explore it. Name the toy and talk about what it does. Demonstrate the toy's movement by activating switch for the child.

Lay child on stomach over towel roll and place mercury headband switch on the head. Position the mercury capsules so that slight head movement will activate the toy. Attach switch to battery-operated toy which is placed in front of child's head.

Assist child in lifting head to look at and/or listen to the toy. May need to assist child several times to become aware of start/stop action and sound of the toy.

Verbally encourage child to make the toy "go" again. Child may also need to be prompted physically by touch to side or top of head. Moving the toy around on the floor in front of the child's head may also provide stimulus for head lifting.

As child's response begins to decrease, a different toy can be introduced to continue to stimulate interest in the activity.

As child develops an understanding of causality and attains better head control, mercury capsules can be repositioned so that greater effort is required to activate toy.

Variations:

Child's position could be changed to a supported sitting position. The same mercury headband switch can be used to encourage midline head control by adjusting the placement of the capsules on the headband. If the same toy is used, it will need to be placed on a table or box at child's eye level. A

(Continued)

Figure 6. Sample ACTT (Activating Children Through Technology) Curriculum Activity. (Continued)

hanging toy or mobile could also be used at a level in which child is required to keep head in midline to activate the music or sound.

Helpful Hints:

The appropriate placement of the mercury capsules should be determined before headband is placed on the child's head, if possible, to reduce frustration on the part of the child. Also the capsules should be secured in place so that head movement elicits consistent activation of the toy.

Adaptations:

Visual Impairment: Use battery-operated toys or a tape recorder which have a variety of different sounds. Assist the child in tactilely exploring the toy and physically orientating to its location. A vibrating pillow may also be used, placed under the child's chest or other position to stimulate head movement to control the vibration.

Auditory Impairment: Use brightly colored toys or a battery-operated light to stimulate child's visual response. Also a vibratory pillow or toy may be used to stimulate head movement.

Motor Impairment: Use a timer attached to switch and toy so that toy will play for several seconds after initial activation. Child is not required to keep his head up to listen to toy. One disadvantage of using a timer for this activity is that it does not give the child direct control of the sound. It is activated for several seconds despite the child's response or head position. For some children this may be needed to stimulate initial head lifting and reduce frustration from physical limitations.

ISSUES

❑ Screening, diagnosis, and referral are linked together as processes that precede assessment and program planning. However, establishing criteria to identify children who are eligible for services represents a multisided issue bounded on one side by available funds (never enough to go around and serve all the children who may benefit), on another by agreement or disagreement about the acceptability of the degree of handicapping conditions necessary before services can be provided, and, on yet another, by questions of efficacy as it is affected by various handicapping conditions and program types.

Screening, diagnosis, and referral precede assessment and program planning.

Further, although some states may have decided on the eligibility requirement for the preschool population from 3 to 5 years of age, the same requirements are not appropriate for children under age 3. For example, if a 6-month delay in a developmental domain is used as a criterion for preschool children, it seems clear that one cannot apply the same criterion to a 3-month-old Down syndrome child. The ratio of the number of months of delay needed to identify a need for services is different for the infant who has been alive only 9 months (a 6-month delay means that the child is delayed by a ratio of 1:3). But when that criterion is applied to a 4-year-old child, the ratio is 1:8. Clearly, the arbitrary number of months delay used during the preschool years is not a fair one to use with children from birth to age 3. Obviously, identified handicaps such as Down syndrome, cerebral palsy, and other biological conditions are candidates for birth-to-3 services. The emphasis on individual family service plans focuses attention on both the child's condition and/or delay as well as the needs of family members rather than on the quantitative amount of the child's delay.

Exhaustive tests when screening results in costly expenditures.

One of the pitfalls in gathering information is collecting too much too soon. For example, doing exhaustive tests when screening to find children with developmental delays results in needless and costly expenditures. Children who are screened and who appear to be functioning at the level typical of their chronological age do not need to go through a battery of tests during screening in order to find out whether they might be eligible for an early intervention program. These children may be rescreened in 6 months if their parents request it or if there are any questions about their development. The full battery of carefully chosen tests and observation instruments comes into play when children who are suspected of having a developmental delay or a potential problem as determined by screening receive further assessment by appropriate professionals. Sometimes rescreening may be all that is needed, particularly if parents report that the child acted in an unusual, nontypical manner during testing, or if the child was ill or afraid of the examiner. Some programs screen their children using the full Battelle Developmental Inventory (Newborg et al., 1984) or the Bayley Scales of Infant Development (Bayley, 1969). This is not necessary during the screening phase, although it may be appropriate during the assessment phase. Overtesting at the screening phase is expensive and uses valuable resources needlessly.

A pitfall is expecting to get needed information from the wrong instrument.

A second pitfall is expecting to get the needed information from the wrong instrument. For example, if the intent is to determine accurately as many of the child's behaviors as possible in order to plan appropriate daily and weekly activities, then using a test such as the Developmental Profile II (Alpern, Boll, & Shearer, 1980) is inappropriate. Rather, a comprehensive test of developmental domains, such as the EPS (Bricker, Bailey, & Gentry, 1985), will yield the needed information. Another example of using the wrong instrument is seen when screening instruments such as the Denver Developmental Screening Test (Frankenburg, 1978) are used in place of a comprehensive set of tests and observations to assess the nature of the child's developmental level and handicapping conditions.

A problem arises when the information gathered in the assessment phase is linked to curricular activities for young children and the curricular activities consist of the test items. This is not a major issue in curriculum-referenced measures since the best of them suggest activities to meet a teaching objective and do not attempt to teach the item specifically (Fewell, 1983a). "Teaching the test" may result in higher scores on tests, but is not likely to lead to greater adaptability and functional behavior on the part of the child or greater comfort in the family. For example, learning to stack three blocks probably will not help the child with cerebral palsy learn to feed himself or herself or to communicate needs. Learning to control switches to activate a toy or to use a communication program is more functional, but does not appear on any developmental tests we have seen. Activities planned for young handicapped children need to be functional. They should help the child

Activities need to be functional.

have an impact on the environment and the people around him or her even though that impact may be small.

While P.L. 99-457 legislates an individualized family service plan, we must remember that families have different needs, different strengths, and a wide range of problems. A continuum of family participation in early intervention might range from the family as primary intervener to the family expecting outside professionals to intervene. A number of factors determine where on the continuum a family might fall, yet early intervention personnel, decision makers, and families themselves must recognize that there are different roles appropriate for family members to take in screening, assessment, and curriculum. Differences in families and their roles are important and must be considered in planning programs for them and their children. All families cannot be expected to take part in the same capacity.

All families cannot take part in the same capacity.

Finally, different professionals have different conceptions about what appropriate intervention activities really are, and so do families. Notions about differences between therapy and developmental activities are found among professionals. The role of play has been gaining increasing attention in programs for handicapped children, a positive step in early intervention. Yet the notion that child-controlled play activities are worthy of serious attention will probably be a point of contention among service providers in the coming years. Taken together with the need to provide integrated intervention activities rather than separate isolated events, developmentally appropriate activities that include a recognition of the importance of play should become the hallmark of early intervention activities.

We should not see a group of three infants pull up to a table and stand there looking at blocks and plastic cups in the middle, out of their reach, and then hear the physical therapist tell their mothers as she takes the manipulative materials away, "We're just working on motor activities now, not cognitive things." Removing the blocks and the cups removes the children's need to stand at the table so they can reach for something that interests them. It also confuses mothers. Integrating motor and cognitive elements in one activity, together with communication and social skills, provides a framework for meaningful, functional activities that make sense to families and provide beneficial experiences to infants and toddlers. Curricular integration is not viewed as an important strategy by all early interventionists, but it can be expected to gain in acceptance in the coming years.

Curricular integration can be expected to gain in acceptance.

SUMMARY

❑ The material in this chapter has been wide ranging, providing an overview of the relationships among screening, assessment, and curriculum in programming for handicapped infants and toddlers and their families, with attention to the potential impact of P.L. 99-457. Each topic can be reviewed in greater depth in a number of sources suggested by the references at the end of this chapter. The intent here was to provide initial, essential information to aid service providers in their efforts to establish infant programs and upgrade the quality of their services. Sharp distinctions between screening and assessment clarify personnel functions and agency responsibilities in interagency efforts. Continued attention to the role of families in the processes has been emphasized. The issues discussed, together with new ones, are likely to be considered and argued by early intervention staff as we move into the full realization of the impact of P.L. 99-457.

REFERENCES

Alpern, G., Boll, T., Shearer, M. (1980). *The developmental profile II.* Aspen, CO: Psychological Development Publications.

Apgar, V. (1953). A proposal for a new method of evaluation of the newborn infant. *Current Researches in Anesthesia and Analgesia, 32,* 260-267.

Barnard, K. (1979). *Nursing child assessment teaching manual.* Seattle, WA: Department of Parent and Child Nursing, NCAST, University of Washington.

Bayley, N. (1969). *Scales of infant development.* New York: Psychological Corporation.

Bennett, F. C. (1982). The pediatrician and the interdisciplinary process. *Exceptional Children, 48,* 306-314.

Brazelton, B. (1973). *Neonatal behavioral assessment scale.* Philadelphia, PA: J. B. Lippincott.

Bricker, D. (1986). *Early education of at-risk and handicapped infants, toddlers, and preschool children.* Glenview, IL: Scott, Foresman.

Bricker, D., Bailey, E., & Gentry, D. (1985). *The evaluation and programming system: For infants and young children.* Eugene, OR: University of Oregon.

Bricker, W. A., & Campbell, P. H. (1980). Interdisciplinary assessment and programming for multihandicapped students. In W. Sailor, B. Wilcox, & L. Brown (Eds.), *Methods of instruction for severely handicapped students* (pp. 3-45). Baltimore: Brookes Publishing.

Brinker, R., & Lewis, M. (1982). Making the world work with microcomputers: A learning prosthesis for handicapped infants. *Exceptional Children, 49,* 168-170.

Bristol, M. M., & Gallagher, J. J. (1982). A family focus for intervention. In C. T. Ramey & P. L. Trohanis (Eds.) *Finding and educating high-risk and handicapped infants* (pp. 137-161). Baltimore, MD: University Park Press.

Brooks-Gunn, J., & Lewis, M. (1981). Assessing young handicapped children: Issues and solutions. *Journal of the Division for Early Childhood, 2,* 91.

Brown, D., Simmons, U., Methvin, J. (1979). *Skills Inventory* (The Oregon Project for Visually Impaired and Blind Pre-school Children). Medford, OR: OREGON Project.

Bzoch, K., & League, R. (1971). *Receptive-expressive emergent language scale.* Baltimore, MD: University Park Press.

Caldwell, B., & Bradley, R. (1978). *Home observation for measurement of the environment.* Little Rock, AR: Center for Child Development and Education, University of Arkansas.

Deppe, J. (1986). *Illinois early childhood state plan.* Springfield, IL: Illinois State Board of Education. Draft submitted for review.

Dunn, L., & Dunn, L. (1981). *Peabody picture vocabulary test* (rev. ed.). Circle Pines, MN: American Guidance Service.

Dunst, C. J. (1981). *Infant learning: A cognitive-linguistic intervention strategy.* Hingham, MA: Teaching Resources.

Fewell, R. (1983a). Assessing handicapped infants. In S. G. Garwood & R. R. Fewell (Eds.), *Educating handicapped infants: Issues in development and intervention* (pp. 257-297). Rockville, MD: Aspen.

Fewell, R. (1983b). The team approach. In S. G. Garwood & R. R. Fewell (Eds.), *Educating handicapped infants: Issues in development and intervention* (pp. 299-322). Rockville, MD: Aspen.

Fewell, R., & Folio, R. (1974). *Peabody developmental motor scales* (rev. ed.). Hingham, MA: Teaching Resources.

Frankenburg, W. K. (1978). *Denver developmental screening test*. Denver, CO: Ladoca Publishing Foundation.

Griffiths, R. (1954). *The abilities of babies*. London: University of London Press.

Griffiths, R. (1970). *The abilities of young children*. London: Child Development Research Center.

Helmstetter, E., Hazel, R., Barber, P., Behr, S., Roberts, S., Guess, D., Weber, L., Behr, B., & Magrab, P. (1985). *A community approach to integrated service system. Project Nexus*. (Contract No. 300 84 0149). Draft available from University of Kansas. Kansas City: University of Kansas.

Horowitz, F., (1982). Methods of assessment for high-risk and handicapped infants. In C. Raney & P. Trohanis (Eds.), *Finding and educating high risks and handicapped infants*. (pp. 101-118). Baltimore, MD: University Park Press.

Hutinger, P. (1986). Sharing centers for handicapped infants and toddlers in rural settings. *Rural Special Education Quarterly, 7*(2).

Hutinger, P. (1987). Computer-based learning for young children. In J. L. Roopnarine & J. E. Johnson (Eds.), *Approaches to early childhood education* (pp. 213-236). Columbus, OH: Charles E. Merrill.

Hutinger, P., Donsbach, P., Cunningham, C., Longanecker, J., & Sharp, J. (1981). *Have wagon: Will travel—sharing centers for rural handicapped infants, toddlers, and their parents* (rev.ed.). Macomb, IL: Macomb 0-3 Regional Project, Western Illinois University.

Hutinger, P., Marshall, S., & McCartan, K. (1983). *Macomb 0-3 core curriculum*. Macomb, IL: Macomb Projects, Western Illinois University.

Hutinger, P., Marshall, S., McCartan, K., Nelson, A., & Hutinger, S. (1986). *CORE* [Computer program]. Macomb, IL: Macomb Projects, Western Illinois University.

Hutinger, P., & McKee N. (1980). The baby buggy: Bringing services to handicapped rural children. *Children Today, 8*(1), 2-5.

Hutinger, P., Mietus, S., Smith-Dickson, B., & Rundall, R. (1985). *Executive summary. Birth to three programs in Illinois: The state of the art*. Macomb, IL: Macomb Projects, Western Illinois University.

Hutinger, P., Perry, L., Robinson, L., Weaver, K., & Whitaker, K. (1986). *ACTT curriculum*. Macomb, IL: Project ACTT, Western Illinois University.

Hutinger, P., Perry, L., Robinson, L., Whitaker, D., & Whitaker, K. (1986). *ACTT starter kit*. Macomb, IL: Project ACTT, Western Illinois University.

Hutinger, P., & Swartz, S. (1980). *Executive summary: Illinois early childhood handicapped research study*. (Project No. P 953062). Springfield, IL: State Board of Education.

Knobloch, H., & Pasamanick, B. (Eds.). (1974). *Gesell and Armatruda's developmental diagnosis—the evaluation and management of normal and abnormal neuropsychologic development in infancy and early childhood* (3rd ed.). Hagerstown, MD: Harper & Row.

Mahoney, G., Finger, I., & Powell, A. (1985). The relationship of maternal behavioral style of the developmental status of organically impaired mentally retarded infants. *American Journal of Mental Deficiency, 90*, 296-302.

Mahoney, G., Powell, A., & Finger, I. (1986). The maternal behavior rating scale. *Topics in Early Childhood Special Education, 6*(2), 44-55.

McCollum, J., & Stayton, V. (1985). Infant/parent interaction: Studies and intervention guidelines based on the SIAI model. *Journal of the Division for Early Childhood, 9*, 125-135.

Milani-Comparetti, A., & Gidoni, A. (1977). *Milani-Comparetti motor developmental scale*. Omaha, NE: Meyer's Children's Rehabilitation Institute.

Miller, J. F. (1981). *Assessing language production in children: Experimental procedures*. Baltimore, MD: University Park Press.

Neisworth, J. T., Willoughby-Herb, S. J., Bagnato, S. J., Cartwright, C. A., & Laub, K. (1980). *Individualized education for preschool exceptional children*. Rockville, MD: Aspen.

Newborg, J., Stock, J., Wnek, L., Guidabaldi, J., & Svinicki, J. (1984). *Battelle developmental inventory*. Allen, TX: DLM Teaching Resources.

Peterson, N. L. (1987). *Early intervention for handicapped and at-risk children*. Denver, CO: Love Publishing.

Powell, M. L. (1981). *Assessment and management of developmental changes and problems in children*. St. Louis, MO: Mosby.

Ramey, C. T., Trohanis, P. L., & Hostler, S. L. (1982). An introduction. In C. T. Ramey & P. L. Trohanis (Eds.), *Finding and educating high-risk and handicapped infants* (pp. 1-17). Baltimore, MD: University Park Press.

Roberts, C. S., & Feetham, S. L. (1982). Assessing family functioning across three areas of relationships. *Nursing Research, 31*(4), 231-235.

Robinson, L. (1986a). Designing computer intervention for very young handicapped children. *Journal of the Division for Early Childhood, 3*(10), 209-215.

Robinson, L. (1986b). Computers provide solid learning base for pre-school children. *Closing the Gap, 5*(5), pp. 1, 18, 25.

Rosenberg, S., & Robinson, C. (1985). Enhancement of mother's interactional skills in an infant educational program. *Education and Training of the Mentally Retarded, 20*, 163-169.

Rosenberg, S., Robinson, C., & Beckman, P. (1984). Teaching skills inventory: A measure of parent performance. *Journal of the Division for Early Childhood, 8*, 107-113.

Rosenberg, S., Robinson, C., & Beckman, P. (1986). Measures of parent-infant interaction: An overview. *Topics in Early Childhood Special Education, 6*(2), 32-43.

Satir, V. 1972. *Peoplemaking*. Palo Alto, CA: Science and Behavior Books.

Sheehan, R., & Gallagher, R. J. (1983). Conducting evaluations of infant intervention programs. In S. G. Garwood & R. R. Fewell (Eds.), *Educating handicapped infants: Issues in development and intervention* (pp. 495-524). Rockville, MD: Aspen.

Simeonsson, R., Huntington, G., Short, R., & Ware, W. (1982). The Carolina record of individual behavior: Characteristics of handicapped infants and children. *Topics in Early Childhood Special Education, 2*(2), 43-55.

Smith-Dickson, B., & Hutinger, P. (1986). *Project RAIN* (Progress Report and Continuation Proposal). Macomb, IL: College of Education, Western Illinois University.

Stillman, R. (Ed.). (F edition, 1977; G edition 1978). *Callier-Azusa Scale*. Dallas, TX: Callier Center for Communication Disorders, The University of Texas at Dallas.

Suarez, T. M. (1982). Planning evaluation of programs for high-risk and handicapped infants. In C. T. Ramey & P. L. Trohanis (Eds.), *Finding and educating high-risk and handicapped infants* (pp. 193-215). Baltimore, MD: University Park Press.

Tjossem, T. (1976). Early intervention: Issues and approaches. In T. Tjossem (Ed.), *Intervention strategies for high-risk and handicapped children*. Baltimore, MD: University Park Press.

Whitaker, D. (1984). *Choices*. [Computer program]. Macomb, IL: Project ACTT, Western Illinois University. (Project No. 024XH 40046)

Whitaker, D. (1985). *Peek 'n' speak*. [Computer program]. Macomb, IL: Project ACTT, Western Illinois University. (Project No. 024BH 50081)

White, B., & Watts, J. (1973). *Experience and environment: Major influence on the development of the young child*. Englewood Cliffs, NJ: Prentice-Hall.

Uzgiris, I., & Hunt, J. McV. (1975). *Assessment in infancy*. Urbana, IL: University of Illinois Press.

SELECTED 0-3 CURRICULA

ACTT Curriculum
Authors: Patricia L. Hutinger, Lori Perry, Linda Robinson, Kathie Weaver, and Kate Whitaker
Available from: Project ACTT, College of Education, Western Illinois University, 27 Horrabin Hall, Macomb, IL 61455.
Date of Publication: 1986
Cost: $40.00 plus shipping (ACTT Starter Kit sold separately)
Format: Paperback
Developmental Ages: Birth–8 years
Adaptations: Visual, auditory, and motor
Comments: The ACTT Curriculum is a supplemental curriculum designed for use in conjunction with existing early intervention programs for young children ages birth through 8 utilizing computer technology. The three primary components of the curriculum include Birth to Three, Three to Five, and Severe and Profound technological applications. Designed to complement the ACTT Starter Kit, the Curriculum contains functional activities, specific hardware and software applications, and adaptations for various handicapping conditions.

Adaptips
Authors: Judy A. Goodrich and Patricia G. Kinney
Available from: Curriculum Adaptations for the Deaf-Blind Project, Center for Professional Development, 105 Taylor Education Building, University of Kentucky, Lexington, KY 40506-0001.
Date of Publication: 1985
Cost: $12.00
Format: Paperback
Developmental Ages: 0–24 months
Comments: The Adaptips Manual is a process approach for adapting curricula to meet the needs of deaf-blind children who function in the sensorimotor developmental stage. The manual is intended to assist teachers in assessment and program planning for young deaf-blind children.

Carolina Curriculum for Handicapped Infants
Authors: Nancy M. Johnson, Ken G. Jens, and Susan M. Attermeier
Available from: Brookes Publishing Company, P.O. Box 10624, Baltimore, MD 21285-0883.
Date of Publication: 1985
Cost: $29.95
Format: Paperback, 278 pages
Developmental Ages: 0–24 months
Adaptations: Visual and motor
Comments: The CCHI, developed for use with severely handicapped infants and toddlers who function in the birth to 2-year range, is a developmentally sequenced curriculum organized into 19 curricular areas (e.g. tactile integration, auditory and space localization, gestural communication). The nine cognition domains are based on Piagetian theory. The gross motor sections were authored by a pediatric physical therapist and extensive drawings illustrate the text. Each objective specifies the position of the child, materials, teaching procedures, and evaluation of performance. Assessment log available.

Developmental Programming for Infants and Young Children
Authors: D. Sue Schafer and Martha S. Moersch
Available from: The University of Michigan Press, Department YB, P.O. Box 1104, Ann Arbor, MI 48106.
Date of Publication: 1981
Cost: $16.00 (Volumes 1-3 Assessment/Applications, Profile, Activities)
Format: Paperback
Developmental Ages: 0–36 months
Adaptations: Auditory, visual and motor
Comments: A developmentally sequenced curriculum which identifies the target behavior, the skill, and appropriate activities. Developmental areas addressed include cognition items that are cross-referenced with Piagetian domains of sensorimotor intelligence.

Hawaii Early Learning Profile (HELP) and HELP Activity Guide
Authors: Setsu Furuno, Carol Hosaka, Barbara Zeisloft, Katherine O'Reilly, Takayo Inatsuka and Toney Allman
Available from: VORT Corporation, P.O. Box 11552K, Palo Alto, CA 94306.
Date of Publication: 1979
Cost: HELP Charts $2.95/set of three; $1.95 (10 or more sets); Activity Guide: $14.95 (1 to 9 copies), $11.95 (10 or more copies)
Format: Paperback, 230 pages
Developmental Ages: 0–36 months
Adaptations: Motor

Comments: A developmentally sequenced curriculum which suggests several activities for each target behavior in developmental areas of cognition, expressive language, gross motor, fine motor, social-emotional and self-help. The home activities are intended to be incorporated into daily family routines.

Infant Learning: A Cognitive Linguistic Intervention Strategy
Author: Carl J. Dunst
Available from: DLM Teaching Resources, P.O. Box 4000, Allen, TX 75002.
Date of Publication: 1981
Cost: $22.00
Format: Paperback
Developmental Ages: 0–24 months
Comments: Curriculum focuses on an "ecological" approach to intervention. Behaviors are developed in the setting and context in which they will be used. This curriculum places emphasis on acquisition of cognitive linguistic competencies and expands the Piagetian theory of sensorimotor development.

HICOMP Curriculum and Guide
Authors: Sara J. Willoughby-Herb and John T. Neisworth
Available from: Charles E. Merrill (reference #410770), Columbus, OH 43216, 800/848-1567.
Date of Publication: 1983
Cost: $60.00
Developmental Ages: 0–60 months
Comments: This curriculum was developed for typical and atypical children and is based on normal developmental theory. Domains include selfcare, communication, motor and problem solving.

Macomb 0–3 Regional Project Core Curriculum (3rd Edition)
Authors: Patricia L. Hutinger, Sue Marshall, and Kathleen McCartan
Available from: Macomb 0-3 Regional Project, Room 27 Horrabin Hall, Western Illinois University, Macomb, IL 61455.
Date of Publication: 1983
Cost: $49.95; CORE (Computer Oriented Record-Keeping Enabler) available separately
Format: Looseleaf notebook, 265 pages
Developmental Ages: 0–36 months
Adaptations: Auditory, visual and motor
Comments: This developmentally sequenced curriculum places great emphasis on functional goals, objectives and activities in six curricular areas (Gross Motor, Fine Motor, Cognition, Communication, Social, and Self Care). The curriculum is divided into three major sections. Part I provides information regarding the curriculum format, target population, and use of the curriculum. Part II is the actual curriculum and Part III is a program planning guide to be used with individual children as programs are developed, implemented and monitored.

The Core Curriculum is intended for use by a variety of professionals, as well as in programs where a single child development specialist has program responsibility.

The CORE (Computer Oriented Record-keeping Enabler) computer program for Apple II and IIe and IBM was designed for use with the Macomb 0–3 Core Curriculum; it enables direct service staff to create and store goals and objectives for IEPs. Available for Apple CP/M (requires Z–80 card), Apple Pascal, and IBM at a cost of $89.95, or purchase Core Curriculum and CORE for $129.95.

Small Wonder (Level 1 and Level 2)
Author: Merle B. Karnes
Available from: American Guidance Service (AGS), Publisher's Building, Circle Pines, MN 55014.
Date of Publication: 1979, 1981
Cost: $92.00 per Level
Format: Kit includes user's guide, activity cards, puppet, picture card stories, ideas
Developmental Ages: 0–36 months
Adaptations: Motor
Comments: Each level contains 150 activity cards based on normal development. A user's guide for each level discusses health, safety, development, and adaptations for physically handicapped or developmentally delayed children.

SELECTED ASSESSMENT INSTRUMENTS

Developmental Measures

Bayley Scales of Infant Development
Author: Nancy Bayley
Available from: The Psychological Corporation, 757 Third Avenue, New York, NY 10017, or Regional Office, The Psychological Corporation, 7555 Caldwell Avenue, Chicago, IL 60648.
Date of Publication: 1969
Age Range: 2–30 months
Comments: A norm-referenced, standardized test accompanied by a rich research base, the data was collected on nonhandicapped children. Reliability and validity data are available. Both a Mental Scale and a Motor Scale provide a Mental Development Index and a Psychomotor Development Index.

Battelle Developmental Inventory
Authors: J. Newborg, J. Stock, L. Wnek, J. Guidabaldi, and J. Svinicki
Available from: DLM Teaching Resources, P.O. Box 4000, Allen, TX 75002.
Date of Publication: 1984
Age Range: 0–8 years
Comments: Norm-referenced, standardized developmental battery, meets the requirements of the Standards for Educational and Psychological Tests. The developmental sequence across five domains is appropriate for developing individual child plans. The domains are Personal-social, Adaptive, Motor, Communication, and Cognitive. However, it is a new instrument which has not yet been subjected to extensive research.

The Callier-Azusa Scale
Editor: Robert Stillman
Available from: The University of Texas at Dallas, Callier Center for Communication Disorders, 1966 Inwood Road, Dallas, TX 75235.
Date of Publication: 1977 (F. Edition) and 1978 (G. Edition)
Age Range: 0–9 years
Comments: Criterion-referenced test for deaf-blind and severely impaired children, includes 18 subscales which assess behaviors in five domains: Motor Development, Perceptual Abilities, Daily Living Skills, Cognition, Communication and Language, and Social Development.

The Evaluation and Programming System for Infants and Young Children (EPS)
Authors: D. Bricker, E. Bailey, and D. Gentry
Available from: The University of Oregon, Eugene, OR.
Date of Publication: 1985
Age Range: 0–3 years
Comments: A criterion-referenced instrument that includes functional goals and objectives, the EPS uses observation, direct testing, and parent report. Six domains are included: Gross Motor, Fine Motor, Communication, Cognition, Self-help, and Social. Each item can become a training objective. Adaptations for sensory and motor impairments are permitted.

The Revised Gesell Developmental Schedules
Authors: H. Knoblach, F. Stevens, and A. Malone
Available from: Medical Department, Harper and Row Publishers, Inc., 2350 Virginia Avenue, Hagerstown, MD 21740.
Date of Publication: 1980
Age Range: 1–36 months
Comments: A norm-referenced assessment of overall development, the test includes five domains of behavior: Adaptive, Gross Motor, Fine Motor, Language, and Personal-Social. It provides developmental quotients and a maturity age score for general development and the five domains cited above.

Sensorimotor Measure

Ordinal Scales of Psychological Development
Authors: I. Uzgiris and J. Hunt
Available from: The University of Illinois Press, Urbana, IL 61801.
Date of Publication: 1975
Age Range: 1–24 months
Comments: A criterion-referenced ordinal scale, to assess the infant's functioning on the sequences within the six stages of the sensorimotor period. These scales are based on a Piagetian framework of cognitive development.

MEASURES ADMINISTERED BY SPECIALIZED PERSONNEL

Milani-Comparetti Developmental Scale
Authors: A. Milani-Comparetti and E. A. Gidoni
Available from: Meyers Children's Rehabilitation Institute, University of Nebraska at Omaha, Omaha, NE 68131.
Date of Publication: 1977
Age Range: 0–2 years
Comments: Measures physical development through "Spontaneous Behavior" and "Evoked Response." Designed for use by a physician, occupational therapist, or physical therapist. Motor development areas include the ability to control head and body, move from one position to another, stand up from a supine position, and move about.

Reflex Testing Methods for Evaluating CNS Development
Author: Mary Fiorentino
Available from: Charles C Thomas Publishers, 301–327 Lawrence Avenue, Springfield, IL 62717.
Date of Publication: 1979
Age Range: 0–6 years
Comments: Tests are designed for those evaluating and treating children with neurophysiological disorders, i.e., pediatricians, physical and occupational therapists. The purpose is to determine neurophysiological reflexive maturation of the central nervous system at the spinal, brain stem, midbrain, and cortical levels.

PARENT REPORT MEASURES

The Developmental Profile II (revised edition)
Authors: G. Alpern, T. Boll, and M. Shearer
Available from: Psychological Development Publications, Aspen, CO.
Date of Publication: 1980
Age Range: 0–12 years
Comments: A norm-referenced and standardized measure, the domains measured are Physical, Self-help, Social, Academic, and Communication. Normally the information is gathered through parent interview.

Minnesota Child Development Inventory (MCDI)
Authors: H. Ireton and E. Thwing
Available from: Behavior Science Systems, Inc., P.O. Box 1108, Minneapolis, MN 55440.
Date of Publication: 1972
Age Range: 6 months–6 years
Comments: The MCDI is standardized and uses the mother's observations to assess her child's development through her response to 320 statements. There are seven scales: Gross Motor, Fine Motor, Expressive Language, Comprehension-conceptual, Situation Comprehension, Self-help, and Personal-social. There is also a summary General Development Scale.

Parent-Child Interaction Measures

Human Interaction Scale
Authors: Burton White and Jean Watts
Available in: Experience and Environment, Volume 1, Prentice Hall, Inc., Englewood Cliffs, NJ.
Date of Publication: 1973
Age Range: Birth–6 years
Comments: An interaction rating scale to use with observations. The scale includes five dimensions: Activities, Initiation Index, Encouragement Index, Interaction Technique, and Compliance Index.

Teaching Skills Inventory
Authors: Steven Rosenberg, Cordelia Robinson, and Paula Beckman
Available from: Journal of the Division for Early Childhood (1984), *8,* 107–113.
Comments: Version 2, which rates the interaction between mother and child, includes 15 items rated on a 7-point scale. It assesses Structure of the Interaction, Maternal Responsivity, Maternal Instructional Skills, and Child Interest.

The Nursing Child Assessment Teaching Scale
Author: L. Barnard
Available from: Department of Parent and Child Nursing, NCAST, University of Washington, Seattle, WA 98105.
Date of Publication: 1979
Comments: This is an observational instrument that can be used to evaluate parent-child behaviors in an interactional context during a teaching situation.

Social Measures

A Social Maturity Scale for Blind Children
Authors: Kathryn Maxfield and Sandra Buckholz
Available from: The American Foundation for the Blind, Inc., New York, NY.
Date of Publication: 1957
Age Range: 0–6 years
Comments: The test was standardized with 484 visually handicapped children and is an adaptation of the Vineland Social Maturity Scale. It is usually administered in a parent interview format.

Vineland Social Maturity Scale (Revised)
Author: Edgar A. Doll
Available from: American Guidance Service, Inc., Publishers Building, Circle Pines, MN.
Date of Publication: 1985
Age Range: Birth–Adult
Comments: A norm-referenced measure to assess social competence in three formats. The survey edition, a questionnaire, assesses four domains (Communications, Daily Living Skills, Socialization, and Motor Skills) and 11 subdomains. Each of the subdomains generates an adaptive level and an age equivalent score.

Curriculum Referenced Measures

Peabody Developmental Motor Scales
Authors: Rebecca Fewell and Rhonda Folio
Available from: Teaching Resources Corporation, Hingham, MA.
Date of Publication: Revised Experimental Edition 1974
Age Range: Birth–7 years
Comments: Gross motor assessment includes reflexes, balance, nonlocomotive, locomotor, and receipt and propulsion of objects. Fine motor assessment includes grasping, hand use, eye-hand coordination and finger dexterity. A program of activities to teach each skill is included.

Skills Inventory (The Oregon Project for Visually Impaired and Blind Preschool Children)
Authors: Donnise Brown, Vickie Simmons, and Judy Methvin
Available from: OREGON Project, Jackson County Education Service District, Medford, OR.
Date of Publication: 1979
Age Range: Birth–6 years
Comments: Although this is not a normed assessment instrument, it can be used to determine performance level for visually impaired or blind children. It includes a Skills Inventory in the areas of Cognition, Language, Self-help, Socialization, Fine Motor, and Gross Motor. Teaching activities are included.

Language and Communication Measures

Protocols for Language Samples and Mean-Length Utterance
Authors: Jon Miller, Thomas Klee, Reha Paul, and Robin Chapman
Available in: Assessing Language in Children, Experimental Procedures, University Park Press, Baltimore, MD.
Age Range: Infants, toddlers, and older children
Comments: Procedures to assess productive language behavior in children based on work with developmentally disabled children. Includes ways to measure pragmatics, morpheme counts, syntax, and semantics.

Receptive-Expressive Emergent Language Scale (REEL)
Authors: K. R. Bzoch and R. League
Available from: University Park Press, Baltimore, MD.
Date of Publication: 1971
Age Range: Birth–3 years
Comments: Intended to identify very young children who may need early language intervention, the scales include auditory perception, auditory association and recall, and auditory-motor learning.

Sequenced Inventory of Communication Development
Authors: Dona Lea Hedrick, Elizabeth Prather, and Annette R. Tobin
Available from: Western Psychological Services, Los Angeles, CA.
Date of Publication: 1978
Age Range: 4–48 months
Comments: The receptive language scale includes assessment of sound and speech awareness, discrimination, and understanding. The expressive scale includes imitating, initiating, and responding. The scale also assesses length of expressive language, grammatic and syntactic structure, and articulation.

SELECTED SCREENING INSTRUMENTS

Screening Measures
Administered by Medical Personnel

Apgar Scales
Author: Virginia Apgar
Available in: Current Research in Anesthesia and Analgesia, 32, 260.
Date of Publication: 1953
Developmental Age: Neonates
Comments: A medical evaluation of fine signs in the newborn infant within minutes after birth. It is a rating system for heart rate, respiration, reflex to stimulation, muscle tone, and color.

Brazelton's Neonatal Behavior Assessment Scale
Author: T. Berry Brazelton
Available from: J. B. Lippincott Co., Philadelphia, PA.
Date of Publication: 1974
Developmental Age: Birth through first month of life
Comments: Provides a measure of physical maturation and responsivity. Includes six stages of state from sleep to crying, 11 specific behaviors, and 16 general behaviors as well as habituation.

Developmental Screening Measures
Administered by Early Intervention Staff

Battelle Developmental Inventory Screening Test
Authors: J. Newborg, J. Stock, L. Wnek, J. Guidabaldi, and J. Svinicki
Available from: DLM Teaching Resources, P.O. Box 4000, Allen, TX 75002.
Date of Publication: 1984
Developmental Age: 0–8 years
Comments: Norm-referenced, standardized test in fine domains; personal, social, adaptive, motor, communication, and cognition. Each domain contains subdomains. A set of testing materials can be purchased.

Denver Developmental Screening Test (DDST)
Authors: W. Frankenburg, J. Dodds
Available from: Ladoca Project and Publishing Foundation, Inc., Denver, CO.
Date of Publication: 1970
Developmental Age: 0–6 years
Comments: Screens gross motor, language, fine motor-adaptive, and personal-social skills. Based on the Gesell Developmental Schedules, the DDST was developed to identify children whose development was normal, abnormal, or questionable.

Denver Prescreening Development Questionnaire (DPDQ)
Authors: W. K. Frankenburg, W. J. van Doorninck, T. N. Liddell, and N. P. Dick
Available from: Pediatrics, 1976, 57(5), 744–753.
Developmental Age: 3–6 years
Comments: Designed to be used together with the DDST, the DPDQ provides information about the parents' perception of their child's level of developmental functioning.

Developmental Activities Screening Inventory (DASI)
Authors: R. Dubose and M. Langley
Available from: Teaching Resources, Inc., Hingham, MA.
Date of Publication: 1977
Developmental Age: 6 months–6 years
Comments: For sensory-impaired preschoolers; covers fine motor, causality-means/ends, number concepts, size discrimination, and seriation. Bricker (1986) suggests that this is an "interim" screening between identification of problems in development and assessment for program planning.

4.
Model Programs for Infants and Toddlers with Handicaps

Merle B. Karnes
and
Vicki D. Stayton

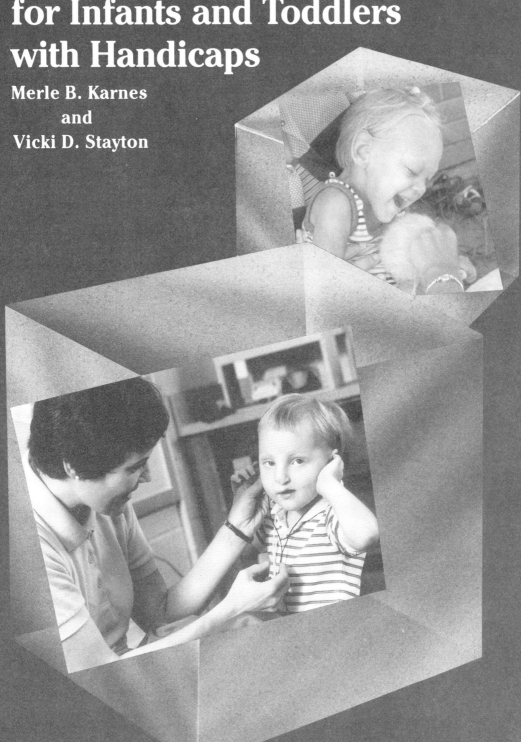

Educators may acquire valuable information by examining exemplary program models.

❑ Since the late 1960s, programs for young children with handicaps have proliferated. As part of this movement, numerous programs for infants and toddlers have been developed. This trend has gained impetus from the passage of Public Law 99-457, the Education of the Handicapped Act Amendments of 1986, with its emphasis on the planning and development of services for infants and toddlers. As new programs are developed, educators may acquire valuable information in the initial planning and development stages by carefully examining the components of exemplary models that have been developed for infants with handicaps.

Peterson (1987) defined a model program as "a program for children in which its content and operational strategies are clearly conceptualized and defined in a manner that assures internal consistency and coherence"(p. 371). Typically, an early intervention model consists of a clearly conceptualized philosophical or theoretical orientation, a set of program goals and objectives, an identified population of children and families, well-qualified staff and provisions for team functioning and staff development, specified service delivery options, established intervention procedures (i.e., assessment, curriculum, materials, and instructional strategies), a model for family involvement, and rigorous program evaluation (Filler, 1983; Peterson, 1987; Sheehan & Gradel, 1983).

National efforts have stimulated development of model programs.

A variety of national efforts have stimulated the development of model programs. The passage of Public Law 90-538, the Handicapped Children's Early Education Assistance Act, in 1968, had the greatest impact on the development of programs for young children with handicaps. This act established the Handicapped Children's Early Education Program (HCEEP), a seed money program designed to assist in developing and demonstrating exemplary services for handicapped children ages birth to 8 years and their families (DeWeerd & Cole, 1976). During 1968-1969, with the assistance of an advisory board, the central staff of the Bureau of Education for the Handicapped (BEH) developed procedures for implementing the legislation. Grants were awarded to projects to develop what became known as First Chance or HCEEP demonstration projects. Over a 3-year funding cycle, the projects were charged with developing and evaluating exemplary practices that could be replicated by other sites. All funded demonstration projects were required to continue the model by local and/or state funding after termination of the 3-year period. Initially, 24 demonstration projects primarily serving children ages 3 to 8 were funded in July, 1969, at the level of one million dollars. From 1969 through 1987, a total of over 500 demonstration projects were funded to serve ages 0 to 8. Of these, at least 200 were demonstration models for the age 0 to 2 population.

Grants were awarded to develop HCEEP demonstration projects.

At least 200 were models for 0–2 population.

Demonstration projects must include the following features to be funded according to the requirements of the federal government:

1. Exemplary services to children that would enhance cognitive, language, motor, and social/emotional development.

2. Professional and nonprofessional staff development.

3. Parent involvement.

4. Collaboration with appropriate agencies, including public school districts.

5. Dissemination of information and materials related to model practices.

6. Program evaluation. (DeWeerd, 1979).

Although the original intent was to fund demonstration projects for a 3-year cycle and then terminate funds, allowing other projects to receive funding, it soon became evident to BEH that the exemplary practices developed by projects should be made available to other interested sites. Thus, in the summer of 1972, P.L. 90-538 funds were made available to projects that had completed the 3-year demonstration cycle and wished to apply for outreach projects to assist other sites in replicating the demonstration model. Adopting or adapting a model whose effectiveness has been demonstrated may prove more desirable for sites with similar needs, populations, and philosophical commitments than developing a model of their own for the following reasons:

- It is costly to develop a model. Over the 3-year cycle of a demonstration site, the government has funded the development and demonstration of models at a cost ranging from $300,000 to $400,000. When a model meets the needs of a site and has been approved by the Office of Special Education Programs for outreach, it can be replicated within a year at another site at a fraction of the cost of developing a new model.

A model can be replicated within a year.

- Some demonstration projects have been evaluated rigorously and have proved worthy of replication. Some even have evidence that the model can be transported to another site and obtain comparable results. If a site has needs that can be met by a demonstrated exemplary program, financial resources, time, and effort can be saved by adopting or adapting the proven model.

- Outreach project staff can be invaluable in conducting inservice training of the replication site staff and can serve as consultants in coping with problems of providing services to infants and their parents.

- Even when the demonstration models are not funded for outreach, the staff are obligated to continue to demonstrate their models and in most cases they are willing to provide some technical services to sites that wish to replicate their models.

Knowledge of federally funded exemplary programs may prove helpful to sites desiring to improve their programs and/or to those initiating programs and seeking an appropriate model to replicate. This chapter, therefore, provides comprehensive information regarding model components based on a survey of HCEEP projects serving infants and toddlers with handicaps and their families. First, survey results of HCEEP demonstration projects that serve children age birth to 2 years and their families are discussed. Second, 12 of these projects are highlighted to provide a more detailed description of program components. Finally, the chapter discusses the implications of the survey for the development and implementation of programs for infants and toddlers with handicaps.

METHOD

❏ The sample for this study was drawn from the 144 HCEEP projects funded from 1981 through 1986 that were included in the annual HCEEP directories compiled by TADS (Technical Assistance Development System) and that reported serving children age birth to 2 years. Both demonstration and outreach projects were contacted; however, outreach projects were asked to report only on their demonstration models.

HCEEP projects have specific guidelines for program development and implementation.

Several factors influenced the selection of HCEEP projects as exemplary models. First HCEEP projects have specific guidelines for program development and implementation. Second, the projects are monitored and evaluated on an ongoing basis. Finally, research suggests that HCEEP projects continue the model demonstration services beyond the federal funding period (Swan, 1980).

Procedures

❏ A questionnaire was mailed to each of the 144 HCEEP projects. The questionnaire, which contains a variety of checklists, Likert scales, and open-ended questions, was designed to obtain comprehensive information regarding the model program. A review of the literature suggested common components of exemplary models and thus influenced the selection of survey questions. Some items were adapted from a needs assessment questionnaire developed for the Illinois Early Childhood State Plan Project (McCollum, 1985). Projects that did not respond to the initial mailing received a second questionnaire, and some sites called to explain why they could not complete the questionnaire. Factors addressed by the survey included agencies involved in administering the program and cooperatively providing services; characteristics of the children served; characteristics of the families served; service delivery options; staffing patterns (including staff development); program facility; a description of the services to children and families (i.e., program philosophy, program goals and objectives, assessment procedures, curriculum, instructional materials, instructional strategies); and program evaluation. (A copy of the questionnaire may be obtained from the first author.)

SURVEY RESULTS

Forty-six percent provide services to infants and toddlers.

❏ Of the 144 projects canvassed, 79 (55%) responded to the initial mailing and another 17 (12%) responded to the second mailing, resulting in 96 returns (67%). Sixty-seven (46%) of the respondents provided services to infants and toddlers with handicaps. Twenty-nine (21%) of the projects are no longer in existence or do not provide services to children from birth to age 2. It is assumed that the programs most active in providing services to young children responded to the survey. The response rate was relatively high when compared with similar surveys (Karnes, Linnemeyer, & Myles, 1983; Karnes, Linnemeyer, & Shwedel, 1981; Trohanis, Cox, & Meyer, 1982).

Results are based on self-reported data.

The following information is a synthesis of the data reported by the 67 projects providing services to infants and toddlers with handicaps and their families. It must be emphasized that the results are based on self-reported data from the written questionnaire.

Program Administration

❏ The most common fiscal agencies for programs are universities (31%), public schools (21%), and private agencies (19%). Other agencies/ programs that administer the infant/toddler projects are listed in Table 1. All of the model projects indicated that they work collaboratively with other appropriate agencies in providing services to children. The agencies most likely to be involved are public schools, universities, state departments of education, state departments of mental health and mental retardation, and local agencies such as county health departments and social services. Programs tend to be located in large cities with populations over 50,000 (40%), but 11% are located in cities with populations of 25,000 to 50,000, 15% in small towns with populations of 2,500 to 25,000, 9% in rural areas, and 25% in areas that are a combination of other types.

Programs tend to be located in large cities.

Characteristics of Children Served

❑ The majority of programs that returned the survey serve children who are at risk for developmental delays (80%), as well as those who have diagnosed handicaps (94%) or developmental delays (92%). Table 2 contains a breakdown by category of the children served in the 67 programs. Services for infants begin at or fairly soon after birth. In all of the programs the children served spread relatively equally across all age ranges: birth to 6 months (18%), 7 to 12 months (18%), 1 to 2 years (30%), and 2 to 3 years (34%). Programs serve an average of 33 children, for a total of 2,125 children in the 67 programs responding. The majority of children are male (61%). Most are Caucasian (57%), with 27% Black, 10% Hispanic, 3% Native American, and 1% Oriental. The remaining 2% are from a variety of cultural and ethnic backgrounds.

Services for infants begin at or fairly soon after birth.

Characteristics of Families Served

❑ The majority of families served are two-parent families (43%); the second largest group represented are single-parent families with the mothers as heads of household (30%). Some children (12%) live in extended families. Another 9% live in foster homes. Only 0.36% live in single-parent families with the father as head of household. Table 3 shows percentages of each type of family structure represented for the 67 projects. Based on income and education levels, the majority of families could be categorized as of lower socioeconomic status (SES). Most of the families (81%) earn less than $20,000 per year, while 43% of the total earn less than $10,000 per year. Of the fathers represented, 65% have a high school education or less; of the mothers, 79% have a high school education or less. Several of the parents have completed only the elementary grades—12% of the mothers and 13% of the fathers.

The majority of families could be categorized as of lower socioeconomic status.

Service Delivery Options

❑ Infant and toddler programs may differ according to the setting in which services occur. Services are usually provided in one of two environments, the child's home or a center such as a school or hospital. Karnes and Zehrbach (1977) described intervention models as representing one of four combinations of these two settings: (a) home participation only, (b) home participation followed by center participation, (c) combination home and center participation, and (d) center participation only. Several factors may affect the service delivery option chosen for a program: geographic location (e.g., rural, urban), the recipient of direct services (e.g., child, parent, or both), program goals and objectives, age of the child who receives services, and the person(s) providing services.

Services are usually provided in the child's home or a center.

Table 1. Agency Administering the Program

Agency	Percentage of Programs Administered by the Agency
University	31
Public school district	21
Private agencies	19
Department of mental health/mental retardation	10
Hospitals	6
Residential schools	4
Association of Retarded Citizens	3
State Department of Education	1.5
United Cerebral Palsy	1.5
Regional health district	1.5
Parent/child center	1.5

Note. Based on 67 projects.

Table 2. Handicapping Conditions of Children Served

Handicapping Condition	Percentage Served
Orthopedically/physically impaired	8
Mentally retarded	14
Health impaired	7
Emotionally disturbed	1
Autistic	1
Speech/language impaired	12
Hearing impaired	2
Deaf	0.33
Visually impaired	2
Blind	1
Deaf-blind	0.28
Multihandicapped	13
Delayed, no specific diagnosis	13
At risk for delay	26
Neurologically impaired	1

Note. Based on a total of 2,125 infants and toddlers in 67 programs.

Table 3. Family Structure

Family Structure	Percentage Served
Two-parent family	48
Single-parent family (mother as head of house)	30
Single-parent family (father as head of house)	0.36
Extended family	12
Foster placement	9
Residential hospital placement	0.18
Unknown	0.76

Note. Based on a total of 2,190 families in 67 programs. The number of families served is larger than the number of children served, because some projects (e.g., Supporting Extended Family Members [SEFAM] provide services directly to family members other than the child).

The majority of respondents to this survey (70%) indicated the availability of the home-plus-center option, while 13% offer home-based only, 12% center-based only, and 5% other. However, respondents reported that the majority of children (52%) are actually served in centers, while 27% are served at home, 15% in the home-plus-center option, and 6% other. The discrepancy between the availability of options and the typical patterns of service seems to be related to the type of intervention services and who is receiving them. The primary focus of many programs is to provide direct services to the child in the home setting. These programs, however, may also provide services for the parent (e.g., support groups) on a regular basis in a center. Table 4 compares availability of options with the typical pattern of services.

The majority are actually served in a center.

The frequency of services also varies across programs. Many programs allow for flexibility in the amount of time per session and the number of sessions per week or month based on the needs of the child and the family. The most typical length of a session is 1 to 2 hours (59%), with the next most typical options being 27% half day, 11% full day, and 3% less than 1 hour. Services are most typically provided 1 to 2 days per week (52%); however, frequency of sessions does vary, with 27% of the programs offering services 3 to 5 days per week, 15% every 2 weeks, and 6% once a month.

Services are most typically provided 1 to 2 days per week.

Staffing Patterns

❑ To maintain high-quality services for children and their families, qualified staff are essential. The number and type of staff vary across programs depending on the programs' goals and objectives, services provided, service delivery approaches, the number of children served, their ages and handicapping conditions, and the needs of the families (Peterson, 1987). Peterson has suggested that the level of training and

Table 4. Service Delivery Options

Service Delivery Options	Availability of Option	Typical Pattern of Service
Home	12%	27%
Center	13%	52%
Home plus center	70%	15%
Other (e.g., daycare homes)	5%	6%

expertise required of the staff may be related to a program's philosophical orientation and the curriculum and instructional strategies employed. Because of the budgetary constraints of many infant and toddler programs, as well as the scarcity of experienced, trained personnel to work with infants and toddlers with handicaps, many programs must plan and implement staff development activities on an ongoing basis.

Respondents to the survey employ and contract with a wide range of professionals. Table 5 provides a list of roles for which the programs employ or contract for staff and the educational levels of those staff. The services of administrators/project directors and coordinators, infant interventionists, physical therapists, occupational therapists, speech therapists, psychologists, paraprofessionals, and volunteers are available to the majority of programs. Many also have the services of nurses, social workers, and family interventionists. It is interesting to note that all professional staff with the exception of two have BS degrees or higher. The survey results show that the infant interventionists provide the majority of services to the child and the family.

Infant interventionists provide the majority of services to the child and the family.

The majority of projects (71%) indicate that some efforts at teaming occur with weekly team meetings being held. Another 8% indicate that teaming is not practiced and one person is responsible for implementing services. Several of the projects (21%), however, provided no information about team practices. Only 22% of those responding to this item identified a teaming model. A transdisciplinary model is used by 11%, interdisciplinary by 9%, and multidisciplinary by 2%. Most of the projects (54%) conduct formal needs assessments and formulate staff development plans. Some (20%) report that staff are involved in regular staff development activities (e.g., local workshops, state conferences) but do not indicate how needs are determined. Others (9%) indicate that staff development activities are planned informally, and 17% provide no information about staff development.

Services to Children

❑ The theoretical or philosophical orientation of the programs for children fall into five categories. Fourteen percent of the projects, however, failed to identify a philosophical orientation. Those which were identified are:

● The child development approach focuses on normal development and assumes that children learn when they are developmentally ready.

Table 5. Model Program Staff.

Staff	Employed by Program	Contracted by Program	Education High School	BS	MS	PhD
Administrator	68	2		6	35	24
Coordinator	48	3		6	28	8
Psychologist	27	11			18	13
Physical therapist	26.2	25		21	20	3
Occupational therapist	31	11		18	15	2
Infant interventionist	100	2	2	46	49	
Speech therapist	44.2	7		6	37	
Social worker	19	4		3	13	
Nurse	21	3		10	6	
Physician	4	18				4
Paraprofessional	62	2	36	11	10	
Volunteer	73	1	56	18		
Teacher	18			9	9	
Family interventionist	28	2	1	13	18	
Evaluation consultant	3	2				4
Child care specialist		1		1		
Respite care provider	1		1			
Dissemination coordinator	1		1			
Concept specialist	1				1	
Vision specialist	1				1	
Nutritionist	1	2			1	
Neurologist		1				1
Psychiatrist		1				1
Editor/writer		1			1	
Counselor		1			1	
Early childhood specialist	1				1	
Consultant	1				1	
Educational diagnostician	1				1	
Infant psychometrist	1				1	
Cultural anthropologist		1				1
Audiologist		1			1	
Computer programmer/ specialist	4				3	1

Note. Figures are for 67 programs. Educational level was not available for some programs.

Typically, the interests of the child and the age-appropriateness of skills are given paramount consideration. The philosophies of 33% of the projects are based on this approach. Six projects specifically mention Piaget, and two cite Erickson.

- The behavioral philosophy adopts the principles of behavior modification and precision teaching. Skills are sequenced, and target behaviors are specified. Slightly over 10% of the projects adopt this approach.

- Developmental learning is a combination of the child development philosophy and the behavioral philosophy. Twenty-five, or 38%, of the projects state that this is the theoretical basis for their programs.

- The medical model was cited only once. This model concentrates on medical diagnosis and therapeutic intervention with the child.

- The transactional model is a dyadic model in which the behavior of each individual—child or adult—influences the behavior of the other partner. The primary intervention is typically with the adult, who is taught to observe and interpret the infant's behavior and respond appropriately to the infant's cues in a dyadic situation. Two programs (3%) use this approach.

Assessment Procedures

❑ Assessment procedures vary across programs. Seventy-two instruments were listed as being used for assessment. Only six of these were cited as being used for screening. Three programs stated that they screen but provided no information about instruments or procedures. Over 50% of the programs rely on referrals and seem not to have well-developed screening programs. Seventeen (25%) of the 67 programs gave no information regarding screening.

Nine programs (13%) refer children to other agencies for diagnosis. For those programs that do conduct diagnostic assessment, 26 instruments were reported. The most frequently used is the Bayley Scales of Infant Development (Bayley, 1969) (9 programs or 13%). The next most frequently used are those developed by the programs (8 programs or 12%). Fourteen programs (21%) gave no information about how the children are diagnosed.

Bayley Scales of Infant Development are used most frequently.

Of the 59 instruments used for ongoing assessment, the Bayley Scales of Infant Development (Bayley, 1969) are used most frequently (approximately 25% of the programs). The Hawaii Early Learning Profile (Furono, Inatsuka, Allman, & Zelsloft, 1979), the Denver Developmental Screening Test (Frankenburg, 1973), the Early Intervention Developmental Profile (D'Eugenio & Rogers, 1975), the Early Learning Accomplishment Profile (Glover, Preminger, & Sanford, 1978), and the Uzgiris-Hunt Scales for Ordinal Development (Uzgiris & Hunt, 1975) were each listed by six to nine of the programs. All other tests cited are used in fewer than six of the programs, and the majority of these were listed as being used in only one or two programs.

Over 70% of the respondents reported that they develop an IEP (individualized education program) for the child. The remainder provided no information.

A variety of curricula are used with the infants to implement IEPs.

A variety of curricula are used with the infants to implement IEPs. Over 60% of the respondents stated that an organized curriculum is used. No information was provided by the other 40%. One-fourth use a project-developed curriculum. Among the projects using a published curriculum, the most popular is the Hawaii Early Learning Program (16%) (Furono et al., 1979); next is the Portage Curriculum (6%) (Bluma, Shearer, Frohman, & Hilliarn, 1976). The Oregon Project curricular approach is used by three programs (4%). The remainder of the projects use curricula cited by no more than two projects each, most by only one.

Approximately 65% of the respondents stated that the staff member most frequently responsible for direct services to the child is the infant interventionist, sometimes referred to as the teacher. Others providing direct services to a much lesser degree are speech and language specialists, occupational therapists, physical therapists, paraprofessionals, social workers, parents, and psychologists. Five percent of the respondents provided no information on this subject.

Thirty-five percent keep logs or anecdotal records.

Approximately 35% of the projects keep logs or anecdotal records on the child. Thirteen percent reported using behavioral reporting techniques. Only 13% of the programs stated that they keep records of case conferences, and only 3% reported keeping attendance records. Three percent computerize their record-keeping system, but only 1.5% use videotapes to record behavior. Nine percent of the programs reported records on pre- and postassessment.

In response to the question, "Are deliberate plans and procedures developed to facilitate transition?", over 65% indicated "Yes," 15% stated "No," and 15% provided no information.

Family Involvement

❑ To receive funding as an HCEEP demonstration program, projects must include a parent involvement component. Thus, parent or family involvement is an important aspect of the projects surveyed. Many (70%) view both the parents and the child as the primary recipients of services. These are the programs that provide home or home and center services to help parents gain skills as the child's primary teachers or to improve parent-child interaction skills, thus enhancing the child's development. Other programs (22%), however, design services primarily for the parents. For example, the Training in Parenting Skills (TIPS) project has developed televised programs for parent education. Of the other projects (e.g., Supporting Extended Family Members), 8% involve fathers, siblings, and grandparents. Whether projects view the primary recipient of services as the child, the parent, or both, the majority (89%) do provide some type of service for both the child and the parent.

Many view both parents and child as primary recipients of services.

Traditionally, family involvement models have been based on the individual (e.g., parent counseling) or the dyad (e.g., parent-mediated interventions such as behavior management). Programs typically offer services for parents rather than the entire family, with the mother as the primary recipient. Families are complex, interdependent systems, however; what happens to one member affects all others (Bailey et al., 1986; Turnbull & Turnbull, 1986). A family systems approach to family involvement considers each family as unique, with its own needs and skills. Such an approach further suggests that for some families noninvolvement in the program may result in more time for the parents to be effectively involved with the children and other family members (MacMillan & Turnbull, 1983). Thus, in planning programs based on a family systems model, projects must assess the needs of families, develop family plans with goals and objectives based on the identified needs, select strategies or services based on these goals and objectives, and use appropriate evaluation techniques.

Programs typically offer services for parents rather than the entire family.

The majority of respondents (38%) indicated that they adhere to a family systems model in designing services to families. Many programs, however, continue to focus on individual parent models: parent training (28%), parent support (10%), behavioral approaches (4%), and psychosocial models (1%). Another 3% of the programs use parent-interaction models. It is interesting that 16% of the projects provided no information regarding their philosophical orientation for designing parent involvement services.

Respondents adhere to a family systems model.

Most of the projects surveyed (65%) conduct some type of family needs assessment. Of the remaining projects, 10% do not conduct needs assessments and 25% did not respond to this item. Procedures for assessing family needs include interviews, questionnaires/checklists, and videotapes. There is no consistency across projects, however, in the procedures used or in the type of information collected. Only 11 (16%) of the 67 projects conduct parent interviews, and only 1.5% use videotapes for assessment purposes. Forty-one different questionnaires/checklists

Most projects conduct family needs assessment.

are used by the projects, but only two of those are used by as many as three projects, with another four inventories used by up to two projects. Some of the questionnaires are standardized instruments, but most of the needs assessments are project-developed.

Although 65% of the projects assess family needs, only 50% develop family plans or incorporate family goals and objectives into the child's IEP. Of the remaining projects, 19% do not develop family plans and 31% did not respond to this item. One might ask, Why assess family needs if family goals and objectives are not developed? For what purpose is the needs assessment information being used?

Why assess family needs if family goals and objectives are not developed?

Most of the projects (79%) reported that they provide some kind of structured service to families. The remaining projects did not respond to this item. In a review of the literature, Welsh and Odum (1981) identified the following six components or kinds of service that are typically included in programs:

1. Social and emotional support.
2. Advocacy.
3. Decision making.
4. Family education/training.
5. Teaching by family members.
6. Communication.

With the exception of decision making, each of these was represented in the responses to the survey. The majority of projects, however, reported that they develop IEPs for children. If family members are involved in the development of those IEPs, then decision making can be included as a family involvement strategy. The most commonly available service is parent education/training through group sessions (37%), followed by program newsletters (28%) and social/emotional support activities through individual sessions (12%) and group sessions (11%). Table 6 lists all the types of services being provided.

The most commonly available service is parent education/training through group sessions.

Only 28% of the projects use a curriculum in the family involvement component. Most (57%) provided no information related to this issue, and 15% admitted that they use no curriculum. Of those that do use a structured curriculum, the majority are project-developed (58%).

In 32% of the projects, the entire team assists with the family involvement component. In 33% of the projects, the person responsible for family services varies depending on project design and family needs. Professionals who are typically involved in these projects include parent/infant specialists, social workers, program coordinators, case managers, and psychologists. Many of the projects (35%) failed to respond to this item.

Program Evaluation

❏ Most of the projects (70%) conduct structured evaluations of their programs based on goals and objectives. These projects did not specify their evaluation models. Outside evaluators are involved in 6% of the projects (no evaluation model specified), while 2% are monitored by outside agencies (e.g., Department of Mental Health/Mental Retardation). The Discrepancy Evaluation Model (Yavorsky, 1978) is used by 2% of the projects, and a single-subject research design by 2%. Only one project is involved in longitudinal research. Another 2% reported that they do not

Only one project is involved in longitudinal research.

Table 6. Family Involvement Services

Services/Strategies	Percentage of Programs Offering Service
Social/Emotional Support Services	
Parental support	
Individual sessions	12
Group sessions	11
Social activities	5
Information about or referral to other agencies	3
Parent-to-parent activities	3
Advocacy Activities	
Parent advisory committees	3
Parent education training	
Parent group sessions	37
Home visits	9
Classroom observations	5
Individual packets	3
Parent-child interaction sessions	3
Lending library	1.5
Fathers' workshops	1.5
Grandparents' workshops	1.5
Siblings' workshops	1.5
Family Members as Teachers	
Home	8
Center	6
Communication	
Newsletters	28
Local media articles	1.5
Progress reports	1.5
Daily notes	1.5
Telephone contacts	1.5

evaluate program effectiveness, and 17% provided no information about program evaluation.

DESCRIPTIONS OF MODEL PROGRAMS

❑ Twelve projects that responded to the survey are described here. The 12 were selected to represent a cross section of philosophical orientations, program goals and objectives, populations served, service delivery options, intervention strategies, and demographic regions (large city, small town, rural area). Another criterion for selection was the distinctiveness or "uniqueness" of services to children and families. Still another was that the answers to the survey were specific enough to allow an accurate description to be written. To determine the accuracy of program descriptions, the initial draft was mailed to each of the 12 projects.

These descriptions should provide sufficient information for readers to select models that may be appropriate for the areas in which they provide services. More detailed information about assessment instruments, products developed, or commercially used instructional materials also can be obtained from the project offices.

DEVELOPMENTAL EDUCATION-BIRTH THROUGH TWO (DEBT PROJECT)

❑ The Developmental Education-Birth Through Two (DEBT) Project is a program of the Lubbock Independent School District, Lubbock, Texas, a city of more than 50,000. The program is unique in that it has been fully funded through Lubbock Independent School District's local tax dollars since 1977 and thus is an integral part of the school system. All appropriate local, regional, and state health, education, and social service agencies participate in service delivery. Approximately 40 agencies involved with young children with handicaps and their families participate in collaborative planning and sharing each month.

Program has been funded through local tax dollars since 1977.

Characteristics of Children Served

❑ The DEBT project serves children between the ages birth through 2 years with a variety of handicapping conditions: (a) orthopedically impaired, 12%; (b) mentally retarded, 4%; (c) health impaired, 16%; (d) speech and language impaired, 18%; (e) visually impaired, 2%; (f) multiply handicapped, 30%; and (g) developmentally delayed with no specific diagnosis, 18%. Thus, the majority of children served have multiple handicaps, with the next two largest groups of children having speech and language impairments or developmental delays with no known cause. The project serves children from a variety of cultural and ethnic groups: (a) 18% Black, (b) 39% Caucasian, (c) 42% Hispanic, and (d) 1% American Indian. Of the children served, 59% are males and 41% are females.

Majority of children have multiple handicaps.

Characteristics of Families Served

❑ The majority of children served by the DEBT project (55%) are members of two-parent families. The remainder live primarily in single-parent families with the mothers as heads of household (17%) or in extended families (19%). Some of the children (7%) live in foster homes. None of the children live in single-parent families with the fathers as head of household. Based on education and income levels, the majority of the families would fall into lower or lower middle SES levels. Twenty-eight percent of the fathers and 25% of the mothers have completed elementary or junior high school only; 50% of the fathers and 56% of the mothers have completed high school; and 13% of the fathers and 19% of the mothers have completed an undergraduate college degree. Information was not available for 8% of the fathers. The

Majority of families fall into lower or lower middle SES levels.

breakdown for income levels is as follows: (a) below $10,000, 22%; (b) $10,000-$15,000, 19%; (c) $15,000-$20,000, 20%; (d) $20,000-$25,000, 31%; (e) $25,000-$50,000, 7%; and (f) above $50,000, 1%.

Service Delivery Options

❑ The DEBT project provides services through a combination home and center-based option. The majority of services, however, are provided in the home setting, where intervention occurs for approximately 1 to 2 hours, 1 to 2 days per week. Intervention sessions focus on both the parent and the child. Therapy sessions (e.g., occupational therapy, physical therapy) may occur in the center, depending on individual children's needs.

Staffing Patterns

❑ The DEBT project employs a variety of professionals and paraprofessionals to provide services to children aged birth through 2 and their families. Efforts are made to function as a modified transdisciplinary team. The recommendations of team members are jointly shared and incorporated into the IEP. Program staff includes one administrator, six infant interventionists, one family interventionist, one speech therapist, two paraprofessionals, one bus driver, one educational diagnostician, and five volunteers. Specialized services are provided contractually. This includes assistance from one psychologist, three physical therapists, one occupational therapist, one speech therapist, and one social worker. The infant interventionist spends the greatest amount of time with the child and the family. Other services, with the exception of the psychologist and the social worker, are readily available as needs are identified.

Efforts are made to function as a modified transdisciplinary team.

All of the persons working with the project, with the exception of the bus driver and the paraprofessionals, have BS degrees or higher. Needs for staff development are determined through periodic individual and group surveys. The project administrator is then responsible for planning appropriate activities, including weekly staff meetings and staff sharing, use of community experts, workshops, and literature reviews.

Services for Children

❑ The DEBT project is a developmentally based combination home and center intervention model. Primary services to children are provided through weekly home visits. Center-based activities include weekly play groups and therapy sessions (e.g., occupational therapy, speech therapy).

Primary services are provided through weekly home visits.

Children are carefully screened and provided with a diagnostic evaluation before being placed in the program. The Denver Developmental Screening Test (Frankenburg, 1973) is the primary screening instrument used. Diagnostic assessment instruments include the Koontz Child Development Scale (Koontz, 1974), the Vineland Social Maturity Scale (Doll, 1965), the Bayley Scales of Infant Development (Bayley, 1969), and the Receptive-Expressive Emergent Language Scale (REEL) (Bzoch & League, 1978). Other assessment instruments or procedures are used depending on individual children's needs. For example, the Hawaii Early Learning Program (HELP) (Furono et al., 1979) is used for program planning.

Each child has an IEP with long-term 3 months and weekly objectives in each developmental area identified as needing intervention. A variety of commercial and teacher-made curricula and materials are used to implement the IEPs. These include the Koontz Child Developmental Program (Koontz, 1974), Hawaii Early Learning Program (HELP) (Furono et al., 1979), Teaching Research Curriculum (Fredericks, 1976), and Teaching Down Syndrome Children (Hanson, 1977). Implementation of the IEP is monitored through daily and weekly records. Daily logs document all services provided including time and cost factors. Anecdotal notes regarding the weekly plans and programs are also recorded.

Implementation of the IEP is monitored through daily and weekly records.

Family Involvement

❑ Parents are an integral part of the DEBT project. The combination home- and center-based model is designed to help parents become effective teachers of their children, find appropriate community resources, and share and explore their feelings with other parents. Through the weekly home visits, parents acquire the skills they need in working with their children. The DEBT project has also been instrumental in establishing a nonprofit center, a Parent Cottage, which provides a homelike environment where parents can meet weekly for sharing and learning. The infant interventionist is primarily responsible for assisting the parents with teaching skills. However, if a child is receiving any type of therapy (e.g., physical therapy, speech/language therapy), that therapist also teaches the parent how to continue the therapy in the home. The family interventionist (parenting consultant) facilitates group meetings.

The infant interventionist is primarily responsible for assisting parents with teaching skills.

Family needs are determined through formal and informal observation, interviews, and completion of a project-developed survey. Goals and objectives for the family are then incorporated into the child's IEP. Daily records of all direct services are maintained. These include services rendered, time spent, staff involved, and costs.

Program Evaluation

❑ Both formative and summative program evaluation data are collected. A variety of information is considered in determining overall program effectiveness: cost, child progress, case studies of children and families, and the ability of individual families to function.

SUPPORTING EXTENDED FAMILY MEMBERS (SEFAM)

❑ The SEFAM project is unique in that it does not provide direct services to children. Instead, services are provided to traditionally underserved family members through three project components. The Fathers Program is designed to provide fathers of handicapped children ages birth to 5 years with information and peer support through a twice-monthly program facilitated by a professional-parent team. The Siblings Program consists of quarterly meetings at which siblings between the ages of 7 and 12 have opportunities to meet other siblings, develop friendships in the context of social activities, meet with group leaders to discuss their concerns, and learn more about their siblings' handicaps. The Grandparents Program also consists of quarterly meetings that provide grandpar-

Services are provided to traditionally underserved family members.

ents of children with handicaps opportunities to access peer support and obtain answers to their questions about their grandchildren's handicaps.

The SEFAM project was initially administered by the University of Washington, Seattle, but is now administered by three agencies. Merrywood School for the Handicapped, Bellevue, Washington, administers the Fathers Program, while the Grandparents Program is administered by the Advocates for Retarded Citizens of King County, Washington. The Siblings Program continues to be offered through the University of Washington. These programs are offered in an urban area (population more than 50,000).

The SEFAM programs supplement, rather than supplant, direct service programs for children with handicaps and their families; therefore, staff do not formally coordinate with other agency staff. An important component of all three programs, however, is the information component, in which SEFAM staff provide family members with information on community resources for the child and the family. Staff routinely refer families to intervention programs for their children and to auxiliary services (e.g., respite care or recreational programs) that would benefit the family system.

Characteristics of Families Served

❑ Families are recruited for the local programs through announcements sent to developmental disabilities centers and hospitals, as well as through newspaper announcements. The family members served by this project are primarily from middle-class, Caucasian, two-parent families. Sixty-one percent of the fathers and mothers have undergraduate college degrees; 22% of the fathers and 6% of the mothers have graduate degrees; 6% of the fathers and 11% of the mothers have only high school educations. The handicapped children in these families have a variety of handicapping conditions: (a) 61% Down syndrome, (b) 11% cerebral palsy, (c) 6% multiply handicapped, and (d) 22% other conditions or syndromes (e.g., hydrocephalus). The majority (56%) of the children with handicaps are male.

Family members are primarily from middle-class, Caucasian, two-parent families.

Service Delivery Options

❑ Meetings for each of the three components are held at a center. The Fathers Program meets for 1 to 2 hours every 2 weeks. Both the Siblings and the Grandparents Programs meet once every 3 months.

Staffing Patterns

❑ Project staff include two coordinators, one for the Fathers Program and one for the Grandparents Program. The Fathers Program also provides outreach services. The outreach component has an administrator and contracts with professionals to fill the roles of evaluator, editor/writer, and programmer. The editor/writer and programmer have master's degrees; the evaluator has a PhD. Other professionals such as psychologists and physical therapists are often called upon to assist with or present at meetings.

Family Involvement

❏ The SEFAM project is based on a family sustems orientation. By serving traditionally underserved members of the child's family (i.e., fathers, siblings, and grandparents), the project staff believe that they can indirectly benefit the handicapped child by making more informed and supported caregivers available, both while the child is young and as the child grows and develops.

The assessment of the family members' needs occurs through administration of the Beck Depression Inventory (Beck & Beamesdorfer, 1974), Inventory of Parents' Experiences (Crnic, Greenberg, Ragozin, & Robinson, 1982), Questionnaire on Resources and Stress (Holroyd, 1974), Family Environment Scale (Moos, 1974), and Parent Role Scale (Gallagher, Cross, & Scharfman, 1981). Family plans are not developed.

Needs are met through scheduled meetings and newsletters.

Family members' needs are met through regularly scheduled meetings and newsletters. The Fathers Program meets twice a month at Merrywood School. *Focus on Fathers*, a newsletter, is published quarterly. Sibling workshops are held quarterly by the Association for Retarded Citizens of King County, who also publish a quarterly newsletter, *Especially Grandparents*. Curricular materials for each component have been developed: *The Fathers Program* (Meyer, Vadasy, & Fewell, 1984), *Sibshops* (Meyer, Vadasy, & Fewell, 1985), and *Grandparent Workshops* (Meyer & Vadasy, 1986).

The SEFAM staff at the University of Washington continue to consult with community staff and assist in the local demonstration programs. This assistance takes the form of help in fundraising, program evaluation, and dissemination.

Program Evaluation

Fathers Program is rigorously evaluated.

❏ The Fathers Program is rigorously evaluated. All of the participating fathers and their wives participate in a longitudinal, field-initiated research study of the impact of program involvement on both parents. Variables investigated are the effects on stress and depression, access to and satisfaction with social supports, family role orientation and satisfaction, and parents' problem-solving skills.

EARLY CHILDHOOD DAY CARE MODEL PROJECT

Purpose is to integrate handicapped into regular day-care settings.

❏ The Early Childhood Day Care Model Project is a program of the Region XIX Education Service Center in El Paso, Texas. The primary purpose of the project is to integrate handicapped infants and toddlers into regular day-care settings. This project, which serves a large city area (500,000+ population), works cooperatively with the Texas Education Agency, Early Childhood Intervention, the El Paso Rehabilitation Center, Life Management, physicians, and other agencies and individuals providing referral and childfind services. Agencies such as Early Childhood Intervention refer handicapped children and their families who need childcare services or an environment for the child that promotes socialization skills.

Characteristics of Children Served

❏ The majority of children involved in the project (64%) are 2 to 3 years of age. All are over 7 months of age. The children represent a variety of handicapping conditions: (a) multihandicapped with cerebral palsy, 58%, (b) health impaired, 19%, (c) speech/language impaired, 8%, (d) developmentally delayed with no known cause, 8%, and (e) visually impaired, 7%. Fifty-four percent of these children are considered moderately handicapped, while another 35% are severely handicapped. The majority of the children served are males (54%). A variety of cultural and ethnic backgrounds are represented: (a) 46% Hispanic, (b) 46% Caucasian, (c) 4% Black, and (d) 4% Oriental.

54% are moderately handicapped, 35% severely handicapped.

Characteristics of Families Served

❏ The parents' incomes and educational levels place most of the families represented in a lower SES. All of the mothers and fathers are high school graduates, with the exception of one father who has an undergraduate college degree. The income levels are as follows: (a) below $10,000, 38%; (b) $10,000-$15,000, 12%; (c) $15,000-$20,000, 27%; (d) $20,000-$25,000, 15%; and (e) $25,000-$50,000, 8%. Most of the families served (60%) are two-parent families.

Service Delivery Options

❏ Children served by the Early Childhood Daycare Model Project are placed in center-based day-care facilities. The majority of children attend the day-care program for 1 to 2 hours 1 to 2 days per week. Attendance, however, ranges from 2 hours 1 day per week to full-day sessions 5 days per week.

Staffing Patterns

❏ The project staff include an administrator, a coordinator, psychologists, and two paraprofessionals. All staff have a minimum of a BS degree, with the exception of one of the paraprofessionals, who is a high school graduate. The staff meet on a regular basis to share information about individual cases and obtain input from team members. Staff attend staff development workshops throughout the year. In addition, any day-care staff who desire additional training are given community college credit to attend workshops at least three times a year.

Staff meet on a regular basis.

Services for Children

❏ The primary goals of the Early Childhood Day Care Model Project are to identify day-care centers willing to accept children with handicaps, to identify families with handicapped children that desire day-care services, and to enroll infants and toddlers in the day-care programs. Children are initially referred to the project by community agencies and physicians, who conduct screenings.

Children are initially referred by community agencies and physicians.

Each child has an IPP (individual program plan) which stresses socialization skills. Curricular and instructional materials vary depending on what is used in the day-care setting. Each child receives direct services from the project paraprofessionals and therapists (e.g., physical therapist). The case manager maintains contact with the center as well as the family.

Family Involvement

❑ Through participation in this project, family members receive some respite from care of the child, and regular work schedules can be maintained. Family needs are determined through initial intake forms and consultation. Records from the referring agencies may also provide information about family structure and family needs. Formal family plans are not developed; however, goals and objectives are determined in the initial consultation.

All parents are invited to support group sessions. Training seminars are also provided. In addition, individual consultations are held on a regular basis with each family. All personal contacts, as well as letters and phone calls, are documented.

Program Evaluation

❑ Program effectiveness is determined primarily by measuring the attitudes of day-care center staff in accepting children with handicaps and the parents' attitudes about leaving their children in the day-care setting.

TUESDAY'S CHILD

Designed for families with increasing conflict in parent/child relationship.

❑ Tuesday's Child was developed in 1980 as the Early Intervention Project at Children's Memorial Hospital in Chicago and became a separate, not-for-profit organization in June 1984. It is designed for families who experience increasing conflict in the parent/child relationship. In these families, day-to-day interactions over going to bed, eating meals, or getting dressed may turn into terrible struggles between the parent and young child. Tuesday's Child offers an intensive parenting program designed to improve the parent/child relationship and offset future problems. It also has a Child Center that provides a carefully planned social and educational environment for the enrolled children. In the Child Center, staff members can observe the child to identify developmental disabilities and can work individually to enhance each child's developmental functioning. A close liaison is maintained with the Chicago Public Schools' early childhood program and suburban early childhood programs.

Characteristics of Children and Families Served

Parents come because of difficulty in managing their children's behavior.

❑ Tuesday's Child serves families with children ages 18 months through 5 years. Parents come to the program because of difficulty in managing their children's behavior. Approximately 45% of the children with behavior problems have concomitant handicapping conditions. These cover a broad range and include hyperactivity/ADD, developmental delays, language problems, pervasive developmental disorders, health problems, and early signs of learning disability. The majority of the children served are male (82%). The family structure is primarily two-parent (89%) and Caucasian (86%).

Service Delivery Options

❏ Tuesday's Child is a center-based model. Parents attend the parenting program twice each week for 2 and 1/2 hours. Children are in the Child Center while their parents are in the parenting program. Children may also attend additional 2 and 1/2 hour sessions in the Child Center. A special 2 and 1/2 hour program for working families is conducted on Saturday.

Staffing Patterns

❏ Tuesday's Child has the following staff: a psychologist (executive director), an MA-level early childhood specialist (program director), two MA-level Child Center teachers, and one 3/4-time BA-level Child Center teacher. The center also has about 40 volunteers each year, many from area universities and colleges. Diagnostic evaluations are completed contractually. Parents who have participated in the program must also serve as paraprofessional trainers for other parents. Child Center teachers provide services to children, while the early childhood specialist, the psychologist, and the paraprofessional trainers have the greatest contact with parents. The Child Center staff have weekly planning meetings. The program director also meets weekly with volunteer Child Center staff.

Parents must also serve as trainers for other parents.

Services for Children

❏ Tuesday's Child is a behaviorally oriented program based on social learning theory. Families are initially screened in a 1 and 1/2 hour interview with a professional staff member while the child is observed in the Child Center program. Parent/child interaction is assessed at each visit to the center using a 10-second interval recording system. The child is observed in the Child Center by the program director and teacher to detect potential developmental problems. If developmental disabilities are suspected, a formal diagnostic evaluation is conducted using instruments appropriate for the individual child.

The child's IEP focuses on social skills, with skill acquisition in other developmental areas considered secondary. Three major areas are identified for each child: compliance with teacher requests, time on task in individual and group activities, and interaction at an age-appropriate level with peers. The curriculum and instructional strategies are based on social learning theory. No specific commercial curricula are used. Teachers meet weekly to record observations on each child's attainment of objectives.

Teachers meet weekly.

Transition into public school programs is facilitated by the staff. The program director makes telephone contact with the school district and frequently attends staffings. The results of diagnostic evaluations are available to the school districts. Many of the children, however, are able to make the transition to regular community preschools without staff involvement.

Family Involvement

❏ The parent component of Tuesday's Child is also based on social learning theory. Each paraprofessional trainer interviews an incoming parent on the child's behavior at home, using the Strengths/Needs

Inventory (Lavigne, 1984). Each parent lists objectives for changing the child's behavior at home. A supervising staff member prioritizes and approves these objectives. The parent then implements the objectives at home. Behavior management strategies are applied and data are collected.

Each parent meets weekly with a paraprofessional and in a parent group.

Each parent meets weekly with a paraprofessional and also participates in a weekly parent group. An important part of parent training is a 20-minute parent/child play session conducted at each visit. In this session, the parent instructs the child to play with a particular toy. The parent issues a new instruction every 2 minutes. During these play sessions, the parent has the opportunity to practice the application of differential social reinforcement under the supervision of a trainer. The parent thus receives feedback and encouragement for attempts to practice use of new child management strategies. The psychologist supervises the paraprofessionals and conducts the majority of parent groups (75%); the early childhood specialist conducts the remainder of the parent groups. After parents complete the training with their child, they are required to serve as instructors for new participants. Parents are also active in disseminating the project (e.g., through a speaker's bureau) and in fundraising activities.

Records of child and parent progress are maintained regularly.

Records of child and parent progress are maintained regularly. Parent/child interactions in specially designed play sessions are graphed. In addition, objectives listed on the Strength/Needs Inventory are monitored and checked off when completed.

Program Evaluation

❏ Observational data from parent-child interactions are used in a single-subject applied behavior analysis design to demonstrate the impact of the program for each parent-child dyad. An evaluation of Tuesday's Child from 1980 to 1983 was recently conducted with the help of an outside evaluator. Results are not yet available.

ADOLESCENT-INFANT DEVELOPMENT PROGRAM

The aim is to assist adolescents in understanding their roles as parents.

❏ The aim of the Adolescent-Infant Development Program is to assist adolescents in understanding their roles as parents by enhancing their understanding of child development and helping them integrate family functions into everyday life. Funded as an HCEEP demonstration project from 1983-1986, the program is now administered by the Howard University Hospital, Department of Pediatrics. Collaborative efforts are maintained with the Washington, D.C., public schools and the Child Development Center of Howard University.

Characteristics of Children and Families Served

❏ Most of the families served by this program could be characterized as lower SES, as indicated by income and education. Most of the parents are high school students, but the program has also begun to serve younger parents, including those in junior high and elementary school. The incomes are all less than $20,000 per year, with the majority falling below $10,000 or between $10,000 and $15,000. The families represent cultural and ethnic minorities. Most are single parent, Black families with the mothers as heads of household. Only a small number are two-parent or extended families. The typical infant is less than a year old, male, and at risk for developmental delays.

Most are single parent Black families.

Service Delivery Options

❏ The service delivery model varies depending on the needs of the parent and child. A combination home-and-clinical model seems prevalent, although most families are served via home visits. The time spent with the parent and child also varies depending on individual needs. Visits range from a half hour to a full day in length and may occur only once every 2 months or as frequently as 5 days a week. The typical pattern, however, seems to be 1 to 2 hours, 1 to 2 days a week.

Most are served via home visits.

Staffing Patterns

❏ Program staff include a half-time administrator, a coordinator, an infant interventionist, a social worker, and an administrative assistant/ dissemination coordinator. All staff except the administrative assistant have an MS degree or higher. The infant interventionist and the social worker are the primary family contacts.

Services for Children

❏ The Adolescent-Infant Development Program is developmentally based and adheres to the theoretical models of Piaget and Erikson. Children are initially assessed with the Brazelton Neonatal Behavioral Assessment Scales (Brazelton, 1973) and the Bayley Scales of Infant Development (Bayley, 1969). Other diagnostic evaluations are obtained from other clinics/resources as needed. The Education for Multi-Handicapped Infants (EMI) (Elder, 1975) is used for programming purposes. IEPs are developed, and the Education for Multi-Handicapped Infants is used along with other curricula to implement IEPs.

Family Involvement

❏ The family component of the Adolescent-Infant Development Program focuses on direct social services. After the birth of the child, the parent's needs are assessed using the Iowa Parenting Skills Needs Checklist. Several strategies are then employed to meet parents' needs. Parents may attend group meetings; they may become involved as volunteers in the center program; they may be provided with informational sheets; and they may learn appropriate games or activities for use with their children.

Program Evaluation

❏ Program effectiveness is measured by the accomplishment of program objectives in quantifiable terms by specifically set criteria. Cost-effectiveness data are also collected.

PROJECT LINKING INFANTS IN NEED WITH COMPREHENSIVE SERVICES (LINCS)

❑ Project LINCS was developed by faculty of the University of Missouri at Columbia. The project is currently administered by the Missouri Department of Mental Health (the Regional Center for the Developmentally Disabled) and the Missouri Department of Health (the community health units). The University of Missouri has a LINCS Outreach Project. The administrative office for the project is in the Central Missouri Regional Center, Columbia, Missouri, Department of Mental Health.

The heart is interagency collaboration.

At the heart of the LINCS program and model is interagency collaboration. The program is designed to provide a systematic process for linking the expertise of regional service centers with community agency personnel who have direct and systematic access to children and families. The project is specific to rural areas where access to services and the unique characteristics of the child and the family require an adapted service delivery model. Using a team approach, regional personnel train designated community agency personnel to assist parents in providing developmental stimulation or implementing specific home-based intervention programs. Initial training is followed by systematic case management contacts and technical assistance. Emphasis on these latter aspects increases the effectiveness of case findings and direct intervention and decreases the professional isolation often characteristic of human service personnel in rural areas.

The focus of the intervention is the general development of children who are at risk for developmental delays or disabilities or who have developmental delays or specific handicapping conditions. The unique features of this model are two: (a) a process for establishing and maintaining regional-community linkage for service delivery in rural areas and (b) consideration of rural/community issues.

Characteristics of Children and Families Served

Project serves birth to 3 in a rural area.

❑ The project serves children from birth to 3 years of age in a rural area of fewer than 2,500 people. The children served are primarily mildly and moderately mentally retarded, but other handicaps are included. The children are predominantly Caucasian; only one is Black. The largest number of children fall into the 2- to 3-year age group. A large percentage of the children come from low-income homes.

Service Delivery Options

❑ The service is delivered in the home, and the length of sessions for children and parents is approximately 1 hour. Most children and their parents are seen at home for 1 hour once or twice a month.

Staffing Patterns

❑ Regional service center personnel use a teaming model to integrate and enhance the expertise of direct service providers in the community. Staff development is the responsibility of the regional service center, and these activities are determined by the regional service center staffing patterns. The staff includes a psychologist, a physical therapist, an occupational therapist, an infant interventionist, a speech therapist, a physician, a nurse, a social worker, and paraprofessionals. All are employed by the regional center, with the exception of the physician and the nurse, who are jointly employed by the regional center and a community agency. A community agency provides the paraprofessionals. The two staff members who are readily available are the nurse and the social service agency paraprofessional. The nurse is the key infant interventionist.

Services to Children and Families

❑ Regional service centers provide inservice training to community agencies concerning case finding strategies, eligibility criteria, referral processes, and screening. The community agency identifies someone to work with families of infants, and the Regional Service Center provides the training. There are no set instruments for developmental assessment; the nature of the population and the choice of instruments are the responsibility of the regional service center. A multidisciplinary evaluation is conducted by regional service center personnel.

In theoretical orientation, the model is ecological and Piagetian. Individualized programs are developed and maintained by the regional service center. A project-developed activity manual and resource guide are used to develop an individualized plan.

Model is ecological and Piagetian.

Family involvement varies depending on the needs of the family and the community agency upon whose caseload they appear. Strategies to involve parents include parent groups, direct teaching of their infants, and work on newsletters.

The regional service center is responsible for transition. It is a case management function of the center to link with the receiving agency.

Program Evaluation

❑ The effectiveness of the program depends on the linkage of regional service centers and community agencies to provide service delivery. The following variables are evaluated with the Concern-Based Appraisal Model:

1. Community agencies' use of critical components on specific intervention strategies referred to as the "Levels of Use" instrument (LOU), which assesses the patterns or areas of concern (SOC), level of skill acquisition, and maintenance in new areas of programming.
2. Agency administration satisfaction with the model and the linkage.
3. A community system—the degree to which interagency coordination occurs and linkages or service networks expand.

PROGRAM FOR CHILDREN WITH DOWN SYNDROME AND OTHER DEVELOPMENTAL DELAYS

❑ The agency that administers the program for children ages birth to 18 months with Down syndrome and other developmental delays is the Child Development Center located at Sumner, Washington. Other agencies that participate in the delivery of services are the Sumner School District,

Division of Developmental Disabilities, Pierce County Health Services, Bureau of Developmental Disabilities, First Christian Church of Sumner, and the Model Preschool Outreach Program, University of Washington. In addition, a close working relationship is maintained with other local public schools and the Association for Retarded Citizens. Referrals to other public agencies such as the Child Development Mental Retardation Center and Children's Hospital and private sources are made when appropriate.

The goal of this birth-to-3 program is to facilitate the development of young children with developmental delays by providing educational programming with the support of physical, occupational, and speech therapy services and to provide support and training to families.

Toddler program is center based.

The toddler program (18 months to 3 years) is center-based, with a strong parent involvement component. Programs at all levels implement the systematic process of instruction, including assessment; establishing goals and objectives; planning a program that allows the child to succeed; implementing the program; and evaluating the program's daily data collection, quarterly IEP updates, and annual pre- and postdata analysis. The curriculum includes instruction in gross and fine motor, cognitive, communication, and social and self-help skill areas. Home programs emphasize activities that can be incorporated into the families' daily routines.

Characteristics are mainstreaming and quality of systematic intervention.

The distinguishing characteristics of this model are the mainstreaming of preschoolers with handicaps with children who do not have handicaps and the quality of systematic intervention with both children and their families. The project also has a hands-on training program that encourages persons from the community, students, and parents to volunteer in the project. The Parent Trainer and Coordinator have developed an innovative method of training that does not intimidate but encourages willing volunteers and trainees.

Characteristics of Children and Families Served

❑ This project serves small towns with populations under 25,000. The children served are at risk for developmental delays or disabilities, have developmental disabilities, or are diagnosed as having disabilities or handicapping conditions. Of the 39 children currently receiving services, 37 are diagnosed as mentally retarded, 1 as health impaired, and 1 as blind. The children's ages range from 0-6 months (2) to 2-3 years (18). Fourteen of the children are between ages 1 and 2, and 5 are between the ages of 7 and 12 months. All are Caucasian. Twenty-two are female and 17 male.

The great majority of the children (31) are from two-parent families. Only 4 are from single-parent families with the mothers as heads of household, and 4 are in foster homes.

Service Delivery Options

Parents have a choice during infant period.

❑ The infant program (birth to 18 months) serves infants and their parents, with the therapist and teacher working individually with infants and parents. Parents have a choice of a home- or center-based program during the infant period. Sessions are 1 to 2 hours in length, and parent and infant are seen one to two times a week. The early preschool (18 months to 3 years) is center-based, with a strong parent involvement component. It meets 4 days a week; sessions are half a day in length.

Staffing Patterns

❑ The project employs an administrator, a parent coordinator, a psychologist, a physical therapist, two occupational therapists, a speech therapist, teachers, and a concepts therapist. Volunteers are also used. Four of the staff have master's degrees; the psychologist has a PhD. Teaming is facilitated by monthly meetings of teachers, parents, and support staff. Classroom staff interact daily with support staff.

Classroom staff interact daily with support staff.

The director is responsible for staff development, and a needs assessment is conducted informally at weekly staff meetings. Staff attend workshops and conferences and consultants are brought in to meet their needs. The Model Preschool Outreach Staff also provide inservice training.

Services for Children

❑ Programs at all levels implement the systematic process of instruction, including assessment, establishing goals and objectives, planning a program that allows the child to succeed, implementing the program, and evaluating the child through daily data collection, quarterly IEP updates, and annual pre- and postdata analysis. The curriculum includes instruction in gross and fine motor, cognitive, communication, and social and self-help skill areas.

Objectives are obtained from the Classroom Assessment of Developmental Skills (Oelwein, Fewell, & Pruess, in press), supplemented with the Brigance Diagnostic Inventory of Early Development (Brigance, 1978). The program uses a developmental approach in all skill areas. Plans for specific intervention strategies are developed jointly by parents, teachers, and support staff, based on specific needs of the child and the family. Learning activities are designed to use the child's natural environment and daily routine at home and school. These activities span the stages of learning—acquisition, practice to proficiency, and transfer and generalization. Positive adult-child interaction is emphasized, using techniques of "turn-taking."

Learning activities use natural environment and daily routine.

Individualized education programs (IEPs) are developed on a yearly basis, with quarterly updates in which all team members, including the parents, participate. Additional teaming is facilitated through monthly meetings of teachers, parents, and support staff. Classroom staff interact with support staff on a daily basis.

The Alpern Boll Developmental Profile (Alpern & Boll, 1972) is the screening instrument used, and referrals come from physicians, the Department of Developmental Disabilities, public schools, parents, and therapists. Instruments used in assessment and diagnostic evaluation are the Classroom Assessment of Developmental Skills (Oelwein et al., in press), Battelle Developmental Inventory (Newborg, Stock, Wnek, Guibaldi, & Svinicki, 1984), Bayley Scales of Infant Development (Bayley, 1969), Peabody Developmental Motor Scales (Folio & Fewell, 1983), and the Sequenced Inventory of Communication Development (Hedrick, Prather, & Tobin, 1984).

Services to Parents

Occupational therapist and teachers are primary staff working with parents.

❏ Parents are involved in a number of ways through newsletters, direct teaching, and monthly parent workshops. The occupational therapist and teachers are the primary staff working with parents of infants. A parent coordinator is responsible for parent meetings and workshops and for training volunteers. The Child Development Center staff maintains a close working relationship with the local public schools, the Division of Developmental Disabilities, the Association for Retarded Citizens, and the Model Preschool Outreach staff of the University of Washington to facilitate transition. In addition, referrals to other public agencies (e.g., Child Development and Mental Retardation Center, Children's Hospital) and to private sources are made when appropriate.

Program Evaluation

❏ Annual monitoring of the program and collection of data are conducted by the Division of Developmental Disabilities and Pierce County Social and Health Services. Data from the Classroom Assessment of Developmental Skills (Oelwein et al., in press) are reported to outreach staff, and complete analyses of individual and group gains are provided.

MACOMB 0-3 RURAL PROJECT

❏ The Macomb 0-3 Rural Project was administered during its development stage by Western Illinois University at Macomb. The McDonough County Rehabilitation Center and the Fulton County Rehabilitation Center now serve as continuants for direct services and demonstration of the model. The foci of the model are (a) providing an effective education/ remediation program for optimal development of handicapped infants in rural areas and (b) helping parents who live in rural areas acquire skills and knowledge to become more effective in dealing with their children. The program serves rural communities with populations of less than 50,000.

Only rural model approved by JDR panel.

This model was one of the first rural federally funded birth-to-3 programs and is the only rural 0-3 model approved by the Joint Dissemination Review Panel at the federal level. This panel reviews the project according to a set of criteria and determines whether or not it is worthy of being nationally disseminated.

Characteristics of Children Served

Most are developmentally delayed.

❏ The children served are those at risk for developmental delays or disabilities, those who have developmental delays, and those diagnosed as having disabilities or specific handicapping conditions. Of the children served, most are developmentally delayed with no specific diagnosis (38%). The second largest category comprises children with speech and language impairments (21%). Others included in the program are children who are orthopedically/physically impaired (2%), mentally retarded (9%), health impaired (15%), visually impaired (2%), multihandicapped (4%), and at risk for delays (9%). Nine percent of the children are 12 months old or younger, 49% are between 1 and 2 years of age, and 42% are between 2 and 3 years of age. The majority of the children (98%) are Caucasian;

the other 2% are Black. Sixty-four percent of the children are male, 36% female.

Characteristics of Families Served

❏ A high proportion of the families (66%) are classified as having low incomes, below $10,000. Only 2% of the families have incomes above $50,000. Of the remaining families, 11% have incomes between $25,000 and $50,000, 2% between $20,000 and $25,000, 13% between $15,000 and $20,000, and 6% between $10,000 and $15,000.

The majority of the fathers (63%) and mothers (60%) have high school educations. However, 30% of the fathers and 33% of the mothers have attended undergraduate school. The other 7% have only an elementary education.

Service Delivery Options

❏ The delivery system is home plus center. Both parent and child are provided services for 1/2 hour to 1 hour per session. On the average, children and parents are seen once a week.

Staffing Patterns

❏ Each of the two demonstration sites is staffed by an administrator (MS), a coordinator (BS), three infant interventionists (BS), a social worker employed by the program, a psychologist, two physical therapists (BS), an occupational therapist, a nurse (PhD), a counselor, and a nutritionist. Of the ancillary staff members, the occupational therapist, physical therapist, parent/infant specialist, speech therapist, and social worker are readily available. The others are available, but not readily. No volunteers or paraprofessionals work in the program. Compared with other staff, the parent/infant specialist spends the greatest amount of time with the infant and the family.

The flexibility of the team working with infants and parents permits shifting of responsibilities. Communication among team members is important to the success of the program. A needs assessment is conducted with staff through the use of a questionnaire, and professional growth goals are defined and activities provided accordingly.

The specialist spends the greatest amount of time with the infant and family.

Services to Children

❏ Referrals come to the project from doctors, hospitals, the Department of Children and Family Services, the Public Health Department, school personnel, mental health centers, and the general citizenry. All children referred to the project receive screening and diagnostic services. Screenings are also conducted periodically in conjunction with community organizations.

The standardized instruments used in developmental assessment are the Receptive-Expressive Emergent Language Scale (REEL) (Bzoch & League, 1978) and the Alpern-Boll Developmental Profile (Alpern & Boll, 1972). In addition, information from the physician and the occupational therapist is obtained the first month the infant receives services. The child's hearing and vision are evaluated by an audiologist and a vision specialist.

Theoretical orientation is Piagetian.

The theoretical orientation of the model is Piagetian. The goals emphasize gross motor, fine motor, cognitive, social, communication, and self-care skills. After 4 weeks of attendance in the program and observation by the parent/infant educator, goals and objectives for the child are determined, taking the parents' concerns into consideration. A core curriculum developed by the project is then implemented.

The core curriculum is based on four sets of principles: (a) general principles of growth and development, (b) selected Piagetian principles related to the sensorimotor and preoperational periods, (c) principles related to language development, and (d) specific therapy techniques for handicapping conditions. The instructional materials used are the Macomb 0-3 Core Curriculum and Have Wagon: Will Travel, the materials used in the sharing centers for parents. The Computer-Oriented Record-Keeping Enabler (CORE) allows the staff to store goals and objectives for the IEPs. The parent-infant educators, also called child development specialists, are responsible for intervention with the infant.

Family Involvement

The parent is the primary change agent.

❑ The basic assumption of the model, so far as the family component is concerned, is that the parent is the primary change agent and that the parent's cooperation and enthusiasm are essential to the success of the program. The project follows a plan for parents similar to the IEP for the child. These plans delineate strengths and needs, the major outcomes expected, criteria, procedures and times for determining success, specific intervention services, and a timeline for services.

Caseworker and social worker are responsible for working with families.

Families are involved in the program through support groups, monthly newsletters, and participation as aides to teachers. The caseworker and social worker are primarily responsible for working with families. They function as consultants, parent/family educators, case managers, counselors, and advocates.

Transition Activities

❑ The Outreach Macomb 0-3 Project participates in local agency activities; provides inservice training; and coordinates efforts among local preschools, public school programs, and Head Start on transition to other programs. The receiving teacher makes observational visits to each child's early childhood program. The early intervention program shares information with the receiving teachers during team meetings and at individual conferences. Written reports are also provided to ensure the child's smooth transition to the next level. The program is evaluated by measuring child progress, parent participation, and staff and parent satisfaction.

MULTI-AGENCY PROJECT FOR PRESCHOOLERS (MAPPS) (0-5)

❑ The MAPPS Project is located at the Developmental Center for Handicapped Persons on the campus of Utah State University. The project works with agencies including rural preschools for the developmentally delayed, Head Start programs, the Navajo Reservation, Air Force

Family Support Centers, and high school programs for adolescent mothers and their infants.

The theoretical orientation of the program is developmental and behavioral. For each child an individualized program is developed and the method of delivery is based on the individual needs of the child and the family. The focus of the MAPPS Project is to provide parents, caretakers, and teachers of children age 0 to 5 years with assessment and appropriate intervention curriculum materials for use in the areas of their deficits.

Theoretical orientation is developmental and behavioral.

Characteristics of Children Served

❏ The 0-2 population served represents a wide variety of handicapping conditions, as well as those at risk for developmental delays or disabilities. Approximately 21% of the children who are served by the project are from 0 to 6 months of age, 21% are from 7 to 12 months, another 21% are from 1 to 2 years, and 37% are from 2 to 3 years. Because the MAPPS Project works with a wide variety of agencies, the gender and ethnic backgrounds of the children represent the local populations in which these agencies exist and vary from year to year. Of the children served, approximately 60% are Caucasian, 20% are Navajo, and the remainder are Black or Hispanic. The total number of children served by agencies currently using the MAPPS model is approximately 500. The majority of children served (63%) are male.

Service Delivery Options

❏ Parents may choose to have their infants served in the home or in the center. Both parents and infants receive 1 to 2 hours of service per session, 1 to 2 days a week. The typical pattern of service for the large majority of clients is home plus center. At 2 1/2 years of age, most toddlers are served in the center and at home.

Typical pattern is home plus center.

Staffing Patterns

❏ The program's administrator and coordinator are both trained at the PhD level. Two psychologists, one physical therapist, two occupational therapists, one infant interventionist, a speech correctionist, a physician, a nurse, a social worker, and five paraprofessionals serve the program as well as volunteers. The professional staff readily available to parents and infants are the physical therapist, the speech therapist (MS), the infant interventionist (MS) and the volunteers. The person who spends the greatest amount of time with the infant is the infant interventionist. A transdisciplinary approach is used.

A transdisciplinary approach is used.

Staff development is ongoing. The director and coordinator take overall responsibility for planning activities based on an assessment of staff needs.

Services for Children and Families

❏ The theoretical orientation of the program is developmental learning (i.e., a combination of developmental and behavioral). Each infant has an individualized program, and the delivery system is based on the individual needs of the infants and their families.

The Battelle Developmental Inventory and Screening Instrument (Newborg et al., 1984), the Peabody Developmental Motor Scales (Folio & Fewell, 1983), the Bayley Scales of Infant Development (Bayley, 1969), the Sequenced Inventory of Communication Development (SICD) (Hedrick et al., 1984), and the Preschool Language Scale (PLS) (Zimmerman, Steiner, & Favatt, 1969) are used to assess the infants. Information from the physician, the occupational therapist, the physical therapist, and the speech therapist is used in the evaluation process.

Assessments are administered yearly.

Assessment results are compiled for program planning for the children and for measuring program effectiveness. Assessments are administered yearly on a pre/post basis.

For children from birth to 3 years of age, the child's developmental level is assessed first. Next, the child's parents are trained to provide the intervention using the Curriculum and Monitoring System (CAMS) (Peterson & Sedjo, 1979) curriculum. Then, families are monitored by phone or in person on a weekly basis. MAPPS also mainstreams children who are developmentally delayed ages 3 to 5 into existing preschool and day-care programs. The project provides these programs with child assessment, teacher training, and curriculum materials.

The Curriculum and Monitoring System (CAMS) (Peterson & Sedjo, 1979), developed by the MAPPS Project, is the primary curriculum used. CAMS is a developmentally sequenced series of teaching objectives that cover skills normally developed from birth to 5 years of age. Each objective is task-analyzed and broken down into small steps. Teaching instructions and mastery levels are specified for each step of the program.

Transition Activities

❑ Attention is given to the transition of the child from one level to another. Appropriate team members participate in conferences with receiving teachers.

Program Evaluation

❑ Infants are tested on a pre/post basis. A parent attitude questionnaire is administered yearly; participating agencies complete a questionnaire to determine agency satisfaction.

THE COPING PROJECT (CHILDREN'S OPTIMAL PROGRESS IN NEURODEVELOPMENTAL GROWTH)

❑ The COPING Project, located at the Johnson Rehabilitation Institute of the John F. Kennedy Medical Center in Edison, New Jersey (a city with a population between 25,000 and 50,000), is designed to enhance the adaptive behaviors of children and families by reducing stressors and developing personal resources needed for effective coping. Intervention

Intervention is personalized for each family.

is personalized for each family based on their needs, stressors, and available coping resources. Services consist of a variety of educational and therapeutic activities for most families; some require supportive counseling. Programming is modified as family needs change over time.

The COPING Project has developed two unique models: the COPING Process Model and the Personalized Learning Model. These models guide team assessment of child and family stressors and resources, team interaction and development of comprehensive service plans, family involvement in planning intervention goals and activities, intervention that addresses adaptive behaviors as well as developmental skills, and intervention that leads to the enhancement of family resources for effective coping.

Characteristics of Children Served

❑ Children admitted to the project are at risk for developing delays or disabilities, have developmental delays, or are diagnosed as having disabilities or specific handicapping conditions. The program serves approximately 135 children, 15% between 0 and 6 months of age, 22% between 7 and 12 months, 30% from 1 to 2 years, and 33% between 2 and 3 years. The population is predominantly Caucasian (67%), with 15% Black, 15% Hispanic, and 3% Oriental. Gender distribution is 41% female and 49% male. There is a wide range of handicapping conditions: delayed with no specific diagnosis (25%), orthopedically handicapped (17%), speech and language impaired (17%), mentally retarded (12%), multihandicapped (12%), health impaired (8%), emotionally disturbed (9%), at risk for delay (4%), autistic (4%), and visually impaired (4%).

There is a wide range of handicapping conditions.

Characteristics of Families Served

❑ Of the families served, 30% have incomes below $10,000 and 57% have incomes between $15,000 and $25,000. Only 13% have incomes above $30,000. The majority (74%) are two-parent families; 22% are single-parent families with the mothers as heads of household. The remaining children (4%) are members of extended families.

Majority are two-parent families.

Service Delivery Options

❑ The delivery systems are home, center, and home plus center. Parents and children are seen twice a week for 2-hour sessions.

Staffing Patterns

❑ The staff include an administrator (PhD), a coordinator (MS), a psychologist (PhD), 2.5 physical therapists (BS), 2.5 occupational therapists (BS and MS), 2 infant interventionists (MS), 2.5 speech therapists (MS), a physician (MD), a nurse (BS), and 2 social workers (MSW). All of these staff are readily available to the project. The speech pathologists, occupational therapists, physical therapists, and teachers spend the most time with the infant.

Services to Children

❑ In addition to informal developmental and clinical evaluation, the Early Coping Inventory (Zeitlin, Williamson, & Szczepanski, 1984), the Hawaii Early Learning Profile (HELP) (Furono et al., 1979), the Uzgiris/Hunt Scales of Ordinal Development (Uzgiris & Hunt, 1975), the Milani-Comparetti Motor Development Screening Test (Pearson, Rice, & Trembath, 1973), and the Developmental Hand Dysfunction (Erhardt, 1982) are used selectively.

Theoretical orientation is developmentally based.

The theoretical orientation of the program for children is developmentally based. The delivery is center-based with home visits. The major focus of the model is adaptive coping. Clinical frames of reference include neurodevelopmental therapy (NDT), sensory integration, and behavior management. Each child has an individualized education (service) program (IEP). Daily notes are taken on the child, and 6-month program reports are written. All team members who work with the child or family contribute information that is integrated into a comprehensive report by the case coordinator.

Family Involvement

❑ The family involvement component uses a family systems approach and a Coping Process Model. The instruments used to access needs are the Coping Inventory (Zeitlin, 1985), the Carolina Parent Support Scale (Bristol, 1983), the Belief Scale (Bristol, 1983), and the Definition Scale (Bristol & DeVellis, 1981).

Among the strategies used to involve parents are parent discussion groups, parent training sessions, individual conferences, counseling/psychotherapy, fathers' nights, topical workshops, and a parents' association. The social worker and the child's primary case coordinator have the major responsibility for working with the families.

Families are seen most frequently by the social worker and primary therapist.

Team members work with parents using the Coping Through Personalized Learning Model. Families are seen most frequently by the social worker and the child's primary therapist. The model consists of decision-making questions that structure team sharing during assessment; data analysis; and the development of goals, objectives, and intervention strategies.

A series of workshops has been designed to provide parents with information concerning the law; their roles, rights, and responsibilities; and the duties of the receiving program and the current IEP. Parent support groups address individual family concerns. Each child's educator writes a transition plan to be sent to the child's new program personnel.

THE FAMILY DAY CARE PROJECT

❑ The Family Day Care Project is housed in Ann Arbor, Michigan, and is administered by the Child Care Coordinating and Referral Service. Other agencies participating in the service delivery of the project are the Washtenaw Intermediate School District, Ann Arbor public schools, the Washtenaw Association for Retarded Citizens, and Eastern Michigan University. The service area is a university town with a population of about 150,000.

Focus is to train family day-care providers.

The focus of the project is to train family day-care providers to care for children with special needs. After training, children are placed with the providers and are supported by weekly or bimonthly visits from the special services coordinator (an early intervention specialist). Parents are counseled, when appropriate, on the necessity of a whole team approach—the school, the provider, the project, and the family—to maximize support and development of the child.

Training sessions for the providers are conducted using adult education models of parent training to deliver information on the care of children ages 0 to 3 with special needs.

Characteristics of Children and Families Served

❏ Children served are at risk for developmental delays or disabilities, have developmental delays, or have been diagnosed as having disabilities or specific handicapping conditions. Thirty children are enrolled. One third of the children (33%) are at risk for delays, 13% are health impaired, and 10% have sensory impairments. Other handicapping conditions represented include mental retardation, emotional disturbance, multiple handicaps, and developmental delays. Most of the children are mildly to moderately handicapped.

Most children are mildly to moderately handicapped.

Children range in age from 0-6 months (17%) to 2-3 years (67%). Ten percent are 7-12 months old, and 6% are 1-2 years old. The program is made up primarily of Caucasian children (83%); 13% are Black and 4% are Hispanic. The majority of the children are male (67%). Of the 30 children served, 22 are from two-parent families; the remainder are from single-parent families with the mothers as heads of the households.

Service Delivery Options

❏ Children are enrolled in family day-care homes. They spend varying hours and days per week in the day-care programs, depending upon the family's and child's needs.

Staffing Patterns

❏ An administrator (PhD), a coordinator (BS), and an early intervention specialist (MS) are employed by the project. The psychologist (MS) is contracted by the program. The intermediate school district supplies the services of a physical therapist, an occupational therapist, a speech therapist, and teacher consultants. All staff—both project staff and those provided by the school district—are readily available. The family day-care provider spends the greatest amount of time with the children. The early intervention specialist spends the most time with the family. Each staff member has a staff development plan, which may include taking classes, attending conferences, and attending inservice sessions.

The early intervention specialist spends the most time with the family.

Services to Children

❏ The Denver Developmental Screening Test (Frankenburg, 1973) is used for screening, and a large battery of other instruments is used by the school district for assessment.

The diagnostic evaluation of the child is conducted by the Washtenaw Intermediate School District or the Ann Arbor Public Schools. The day-care experience supports the work that the special education staff have proposed in their individualized education programs (IEPs). The children with handicaps are integrated into the family day-care home, and the home is provided with activities to achieve the goals delineated by each child's IEP. Logs are kept on the child by the special services coordinator.

Children with handicaps are integrated into the family day-care home.

Services to Families

❏ The Family Day Care Rating Scale (Harms & Clifford, 1984), an adapted version of *Attitudes of Educators Toward Exceptional Children*

(Haring, Stern, & Cruickshank, 1958), and the case study analysis are used to assess family needs. An early intervention specialist is responsible for working with the families.

The Family Day Care Project is a model based on collaboration among the school system, the family day-care providers, and the parents. Its goal is to deliver comprehensive services to working families who have children with special needs. Frequent meetings are held with staff from agencies serving the family, defining the roles of each agency in meeting the family's needs.

Transition Activities

Conferences are held with the receiving teacher.

❑ Conferences are held with the receiving teacher when a child is ready to be placed at the next level. Since family day care includes both before-and after-school care, many of the children continue in day care for several years.

Program Evaluation

❑ The effectiveness of the program is assessed by administering a pre/post attitudinal survey and by analyzing changes in scores on the Family Day Care Rating Scale (Harms & Clifford, 1984).

The project is disseminated through speeches at local, state, and national conferences and through newsletters and local media coverage.

The unique feature of this model is the coordination of day care with other childhood special education programs. Specialized day care is offered to families who otherwise would not have this service.

CHILDREN WITH HEARING IMPAIRMENTS IN MAINSTREAMED ENVIRONMENTS (CHIME)

The project has a working agreement with area hospitals and clinics.

❑ Project CHIME is administered by the Nassau County BOCES (Board of Cooperative Educational Services), whose administrative office is in Westbury, New York. The project has a working agreement with area hospitals and clinics. The focus of the project is the education and mainstreaming of 2- to 3-year-old Caucasian children who have hearing impairments with nonhandicapped children in neighborhood nursery schools. The communities served have populations of 25,000 or less.

Characteristics of Children and Families Served

❑ All of the children enrolled in the demonstration project are between the ages of 2 and 3 years. The majority (51%) are female. Most of the children (86%) are from two-parent families; only 14% are from single-parent families.

Service Delivery Options

❑ The children participating in the project attend the BOCES Program for Children with Hearing Impairments 5 days a week. Two to 3 mornings each week, they are mainstreamed with their nonhandicapped peers in local nursery schools within their home communities for sessions of approximately 1 to 2 hours.

Staffing Patterns

❑ The staff include a project director and a project coordinator. The latter works full time for CHIME. In addition, a psychologist, audiologist, and teacher/trainer, all trained at the master's level, are available to the project. Occupational and physical therapy services are also available as needed from the Program for the Hearing Impaired. All project staff work with both the children and their parents. The staff meet twice a month to discuss progress of the youngsters and any special needs that may require staff attention. The project director and coordinator are responsible for the staff meetings. Information about the availability of the program is disseminated through a project brochure and the agency newsletters of Nassau BOCES.

Staff meet twice a month to discuss progress of the youngsters.

Services for Children

❑ Screening and casefinding are conducted by a team that includes the administrator, the psychologist, the audiologist, and the teacher/trainer. The assessment instruments used to develop profiles of children involved in CHIME are the SKI-HI Language Development Scale (Watkins, 1979), the McCarthy Scales of Children's Abilities (McCarthy, 1972), and the *Meadow-Kendall Social Emotional Assessment Inventory for Deaf Students* (Meadow, Karchmer, Peterson, & Rudner, 1980). For diagnostic evaluation, the psychologist uses the Developmental Test of Visual Motor Integration (Beery & Buktenica, 1967), Early Learning Accomplishment Profile (E-LAP) (Glover et al., 1978), and Test for Auditory Comprehension of Language (TACL) (Carrow-Wolfolk, 1985).

Project CHIME is based on the theoretical assumption that very young children with hearing impairments need opportunities to learn and play while interacting with their hearing peers. Mainstreaming them, especially in structured settings, aids in their language development, provides important peer models, and helps develop cognitive and social skills.

Once a child is selected for the program and the parents agree to the mainstreaming experience, project staff visit the local nursery school where this will take place. The staff of the nursery program are trained to work with a child with a hearing impairment and in the use of special equipment such as the auditory trainer, a device that enhances communication between the teacher and the student. Training of staff is ongoing through periodic consultation services from the project.

Before the child is mainstreamed, this goal becomes part of the child's individualized education program (IEP). The IEP is developed in September and updated in January; final assessment of progress is made in June. Parents participate in the development of the IEP.

Once a child enters the mainstream program, progress is monitored on a weekly basis.

Project CHIME has developed an adapted curriculum to be used in mainstreaming by the participating nursery schools. The curriculum stresses language skills, comprehension, and auditory training. Once a child enters the mainstream program, progress is monitored on a weekly basis through case conferencing with staff members as necessary.

Family Involvement

❏ Parent education is an important part of the project. Workshops are held monthly, and minutes are kept. Parents receive extensive training to help them understand their children's development and needs, especially in relation to the hearing world. They also learn to work with their children at home so that the mainstreaming experience will be beneficial for both the parent and the child.

DISCUSSION OF FINDINGS AND IMPLICATIONS FOR PRACTICE

A variety of agencies take the lead in administering programs.

❏ At present, a variety of agencies take the lead in administering programs for infants and toddlers with handicaps. The fiscal agents for most of the programs responding to this survey are universities or public school districts. In that respect, the findings differ markedly from those of a survey conducted 5 years ago in which hospitals were one of the primary fiscal agents for the majority of respondent programs (Trohanis et al., 1982). This shift may indicate a difference in sample populations. It may also indicate an increased interest in the development of infant programs on the part of educational agencies. Whatever the reasons, procedures for cooperation and for determining which agency should serve as head are critically needed, especially with the passage of P.L. 99-457, which stipulates that states applying for program development funds in the area of birth-to-2 services must identify a lead agency and establish an interagency council.

Procedures for cooperation and for determining which agency should serve as head are critically needed.

Analysis of the survey data suggests that infant/toddler programs do not have consistent, well-defined procedures for identifying children with handicaps (i.e., casefinding and screening). The majority of children served by the projects are initially identified through referrals from other agencies. Further, most of the children are those with more readily identified moderate or severe handicaps. Children at risk for developing handicaps and those with milder handicaps seem underrepresented. This suggests the following:

1. Limited funding for birth through 2 programs may result in services for those with more severe handicaps.
2. Identification procedures are not adequately refined to identify children who are at risk or have milder handicaps.
3. Staff in birth through 2 programs may not be trained or have experience in identification and screening procedures, and thus rely primarily on referrals.
4. Parents of children with more severe handicaps may be more likely to demand services.

Professionals tend to be more committed to remediation than to prevention.

5. Professionals tend to be more committed to remediation than to prevention; thus, services may be withheld until delays become obvious.
6. Medical professionals are often reluctant to suggest that infants and toddlers are handicapped or at risk.

These concerns and problems may be reduced by: (a) developing stable funding sources with allocations sufficient to identify children at risk for developing handicaps, as well as those with moderate and severe handicaps; (b) developing preservice and inservice programs to train birth-to-2 staff in systematic casefinding and screening procedures; (c) stressing interagency collaboration in developing and implementing identification procedures; and (d) promoting awareness among parents, professionals, and other citizens as to the importance of intervention even with children who are at risk or who have mild handicaps.

At a time when the divorce rate and the number of pregnancies among unmarried teenagers are increasing in the United States, families served by the HCEEP infant/toddler projects tend to be two-parent families. This suggests that the more stable two-parent families may be the ones that seek services.

Professionals providing services in the surveyed programs tend to have at least a BS degree and come from a variety of disciplines. The data do not indicate, however, whether or not these professionals have specific training and experience in working with infants and toddlers who have handicaps. Personnel preparation programs in early childhood special education (ECSE), birth to 2 years, have only recently been developed and are limited in number. This suggests that many of the staff involved in these model projects may not have training in working with children in this age group. Inconsistencies noted in assessment procedures, the selection of assessment instruments, the selection of curricula, and involvement of families lend additional support to the notion that staff may not have formal training in providing birth-to-2 services.

Personnel preparation programs are limited in number.

Slightly more than half of the projects reported that staff development activities are based on identified needs, with little information about the intensity of such activities. Inservice training should be a high priority budget item in such programs. This is a relatively new field, with knowledge about infants and toddlers with handicaps and strategies for providing services increasing rapidly; thus, inservice must be ongoing and personnel preparation programs must be developed at the preservice level. In addition, research regarding best practices for both preservice and inservice education in ECSE (0-2) is needed, as well as research for best practices related to direct services for children.

Inservice should be a high priority budget item.

All the projects but one indicated a specific philosophical orientation, with developmental learning being the preferred model. Program practices, however, do not always seem consistent with the stated philosophical model. Several concerns can be addressed in the area of assessment:

Practices do not always seem consistent with the stated philosophical model.

1. Identification and screening procedures are not well defined.
2. The selection and use of assessment instruments appears inconsistent across projects.
3. In many programs, assessment instruments seem to be used for purposes other than those for which they were designed (e.g., diagnostic instruments used for ongoing assessment).
4. Few programs seem to link assessment with curriculum development.

Furthermore, criteria for selecting curricula are not evident. Many curricular programs are used, and often they do not match the assessment instruments. Record-keeping procedures also are not well delineated. The majority of programs (65%) do plan specific transitional activities, but none of them reported follow-up activities or evaluation strategies to determine whether transition is successful. These concerns underscore

Curricular programs often do not match assessment instruments.

the need for careful monitoring of programs, as well as the need for high-quality inservice and preservice training.

Most programs reported a family systems approach to working with families. They also reported conducting needs assessments and developing family plans. Staff skills and training in working with families via a family systems model may be questioned, however, since family involvement components do not seem to address the unique needs of individual families. Only 15% of the programs that conduct needs assessments do not develop family plans. Furthermore, a limited number of family involvement strategies seem to be implemented, with parent training and support groups and newsletters being the most popular. Only two programs specifically indicated that they provide services for siblings while only one addresses the needs of fathers and grandparents. As with

Need for training to work with families is indicated.

other program components, the need for training to work with families is indicated. Successful implementation of a comprehensive family involvement program requires the commitment of professionals, many of whom are educated and experienced in working with children, but who may have little or no formal training to work with families.

REFERENCES

Alpern, B., & Boll, T. (1972). *Developmental profile.* Indianapolis: Psychological Development Publications.

Bailey, D. B., Simeonsson, R. J., Winton, P. J., Huntington, G. S., Comfort, M., Isbell, P., O'Donnell, K. J., & Helm, J. M. (1986). Family-focused intervention: A functional model for planning, implementing, and evaluating individualized family services in early intervention. *Journal of the Division for Early Childhood, 102,* 156-171.

Bayley, N. (1969). *Bayley scales of infant development.* New York: The Psychological Corporation.

Beck, A. T., & Beamesdorfer, A. (1974). Assessment of depression: The depression inventory. In P. Pichot (Ed.), *Psychological measurements in psychopharmacology: Modern problems in pharmacopsychiatry* (Vol. 7, 151-169). Basel, Switzerland: Karger.

Beery, K. E., & Buktenica, N. (1967). *Developmental test of visual-motor integration.* Chicago: Follett.

Bluma, S., Shearer, M., Frohman, A., & Hilliarn, J. (1976). *Portage guide to early education.* Portage, WI: Portage Project.

Brazelton, T. B. (1973). *The neonatal behavioral assessment scale.* Philadelphia: J. B. Lippincott Company.

Brigance, A. (1978). *The Brigance diagnostic inventory of early development.* North Billerica, MA: Curriculum Associates.

Bristol, M. M. (1983a). *Carolina parent support scale.* Chapel Hill, NC: University of North Carolina, Frank Porter Graham Child Development Center.

Bristol, M. M. (1983b). The belief scale. In M. M. Bristol, A. Donovan, & A. Harding (Eds.), *The broader impact of intervention: Assessing family stress and support.* Chapel Hill, NC: University of North Carolina, Frank Porter Graham Child Development Center.

Bristol, M. M., & DeVellis, R. (1981). *The definition scale.* Chapel HIll, NC: University of North Carolina, Frank Porter Graham Child Development Center.

Bzoch, K. R., & League, R. (1978). *Receptive-expressive emergent language scale.* Austin, TX: Pro-Ed.

Carrow-Wolfolk, E. (1985). *Test for auditory comprehension of language* (rev. ed.). Allen, TX: Developmental Learning Materials.

Crnic, K., Greenberg, M. T., Ragozin, A., & Robinson, N. (1982). *Inventory of parents' experiences.* Seattle: University of Washington, Child Development and Mental Retardation Center.

D'Eugenio, B. B., & Rogers, S. (1975). *The early intervention developmental profile.* Ann Arbor: Early Intervention Project for Handicapped Infants and Young Children.

DeWeerd, J. (1979, December). *Handicapped Children's Early Education Program: A retrospective.* Paper presented at the Handicapped Children's Early Education Conference, Washington, DC.

DeWeerd, J., & Cole, A. (1976). A handicapped children's early education program. *Exceptional Children, 43,* 155-157.

Doll, E. A. (1965). *Vineland social maturity scale.* Circle Pines, MN: American Guidance Service, Inc.

Elder, W. B. (1975). *EMI assessment scale.* Charlottesville, VA: Education for Multihandicapped Infants.

Erhardt, R. (1982). *Developmental hand dysfunction.* Laurel, MD: Ramsco Publishing Company.

Filler, J. W. (1983). Service models for handicapped infants. In S. G. Garwood & R. R. Fewell (Eds.), *Educating handicapped infants* (pp. 369-386). Rockville, MD: Aspen.

Folio, M. R., & Fewell, R. R. (1983). *Peabody developmental motor scales.* Hingham, MA: Teaching Resources Corporation.

Frankenburg, W. K. (1973). *Denver developmental screening test.* Denver, CO: LADOCA Publishing Foundation.

Fredericks, H. D. (1976). *Teaching research curriculum for moderately and severely handicapped.* Springfield, IL: Charles C Thomas.

Furono, S., Inatsuka, T. T., Allman, T. L., & Zelsloft, B. (1979). *The Hawaii early learning profile.* Palo Alto, CA: VORT Corporation.

Gallagher, J. J., Cross, A. C., & Scharfman, W. (1981). Parental adaptation to the young handicapped child: The father's role. *The Journal of the Division for Early Childhood, 3,* 3-14.

Glover, M. E., Preminger, J. L., & Sanford, A. R. (1978). *The early learning accomplishment profile.* Winston-Salem, NC: Kaplan School Supply.

Hanson, M. (1977). *Teaching your Down's syndrome infant: A guide for parents.* Baltimore: University Park Press.

Haring, N., Stern, G. G., & Cruickshank, W. M. (1958). *Attitudes of educators toward exceptional children.* Syracuse, NY: Syracuse University Press.

Harms, T., & Clifford, R. (1984). *Family day care rating scale.* Chapel Hill, NC: University of North Carolina, Frank Porter Graham Child Development Center.

Hedrick, D. A., Prather, E. M., & Tobin, A. R. (1984). *Sequenced inventory of communication development.* Los Angeles: Western Psychological Services.

Holroyd, J. (1974). The questionnaire on resources and stress: An instrument to measure family response to a handicapped family member. *Journal of Community Psychology, 2,* 92-94.

Karnes, M. B., Linnemeyer, S. A., & Myles, G. (1983). Programs for parents of handicapped children. In R. Haskins (Ed.), *Parent education and public policy* (pp. 181-210). Norwood, NJ: Ablex.

Karnes, M. B., Linnemeyer, S. A., & Shwedel, A. (1981). A survey of federally funded model programs for handicapped infants: Implications for research and practice. *Journal of the Division for Early Childhood, 2,* 25-39.

Karnes, M. B., & Zehrbach, R. R. (1977). Alternative models for delivering services to young handicapped children. In J. B. Jordan, A. H. Hayden, M. B. Karnes, & M. Woods (Eds.), *Early childhood education for exceptional children* (pp. 20-65). Reston, VA: The Council for Exceptional Children.

Koontz, C. (1974). *Koontz child development program: Training activities for the first 48 months.* Los Angeles: Western Psychological Services.

Lavigne, V. (1984). *Strength/needs inventory.* Chicago: Tuesday's Child.

MacMillan, D. L., & Turnbull, A. P. (1983). Parent involvement with special education: Respecting individual preferences. *Education and Training of the Mentally Retarded, 18*, 5-9.

McCarthy, D. (1972). *McCarthy scales of children's abilities.* New York: The Psychological Corporation.

McCollum, J. A. (1985). Parent/infant interventionists: Survey of roles, characteristics, and needs. Springfield, IL: Illinois State Board of Education.

Meadow, K. T., Karchmer, M. A., Peterson, L. M., & Rudner, L. (1980). *Meadow/Kendall social emotional assessment inventory for deaf students.* Washington, DC: Gallaudet College, OUTREACH, Pre-college Programs.

Meyer, D. J., & Vadasy, P. F. (1986). *Grandparent workshops: How to organize workshops for grandparents of children with handicaps.* Seattle: University of Washington Press.

Meyer, D. J., Vadasy, P. F., & Fewell, R. R. (1984). *A handbook for the fathers program: How to organize a program for fathers and their handicapped children.* Seattle: University of Washington Press.

Meyer, D. J., Vadasy, P. F., & Fewell, R. R. (1985). *SIBSHOPS: A handbook for implementing workshops for siblings of children with special needs.* Seattle: University of Washington Press.

Moos, R. (1974). *Family environment scale and preliminary manual.* Palo Alto, CA: Consulting Psychologists Press.

Newborg, J., Stock, J., Wnek, L., Guibaldi, J., & Svinicki, J. (1984). *Battelle developmental inventory.* Allen, TX: DLM Teaching Resources.

Oelwein, P. L., Fewell, R. R., & Pruess, J. B. (in press). *Classroom assessment of developmental skills (CADS).* Seattle, WA: University of Washington Press.

Pearson, P., Rice, L., & Trembath, J. (1973). *Milani-Comparetti motor developmental test.* Omaha, NB: Meyer Children's Rehabilitation Center.

Peterson, A., & Sedjo, K. (1979). *Curriculum and monitoring system.* New York: Walker Educational Book Corporation.

Peterson, N. L. (1987). *Early intervention for handicapped and at-risk children: An introduction to early childhood special education.* Denver, CO: Love.

Sheehan, R., & Graedel, K. (1983). Intervention models in early childhood special education. In S. G. Garwood (Ed.), *Educating young handicapped children: A developmental approach* (pp. 475-514). Rockville, MD: Aspen.

Swan, W. W. (1980). The Handicapped Children's Early Education Program. *Exceptional Children, 47*(1), 12-16.

Trohanis, P. L., Cox, J. O., & Meyer, R. A. (1982). A report on selected demonstration programs for infant intervention. In C. T. Ramey & P. L. Trohanis (Eds.), *Finding and educating high-risk and handicapped infants* (pp. 163-191). Baltimore, MD: University Park Press.

Turnbull, A. P., & Turnbull, H. R. (1986). *Families, professionals, and exceptionality: A special partnership.* Columbus, OH: Merrill Publishing Company.

Uzgiris, I. C., & Hunt, J. (1975). *Assessment in infancy: Ordinal scales of psychological development.* Urbana, IL: University of Illinois Press.

Watkins, S. (1979). *SKI-HI language development scale: Assessment of language skills for hearing impaired children from infancy to five years.* Logan, UT: Utah State University, Project SKI-HI.

Welsh, M. A., & Odum, C. S. (1981). Parental involvement in the education of the handicapped child: A review of the literature. *Journal of the Division for Early Childhood, 3*, 15-25.

Yavorsky, D. K. (1978). *Discrepancy evaluation: A practitioner's guide.* Richmond: University of Virginia, Evaluation Research Center.

Zeitlin, S. (1985). *Coping inventory.* Bensenville, IL: Scholastic Testing Service.

Zeitlin, S., Williamson, G. G., & Szczepanski, M. (1984). *Early coping inventory.* Bensenville, IL: Scholastic Testing Service.

Zimmerman, I. L., Steiner, U. G., & Favatt, R. L. (1969). *Preschool language scale.* Columbus, OH: Charles E. Merrill Publishing Company.

5.
Parent Involvement in Early Childhood Special Education

**Cordelia C. Robinson,
Steven A. Rosenberg,
and
Paula J. Beckman**

❑ In this chapter we will discuss the nature of parent involvement in early childhood special education. Within that general theme we will look at the rationale for parent involvement, ways in which parents have been involved in programs, and the requirements for parent and family involvement as identified in the new legislation, Public Law 99-457, the Education of the Handicapped Act Amendments of 1986. We will identify our assumptions about meaningful parent involvement. Next we will discuss models that have been proposed for the study of families. Within these models, we will identify variables that have been demonstrated to relate to the manner and/or success of parent involvement. We will provide some specific illustrations as to how these variables have been demonstrated to affect parent involvement and from those examples draw implications for developing individualized family service plans as required under P.L. 99-457. Finally, we will discuss implications of these examples for evaluating parent involvement within the context of individualized family service plans.

RATIONALE FOR PARENT INVOLVEMENT

Parent involvement has become an almost universal characteristic.

❑ Emphasis upon parent involvement has become an almost universal characteristic of early intervention programs for handicapped infants and toddlers. However, when programs involving direct intervention with handicapped infants began to gain momentum in the early 1970s, the nature of parent involvement was markedly different from what we see in intervention programs today. Parents were expected to play an instrumental role in the day-to-day intervention activities with their children, and several arguments were offered to justify this. Initially, professionals working in the field of early intervention involved parents in order to extend the impact of intervention. Three reasons have been cited by professionals and parents advocating for legislation that requires parent involvement in intervention programs:

Parents were expected to play an instrumental role in day-to-day activities.

1. Since the child spends the bulk of his or her time with parents, the more knowledgeable they are about child development strategies and activities, the greater the impact of intervention.
2. Parent/child interaction and its relationship to child development was used as a rationale for involving parents in their children's educational programs.
3. Lack of personnel available to work with young handicapped infants makes parent involvement necessary.

ISSUES IN THE DESIGN OF PARENT INVOLVEMENT

Goals of parent involvement need to be clarified.

❑ As the number of early intervention programs has increased over the past 10 to 15 years there has been a corresponding increase in the number of strategies used to involve parents in their children's educational programs. In order to evaluate these various strategies, a number of issues must be considered. First, the goals of parent involvement need to be clarified. Currently, parent involvement assumes a partnership between parents and professionals. Therefore, in programs the meaning of equal partnership must be established and how equal status on the team for parents and professionals can be achieved in light of their probable differences. These include differences in their knowledge of disabling conditions and in their respective roles. Finally, when methods for involving parents are designed, individual differences in both family constellation and cultural style need to be accommodated.

ASSUMPTIONS REGARDING PARENT INVOLVEMENT

❏ In identifying variables that may affect the level and nature of parent participation in early intervention programs, we are making a number of assumptions about parent participation. First, we assume that parent participation is a necessary component of programming for infants and young children. We assume this because young children spend the majority of their time in the family context and need to be looked at in this context. In addition to this logical argument, there is a multitude of written materials and personal testimony from parents and professionals working in the field of early intervention regarding the essential nature of parent involvement. Second, we assume that the primary reason for involving parents is the impact of such involvement upon child development. We also assume that intervention strategies must be flexible and negotiated with families in order to accommodate differences in family styles and in the manner and intensity of parent involvement. Finally, we assume that parents must assist in designing and implementing the service system in which they will participate.

We assume parent participation is a necessary component.

Parents must assist in designing and implementing the service system.

CHANGES IN THE NATURE OF PARENT INVOLVEMENT

❏ We, as well as others in the field of intervention with young disabled children, have noted how parent involvement has changed over the past two decades (Foster, Berger, & McLean, 1981; Rosenberg, 1977; Wiegerink, Hocutt, Posante-Loro, & Bristol, 1980). A number of factors have influenced those changes, including an emphasis upon parent-mediated instruction, program reports indicating variability of level of family participation in parent-mediated intervention, changing family patterns, and introduction of family systems theory. Historically, professional efforts directed toward helping families with disabled children focused upon parents and children separately. Efforts directed toward parents used counseling techniques and focused on acceptance of and adjustment to the child with a disability. Professional efforts to enhance child development were committed to the direct treatment of the child. But changes occurred because of the growing compensatory education movement directed toward families with children considered to be at developmental risk due to conditions of poverty. This movement promoted an emphasis upon direct involvement of parents in instruction of their children.

Historically, efforts focused on parents and children separately.

PARENT-MEDIATED INSTRUCTION

❏ There is now increasingly widespread acceptance of the importance of having parents directly involved in the education of their young children who have developmental problems. As the practice of involving parents became common, and as efforts to teach parents intervention techniques increased, so did reports that the strategies of parent-mediated intervention did not work in all cases. One explanation offered for this lack of uniform success was the lack of individualized strategies for involving parents in the process of parent-mediated instruction.

Aspects of the family influence the capacity to nurture its children.

Aspects of the family, the characteristics of its members, and the total context in which it exists greatly influence its capacity to nurture its children. At times, professional efforts are most profitably directed toward providing supports that enable parents to exercise their caretaking skills effectively. Interventions that focus on the family, parents, or social and economic context are necessary when the conditions of life make it impossible for parents to perform their child-rearing functions adequately. Under these circumstance, no direct form of intervention aimed solely at the child is likely to have substantial impact. Instead, the needs of all family members must be addressed.

Needs of all family members must be addressed.

CHANGING FAMILY PATTERNS

Parent-mediated instruction was derived from the compensatory education model.

❑ Foster et al. (1981) have pointed out that parent-mediated instruction for families with disabled children was derived primarily from the compensatory education model. The model assumed that the deficiencies of low-income children in school-related tasks derived from deficiencies in their home environments. While this deficit model was reasonably congruent in the early First Chance projects that served mildly handicapped children, as more multiply and severely handicapped children came to be served in early intervention projects, the original assumptions and techniques of parent involvement were found to need examination.

This changing pattern included increased number of single-parent households.

Another changing pattern that affected the assumptions and strategies of parent-mediated intervention was the larger context of the American family. This changing pattern included the increased number of single-parent households in which the custodial parent is the mother, the concomitant feminization of poverty, and in the remaining two-parent households, the greater likelihood of both parents working outside the home (Bristol, 1987; Foster et al., 1981). In this regard, Foster and associates pointed out that most strategies of parent-mediated intervention assume a nonworking parent who has time to integrate the recommended interventions into the daily routine.

As more and more intervention programs were developed with professionals and parents involved, there were more opportunities to see variations in strategies and, of course, variations in outcome. Also, there was an increase in the number of people calling for research to help understand variations in outcomes. Most often these people suggested that concepts used in clinical work with families would be helpful in developing a better understanding of variations in outcomes and subsequently in individualizing intervention strategies so as to produce more uniformly successful outcomes (Dunst, Cooper, & Bolick, in press; Foster et al., 1981; Rosenberg, 1977; Turnbull, Summers, & Brotherson, 1986). In the next part of this chapter, we will examine theories of family functioning and propose a system for classifying variables that appear to be common across theories of family functioning and are likely to affect the success of intervention strategies.

MODELS OF FAMILY FUNCTIONING

❏ Historically, theorists interested in the study of families have proposed several different models from which to view family functioning. Most of these models were not originally developed as a means for studying families of handicapped children. However, in recent years a number of investigators have acknowledged the usefulness of these theoretical approaches as a way to understand the impact of a handicapped child on the family. In this section, several of the most prominent approaches will be briefly reviewed, variables that are common across the models will be identified, and implications of these models for interventionists will be described.

Theorists have proposed different models.

Family Systems Theory

❏ The family systems approach has been receiving increasing attention by investigators studying families of handicapped children. This approach is based on the general systems theory as described by Von Bertalanffy (1968). Essentially, this theory asserts that all living systems are composed of a number of parts that are interdependent in the sense that influences associated with one part of the system are likely to affect other parts. Interaction of the parts creates features of the entire system that are not present in any of the parts individually. More recently, family systems theory applications have been extended to families of handicapped children (Dunst, et al., in press; Fewell, 1986; Turnbull et al., 1986). The family systems theory has been an important contribution to our understanding of family functioning. Investigators have recognized that in order to understand family functioning, they cannot simply consider individual members in isolation. Rather, relationships among members and the ecological context in which the families exist must be considered as well (Bronfenbrenner, Avgar, & Henderson, 1977).

General systems theory asserts that all living systems are composed of a number of parts.

ABCX Model

❏ Another model of the impact of events upon families is the ABCX model, originally developed by Hill (1949). Hill's model has been the basis of a longstanding interest in the general literature regarding family relations. Essentially, the ABCX model provides a framework in which a family's reactions to stressful events may be considered.

The ABCX model provides a framework in which reactions to stressful events may be considered.

Briefly, the ABCX model includes four major components. The stressor event (A) interacts with the family's resources (B) and the family's definition of the event (C) to determine the extent to which the event becomes a crisis for the family (X). Several decades of research on stressful events have been based on Hill's model, and components of the model have been elaborated and given considerable attention in the literature. However, only in recent years has the ABCX model been applied to families of handicapped children (Wikler, 1986).

The model is important because the components allow investigators to understand the considerable variability with which families react to the birth of a handicapped child. Thus, when applied to families of handicapped children, the ABCX model may help us explain why some adjust exceedingly well, while for others the experience is devastating. By looking at variability in family reactions to stress, it may be possible to devise individualized strategies to assist families who are having difficulty. For example, the A factor, the stressor event, has been as a life event or transition capable of producing a change in the family social system (McCubbin & Patterson, 1983). Hill distinguished normative stressors from those that are nonnormative. The birth of a handicapped child is generally considered a nonnormative stressor.

Birth of a handicapped child is considered a nonnormative stressor.

In Hill's model, the family's response is likely to be determined by the family's crisis-meeting resources (the B factor). The B factor includes such variables as individual characteristics of each family member, social support, family interaction patterns, and other similar variables. Indeed, in recent years researchers have found that the availability of social support mediates the extent to which families report increased stress following the birth of a handicapped child (Beckman, Pokorni, Maza, & Balzer-Martin, 1986; Bristol, 1979; Bristol, Gallagher, & Schopler, 1987; Crnic, Friedrich, & Greenberg, 1983; Gallagher, Beckman, & Cross, 1983). Thus, there seems to be growing evidence to document the importance of Hill's B factor, that is, family resources, in understanding variability among families in their adjustment to a child who is handicapped.

Hill's C factor, the family's perception of the event, has received less direct attention in the literature but is a potentially important factor. Although few studies of stress acknowledge the importance of the individual's perception of the event in producing stress, many measures of family stress essentially measure the respondent's perception of the effect of various life events. In order to fully understand the effect of this component of Hill's model, more research is needed to distinguish it from the other factors in the model and to look at differences in perception of the importance of various events among different family members. For example, do mothers and fathers perceive the same things as stressful? How do differences in their perceptions influence family functioning in regard to the resources brought to bear or the coping strategies that are used?

The family's perception is an important factor.

Family Life Cycle Model

❑ A third approach which has frequently been used to view families is a family development or family life cycle model (Duvall, 1957; Mederer & Hill, 1983). Essentially, family development theory deals with the issue of family change over time. Families are believed to go through a life cycle demarcated by key stages. Stages are established based on three criteria: (a) a change in family size, (b) the developmental stage of the oldest child, and (c) the work status of the breadwinner. Eight stages were originally proposed by Duvall; however, over the years, the number of stages has been modified by different investigators. Duvall's original stages include (a) the establishment stage, (b) first parenthood, (c) family with preschoolers, (d) family with school-age child, (e) family with adolescents, (f) family as a launching center, (g) family in middle years, and (h) family in retirement.

Families are believed to go through a life cycle demarcated by key stages.

Functions of the family and the roles played by various family members are thought to change based on the family's developmental stage. It is in the transition from one stage of the cycle to the next that the most potential for stress exists. Turnbull et al. (1986) have incorporated the notion of family life cycles into their thinking about the effects of handicapped children on families. They point out that, in addition to normal transitions, families of handicapped children are likely to experience additional stress associated with transitions. Since stages are grounded in the age of the oldest child, families of handicapped children may not experience transitions when they are expected, or both the stages and the transitions may be unusually long.

Families of handicapped children are likely to experience additional stress associated with transitions.

Several considerations are important when attempting to apply the family development model to families of handicapped children. First, the nature of the family has changed dramatically in recent years. There is a growing number of "blended" families, children who participate in multiple households, and families headed by single parents. For these families, clear stages are often difficult to identify and there may be multiple transitions. Second, the life cycle approach assumes that the impact of a crisis will be greater when a family is in transition from one stage to the next than when a family is within a stage period. While transitions may tend to be difficult, it is important not to ignore the rather significant changes that can occur within a particular stage. This is especially true for families of high-risk or handicapped infants. During infancy, there are numerous milestones that may not be achieved when they are expected. Failure to achieve milestones may be a continuing source of stress during the first few years of life. For high-risk infants hospitalized for long periods of time, the weeks of hospitalization may be highly stressful. Thus, while the life cycle approach to families is useful, focusing on the stress of transitions may cause professionals to overlook important sources of stress that occur for families within stages.

There is a growing number of "blended" families.

Failure to achieve milestones may be a continuing source of stress.

Transactional Model

❑ The fourth model we will consider is the transactional model. The transactional model was orginally developed by Sameroff & Chandler (1975) to account for the difficulty professionals often have in predicting developmental outcome for high-risk infants. They argue that neither biological nor environmental factors alone are sufficient predictors of outcome for high-risk infants. Although it is more useful to view outcome for high-risk infants in terms of the interaction between biological and environmental events, even an interactional model is insufficient to account for variations in outcome. Sameroff & Chandler urged the adoption of a transactional approach, which acknowledges the interaction between environmental and biological contributors to development, but argues that these factors alter the impact of each upon the other over time. Thus, biological and environmental variables interact at time one to produce changes in each other. These changed biological and environmental variables then interact at time two, and so on. The term *transactions* refers to the dynamic process of change over time that can be used to explain development.

Transaction refers to dynamic process of change over time.

Beckman (1983, 1984; Beckman-Bell, 1981) has applied this approach to explain stress in families. Characteristics of the child, the family, and the ecological context in which the family functions interact over time to produce changes in one another. For example, if an infant is irritable, difficult to console, and irregular in sleep-wake patterns, these characteristics may influence the family in many ways. The sleep of other family members may be disturbed, ultimately resulting in chronic fatigue, and interaction patterns between the parents and the infant may be disrupted. Over time, these events may continue to influence the family. The marital relationship may suffer, there may be less time spent with nondisabled siblings and other family members, and the child's development may be adversely affected.

COMMON VARIABLES

Interventionists may not always find these theories useful.

❑ Although the theoretical models described herein are useful in understanding family functioning, none were specifically formulated as a way to understand the issues faced by families of handicapped children, nor do they always have direct implications for interventionists. As a result, interventionists may not always find these theories useful for developing interventions for families. In the remainder of this section, we will illustrate how the theoretical models can be used as a basis for designing interventions.

It is useful to identify variables common across models.

Input variables are not readily changed.

To apply family theory to the study of families with disabled infants, it is useful to identify variables that are common across theoretical models. For purposes of discussion in this chapter, we have placed variables in one of three categories: input variables, mediating variables, and output variables. Input variables are those factors that are identifiable at the point the child and family are first seen and that may influence family functioning. Input variables are the "givens" of family life—variables that families bring with them and that are not readily changed. Inputs include the stressors that impinge on the family, its income, the education and intellectual attainments of its members, their health and disability characteristics, and their stage in the life cycle.

Mediating variables are more readily changed.

Mediating variables are those factors that are likely to influence a family's ability to adjust to changes and cope with crisis. Mediating variables are characteristics of the family that are more readily changed. They influence the impact of input on the family's ability to contribute to the well-being and development of its members. Examples include available resources (e.g., time, money, programs available); social support (e.g., neighbors, friends, extended family members who can provide social support); internal coping strategies (e.g., psychological strategies used by individual members or the family to alter their perception of the situation, such as identifying aspects of the situation that can be changed); cohesiveness and consensus; adaptability; patterns of interaction among individual members; and the ability of members to communicate needs and feelings.

Output variables include measures of child and family outcomes.

Output variables include child outcomes (e.g., measures of child development, behavior, health) and measures of family outcomes (e.g., level of stress, cohesiveness among family members, physical and emotional health of family members). Finally, it is important to remember that families change over time, and what was initially to be considered an "output variable" may later become an "input" to the system.

ILLUSTRATIONS OF THE IMPACT OF SELECTED VARIABLES

❑ Many variables influence parental involvement in early education programs. In assessing and serving individual families, it is helpful to understand the events and circumstances that hinder parent involvement with their children's programs. This information allows us to determine which supports are most likely to help them become satisfied participants in their children's education.

Impact of Resources

❑ Resources can refer to both emotional and physical factors. A family must have sufficient control of quantities of food, shelter, and manpower to maintain itself and its disabled member. In addition, the family must have emotional support in order to continue functioning under emotionally trying circumstances. Bronfenbrenner (1975) pointed out that inadequate nutrition and health care, poor housing, lack of education, limited income, and the necessity for long or unusual working hours all constitute components of an environment that can sap parents of time and energy. Additional data arguing that adequate resources are required if families are to be able to support an intervention can be found in the work of Patterson, Cobb, and Ray (1973), who observed that mothers lacking financial and manpower resources had difficulty learning child management techniques.

Resources refer to both emotional and physical factors.

Personal and social resources must also be considered. Parental depression (McLean, 1976) or psychopathology, chronic illness, limited intellectual abilities (Kaminer, Jedrysek, & Soles, 1981; Rosenberg & McTate, 1982), and adverse family relationships are individual and family characteristcs that can also limit parental willingness and capacity to become involved in program activities. It is well documented that a retarded child makes taxing emotional and physical demands on family members (Farber, 1960; Holt, 1958; Mercer, 1966), as do a child's physical disabilities (Mercer, 1966; Walker, Thomas, & Russell, 1971), oppositional behaviors (Berkowitz & Graziano, 1972), and chronic illness (Crain, Sussman, & Weil, 1966).

Personal and social resources must be considered.

Exhaustion, a side-effect of keeping disabled children at home (Holt, 1958), is associated with the institutionalization of such children (Mercer, 1966). Lonsdale (1978) reported that parents of disabled children experience increases in tension, illness, and/or ability to work. This unfortunate reaction may be expected to adversely affect parents' involvement in programs for their disabled children.

Intervention Focused on Resources

❑ Families with severely handicapped children often require substantial manpower and financial resources. To deal with this resource problem, Wolfensberger (1969) argued that such families should be eligible for housekeeping assistance, day care, and income subsidy so that they may continue to maintain the child in their home. The family's social network may prove to be another source of emotional and material assistance. Supportive interventions that reduce parental distress should have a positive effect on children. For example, children have an improved rate of recovery from surgery when efforts are made to reduce the anxiety of their mothers (Skipper & Leonard, 1968).

Interventions that reduce parental distress have a positive effect on children.

Impact of Expectancies and Goals

❑ Parents' personal characteristics also influence their willingness and ability to become involved in early intervention programs. In particular,

Gratifications of infant care can be reduced when the child is severely handicapped.

parents' expectancies and goals for their children affect their involvement in program activities (Rosenberg, 1977). Their aspirations for their child are generally perceived as thwarted when the child is diagnosed as handicapped. To a great extent, this is the result of society's devaluation of disabled people and the consequent devaluation of parenting disabled children. Because of this, the parents begin to question many of the goals that are commonly held for children. In addition, many of the gratifications of infant care, such as the observation of rapid development, expectations of future growth and development, and social pride, can be greatly reduced when a child is severely handicapped. It is not surprising that some parents are ambivalent about committing themselves to what they may perceive as a lifetime of unrewarding and futile effort.

Parental goals and values also affect participation in program activities. Parents who can value their children regardless of their attainments will have an easier time investing in the education and development of their young children than will parents who are highly concerned with the social status of their families and children. In this connection, Rosenberg (1977) found that, among mothers of handicapped infants, those who placed greater emphasis on economic goals and social status were judged to be less involved in their children's educational programs.

Intervention in Expectancies and Goals

Time-limited agreements allow parents to control their involvement.

❑ In cases where parents are reluctant to involve themselves in intervention programs, short-term contracting may provide a reduction of parental anxiety and shift parental perception from long-term commitment, which they may find overwhelming, to more acceptable periods of days or weeks. Where needed, succeeding contracts may be lengthened and, in time, eliminated altogether. The use of time-limited agreements allows parents to control their involvement and permits them a trial period in which to familiarize themselves with their program responsibilities. This procedure is common in behavioral therapy (Knox, 1971). Other procedures may also be used in generating parental involvement; naturally, the particular strategies used will vary for different families.

Impact of Consensus

Marital discord is associated with failure to learn child-rearing skills.

❑ Family members must reach some agreements about the nature of their goals, the allocation of tasks, and the coordination of activities, including child care and therapy. Where there is a lack of consensus among parents regarding the execution of household and therapeutic activities, or where parents and professionals differ over home program goals, the treatment of the child will suffer. For example, parents who differ intensely over issues related to child care will be unable to agree on activities related to their child's program. Patterson, Cobb, and Ray (1973) have observed that marital discord is associated with failure to learn child-rearing skills.

Conflict between retarded children and members of their families or with schools is thought to be associated with the institutionalization of retarded persons (Mercer, 1966). When there is a lack of consensus between spouses, and the father is unfamiliar with the rationale for the procedures his wife uses, Radin (1972) suggested that the father be involved in the program in ways that are consistent with his role in the family. She found that involved fathers were more likely to reach agreement with their wives and project staff on goals and procedures than were fathers who remain uninvolved. Beyond this, the capacity of parents to resolve their differences can be enhanced by teaching them ways to negotiate and seek compromise solutions (Weiss, Hops, & Patterson, 1973).

Intervention on Consensus

❑ Where consensus between parents and program staff breaks down, negotiation procedures can be employed to reduce conflicts. Differences over goals and procedures can be pinpointed, the alternatives considered, and the advantages and disadvantages of the various possibilities discussed by parents and staff. Ultimately, a compromise solution can be designed and, where needed, the agreement recorded as a written contract.

Summary

❑ We have provided a few illustrations of how some of the variables typically looked at in models of family functioning have been studied in families with a disabled member. It is apparent that the concepts called for in P.L. 99-457 to be included in the design of individual family service plans (IFSPs) are consistent with both clinical and research findings in the field of early childhood special education.

Concepts are consistent with clinical and research findings.

THE INDIVIDUALIZED FAMILY SERVICE PLAN

❑ P.L. 99-457, passed in the fall of 1986, extends the concept of the individualized education program to include a statement of the family's strengths and needs in relation to the child in the form of an IFSP. The intent of this legislation is for the IFSP to become the basis for work with disabled children and their families. Regulations already stipulate that the IFSP must contain the following:

1. Description of the child's present level of developmental functioning.
2. Statement of the family strengths and needs that are relevant to facilitating child growth and development.
3. Statement of anticipated outcomes as a result of enhancing family functioning.
4. Description of the services needed by child and family.
5. Dates of initiation and conclusion of services.
6. Identification of the case manager.
7. Description of the steps for transition of a child from present program to next program.

The family-oriented approach mandated by this legislation addresses children's needs within the context of their family's needs. The literature cited in this chapter points to the need for services for young children that are individualized not just for the child, but for the family as well. However, systems (especially systems that serve a large number of people) are notorious for becoming less flexible over time in what occurs in the implementation of policies and procedures. As professionals across

They must be aware of the complexity of the mission and need for flexibility.

disciplines continue to work in early childhood special education and embark upon implementation of P.L. 99-457, they must be aware of the complexity of the mission and the need for flexibility in the design of guidelines for IFSPs.

INDIVIDUALIZING THE FAMILY SERVICE PLAN

❏ In 1982, Turnbull and Turnbull pointed out that despite program variations, early childhood special education programs shared the following implicit assumptions or beliefs regarding parent involvement in programs:

1. The parents (and the child) should be part of the process from which they are so often removed—a belief in shared decision making.
2. Parent participation should increase the appropriatenesss of the educational services—a belief in parent involvement as a means of ensuring that schools satisfy their legal obligations to children.
3. Parents should receive counseling and training to prepare them to be part of the education of their child at home—a belief in the role of parent as teacher (p. 116).

Turnbull and Turnbull's point was that we need to examine our assumptions regarding parent involvement and become open to the fact that not all parents want or have the resources to strive for these idealized roles of decision maker, advocate, and teacher. Just as the kinds of educational activities and the manner of their presentation should be adjusted to the characteristics of each individual child, so too should programs attempt to accommodate the characteristics of families served. Effective support of family involvement requires adjusting the nature and level of involvement of the program to best fit the needs of children and their parents.

Programs should attempt to accommodate characteristics of families.

FAMILY-FOCUSED APPROACHES

❏ Over the past several years, groups involved with the delivery of services to infants have cited the need for consideration of a number of issues if our approaches are to be family-focused (Bailey et al., 1986; Olson, Bostick, Jones, & Tate, 1987). While these approaches have varied in specific elements, they share a common problem-solving approach. Recommended problem-solving steps include (a) designating a case coordinator; (b) assessing child and family needs and strengths; (c) reviewing assessment findings with the family; (d) holding a staff conference to discuss any specific child or family strengths, resources, or deterrents that need to be highlighted before meeting with the family to select goals; (e) holding an IFSP meeting; (f) implementing services, and (g) monitoring services and revising the IFSP as needed.

Goals and objectives can correspond with changing needs.

This problem-solving format provides professionals and family members with information on which to base the cycle of steps, which includes planning, intervention, and revision. When this process is used, goals and accompanying objectives can correspond with the family's changing needs and circumstances. In addition, the parents have opportunities to determine their own goals and comment on evaluation findings.

The evaluation and planning process must be coordinated; this is generally done by a professional who is able to maintain contact with family and other team members. It is the coordinator's responsibility to see that everyone at the IFSP meeting has an opportunity to be heard. The coordinator is also responsible for checking with the team, including the parents, to determine how successfully the IFSP is being implemented.

ASSESSMENT OF CHILDREN AND FAMILIES

❏ Approaches to the assessment of handicapped children and their families vary considerably across programs (e.g., Bailey et al, 1986; Olson et al., 1987; Rosenberg, Robinson, & McTate, 1981; Turnbull & Turnbull, 1986). For the purposes of the IFSP, assessment of the child should determine current level of development in cognitive, motor, communication, psycho-social and self-help skills. As with IEPs, these findings should be based upon data derived from nondiscriminatory measures and should reflect a multidisciplinary approach to assessment.

Findings should be based on nondiscriminatory measures and reflect a multidisciplinary approach.

Parent-child interaction is an important area for assessment when serving young children who have handicapping conditions. For young children, interactions with their parents are an enormously important source of learning and mutual enjoyment. These interactions are frequently made difficult by handicapping conditions. Responsivity and sensitivity, along with other parent characteristics, have become common elements in intervention strategies that emphasize parents' ability to read and respond to their children's communicative cues. Such an emphasis is appropriate since there is evidence that infants' handicaps can alter their interactive capacities in ways that impair their ability to contribute to enjoyable exchanges with their parents. For example, they may respond slowly to their parents or use atypical modes for communicating their interest. As a result, interactions may be less enjoyable and may occur less frequently. Parents may be more directive toward their handicapped infants, and they may have difficulty recognizing and responding to their infants' communications and expressions of interest. It is easy to see that these responses by parents can result in decreases in child involvement in activities; in turn, this may further complicate parental efforts to find mutually satisfying patterns of interaction.

Fortunately, parents and their handicapped babies can be helped to establish mutually satisfying interactions that foster child growth. Several characteristics of enjoyable parent-infant interactions promote child development. Parents should be responsive to their children's interests and moods when interacting with them; wherever possible, children should be encouraged to initiate exchanges and select materials. Active responding by children should be sought rather than the passive responding associated with extensive use of prompting or physical guidance and there should be a match between children's developmental capacities and the developmental level of the tasks and communications presented to them. Feedback regarding performance on curricular activities should be informative and positive in affect. Parents can be assessed on these dimensions. The information obtained during assessment can be used to give them specific instructions and explanations for

Parents should be responsive to their children's interests and moods.

making the most of interactions with their children (Rosenberg & Robinson, in press).

The third area for assessment is the family—its inputs, mediators, and outputs. Assessment of a family's input characteristics provides information about the composition of the family. A knowledge of mediators reveals the procedures the family uses to resolve conflict, the coping abilties of its members, and the extent to which members agree with each other on important issues, as well as the availability of resources and social supports. Output information addresses the family's current level of functioning.

Input information begins with the family's composition and structure.

Input information begins with the family's composition and structure. Composition includes family members, their ages, educational attainments, and employment status. Also included is information about the health of family members and the caretaking needs of the children. Boundary permeability or cohesion of the family structure may be evaluated first. A family's external boundaries maintain the distinction between the family and the rest of the world and influence the level of cohesion among members. Boundaries within the family define the subsystems that comprise the family and regulate interaction by determining who is included in making decisions affecting family life and the extent to which individuals affect one another by their actions and outcomes (Minuchin, 1974). The boundaries of the family can be assessed by observing the family's openness to new ideas and materials from the outside world.

Family boundaries are also assessed by interview and self-report questions.

Boundary maintenance and permeability is also indicated by the extent to which families seek to participate in decisions that affect family members and regulate the flow of people and materials into their household. The state of the family's boundaries is also assessed by interview and self-report questions that ask (a) the extent to which they feel that their roles as parents have been taken over by people from outside the family, and (b) the number of agencies with which the family is involved. Internal family boundaries are assessed by determining which members are involved in decision making (Rosenberg, 1977). In instances in which members are inappropriately involved in or excluded from decision making, or, for example, where decision making has been turned over to outsiders, this would be noted as a problem. Strategies for decision making would be addressed with the family.

Family's material resources must be assessed.

A family must have adequate material and social resources to maintain itself and its members. In addition, the family must have the emotional strengths and problem-solving skills needed to permit its continued functioning under stressful circumstances. Each family's material resources must be assessed by determining its income, the state of its housing, and access to transportation. In this connection we also consider parents' level of education, employment history, and job-related skills. Psychological strengths of family members are assessed by history and emotional and intellectual abilities are evaluated through clients' self-reports and worker observations. The availability of support from extended family and friends is also assessed (Peterson, 1981; Rosenberg, 1977).

Mediating variables include consensus among members.

Mediating variables influence the processes by which families are able to use their resources and the efforts of their members to produce a functioning household. These include consensus or the extent of agreement among members regarding goals, priorities, and the division of labor; information about how family members relate to one another; and information about coping skills of family members.

A knowledge of consensus among family members is useful because families must reach some stable arrangements with regard to their goals, the allocation of tasks, and the coordination of family activities, particularly child-related tasks, if they are to be effective caregivers. Where there is a lack of consensus among parents and professionals over home program goals, the care and treatment of the child may be expected to suffer. Consensus between spouses and between professionals can be assessed by self-reports (e.g., Olson et al., 1987; Rosenberg, 1977) as well as by less formal discussions.

Coping is often mentioned as an important determinant of a family's health. A family's capacity to cope is determined by the effectiveness of the strategies used by the family as a whole and by individual members to continue orderly functioning despite changing circumstances. One useful inventory of coping strategies is F-COPES (McCubbin, Olson, & Larsen, 1981), a self-report measure that asks respondents to indicate the extent to which they use certain coping strategies. Family level outcomes may be assessed in terms of the extent to which the family meets its member's fundamental needs for the maintenance of life and health as well as for less basic necessities such as love and an environment that is supportive of personal development.

Coping is an important determinant of a family's health.

Several measures of task allocation in the family are also available (Olson et al., 1987; Gallagher, Scharfman, & Bristol, 1984). These are self-report instruments that ask respondents to indicate the extent to which parents participate in tasks required for the maintenance of the family.

After the assessment phase is completed, the family meets with the assessment team to review the findings. Parents are given information about their child's developmental status. The family evaluation results are also reviewed; the extent to which the family believes these results accurately reflect their present status is determined. This step is particularly useful where the evaluation relies mainly on self-report measures that do not involve conversation between the family and professionals. In addition, preliminary discussions of child and family needs and goals occur at this point.

The family meets with the assessment team to review findings.

A staffing is held after the family and child assessment data have been collected. Staff representing all disciplines involved with the child and family attend and review findings. A family goal worksheet such as that included in Figure 1 can be used to structure this meeting.

An IFSP planning conference with the family is then held to identify and finalize both child educational goals and family goals; family members and professionals select goals regarding the family's and the child's needs and identify strategies for achieving those goals. Professionals and family members should discuss methods for overcoming obstacles that interfere with completion of a desired activity or goal. A plan is developed for reevaluating the goal or associated objectives if necessary. A commitment is written itemizing goals, describing how and when goals will be evaluated for completion, and setting up a time line. This family goals worksheet should also list the person responsible for the goal and the resources available to assist in the completion of the goal.

An IFSP conference is held to identify child and family goals.

Once developed, a family goal worksheet (Figure 1) based on family plans usually does not remain static. After being implemented, an intervention plan must be reviewed where necessary and modified so that it reflects changes in the needs and circumstances of the family and

An intervention plan must be reviewed and modified.

Early Childhood Special Education: Birth to Three

Figure 1. Family Goal Worksheet.

FAMILY GOAL WORKSHEET   FAMILY NAME _____ CHILD NAME _____

AGE _____

Family/Child Needs	Family Resources	Goal	Competing Needs or Deterrents to Success	Recommended Methods
Motor development needs	Coping strategy: Family high on use of external support. Family Responsibility Checklist shows Mom doing 90% of household tasks. Dad indicates his desire to share more responsibility. Family is rigid and enmeshed on FACES and scales. Large group of extended family and friends who are willing to offer support.	Physical therapy twice weekly.	Lack of transportation. Father has varied work schedule. Four other young children in the home. Mom has heavy time commitment to family and other children.	Physical therapy should be offered in the home, or obtain assistance from extended family and friends to bring child in to appointments.
Financial resources needed to cover services to infant	Coping strategies: Family high on use of external support. Mom is assertive in her communication with agencies. Family is living on a minimal budget. Hospital bills for infant's delivery as yet unpaid.	Increasing skill in accessing local and state resources to obtain SSI or Medicaid support.	Father's pay is variable, thereby influencing status on Medicaid. Father is hesitant to take state assistance.	Work with Mom to obtain SSI coverage for infant. Meet with Dad to discuss financial needs of infant.

Note: From Olson, Bostick, Jones, & Tate (1987). Reprinted with permission.

its members. Information about family members' responses to intervention provides the feedback with which each plan's appropriateness is evaluated. This feedback also guides modification of the plan. Plans are most frequently modified by changing treatment goal priorities as additional goals are added when unanticipated problems arise. Second plans also must change when intervention strategies are found to be ineffective.

CONCLUSION

❑ In our conceptual model of how individualization of the family service plan can occur, we indicate that the characteristics of the child, family, and program interact and that program development needs to be responsive to those characteristics. In that regard, we want to highlight one dimension of that responsibility for flexibility and adaptation. In addition to being responsive to the child's educational and habilitative needs and the family's resources, both material and supportive, for meeting those needs, programs should set a tone of negotiability in the development of the IFSP. The framework of the negotiation cannot be based upon those assumptions regarding parent participation that Turnbull and Turnbull (1982) pointed out were implicit in early childhood special education programming rhetoric. Rather, the negotiation of the IFSP should be entered into without preconceived solutions.

Programs should set a tone of negotiability in the development of the IFSP.

We have many strategies and approaches, and it is our responsibility to design our programs so that all of our strategies are used in appropriate situations. This is the same basic philosophy that underlies the development of individualized education programs (IEPs). Yet we find ourselves attending IEP meetings for which the outcomes are, in large measure, prepared in advance. The defense frequently offered for such advance preparation is that parents are not really prepared to write goals and strategies. Of course, in many cases they are not, at least initially. Frequently, the atmosphere at such meetings is so intimidating, albeit unintentionally, that parents have to be seasoned veterans to feel they can contribute. The same danger of lack of parent participation exists in the construction of an IFSP. The program and staff are responsible for preventing an atmosphere that opposes professionals with the "answers" to parents who feel that they have nothing to contribute.

REFERENCES

Bailey, D. B., Simeonsson, R. J., Winton, P. J., Huntington, G. S., Comfort, M., Isbell, P., O'Donnell, K. J., & Helm, J. M. (1986). Family focused intervention: A functional model for planning, implementing and evaluating individualized family services in early intervention. *Journal of the Division for Early Childhood, 10,* 156-171.

Beckman, P. J. (1983). Influence of selected child characteristics on stress in families of handicapped infants. *American Journal of Mental Deficiency,88* (2), 150-156.

Beckman, P. J. (1984). A transactional view of stress in families of handicapped children. In M. Lewis (Ed.), *Beyond the dyad,* (pp. 281-298). New York: Plenum.

Beckman, P. J., Pokorni, J. L., Maza, E. A., & Balzer-Martin, L. (1986). A longitudinal study of stress and support in families of preterm and full-term infants. *Journal of the Division for Early Childhood, 11*(1), 2-9.

Beckman-Bell, P. J. (1981). Child-related stress in families of handicapped children. *Topics in Early Childhood Special Education, 1*(3), 45-53.

Berkowitz, B. P., & Graziano, A. M. (1972). Training parents as behavior therapists: A review. *Behavior Research and Therapy, 10,* 297-317.

Bristol, M. M. (1979). Maternal coping with autistic children: Adequacy of interpersonal support and effect of child's characteristics. Unpublished doctoral dissertation, University of North Carolina, Chapel Hill.

Bristol, M. M. (1987). Methodological caveats in the assessment of single-parent families of handicapped children. *Journal of the Division of Early Childhood, 11*(2), 135-142.

Bristol, M. M., Gallagher, J. J., & Schopler, E. (1987). *Home environments: Child disability, parental adaptation, and spousal instrumental and expressive support.* Paper presented at the Biennial Meeting of the Society for Research in Child Development, Baltimore.

Bronfenbrenner, U. (1975). Is early intervention effective? In B. A. Friedlander, G. M. Sterrit, & G. E. Kirk (Eds.), *Exceptional infant: Assessment and intervention* (Vol. 3, pp. 449-475). New York: Brunner/Mazel.

Bronfenbrenner, U., Avgar, A., & Henderson, C. (1977). *An analysis of family stresses and supports.* Unpublished manuscript.

Crain, A. J., Sussman, M. G., & Weil, W. B. (1966). Effects of a diabetic child on marital integration and related measures of family functioning. *Journal of Health and Human Behavior, 7,* 122-127.

Crnic, K. A., Friedrich, W. N., & Greenberg, M. T. (1983). Adaptation of families with mentally retarded children: A model of stress, coping and family ecology. *American Journal of Mental Deficiency, 88,* 125-138.

Dunst, C. J., Cooper, C. S., & Bolick, F. A. (1984). Social support and prevention of maltreatment of handicapped children: Issues for families. In J. Garbarino, P. E. Brookhauser, & K. Authier (Eds.), *Special children, special risks: The maltreatment of children with disabilities.* New York: Aldine DeGruyter.

Duvall, F. M. (1957). *Family development.* Philadelphia: Lippincott.

Farber, B. (1960). Family organization and crisis: Maintenance of integration in families with a severely mentally retarded child. *Monographs of the Society for Research in Child Development, 25,*(1, Serial No. 75).

Fewell, R. R. (1986). A handicapped child in the family. In R. R. Fewell & P. F. Vadasy (Eds.), *Families of handicapped children: Needs and supports across the life span.* Austin, TX: ProEd.

Foster, M., Berger, M., & McLean, M. (1981). Rethinking a good idea: A reassessment of parent involvement. *Topics in Early Childhood Special Education, 1*(3), 55-65.

Gallagher, J. J., Beckman, P., & Cross, A. H. (1983). Families of handicapped children: Sources of stress and its amelioration. *Exceptional Children, 50,* 10-19.

Gallagher, J. J., Scharfman, W., & Bristol, M. M. (1984). The division of responsibilities in families with preschool handicapped and nonhandicapped children. *Journal of the Division of Early Childhood, 18,* 3-11.

Hill, R. (1949). *Families under stress.* New York: Harper and Row.

Holt, D. S. (1958). The home life of severely retarded children. *Pediatrics, 22,* 744-755.

Kaminer, R., Jedrysek, E., & Soles, B. (1981). Intellectually limited parents. *Developmental and Behavioral Pediatrics, 2*(2), 39-43.

Knox, D. (1971). *Marriage happiness: A behavior approach to counseling.* Champaign, IL: Research Press.

Lonsdale, G. (1978). Family life with a handicapped child. *Child: Care, Health and Development, 4,* 49-120.

McCubbin, H. C., Olson, D. H., & Larsen, A. S. (1981). *F-COPES: Family Crisis Oriented Personal Scales.* St. Paul: University of Minnesota, Family Social Science.

McCubbin, H., & Patterson, J. (1983). Family stress adaptation to crises. A double ABCX model of family behavior. In H. McCubbin, M. Sussman, & J. Patterson (Eds.), *Advances and developments in family stress theory and research.* New York: The Haworth Press.

McLean, P. D. (1976). Parental depression: Incompatible with effective parenting. In E. J. Mash, L. C. Handy, & L. A. Hammerlynck (Eds.), *Behavior modification approaches to parenting,* (pp. 209-220). New York: Brunner/Mazel.

Mederer, H., & Hill, R. (1983) Critical transitions over the family life span: Theory and research. In H. McCubbin, M. Sussman, & J. Patterson (Eds.), *Social stress and the family: Advances and developments in family stress theory and research,* (pp. 39-60). New York: The Haworth Press.

Mercer, J. R. (1966). Patterns of family crisis related to reacceptance of the retardate. *American Journal of Mental Deficiency, 71,* 19-32.

Minuchin, S. (1974). *Families and family therapy.* Cambridge: Harvard University Press.

Olson, J., Bostick, M., Jones, C., & Tate, L. (1987). The parent profile: A systems approach to assessing and selecting family goals. *Family involvement with at-risk and handicapped infants: An HCEEP model demonstration project.* Moscow: University of Idaho, Warren Center on Human Development.

Patterson, G. R., Cobb, J. A., & Ray, R. S. (1973). A social engineering technology for the retraining of aggressive boys. In H. Adams & L. Unikel (Eds.), *Issues and trends in behavior therapy.* Springfield, IL: Charles C Thomas.

Peterson, P. (1981). *Stressors, outcome dysfunction, and resources in mothers of children with handicaps.* Unpublished doctoral dissertation, University of Nebraska, Lincoln.

Radin, N. (1972). Three degrees of maternal involvement in the preschool program: Impact on mothers and children. *Child Development, 43,* 1355-1364.

Rosenberg, S., & McTate, G. (1982). Intellectually handicapped mothers: Problems and prospects. *Children Today, 2,* 14-26.

Rosenberg, S., Robinson, C., & McTate, G. (1981). Assessment and planning in in-home services. In M. Bryce & J. Lloyd (Eds.), *Treating families in the home: An alternative to placement,* (pp. 84-97). Springfield, IL: Charles C Thomas.

Rosenberg, S. A. (1977). *Family and parent variables affecting outcomes of a parent-mediated intervention.* Unpublished doctoral dissertation, George Peabody College for Teachers, Nashville, TN.

Rosenberg, S. A., & Robinson C. (in press). Interactions of parents with their young handicapped children. In S. Odom & M. Karnes (Eds.), *Early intervention for infants and children with handicaps: An empirical base.* Baltimore: Paul H. Brookes.

Sameroff, A. J., & Chandler, M. J. (1975). Reproductive risk and the continuum of caretaking causality. In F. D. Horowitz (Ed.), *Review of child development research* (Vol. 4, pp. 189-244). Chicago: University of Chicago Press.

Skipper, J. K., & Leonard, R. C. (1968). Children, stress, and hospitalization: A field experiment. *Journal of Health and Social Behavior, 9,* 275-287.

Turnbull, A. P., Summers, J. A., & Brotherson, M. J. (1986). Family life cycle. In A.P. Turnbull & H. R. Turnbull (Eds.), *Families, professionals and exceptionality: A special partnership.* Columbus: Merrill Publishing.

Turnbull, A. P., & Turnbull, H. R. (1982). Parent involvement in the education of handicapped children: A critique. *Mental Retardation, 20*(3), 115-122.

Von Bertalanffy, L. (1968). *General systems theory.* New York: George Brazilier.

Waisbrain, S. (1980). Parents' reactions after the birth of a developmentally disabled child. *American Journal of Mental Deficiency, 84,* 345-351.

Walker, J. H., Thomas, M., & Russell, I. T. (1971). Spina bifida—and the parents. *Developmental Medicine and Child Neurology, 13,* 462-476.

Wiegerink, R., Hocutt, A., Posante-Loro, R., & Bristol, M. M. (1980). Parent involvement in early education programs for handicapped children. In J. J. Gallagher (Ed.), *New directions for exceptional children: No. 1. Ecology of exceptional children,* (pp. 67-85). San Francisco: Jossey-Bass.

Weiss, R. L., Hops, H., & Patterson, G. R. (1973). A framework for conceptualizing marital conflict. In L. A. Hammerlynck, L. C. Handy, & E. J. Mash (Eds.), *Behavior change: Methodology, concepts, and practice. The Fourth Banff Conference on behavior modification,* (pp. 309-342). Champaign, IL: Research Press.

Wikler, L. M. (1986). Family stress theory and research on families of children with mental retardation. In J. J. Gallagher & P. M. Vietze (Eds.), *Families of handicapped persons: Research, programs, and policy issues,* (pp. 167-195). Baltimore: Brookes.

Wolfensberger, W. (1969). A new approach to decision-making in human management services. In R. B. Kugel & W. Wolfensberger (Eds.), *Changing patterns in residential services for the mentally retarded,* (pp. 367-381). Washington, DC: President's Committee on Mental Retardation.

6.
Staffing Patterns and Team Models in Infancy Programs

Jeanette A. McCollum
and
Mary-alayne Hughes

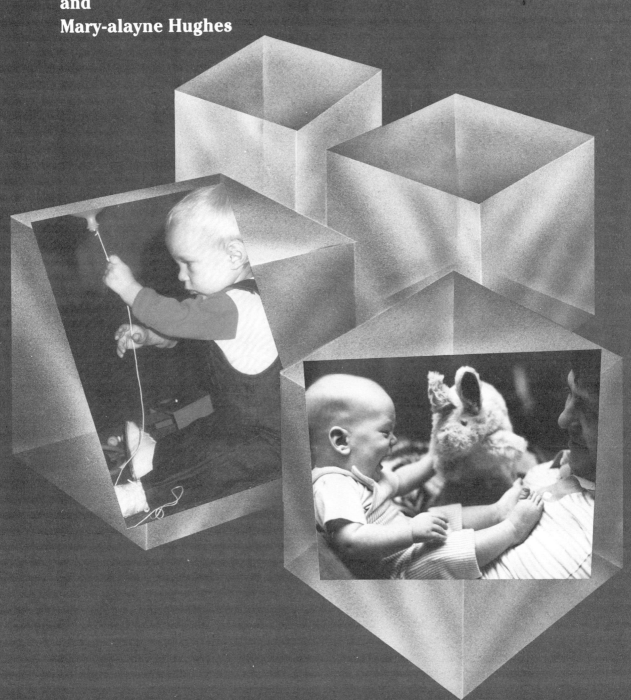

Provisions of P.L. 99-457 have major implications for staffing.

❑ The provisions of P.L. 99-457, The Education of the Handicapped Act Amendments of 1986, have major implications for the staffing of early intervention programs. The most obvious application is the requirement that early intervention services include a multidisciplinary assessment and a written individualized family services plan (IFSP) developed by a multidisciplinary team that includes parents.

Other provisions less obviously related to staffing nonetheless will also influence roles filled by personnel in these programs, thus influencing the training necessary to prepare professionals for these roles. First, eligibility definitions are written in such a way that, subject to further definition by individual states, children served will display a wider range of needs, necessitating not only increased knowledge on the part of individual service providers, but an expanded range in the types and intensity of services provided. Second, the staff providing services to any one family may represent multiple disciplines, and some of them may not be employees of the primary intervention program. New definitions of "staff," "team," and "collaboration" undoubtedly will emerge.

Children served will display a wider range of needs.

New definitions of "staff," "team," and "collaboration" will emerge.

The law, while certainly a major force in determining the future direction of staffing patterns and team models, is just one indication, and in part a culmination, of a more general and increasingly evident concern with staffing issues (Bricker & Slentz, in press; "CEC session identifies," 1984; *Guidelines for infant personnel,* 1984; *Statement of the Division,* 1986). One area of primary concern has been the delineation of disciplines to be included on early intervention teams. Overlaying this question are the thornier ones of the role definitions of these disciplines and the processes through which professionals working with any single family will interact with one another.

Issues related to staffing of early intervention programs are particularly salient at the present time. State plans are being developed which will set standards both for who should be included on teams and for licensing and training of these personnel. Simultaneously, even as role definitions are still evolving, colleges and universities are being called upon to offer training to meet the increased need for personnel uniquely qualified to work with infants with special needs and their families. Collaboration among personnel has become one of the primary concerns of personnel training.

Colleges and universities are called upon to offer training.

The purpose of this chapter is to report and reflect on the results of a study designed to clarify the staffing and teaming options currently used by intervention programs. Prior to reporting these results, an introduction to team models will be provided through a brief review of the literature. The interested reader is referred to Woodruff and McGonigel (Chapter 8) for a more extensive description.

MODELS OF TEAM ORGANIZATION

❑ Teams comprise at least three different but interrelated factors: (a) structure (who is on the team), (b) function (what they do), and (c) interaction (how they do it; i.e., how they interact/communicate) (cf. Golin & Ducanis, 1981). Structure is dependent on many factors (Campbell, 1982; Fewell, 1983): age and handicapping condition of the person to whom services are to be delivered, availability of staff, funding, parent preferences, geographic location, ecology of the family unit, and theoretical orientation. The structure of the team also might be expected

Structure is dependent on many factors.

Figure 1. Hierarchy of Service Delivery Interaction.

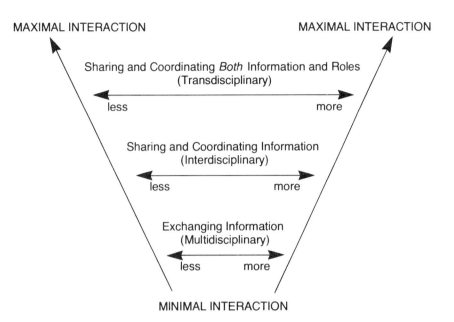

to vary for different programmatic functions (e.g., assessment, IEP development, intervention). Moreover, the word "team" implies a certain level of interaction: it is not merely an association, but rather a commitment to work together toward a common goal. Brill (1976) described this team interaction synergistically, as a "...transactional process, out of which evolves a totality that is greater than that which can be achieved by any of the individuals working alone or alone in summation" (p. 23).

Although structure and function influence the nature of the team, the interaction among team members appears to be the component that distinguishes among the various types of team models, to the extent that the manner of interaction is reflected in the nomenclature of special education service delivery team models: multidisciplinary, interdisciplinary, and transdisciplinary. This interaction can be conceptualized on a hierarchical basis from minimal to maximal levels of interaction: (a) exchanging information (multidisciplinary), (b) sharing and coordinating information (interdisciplinary), and (c) sharing and coordinating both information and roles (transdisciplinary). These three levels are illustrated in Figure 1, which reflects the additive nature of the characteristics of these team models.

Interaction component distinguishes various types of team models.

Multidisciplinary Team

❏ A *multidisciplinary* team is a group of professionals who perform related tasks independently of one another. They constitute a "team" only by association. Examples of this approach are evident in the medical field. Professionals of many different disciplines are often needed to provide services. However, evaluations and consultations are independent, and there is no ongoing coordination of information between team members (Bennet, 1982; Fewell, 1983). Instead, there is diffusion of responsibility (Beck, 1977), with individuals viewing their roles as separate from those of other team members. Recommendations may be communicated via

A multidisciplinary team performs related tasks independently of one another.

individual written reports or by talking directly to the patient (Fewell, 1983). In some cases the information may be collected by or sent to one team member who then interprets that information and presents the recommendations (Hart, 1977). Individual reports may also be presented at staff meetings (McCormick & Goldman, 1979). However, the purpose of exchanging information is to present the goals and plans of each discipline, not to coordinate across disciplines.

A strength of the multidisciplinary model is that more than one discipline is involved. With input from a group of people, there is more expertise available with which to make decisions, and less chance for one person's mistakes or biases to determine the course of events. However, this model has numerous weaknesses because of the nature of the independent roles and minimal interaction among team members. The process is one of piecing information together rather than coordinating information to form a unified, coherent picture. By definition, the multidisciplinary model is a "team" model only in a very loose sense. The minimal interaction of its members does not allow for the dynamics that lead to team cohesion and commitment. Hence, there may be no team consensus.

There are weaknesses in this model because of independent roles and minimal interaction.

Interdisciplinary Team

❏ An *interdisciplinary* team is a group of professionals who perform related tasks independently, but interact with each other in order to coordinate their efforts. Interdisciplinary team members constitute a "team" by their sharing of information to reach a common goal. The intent is that the goals and activities of each discipline will support and complement those of other disciplines. McCormick and Goldman (1979) have pointed out that theoretically there are three team commitments: group decision making, a unified service plan, and opportunity for interaction among the various disciplines. To facilitate this flow of information among team members, one person usually functions as a case manager (McCormick & Goldman, 1979).

An interdisciplinary team performs related tasks independently but interact with each other.

One person functions as a case manager.

The strengths of the interdisciplinary team model are in the efforts to share and coordinate information. However, one possible drawback is the influence of "professional turf" (Fewell, 1983). Some team members may define their roles and expertise more rigidly to protect their professional identity. This type of attitude would strain the functioning of an interdisciplinary team. Another inherent drawback may be the potentially ambiguous role of the case manager. Having one person coordinate information and facilitate team meetings is sound administrative practice in terms of efficiency and productivity. However, if the case manager were to assume an autocratic, decision making role in addition to the administrative role, then recommendations would be unilateral rather than interdisciplinary.

Strengths are in the efforts to share.

If the case manager were to assume an autocratic role, recommendations would be unilateral.

Transdisciplinary Team

❏ A *transdisciplinary* team is a group of professionals who perform related tasks interactively by sharing not only information but also roles. They constitute a "team" through their highly coordinated efforts to interact with one another. What makes the team "transdisciplinary" is the characteristic of sharing roles (role release); "...rather than being apportioned among the disciplines according to their specialty, interven-

A transdisciplinary team shares roles.

tion becomes the responsibility of one (or possibly, two) team member(s). The other team members are available on a continuing basis for consultation and direct assistance" (McCormick & Goldman, 1979, p. 154). When extended to the area of assessment, transdisciplinary teaming is often called *arena assessment* because one person does the testing while the other team members (including parents) observe (Wolery & Dyk, 1984).

Arena assessment is one form of transdisciplinary teaming.

Another characteristic of a transdisciplinary team is that team members accept and accentuate each other's knowledge and strengths to benefit both the team and the child (Lyon & Lyon, 1980). Staff development in the form of mutual training is basic to the concept of role release, enabling each member to assume and implement disciplinary aspects of the roles of other members. Lyon and Lyon (1980) defined role release as a sharing of information and skills between two or more members. It may occur at three increasing levels of complexity: sharing general information, teaching others to make specific judgments, and teaching others to perform specific actions. The first two levels pertain to the sharing of information while the third level pertains to the sharing of roles. Although the concept of role release is usually associated with transdisciplinary teaming, it is obvious that the first two levels apply in increasing degrees to the other team models as well. The third level of role release is a feature only of the transdisciplinary model.

Role release is a feature of the transdisciplinary model.

The literature on transdisciplinary teaming in special education indicates that the teacher is usually the key facilitator of role release (Lyon & Lyon, 1980), since that role is often central in the educational process. Hence, the teacher is not only a specialist but also a generalist. Bricker (1976) has proposed that the teacher become an "educational synthesizer" whose responsibility would be to "...seek information from a variety of specialists and then integrate such inputs into intervention procedures that can be implemented daily by a classroom staff member or parent" (Bricker, 1976, p. 96). An educational synthesizer would be responsible not only for administrative case management, but also for program implementation. More recently, a similar role has been advocated for the infant interventionist (Fewell, 1983). Likewise, related service personnel must be able to function as both generalists and specialists on early intervention transdisciplinary teams. Examples of intervention strategies include integrated therapy (providing therapy in the classroom and/or other natural environments as opposed to segregated environments) and consultation.

The teacher may be a specialist and generalist.

Service personnel also must function as generalists and specialists.

The high degree of interaction and coordination required by the transdisciplinary model is a strength but also a potential area of weakness. Sears (1981) concluded that variables that may contribute are role ambiguity (team members' uncertainty about their roles), role conflict (job expectations that conflict with one another), and role release (loss of "professional identity" due to role sharing). However, these potential weaknesses may be outweighed by the following strengths: increased agreement among members as to the acceptability of decisions (Cooper & Wood, 1974); greater willingness to implement decisions (Bass & Leavitt, 1963); and enhancement of opportunities for team members to learn from one another (Wolery & Dyk, 1984). Benefits for the child include increased services regardless of budgetary restrictions; decreased fragmentation of services; maximized intervention time; continuity and consistency of services; and holistic treatment (Sears, 1981).

Weaknesses may be outweighed by strengths.

STAFFING PATTERNS AND TEAM MODELS AS APPLIED IN CURRENT PROGRAMS

Lines between models are not clear.

❑ Rarely is theory applied in toto to specific situations. Although the literature gives some guidance in relation to differences and similarities in team models, the lines between models are not yet clear. Much confusion exists as to how programs actually organize components to facilitate interactions between disciplines; how well the three models describe these organizational systems; and what programmatic variables appear to be related to team models. The purpose of this section is to address these issues, using results derived from an in-depth telephone interview with administrators in 10 infant intervention programs.

An initial list of 26 programs was constructed.

Programs* contacted for telephone interviews were selected from among demonstration projects funded through the Handicapped Children's Early Education Program (HCEEP). An initial list of 26 programs was constructed, containing all programs that: (a) served children aged birth to 3; (b) were in their second or third year of funding, or were in the first year beyond their 3-year grant but still functioning in a service delivery capacity; (c) functioned as comprehensive service delivery systems; and (d) served a wide range of children and families (i.e., were not limited to some specific subcategory). From the resulting list of 26 programs, 10

From 26 programs, 10 were selected.

were selected using a table of random numbers. Administrators of these programs were contacted to establish appointments for telephone interviews lasting approximately 1 to 1 1/2 hours.

A structured format was developed including questions related to demographic variables; disciplines that were part of the program staff or available on a consultant basis; and roles and interactions of these individuals during assessment, IEP development, and intervention. All interviews were conducted by one of the authors (MH). However, several interviews were audiotaped so that the completeness of written materials could be reviewed by both authors.

Interviews were used to develop examples of team models.

Quantitative descriptions of the programs were derived by summarizing data related to several demographic variables, types of staff available, and team models characterizing the programs at each of the three stages of the program process (assessment, IEP development, intervention). Interviews then were used to develop examples of team models as applied at the three different stages of the program process. Finally, based on these descriptions, generalizations were derived related to components of teaming that appear to characterize major differences among team models as implemented in these programs.

Of the 10 randomly selected programs, 2 were part of the public school system and 1 was funded through a university; the remaining 7 were associated with public (e.g., Public Health) or private (e.g., Association for Retarded Citizens) agencies. Three served urban areas, while the

---

*Clay County Coordinated Preschool Program, Moorhead, MN; Early Childhood Program, Stark County Board of Mental Retardation/Developmental Disabilities, Canton, OH; HOPE (Helping Others Through Parent Education) Preschool Program, Birmingham, AL; Madison Area High Risk Project, Huntsville, AL; Parson's Regional Early Intervention Program—Evaluation, Demonstration, and Dissemination (PREP-EDD), Parsons, KS; Preparing Educational Programs for Special Infants Project (PEPSI), Clarksburg, WV; Project Dakota, Eagan, MN; Southern Appalachian Early Intervention Program, Johnson City, TN; Washington County Children's Program, Machias, ME.

others were located in less populated areas, serving a mixture of suburban, small town, and rural populations. All programs were noncategorical and accepted children having a wide range of disabilities and delays. Most of the programs provided services beyond their local areas, with five being county-wide and four serving several counties. The majority of programs (seven) combined center- and home-based services. Two were exclusively center-based, but provided home services if necessary. Only one program was totally home-based. Most programs, while having one or two primary service delivery patterns, also reported providing services through other avenues if needed.

All were noncategorical.

The majority combined center- and home-based services.

Program Staffing Patterns

❏ *Staff Availability.* In each of the 10 programs, the staff role that was most central to service delivery functioned as both primary interventionist and primary coordinator of services to the child and family. This role did not fall exclusively into the domain of any one discipline, and titles varied tremendously among programs; teacher (the most common), facilitator, developmental specialist, home trainer, home advisor, and home therapist. For purposes of clarity, the term *developmental specialist* (DS) will be used throughout this chapter to designate this central role.

Developmental specialist will be used to designate this central role.

Professional training in early childhood education or special education was the most common background of the DSs, and many of these individuals were certified teachers. In addition, persons from other disciplines, particularly speech/language therapists, also served in this role. However, this tended to occur only in programs that had several people serving as developmental specialists, and in each case, at least one DS was an educator. The majority of programs (6 out of 10) reported having only one DS.

Many were certified teachers.

In only one program was the DS position filled by nondegreed people. Other programs, however, used people at paraprofessional levels, or people with specializations but without certification, as part of a larger intervention team with degreed or certified professionals.

Of people from other disciplines who were typical full-time staff members, speech/language therapists were the most common, filling positions in 9 of the 10 programs. Four programs reported having full-time occupational therapists, while two had full-time physical therapists, two had full-time nurses, and three had full-time psychologists. In each case where a full-time psychologist was reported, this individual served primarily as program coordinator/director, but performed psychologist functions when needed. Although all programs reported having a coordinator/director, in several cases this individual also functioned part time as a DS. Other examples of multiple roles were common, such as one program in which an LPN served a specialized role in relation to medical issues and also as a paraprofessional in a center-based classroom. A small number of programs (1-2) employed part-time (less than 50%) personnel as speech/language therapists and occupational therapists. Other full- or part-time staff mentioned by one to two programs were motor development specialist, certified occupational therapy associate, and social worker.

Speech/language therapists were the most common.

All reported a coordinator/director.

Many of the programs used parent agencies or outside community agencies to supplement core staff. Thus, very few consulting staff were hired on a private basis. Other outside staff included public health nurses, mental health specialists, and psychologists. The roles performed by

Many used parent or outside community agencies to supplement core staff.

these individuals ranged from consultation only, to direct services, to functioning as part of the core team. In one case, a professional from another agency had full responsibility for a caseload of families.

Core Staff Roles: Team Structure. Two questions were used to obtain general information related to (a) staff titles (disciplines) included on *every* team and (b) the *typical* core team as it would be constituted for any particular child and family. Parents were named as part of every team by all 10 programs. Of staff members, the title most consistently represented was the DS; this individual was part of every team in 9 out of 10 programs. For 3 programs, this was the *only* staff member represented on every team. Typical core teams formulated for any particular child and family generally were reported to include at least one discipline and (usually more) in addition to the team members described above, often on an "as-needed" basis. Therapists were the most common. Hence, with the exception of the DS and the parent, there was a great deal of variability in disciplines comprising the typical core team.

Parents were a part of every team.

The DS was part of every team in 9 out of 10 programs.

With the exception of the DS and parent, there was variability in the core team.

Examples of Team Processes

❑ Multidisciplinary, interdisciplinary, and transdisciplinary team models are based on the involvement of multiple disciplines in providing early intervention services. Professionals functioning under a multidisciplinary model, although interacting with the same client, perform their respective tasks independently. Interdisciplinary teams, in contrast, perform their tasks independently, but share information with each other so that services to the client may be coordinated. In transdisciplinary teams, professionals from different disciplines share not only information but roles, with the aim of blending goals and intervention into a unified whole.

A brief review of data obtained from the interviews suggested that the team model adopted often varied according to the staff available. However, the model adopted also tended to vary across different programmatic functions. In general, the most prevalent model at the assessment stage was multidisciplinary (5 out of 10 programs). During the IEP development and intervention stages, interdisciplinary models were most common (7 programs). Applications of a transdisciplinary teaming model were least common; when this did occur, it was most likely to be during the assessment function.

The team model varied according to staff available.

Transdisciplinary teaming models were least common.

Combinations and variations of models were common.

Thus, within any program, staffing patterns and teaming models were not necessarily consistent across the three programmatic functions examined. Rather, combinations and variations of models were more common. A sampling of applications by programmatic function follows.

Assessment Function. An application of a multidisciplinary model to the assessment phase can be seen in a program in which the DS first screens the infant in the home in order to determine eligibility. Once this is determined, the DS conducts further assessment of the infant, again in the home setting, while other assessments are conducted in the center by therapists. Each professional writes a summary report of his/her assessment, to be shared later with other evaluators and the parents.

Each professional writes a summary report.

None of the sample programs demonstrated a purely interdisciplinary model during assessment. Characteristics of an interdisciplinary team model, however, did occur in combination with other team models. One program, for example, combines components of the interdisciplinary and transdisciplinary models. Two professionals (educator, speech/language therapist) and the parent serve as an initial evaluation team. Testing occurs in the center. Three tests are given; however, the three tests are scored during the same session, with all team members present. Following this initial assessment, the family comes to the center again for additional assessment performed along more traditional disciplinary lines by physical therapists, occupational therapists, and (for most) a physician. The original team members participate as observers. A team meeting is held with all evaluators present to share this information.

One rural program provided an example of a more purely transdisciplinary model, closely fitting Wolery and Dyk's (1984) description of an arena assessment. Members of a team—educator, speech/language therapist, and occupational therapist—share the same caseload from initial assessment through exit from the program. Prior to assessment, the lead role (DS) is assigned to one of the three team members; this role is maintained throughout. Team members and parents decide what should be assessed and where the assessment should occur. Testing is done by the DS, with all team members (including parents) commenting and helping. Immediately after the assessment, observations are shared, with all members contributing data to all developmental areas. Parents are asked to contribute their observations first, with other team members supplementing as needed.

One rural program provided an example of a transdisciplinary model.

Testing is done by the DS with all team members commenting and helping.

Program Planning Function. There were no examples of programs that functioned along purely multidisciplinary lines during this stage. During plan development, disciplines come together to share information for the purpose of developing a common and agreed-upon mutual document closely fitting the earlier definition of the interdisciplinary model. In the majority of programs, however, there are variations in how the interdisciplinary model is applied, primarily reflecting the inclusion of some components of one of the other models.

During plan development disciplines come together.

One example of an interdisciplinary/transdisciplinary combination was provided by a rural program. In this program, an initial meeting is held with the larger evaluation team (including core team members and additional evaluators) to summarize assessment information with the parent and to discuss eligibility and services available. A second meeting is used to actually write the plan; only the core team (three disciplines) and parents are involved at this stage, with one core team member taking the primary DS role. All members contribute goals for all developmental areas.

Another rural program provided an example of plan development that relies on a more purely transdisciplinary model. Immediately following assessment, in which the parent participates as an active member, all team members contribute to a written summary of strengths and needs, followed by joint discussion of goals. This summary forms the basis of the plan, written at a later date by the parent and the DS.

Immediately following assessment, all team members contribute to a written summary.

Intervention Function. For a variety of reasons, deciding which team model was most descriptive of a program's approach proved to be even more difficult at the intervention stage than for assessment and plan development. First, "team" may be defined at several different layers including the following: the core team that assumes primary responsibility for ongoing, frequent contact with the family; the core team plus adjunct or ancillary staff who provide services on a less regular basis; and a still larger team composed of the above plus personnel from all agencies

"Team" may be defined at several different layers.

Models may differ depending on the particular needs of different families.

Intervention using a multidisciplinary model was rare.

The interdisciplinary model was the most common team model at the intervention stage.

DS and parent observe therapy groups.

involved with the child and family. A different team model may (or may not) describe the characteristics of team interaction at any or all of these layers. A second difficulty in describing team models at the intervention stage is that models may differ depending on the particular needs of different families. Despite these variations, it is possible to provide examples of typical applications of different team models, particularly if we restrict ourselves to the core team.

Intervention using a multidisciplinary model was rare. In very few programs did professionals provide direct services to the child and family that were physically isolated from professionals from other disciplines. In one program fitting primarily the multidisciplinary team model, one professional conducts small-group sessions with two or three infants on a twice weekly basis. Another example was provided by a service delivery system in which infants receive services from several professionals per visit, with time scheduled into different blocks for each professional. A home-based program in which each team member goes separately to the home provides still a third example. Ordinarily, where the multidisciplinary model was applied, it tended to describe an aspect of intervention that was only one part of a larger set of services.

The interdisciplinary model was by far the most common team model at the intervention stage, and took a variety of forms. One center-based program serves infants in small groups, using a team consisting of one professional from each of three disciplines (educator, speech/language therapist, occupational therapist). Weekly meetings are used to update objectives and plan intervention sessions. Within the classroom, children are rotated among the three disciplines, so that service delivery is on a one-to-one basis with each discipline.

A program illustrating aspects of both the interdisciplinary and transdisciplinary models provides home-based and center-based intervention on alternate weeks. Home services are provided by a DS alone, while center-based sessions are provided by a DS and a therapist together, but working with different children. Additional therapy is provided once each month in various locations around the service delivery area. The DS observes these sessions and provides follow-up in the home. Another program with a similar system of alternating weeks uses center-based groups primarily as therapy groups. All therapists serve on a contractual basis, but they come to the center to provide services. The DS and the parent observe therapy groups and follow through with therapy procedures. The DS and the therapists meet once a month to share information.

Several programs provided services that fit within a transdisciplinary team model. In one program, team members (educator, speech/language therapist, physical therapist) meet weekly to develop intervention activities that combine goals of all three disciplines, thus exemplifying the "integrated therapy" approach mentioned earlier. Sessions occur in a variety of settings including home, small groups, and clinics (infant and parent with team in center). The clinic is the primary delivery mode and involves all three team members. The emphasis of teaming is on working together to show the parent how to work with the child. Parents are involved as active participants in service delivery in all three settings, and their mental health is also viewed as a focus of service delivery.

Another program in which the team functions under a more purely transdisciplinary model is one in which each member of a three-person team (speech/language therapist, occupational therapist, educator) functions as a generalist (DS) as well as a specialist. Primary responsibility for children and families is rotated equally among the three so that each serves as general interventionist for one third of the total caseload and as specialized consultant to the other two team members for the other families. Each child and family, therefore, receive direct services from only one professional. However, each professional is accountable for his or her own area of expertise, and teams meet for approximately 6 hours weekly to coordinate services. The philosophy in this program is that the team members serve as consultants to the family, with the family implementing the intervention plan.

Caution is required in attempting to apply team models to the intervention function: If intervention is defined only as direct delivery of service, team models that appear to characterize particular program components may be deceptive. Models are defined not by where or even by whom the intervention is implemented, but rather by the interaction among team members. Ongoing planning is integrally related to the actual intervention, and team models, therefore, must take both planning and intervention into account. For example, a center-based intervention session that on the surface appears to be operating along multidisciplinary lines may have been jointly planned by all disciplines, with each team member then implementing an integrated therapy activity.

Caution is required in attempting to apply team models to the intervention function.

Program Components Supporting Team Models

❑ Despite the many variations in how models were applied to different program functions, and despite the small number of programs interviewed, several interrelated program components emerged as particularly useful for characterizing programs in relation to team models. Moreover, particular aspects of these components tended to appear together as clusters, representing the specifics that support the interaction hierarchy presented earlier in Figure 1.

Role Release. *Role release* (or role blending), representing the extent to which team members perform along disciplinary lines, was identified in the literature reviewed as the feature that best distinguishes among team models. At the base of the hierarchy shown in Figure 1, disciplines provide separate services (multidisciplinary); interdisciplinary teams build upon this by coordinating these services toward mutual goals; finally, one discipline acts as consultant to another or disciplines engage in joint planning/intervention (transdisciplinary). When there is no distinction among disciplines in the implementation of services, complete role release is occurring.

When there is no distinction among disciplines, complete role release is occurring.

Although role release often is seen as a distinguishing characteristic of the transdisciplinary model, it may be more useful to regard this variable as a continuum (from "less" to "more") within each team model, since teaming that was predominantly one model often also contained elements of another. For example, intervention carried out along disciplinary lines but within the same room at the same time would fall into an interdisciplinary rather than a transdisciplinary model. However, the close physical proximity of team members almost certainly would foster some degree of role blending among disciplines.

Teams demonstrating more role release also appeared to have core teams with more stable memberships—core teams consistently composed of the same individuals. In programs where professionals functioned along more disciplinary lines, core teams tended to be formed for each case. It might be expected that role release would be more easily accomplished where team membership was ongoing, and several respondents in fact mentioned that teams must build ongoing relationships.

One additional aspect of role release that deserves attention, and which varied even within teams employing a transdisciplinary model, was whether the release was unidirectional or bidirectional. A major advantage of the transdisciplinary approach is that goals and methods of different disciplines can be integrated and implemented by a single person. This is in congruence with the "educational synthesizer" role mentioned earlier. The most common approach to accomplishing this was for one team member to assume primary responsibility for service delivery while other members were available on a continuing basis for consultation and assistance (McCormick & Goldman, 1979). The issue here is that when one discipline (usually an educator) is always placed in the role of primary interventionist while other disciplines consistently act as consultants, role release is unidirectional. In contrast, where the role of primary interventionist is shared equally among disciplines, with all disciplines (including the educator) taking equal responsibility for the consulting role, role release is bidirectional.

Communication was another program component which differentiated among team models.

Communication. *Communication among disciplines* was another program component that clearly differentiated among applications of different team models. Variations in this component, as in the definition of roles, appeared to be directly and logically related to the extent of role release among disciplines.

Communication patterns in the programs interviewed varied in both frequency and type. Teams exemplifying more role release tended to be characterized by (a) more frequent communication; (b) more different types of communicative mechanisms (e.g., formal staffings, planning sessions, written materials, informal interactions); (c) greater emphasis on face-to-face interaction; (d) team meetings directed toward a wider variety of purposes; and (e) more emphasis on ongoing communication related to joint planning and integrated intervention. This supports the hierarchical nature of Figure 1, in which higher levels build upon, rather than replace, lower levels of interaction.

Three different strategies consistently appeared in teams with a high degree of role release.

In addition, three different strategies consistently appeared in teams with a high degree of role release: arena assessment, integrated therapy, and consultation. Each of these emerged as vehicles for supporting the high levels of communication needed for role release, as each provided a format through which particular disciplines could assume the roles of other disciplines.

The generalist/specialist distinction is useful for understanding variations in the DS role.

Role of the Developmental Specialist. In this study, *the developmental specialist* appeared to play the central staff role in all programs. However, the role varied considerably in relation to team model and extent of role release. The generalist/specialist distinction is a useful one for understanding the variations found in the DS role. "Specialist" applies to knowledge and skills specific to one discipline, while "generalist" relates to broader-context knowledge and skills such as working with families and working in a team situation with other disciplines. In teaming, the knowledge and skills that are shared or released to other disciplines are specialist knowledge and skills, and *any* discipline filling the DS role requires not only specialist knowledge and skills, but generalist knowledge and skills as well.

From these interviews, it was clear that the DS role was more often shared among disciplines in programs using transdisciplinary teams than in programs using other team models. In the literature related to older children with severe handicaps, individuals assuming this central role are assumed to be educators; however, this was not always true of these early intervention programs. Hence, education may best be thought of as one of the specialties represented on a team, having its own specialized contribution to make to that team. New terminology is needed to characterize both the educator who is a specialist in early intervention and the role of the DS (regardless of discipline), rather than regarding this as the same individual. This is not to say that programs could not, if they chose, use the same disciplines in the DS role, but only that clarification is needed between the specialist and generalist aspects of the role.

Education may be best thought of as one of the specialties on a team.

One obvious way in which the DS role varied across team models was that, as role release increased, the DS assumed more aspects of the specialist roles of other disciplines, particularly in the intervention function. A somewhat less obvious variation was related to *case management,* which emerged as a component that is highly related to differences in the application of different team models. From these interviews, differentiation between models appeared to be based on both *when* the case manager was assigned, and *how stable* this individual remained across program functions. The most typical pattern in the programs interviewed was for a DS to fill the case manager role for all functions. Programs using team models with a higher degree of role release tended to assign a case manager at an earlier point in the program process and to retain that manager throughout all program functions. Moreover, this person was always the DS. In contrast, programs functioning along more disciplinary lines tended to assign the case manager somewhat later in the process; to assign different case managers for the different functions; and/or to place case management outside the team (e.g., with a professional who was not part of the core team, or who was part of another agency).

As role release increased, the DS assumed more aspects of the specialist roles of other disciplines.

The most typical pattern was for a DS to fill the case manager role for all functions.

Role of Parents. The *role of parents* also was a program component which differentiated among team models. However, the relationship between model and parental role was not as clear as for other program components. All programs named parents as members of every team. However, within any particular program function, the team model most descriptive of program staff was rarely also completely descriptive of the parents' involvement. The role of parents was most clearly related to the team model in the transdisciplinary approach. Teams displaying more role release among disciplines also tended to assign parental roles that were more similar to their own. One program, in fact, indicated that the adoption of a team model with high degrees of role release among staff members was a result of its philosophy related to the role of families in early intervention.

The role of parents differentiated between team models.

Families have a unique, extremely important, and central role on early intervention teams. However, team models that describe relationships among disciplines may not be entirely appropriate for describing the relationship between various disciplines and the parent. Families are *both* participants in and recipients of services. How they participate and what they receive must be based on their individual desires and needs. That is, the team model cannot completely structure parental interactions with

Families have a unique, extremely important, and central role.

the other team members. New models are needed that will clarify the relationships between the team model and parental role.

DISCUSSION

❑ Public Law 94-142 and the more recent P.L. 99-457 both specify that services to handicapped children be provided by a multidisciplinary team of professionals. The word multidisciplinary is used, however, to refer to the number and types of people to be involved in service delivery; the actual team interaction process is not defined (Pryzwansky, 1981; Sears, 1981). Modifications in the manner of interaction between team members have led to two other team models: interdisciplinary and transdisciplinary. Hence, these three words are used to represent three seemingly distinct team models that represent a hierarchy (from multidisciplinary to transdisciplinary) of increasing interaction and role release among disciplines. However, terminology has become a major roadblock to understanding because the three terms are often used interchangeably in the literature as well as in the field (Lyon & Lyon, 1980). In the current study, for example, although all 10 programs defined themselves as functioning within a particular teaming model, the terms used to describe the model did not necessarily reflect what was actually occurring within the program.

P.L. 94-142 and P.L. 99-457 specify services be provided by a multidisciplinary team.

Terminology has become a major roadblock.

Some of the reasons why terminology may be so confusing became apparent in the course of this study. Few programs demonstrated a pure application of any one model. Rather, it was common for team models to vary across programmatic functions. Even within a particular function, different team models were often applied to the different service delivery patterns available in the program (e.g., center, home). Still another source of variation arose from how comprehensively the word team was used. In most programs, at least three layers of personnel were readily apparent:

At least three layers of personnel were readily apparent.

1. A small core team of professionals (1-3 people) delivering direct, ongoing services to children and families—usually part of the regular program staff;
2. A second layer of professionals functioning in an adjunct role, whose specialties directly influenced service delivery and who might or might not be employed as program staff;
3. A third layer, usually from other agencies, who had far less frequent contact with children and families or who served the same children and families in capacities different from those offered by the program staff.

It is apparent that different team models may, but do not necessarily, characterize these three levels. Broad and imprecise application of terminology for team models not only obscures these variations, it no doubt contributes to sustaining the confusion. It is important that terminology and understanding be clarified, both to facilitate communication and to enable programs to make rational judgments related to their own teaming processes.

Interaction among team members and role release were identified from the literature as the team components most salient in distinguishing among the three team models. However, an underlying and even more pervasive factor appears to be the *purpose* of forming the team and what is to be accomplished by interaction among team members. All other variables that tend to differentiate among models appear to be extensions of, and to both reflect and support, these different purposes.

Relating this back to Figure 1, the first level (multidisciplinary) provides a model in which information is exchanged, if at all, in order to *obtain awareness and understanding among disciplines.* There is no intent to influence other disciplines in carrying out their tasks, but only to exchange among disciplines the knowledge of what each is doing. At the second level (interdisciplinary), the purpose for which the team is established is to *coordinate services among disciplines,* so that each supports the other. The intent is to influence other disciplines to the extent that each discipline takes into account, and is directed toward similar goals as, the others. At the third level (transdisciplinary), the team is established in order to *enable each member to implement, in part or in whole, the disciplinary roles of other members.* This study indicated that these three levels of intent were supported by differential application of several other interrelated program components, which often appeared together as clusters (role release, communication patterns, roles of the staff and parents, case management).

Multidisciplinary provides a model in which information is exchanged.

Interdisciplinary is to coordinate services.

Transdisciplinary is to enable each member to implement the roles of other members.

It is clear that mitigating factors such as geographic location and availability of staff will, to some extent, determine program structure and team model. The current study, however, found no consistent relationship between team model and whether the programs were urban or rural, served small or large geographic areas, or used full-time, part-time, or consulting staff on their core teams. Rather, the determining factor appeared to be the philosophy of the program. This was particularly true of applications of the transdisciplinary model. While there were fewer examples of this model, the choice appeared to be not only conscious and purposeful, but also more consistently applied across program functions. Program structures grew from and supported the philosophy. In contrast, examples of applications of other team models appeared to be less of a conscious choice; the label fit the characteristics of the program, rather than vice versa. It is revealing that, among these 10 programs, those with more features of the transdisciplinary model were also those with written philosophy statements.

Those with more features of the transdisciplinary model were also those with written philosophical statements.

This greater cohesiveness within programs that apply more elements of the transdisciplinary model may result from the fact that this model has been the most extensively described in the literature. Despite this, it is interesting to note that the model is not generally well understood. For example, arguments for and against using a transdisciplinary approach often appear to be the same; cost effectiveness and optimal use of specialized disciplines are cited for both points of view. More careful description of philosophy and program components related to the different models, as well as consideration of differential application of models for different purposes, might also be extremely useful.

IMPLICATIONS

❏ This study was based on interviews from only 10 programs. Therefore, generalizations drawn must be regarded with caution, and they should become topics and hypotheses for future research. Given this caveat, however, the depth of the interviews yielded a rich array of data that can be used to give direction to both program operation and personnel training.

Conscious Choice of Model

Conscious choices can be made concerning the application of program model.

❏ For service delivery programs, this study indicated that conscious choices can be made concerning the applications of program model. Factors such as geographic location, staff availability, relative cost of different kinds of personnel, and size of caseloads certainly will influence these choices. It appears, however, that the program's teaming philosophy can be an equally influential factor. Creative use of settings and careful definition or redefinition of staff roles to support the chosen philosophy were used by these programs to overcome many of the constraints imposed by other factors.

Flexibility

The same team model does not have to apply across all program functions.

❏ Two sources of flexibility are available to programs in considering these choices. First, the same team model does not necessarily have to apply across all program functions. By implication, programs could choose to use different models for different functions (e.g., applying a transdisciplinary arena assessment approach but using an interdisciplinary intervention approach). Another implication is that programs wishing to change team models have the option of doing so gradually; that is, one function, or even part of one function, at a time.

Flexibility lies in the differing layers of staff expertise.

A second source of flexibility lies in the differing layers of staff expertise available to the program. This study indicated that the core team is not necessarily composed only of disciplines employed directly by the program itself; in some cases, outside consultants function as members of the core team. Hence, choice of team model for each programmatic function can vary in relation to creative definitions of interactions among staff in the different layers. Moreover, the team model chosen may differ among layers; while the core team may function as a transdisciplinary team, personnel from other agencies working with that same infant and family may more effectively function as an interdisciplinary or multidisciplinary team.

Purpose

Openness, cooperativeness, and willingness to share and listen were named as necessary personal characteristics.

❏ The purpose of teaming appears to be the single factor most reflective of teaming philosophy and, therefore, the most pervasive guide for making choices. Once the purpose is agreed upon for each programmatic function, program components and strategies can be developed to support them. These plans should include careful definition of each complex set of components related to team models: roles of staff and parents, role release, case management, and communication systems. Conscious choice of team models implies team commitment to those choices. Respondents to this study indicated that attitude was the single most important factor influencing the success of teaming. Openness, cooperativeness, and willingness to share and listen were all named as necessary personal characteristics. A common philosophy and orientation to service delivery also was mentioned. All in all, recognition and clarification of team goals are imperative, as is participation by team members in making these choices.

Training of Personnel

❑ In relation to personnel training, this study indicated that to function as team members, all disciplines serving on core teams in early intervention programs need to be prepared to function not only as specialists in their own disciplines, but as generalists as well. The greater the degree of role release, the more essential is this training. Specialist training implies that for any discipline, intervention with infants and their families will differ from that for older children (Bricker & Slentz, in press; "CEC session identifies," 1984). Specialization in infancy is necessary not only to ensure high-quality intervention by each discipline, but also to build trust and confidence between team members in what other disciplines have to offer, so that information and roles will be shared. Generalist training implies that each discipline has some basic knowledge of the terminology and strategies of other disciplines as well as of family processes and needs, community support systems, and teaming processes. Training for the developmental specialist's generalist role (regardless of discipline) seems especially critical. In the programs interviewed, this individual assumed major responsibility for coordination of services, team leadership, and intervention regardless of the team model employed.

All disciplines on core teams need to function as specialists and generalists.

Careful consideration must also be given to where and when training for these many roles should occur. Few of the programs interviewed reported having any formal inservice training related to teaming. Those with team models using greater role release did indicate, however, that new staff often spent an apprenticeship period with other staff in order to orient themselves and internalize the teaming philosophy.

Several programs also indicated that orientation toward teaming was closely evaluated during the interview process. It seems apparent that training for specialist roles in early intervention should become part of the preservice training of each discipline. Generalist training, in contrast, needs to be integrated across disciplines, and may need to extend across the preservice and inservice levels. Training in teaming processes, in particular, must be ongoing for every team as it undergoes modification and restructuring.

Training in teaming processes must become ongoing.

Need for Research

❑ Further research is needed to expand and clarify the results of this study. Observational research could determine whether or not the patterns emerging from these interviews actually do characterize team models in practice as well as in the perceptions of the respondents. Research also is needed to determine the relationship between different team models and outcomes such as parent and staff satisfaction, cost of services, and efficiency and effectiveness of service delivery. The current study indicates that programs can exercise a great deal of flexibility in making conscious choices related to applying team models. Further data are needed to support these decisions.

REFERENCES

Bass, B. M., & Leavitt, H. J. (1963). Some experiments in planning and operating. *Management Science, 9,* 574-585.

Beck, R. (1977). Interdisciplinary model: Planning distribution and ancillary input to classrooms for the severely/profoundly handicapped. In E. Sontag, J. Smith, & N. Certo (Eds.), *Educational programming for the severely and profoundly handicapped* (pp. 397-403). Reston, VA: Division of Mental Retardation, The Council for Exceptional Children.

Bennett, F. C. (1982). The pediatrician and the interdisciplinary process. *Exceptional Children, 48*(4), 306-314.

Bricker, D. (1976). Educational synthesizer. In M. A. Thomas, (Ed.), *Hey, don't forget about me* (pp. 84-97). Reston, VA: The Council for Exceptional Children.

Bricker, D., & Slentz, K. (in press). Personnel preparation: Handicapped infants. In M. C. Wang, M. C. Reynolds, & H. J. Walberg (Eds.), *Handbook of special education: Research and practice* (Vol. 3) Elmsford, NY: Pergamon Books.

Brill, N. I. (1976). *Teamwork: Working together in the human services.* Philadelphia: J. B. Lippincott.

Campbell, P. H. (1982). Individualized team programming with infants and young handicapped children. In D. McClowry, A. Guilford, & S. Richardson (Eds.), *Infant communication development, assessment and intervention* (pp. 147-186). New York: Grune and Stratton.

CEC session identifies issues in training personnel to work with handicapped/risk infants. (1984, May-June). *DEC Communicator, 10*(3).

Cooper, M. R., & Wood, M. T. (1974). Effects of member participation and commitment in group decision making on influence, satisfaction, and decision riskiness. *Journal of Applied Psychology, 59*(2), 127-134.

Fewell, R. R. (1983). The team approach to infant education. In S. G. Garwood & R. R. Fewell (Eds.), *Educating handicapped infants: Issues in development and intervention* (pp. 299-322). Rockville, MD: Aspen.

Golin, A. K., & Ducanis, A. J. (1981). *The interdisciplinary team.* Rockville, MD: Aspen.

Guidelines for infant personnel training programs. (1984, September). Developed at a meeting held at George Washington University, Washington, DC.

Hart, V. (1977). The use of many disciplines with the severely and profoundly handicapped. In E. Sontag, J. Smith, & N. Certo (Eds.), *Educational programming for the severely and profoundly handicapped* (pp. 391-396). Reston, VA: Division of Mental Retardation, The Council for Exceptional Children.

Lyon, S., & Lyon, G. (1980). Team functioning and staff development: A role release approach to providing integrated educational services for severely handicapped students. *The Journal of the Association for the Severely Handicapped, 5*(3), 250-263.

McCormick, L., & Goldman, R. (1979). The transdisciplinary model: Implications for service delivery and personnel preparation for the severely and profoundly handicapped. *AAESPH Review, 4*(2), 152-161.

Pryzwansky, W. B. (1981). Mandated team participation: Implications for psychologists working in the schools. *Psychology in the Schools. 18,* 460-466.

Sears, C. (1981). The transdisciplinary approach: A process for compliance with Public Law 94-142. *The Journal of the Association for the Severely Handicapped, 6*(1), 22-29.

Statement of the Division for Early Childhood of the Council for Exceptional Children and Interact—The National Committee for Young Children with Special Needs and Their Families (1986, March). Testimony submitted to the Subcommittee for the Handicapped of the U.S. Senate, Washington, DC.

Wolery, M., & Dyk, L. (1984). Arena assessment: Description and preliminary social validity data. *The Journal of the Association for the Severely Handicapped, 9,* 231-235.

7.
Defining the Infancy Specialization in Early Childhood Special Education

Eva K. Thorp and Jeanette A. McCollum

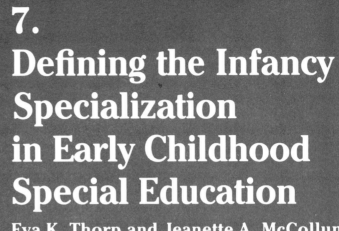

A final delineation of competencies may be somewhat premature.

❏ For early childhood special education, as for other professions associated with early intervention programs, the infancy period represents a new and still emerging area of specialization. From this perspective alone, a final delineation of competencies needed by the early childhood special educator specializing in infancy may be somewhat premature. Currently, however, there is common agreement on one overarching theme that characterizes infant services; that is the need for flexibility in service delivery. It has even been suggested that, rather than reflecting uncertainty, this very flexibility is quite desirable and may be a unique feature of infant services (Dunst, 1983; Ensher & Clark, 1986). While P.L. 99-457, the Education of the Handicapped Act Amendments of 1986, may result in a bit more homogeneity as standards for services are set, this new law also allows much flexibility in service delivery patterns.

P.L. 99-457 allows much flexibility in service delivery patterns.

Such variations in service delivery influence the roles that the educator fills; these variables provide an important context within which the question of competence must be placed. Thus, the question of competencies needed by early childhood special educators is intertwined with other issues for which guidelines are still emerging. These are addressed in the first part of this chapter.

The question of competencies needed is intertwined with other issues.

While it is true that the field is still in the process of consolidating, the topic of what constitutes competence in the infant special educator and how this is similar to or different from competencies needed by other professionals specializing in infancy has been the subject of wide discussion. A number of sources of information, therefore, are available; these are synthesized in the second section of the chapter.

The final section offers a conceptual model that may be used in considering issues related to delineating personnel standards for service programs, specifying licensure structures for personnel, and designing personnel training programs. These issues can be expected to assume considerable importance in the coming years, since, for example, it has been reported that as many as 90% of the states lack sufficient personnel to serve the infant population (Meisels, Harbin, Modigliani, & Olson, 1986).

As many as 90% of the states lack sufficient personnel to serve the infant population.

CONTEXT VARIABLES RELATED TO DEFINITIONS OF COMPETENCIES

Service Delivery Pattern

❏ Several aspects of service delivery have implications for the range of competencies needed by the early childhood special educator specializing in infancy. The term *early intervention* is an umbrella covering many types of services funded by a variety of different public agencies and private providers. Determining an appropriate configuration of available services is a task that must be completed by each state, and ultimately by each local area. The configuration of services will be influenced heavily by factors such as geography, population density, funding patterns, and differing philosophies. In some areas, many services may be drawn together under one agency, while in others different services may remain in the hands of different providers. The frequency and intensity of services also may vary widely.

The frequency and intensity of services may vary widely.

Early education is but one piece of early intervention. Early childhood special educators working as infant special educators are probably most often employed in comprehensive service delivery systems in which a variety of services (social, educational, therapeutic) are available through the same agency, or in which these same services are coordinated for individual families. Although the early childhood special educator would less commonly be employed by those systems providing primarily one specialized type of service (e.g., medical), this type of employment also appears to be increasingly common (Sweet, 1981). The overall array of early intervention services provided by the particular program, and the unique part played by early education as one piece of the total configuration, will heavily influence the competencies needed by the infant special educator employed in that program.

The overall array of services provided will influence the competencies needed by the infant special educator.

Program Purpose and Goals

❑ A second type of variable with implications for personnel competence is the overall purpose, and corresponding goals, of the particular program. One such factor is the population eligible for services. A program limited to serving families in which infants manifest severe disabilities, for example, may be very different from one in which infants are eligible on the basis of being environmentally at risk.

A related variable is the question of who is or should be the primary recipient of services. Is the infant the primary service recipient, as may tend to be the case in medical or therapeutic settings? Are family goals the primary focus, as might be true in a public health or public welfare agency? Is the focus infant goals, approached through teaching the parent to be the primary interventionist, as might be the case in a rural program with limited staff?

Who is or should be the primary recipient of services?

While the family focus philosophy underlying P.L. 99-457 may bring programs somewhat closer together in this respect, different answers to such questions will continue to be influenced by philosophy, geography, and resource allocation. They will have different implications for the roles that infant special educators employed in various settings might fill.

Participation of Disciplines

❑ Intertwined with each of these issues is the question of what disciplines are available within the particular early intervention program and how these disciplines relate to one another. Intervention programs vary in terms of who is included on the early intervention team. Programs employing early childhood special educators range from one-person programs, to those in which the educator is one member of an interdisciplinary direct service team, to those in which the educator participates in a medically oriented diagnostic team. Many disciplines in addition to education should and do engage in early intervention: physical and occupational therapists, speech pathologists, nurses and physicians, nutritionists, social workers, and psychologists are among the most common. Almost all programs, particularly the more comprehensive ones, appear to have someone who functions as a primary interventionist and case manager for each family. Many times the person filling this role is the early childhood special educator (see McCollum & Hughes, Chapter 6).

Intervention programs vary in terms of who is included on the intervention team.

Almost all programs appear to have someone who functions as a primary interventionist and case manager.

Competencies needed are related not just to who is available, however, but also to how roles are defined in the particular program. While the early educators are the experts in infant learning and in developmental and environmental variables related to learning, they may also often function as primary direct service providers and case managers for families. The teaming model employed greatly influences the extent of knowledge required about other disciplines (see McCollum & Hughes, Chapter 6 and Woodruff & McGonigel, Chapter 8).

In summary, much variation exists in the roles for which the early childhood special educator specializing in infancy must be trained. Infant service delivery varies widely in the settings in which services occur. Intervention may occur in a hospital nursery prior to an infant's discharge, in a home, or in the center—more typical of early childhood programs. The content and process of intervention may vary in each of these settings, depending on frequency of service delivery as well as on the professional composition of the service delivery team. It seems clear that no single model, no single service site, no set number of contact hours is *most appropriate for all infants and their families. Rather, service delivery must take into account the unique infant, the family's needs, and the intra- and interagency climate in which services are being planned. The professional must be prepared to adjust to each of these variables ("CEC session...," 1984; Farel et al., 1987; Geik, et al., 1982; NCCIP, 1985).*

Service delivery must take into account the unique infant, the family's needs, and the intra- and interagency climate.

Uniqueness of Birth-to-3 Services

❑ Despite the wide variability in service context, there are common themes that guide infant service delivery and clearly differentiate it from early childhood service delivery (Bricker & Slentz, in press). These themes determine the unique competencies of the infant interventionist. With regard to the field of early childhood special education, they suggest those competencies specific to working with infants and those shared by the entire discipline of early childhood special education. These themes include (a) the role of the family in the life of the infant; (b) the unique nature of the infant as learner and the related implications for instruction; and (c) the significance of specific medical issues salient in infancy.

There are common themes that guide infant service delivery.

Role of the Family. In a recent survey of university programs preparing early childhood special educators, 78% of respondents reported feeling that the parent should be the primary focus of infant intervention efforts (Bricker & Slentz, in press). The primacy of the family in infant services seems to be the most widely agreed upon principle of infant service delivery: All articles reviewed for this chapter identified families as key to programming.

Infancy is the period of greatest dependency of the young child. The family environment can affect the future development of the child positively or negatively. Central to the infant's learning and future development is the attachment relationship. The patterns of interactions with significant adults in infancy provide understandings that serve to organize future social and object learning for the young child. Consequently, it is critical that interventionists support this attachment relationship, rather than ignore or impede it. This is especially important with ill or handicapped infants, who may be at greatest risk for interactional failure.

Central to the infant's learning and future development is the attachment relationship.

Infancy is also a period of reorganization for the family. Parents are adjusting to seeing themselves as parents. Successful adaptation to parenthood is aided by feelings of competence in interacting with one's infant. Thus, programs must attend to bolstering parental competence and self-worth during this period of relationship-building (NCCIP, 1985).

Nature of the Infant as Learner. Several features of the infant as learner suggest early intervention practice and, in turn, suggest competencies. First is the central role that social interaction plays in organizing future learning and competence. Consequently, a key focus of infant intervention should be fostering social and communicative competence in the infant (Dunst, 1983).

A key focus of infant intervention should be fostering social and communicative competence in the infant.

Second, the infant may be less likely to benefit from group interventions than a preschool-age child. Consequently, infant intervention is more frequently individual-focused than group-focused. The professional must view the quality and structure of the dyadic interaction as being as central to intervention as any materials or specific treatments.

Third, the developmental plasticity of at-risk infants makes it difficult to predict outcomes for them, and it suggests that environmental interventions can maximize those outcomes. Further, the nature of sensorimotor learning suggests that the infant learns best through active exploration of the environment. Consequently, the professional may be required to abandon direct instructional strategies and instead become adept at constructing environments that are optimally challenging and enable opportunities for exploration and building upon previous learning.

Finally, infancy is a period of continuing biological organization. Interventions need to be sensitive to the infant's state and the limitations it places upon intervention. Scheduling of intervention must be flexible and sensitive to the infant. Interventionists need to be aware of the degree to which each infant has developed some internal controls for managing environmental stimulation and be able to plan interventions that will assist the infant in that process (Als, Lester, Tronick, & Brazelton, 1982; Vanden Berg, 1985).

Scheduling of intervention must be flexible and sensitive to the infant.

Medical Issues. Several medical issues play particularly significant roles in infant service delivery. First, intervention may begin with infants even prior to discharge from a hospital setting. Consequently, an infant interventionist must be comfortable in that setting, be familiar with the significant vocabulary of that setting, and be aware of the limitations that an infant's medical status may place upon intervention (Bailey, Farel, O'Donnell, Simeonsson, & Miller, 1986; Ensher & Clark, 1986).

Second, infants who are medically fragile, for example those with chronic lung disease associated with prematurity, may achieve a degree of medical stability that enables them to be discharged home; however, they may continue to depend on the assistance of medical technology for survival. Such technologies present a whole host of challenges to families and to professionals working with the infants and their families. Professionals must have some degree of familiarity with these technologies and implications for limitations to intervention. They must further be aware of the many community agencies likely to be involved in treatment efforts with these infants.

Finally, infancy is likely to be a time of continuing uncertainty with regard to medical diagnosis. Thus, infant special educators must have specific knowledge to assist families in negotiating the medical system as they seek diagnosis and treatment.

Infant special educators must have specific knowledge to assist families in negotiating the medical system.

COMPETENCIES OF INFANT SPECIALISTS

❏ An early statement of the qualities of an infant interventionist can be found in a 1981 position paper of the Division for Early Childhood (Cohen, Givens, Guralnick, Hutinger, & Llewllyn, 1981). Since that time, there has been continued elaboration of these qualities. The task of delineating specific skills and abilities of professionals who choose to work with high-risk and handicapped infants and their families has been addressed by universities preparing infant services personnel (Bailey et al., 1986; Bricker & Slentz, in press; Farel, Bailey, & O'Donnell, 1987; Geik, Gilkerson, & Sponseller, 1982; *Guidelines for infant personnel training programs,* 1984; Mallory, 1983; Northcott, 1973); by state agencies (Illinois State Board of Education, 1985; Williamsburg Area Child Development Resources, 1985); by consumers and professionals in the field (Fewell, 1983; Garland, 1978; Healy, Keesee, & Smith, 1985; Hutinger, 1984; McCollum, 1987; Ryan, 1982); and by national education and advocacy organizations ("CEC session...," 1984; Cohen et al., 1981; National Center for Clinical Infant Programs, 1985; National Easter Seal Society, 1986; Weiner & Koppelman, 1987). There is substantial agreement among these diverse groups about the competencies required for infant service. It is significant to note that most of these discussions have occurred within the past 5 years. Thus, it must be expected that, as this field grows and matures, the competencies described will represent a working outline that should and will be modified further as experience with infant service delivery increases.

These skills are required of all members of the infant service team.

The following discussion is divided into two parts. The first addresses those skills required of professionals, whatever their disciplinary training, who will be interventionists with infants with special needs and their families. These skills are required of all members of the infant service team, whether or not they serve as primary provider. These competencies will be termed the *common infancy core.*

These competencies will be termed the common infancy core.

In addition to common infancy core competencies, any professional involved in infant intervention would possess the competencies of his or her larger discipline, as well as specialized infancy-related competencies unique to that discipline. The second section discusses the infancy specialization competencies of the early childhood special educator. Hence, the early childhood special educator specializing in infancy would be expected to be trained in the total array of competencies discussied in these two sections.

Common Infancy Core

❏ The common infancy core competencies fall into four broad categories of knowledge and skill:

- Those that are infant-related.
- Those that are family-related.
- Those that are related to functioning as an effective member of a service delivery team.
- Those that are related to functioning as an interagency advocate for a child and his or her family.

There are also a variety of personal qualities that appear to be especially critical for any professional involved in infant service delivery.

Infant-Related Competencies. It has been suggested that the central competency that organizes all other infancy-related competencies is the ability to learn from observation (Healy, Keesee, & Smith, 1985; NCCIP, 1985). The subtleties of infant behavior and the often fleeting nature of their responses require that the infant interventionist be adept not only at eliciting behavioral responses for the purpose of assessment and intervention but also at deriving information through systematic observation.

The central competency is the ability to learn from observation.

To make skilled use of observation requires an understanding of normal infant development. There must be sensitivity to the remarkable rate of development in infancy as well as an understanding of the unique relationship among domains of development in infancy. There must also be an understanding of atypical development and the potential medical complications of infancy. Given the increased survival of younger and more medically fragile infants, a knowledge of the potential impacts of prematurity on infants is vital, as is an understanding of the unique characteristics of the premature infant. A healthy understanding of the unknowns with regard to the development of premature infants would also be desirable.

There must be sensitivity to the rate of development.

Knowledge of potential impacts of prematurity is vital.

The infant interventionist must be able to assess infants, using the strategies of his or her own particular discipline, for the purpose of planning appropriate interventions. This may require the ability to obtain assessment information through observation of another professional actually assessing an infant—as in a transdisciplinary model. It may further require the ability to conduct assessments in collaboration with parents, in some instances actually coaching the parents to perform assessment items.

Family-Related Competencies. Families have come to be seen as resourceful collaborators in infant services in the assessment, planning, and intervention processes. There is increasing recognition that the central competency related to family services is increasing the ability to support family strengths rather than focusing on family deficits or grieving as the central force in family life (Dunst & Trivette, in press).

The central competency is increasing the ability to support family strengths.

To accomplish these goals the infant service provider must have an awareness of family systems, of the roles of different family members in the life of the family, of the degree to which a family is part of a larger social network, and of the impact that network might have upon the intervention process. The provider must be sensitive to different family constellations and the way in which the family defines itself (Geik et al., 1982).

The provider must be sensitive to family constellations.

A family-focused program provides support to family members in developing patterns of interaction with their infants that will undergird future learning. This requires that professionals attend to the family environment of the infant, that they recognize family strengths, and that they possess an understanding of sources of vulnerability in families— sources of vulnerability unique to the transition to parenthood, to the particular family and to adaptation to an infant with special needs, as well as those resulting from social and economic pressures (NCCIP, 1985). This further requires that professionals possess skill in relating to adults in the family and in supporting and assisting parental competence to enable family members to fulfill their roles in supporting and nurturing the infant in preparation for his or her entry into the world (Cohen et al., 1981).

Teaming Competencies. Providing coordinated services to special needs infants and their families requires a great deal of interdisciplinary collaboration. Two broad categories of skills are needed. The first requires that team members from multiple disciplines have a common vocabulary that enables them to share their disciplinary expertise, to plan interventions jointly, to incorporate parents in planning, and to incorporate shared disciplinary knowledge into their own interventions. The second requires that each team member possess the process skills necessary to work with others as part of an effective decision-making and treatment unit.

Coordinated services require interdisciplinary collaboration.

The first category of skills—the ability to integrate knowledge from other disciplines into one's own disciplinary interventions—suggests several competencies. Each infant intervention team member acts as consultant to the other team members. This requires the ability to translate the central concepts of one's own discipline for other professionals in a way that will enable them to integrate the concepts as necessary into their own interventions. For example, the special educator, versed in cognitive development, learning, and motivation, can suggest to a physical therapist a cognitively motivating activity around which to organize a movement intervention. Similarly, a physical therapist can demonstrate to a special educator specific positions that will promote function during a learning activity. In pursuing this common vocabulary, all team members will be better able to provide integrated services to the child and promote carry-over in many settings (Bailey et al., 1986; Bricker & Slentz, in press).

Each acts as a consultant to other team members.

The team process skills necessary for the infant interventionist include an understanding of models of team functioning. This includes an understanding of the ways in which team functioning is influenced by the staff available and the purpose of the team. It also requires an understanding of the ways in which performance of a disciplinary role in both assessment and service delivery might be influenced by a particular model of team functioning, for example, transdisciplinary versus interdisciplinary (McCollum & Hughes, Chapter 6).

Team process skills include an understanding of models of team functioning.

Finally, possessing team process skills requires an understanding of (a) communication strategies that promote effective teamwork; (b) approaches to decision making and conflict resolution appropriate to interdisciplinary teams; and (c) the unique role contribution of team membership and team leadership (Geik et al., 1982).

Team process skills require an understanding of communication strategies.

Interagency and Advocacy Skills. Given the interagency climate in which infant services are provided, infant interventionists must have an understanding of the larger service delivery context. Given the language of P.L. 99-457 and the emerging picture of varying lead agencies (NASDSE, 1987), this will continue to be a critical competency. Infant interventionists must be aware of the legislative initiatives that guide infant service delivery locally, at the state level, and nationally. They must be aware of parental rights and of their own associated professional responsibilities. They need to be aware of the range of services available to a particular infant and family in the community and how to access those services. Finally, they must be able to apply their teaming skills to working with representatives of other agencies on behalf of a particular family. They must be able to "de-discipline" themselves in order to avoid duplicating services, instead making best use of the broad range of resources available in any community (Bailey et al., 1986; Ensher & Clark, 1986; NCCIP, 1985).

Infant interventionists must be aware of legislative initiatives.

They must be able to "de-discipline" themselves.

Personal Attributes of the Infant Interventionist. One category of competency deserves special attention because it crosses all disciplines and is of equal import to all. That is the set of personal attributes necessary to function successfully as an interventionist.

One category crosses all disciplines.

This category presents many questions: How do we measure these attributes? Must someone enter a training program already possessing them? Which can be learned? Which require experience? Which are central? Which are nice but not critical? Despite such questions, we report the following competencies because there is substantial agreement about their importance (Bricker & Slentz, in press; "CEC session...," 1984; NCCIP, 1985).

1. *Flexibility.* The infant specialist must be prepared for the fact that things may not go as planned. A child may be sleeping, may be ill; parents may have suffered a crisis; plans must change.

2. *Maturity.* There is a need for great sensitivity. Families with new infants are readjusting their own identities as families. The infant specialist must step cautiously around these emerging boundaries, valuing the relationship parents have with their infants, and resisting the temptation to shape the family to his or her own definition. It has been suggested that infant interventionists must themselves be parents. While systems cannot realistically apply such a requirement, the idea does suggest that special attention be paid to these family competencies and that the infant service provider must have great appreciation for the sorrows and also the joys associated with parenting a special needs infant (Geik et al., 1982). Certainly if infant interventionists are not parents, their professional behavior should suggest to parents that they understand the family experience and can be trusted.

3. *Independence.* Infant specialists often work alone, not in the safety of a classroom under the umbrella of a larger system. Thus, the infant specialist needs to be able to take initiative, to step comfortably into many medical, social service, and educational settings, and to work productively in home settings.

4. *Willingness to share.* Since disciplines overlap in infant services, the infant specialist must be willing to share knowledge rather than protect it. Interventionists must also be comfortable with what they do not know. Sometimes they must be prepared to drop altogether their disciplinary cloak in response to the needs of parents or children.

5. *Tolerance.* Finally, and perhaps most important, the infant interventionist must have great tolerance for change (NCCIP, 1985). The field is changing; legislative mandates are changing; disciplinary knowledge is changing; individual families are constantly changing. Change is inherent in the speciality, and tolerance for change—perhaps even a preference for change—is a significant competency.

Infancy Specialization in Early Childhood Special Education

❑ The competencies just described represent a common core necessary for any professional working in the area of infant service delivery. As such, they would also apply to the infant special educator, whether functioning as the sole child development specialist in a rural infant program or as a special educator on an infant service team with a full complement of interdisciplinary professionals. In addition to these core competencies, infant special educators also must possess the competencies that tie them to the larger discipline of early childhood special education, as well as those specialized competencies that are the early childhood special educator's unique contribution to infant service delivery.

Infant-Related Competencies. Infant special educators are experts in infant cognitive, social, and affective development. This requires an understanding of sensorimotor intelligence and the nature of the problems that become the focus of infant learning. Based upon this understanding of infant learning, infant special educators must possess the formal and informal assessment skills to be able to analyze each infant's understanding of his or her environment and then apply what has been learned to planning intervention (Illinois State Board of Education, 1985).

Infant special educators must possess formal and informal assessment skills.

The assessment skills required of infant special educators include being able to (a) use observation as an assessment and (b) derive central assessment information from observing the infant alone at play, from observing other professionals' assessments, and from guiding parents as partners in assessment. Infant special educators must be able to integrate information from formal and informal tests as well as observations to answer specific questions about the infant's development, about the impact of handicaps on development, and about the role of temperamental and affective style in learning.

The contribution of the infant special educator to intervention lies in the ability to construct learning environments that provide opportunities for the infant to accomplish the learning objectives set jointly by the family and professionals. This requires the ability to integrate knowledge of the child derived from all disciplines involved with the child into construction of these environments, and to plan developmentally appropriate and challenging interventions. The special educator must be able to incorporate into the intervention specific environmental adaptations such as positioning and translate the intervention goals into intervention settings and activities that have meaning and value for parents (National Easter Seal Society, 1986; NCCIP, 1985).

The special educator must be able to incorporate specific environmental adaptions.

Finally, infant special educators must be adept at instructional and interactional strategies that promote learning and development in infancy. Infant interventionists must be able to support the parent-child interaction as central to intervention and assist parents in using the home setting as a learning environment. They must possess the skills of data collection and evaluation that enable them to judge the appropriateness of interventions and the directions in which they might go.

Infant special educators must be adept at instructional and interactional strategies that promote learning and development.

Family-Related Competencies. The family intervention skills required of infant special educators are those of collaborator and consultant (Geik et al., 1982). They must possess the skills to include parents in planning and intervention. This requires valuing family priorities as highly as program priorities. It requires knowledge of strategies for assessing family needs, as well as for assessing the resources families themselves can bring to bear in meeting these needs. Where outside resources are required, interventionists need to be able to assist families in accessing resources. Family consultant skills further include the ability to promote interaction between parent and child. Interventionists must be skilled in working through the families, as well as in working directly with infants.

Family intervention skills are those of collaborator and consultant.

The unique family-related task of infant special educators might best be termed *intervention coaching*. They must be able to assist families in identifying and promoting those aspects of their interactions with their child and those aspects of the home environment that most seem to facilitate learning. As intervention coaches, infant special educators must be able to assist families in problem-solving ways in adjusting the home environment to better facilitate learning. They must further be able to translate family goals into workable educational units. They must therefore have such a clear understanding of each child's developmental status and needs that they are able to adjust intervention strategies to settings relevant to the life of the family. This might include such diverse settings as church, a shopping mall, or a restaurant.

It is often the case that the infant special educator is the primary agent for delivery of home-based services. In that role the interventionist is a guest in the home of the family, and must be sensitive to that status. In the intimacy of the home setting, the interventionist will very likely gain information about the family that will facilitate understanding of family needs as they relate to the family's ability to participate in intervention with their child. This information becomes central to team planning and to the educator's own plan of action. It also requires the ability to balance confidentiality with sharing information with appropriate team members.

They must be able to translate family goals into workable educational units.

Teaming Competencies. The teaming competencies discussed in the common core competencies relate as well to infant special educators. They must possess the process skills of team membership and team leadership that promote communication and problem solving on the team. They must also be able to translate the language of their discipline so that the team can incorporate cognitive, affective, and social information while developing an integrated program plan for a child. Similarly, they must be able to integrate the knowledge provided by other disciplines into planning educationally relevant interventions.

Additionally, funding and staffing patterns are such that infant special educators are often the full-time primary agents of service delivery, with other disciplines functioning as consultants or providing less frequent direct treatment. In those instances, the educators must possess the skills of case coordinator, of "educational synthesizer" (Bricker, 1976). They must be able to translate and integrate for families the information from multiple disciplines and assist families in carrying out recommendations from the other disciplines concerned. Finally, they must possess what might best be termed the humility or self-knowledge to know when it is appropriate to call upon other disciplines to assist in intervention with a particular child and family.

Interagency and Advocacy Competencies. The contribution of infant special educators in this area of competency is their knowledge of the special education and early childhood service delivery system as it fits into the larger interagency system of the local community, the state, and the nation. Consequently, infant special educators should be well versed in relevant special education legal mandates related to services for special needs children and their families. They must clearly understand the procedural safeguards of all legislation and be able to provide families with knowledge of their rights under any legislation that applies.

They must understand the procedural safeguards of all legislation.

Infant special educators must understand state and local regulations as they relate to federal policy—specifically, how such regulations affect the referral and intake process, timeliness of evaluation, program planning, review, and referral to the next placement. In the latter regard, infant special educators offer to teams a knowledge of early childhood and special education placements available in the community that are most appropriate to each child's future educational needs. Thus they function as transition specialists within early intervention programs.

Educators should be aware of formal and informal community resources.

Finally, educators should be aware of formal and informal community resources providing case advocacy and advocacy training for parents of children with special needs. Infant special educators must be able to walk the fine line between being system employees and active advocates for children and their families.

A MODEL AND SOME RELATED ISSUES

❏ It is clear that careful attention must be given to the specialized training needs of early educators who choose to work with infants and their families. However, the development of programs directed toward this need is itself still in its infancy. Few states currently have certification standards that require such training (Bricker & Slentz, in press). Although federal funding of personnel preparation programs has begun to yield some excellent models, training is not yet widespread (Brown & Thorp, 1986). Moreover, while some programs are beginning to prepare personnel for this specialization, the extent of specialized training varies tremendously across programs (Bricker & Slentz, in press). This situation undoubtedly will undergo rapid change as states reply to the mandates of P.L. 99-457 to implement full services by 1990.

Development of programs is still in its infancy.

Extent of specialized training varies across programs.

Preparing personnel for a specialization in infancy is a challenge that must be faced not only by early childhood special education, but by other disciplines as well. As states choose lead agencies and develop comprehensive plans for service delivery, personnel standards must be developed. The implications of these standards for certification and licensure must also be addressed.

As states choose lead agencies, personnel standards must be developed.

There is now substantial agreement in the field about the competencies needed by infant interventionists. Discussions related to competence have given way to new issues concerning how these competencies are to be acquired and at what level of expertise. Is it a lofty goal that all professionals working with special needs infants possess all of the competencies described in the preceding sections? Is it, in fact, a necessary goal? For example, should a paraprofessional possess the interagency and advocacy knowledge that a program administrator possesses? Which competencies are necessary for which program roles? Educators need to examine the categories of competencies provided here and use them as a guide to describe the specific competencies required of individuals in different roles.

Which competencies are necessary for which program roles?

Attention must be paid to both differentiated preservice and inservice training.

A second issue that should become the focus of ongoing discussion is the degree to which some competencies are to be required of entry level professionals and which are to be required or refined as a result of experience. Clearly, attention must be paid to both differentiated preservice and inservice training (Healy et al., 1985). Again using the categories of competencies described in this chapter, planners and trainers could develop a framework by which competencies are identified as acquired in preservice training, as a result of continuing education or inservice training, or as a part of on-the-job experience. A related question concerns who is to provide specialized training to these personnel, and at what level.

Figure 1 provides a conceptual model for addressing these important questions. The circle as a whole represents all disciplines that might be included on an early intervention team, with each wedge depicting one discipline (e.g., education, social work, medicine). The varying width of the wedges indicates the varying degrees to which different disciplines may be involved in early intervention programs.

Within each wedge, there is a general body of knowledge and skill (Level I) that a professional belonging to that discipline will be assumed to possess (e.g., the professional knowledge of speech and hearing science or early childhood special education). Level II represents the more specialized disciplinary content related to the infancy period. For many disciplines, including early childhood special education, Level II is a new specialization, with new content. For example, most speech and language pathologists, occupational therapists, and social workers do not currently receive specialized training for the infancy period. It is not yet clear how this new content will be integrated into professional training and licensure structures which, until now, have been restricted primarily to Level I. What is clear, however, is that training and licensing at Level II is a disciplinary responsibility that must be addressed by each discipline. One primary focus of this chapter, for example, has been the delineation of Level II content for the early childhood special educator.

In contrast to Levels I and II, which represent disciplinary specializations, Level III contains a core of common knowledge and skill needed by all professionals working in early intervention. These have been elaborated in previous sections. Level III is not clearly the domain of any one particular discipline, and there may be many advantages to providing this common core throught an *inter*disciplinary training setting.

Most speech and language pathologists, occupational therapists, and social workers do not currently receive specialized training for the infancy period.

Figure 1. *A Model for Conceptualizing Training and Licensure of Infant Specialists from Different Disciplines.*

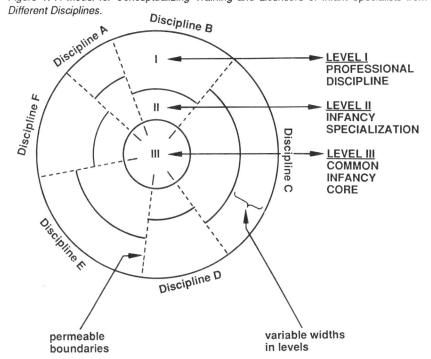

Boundaries between levels must be flexible.

Another important feature of Figure 1 is the permeability of the boundaries between disciplines. The nature of the infant and his or her developmental needs demands that each discipline have access to and understanding of the interrelationships among disciplines. This may be illustrated, for example, by the early educator's need to understand medical terminology. Boundaries between levels also must be flexible, as shown in the varying width of Levels I and II; in any one discipline, the lines between Levels I, II, and III may be less distinct than in another discipline.

For states or professional organizations developing personnel standards for early intervention, Figure 1 can guide thinking and problem solving in relation to licensure and certification, who should provide training in relation to any particular discipline/level combination, and when this should occur during the professional training period. For any particular personnel preparation program in early childhood special education, the issues to be addressed are: What content can the program reasonably offer (Levels I, II, and III) at a high level of quality? Which disciplines should be encouraged to participate in this training and at which level? How should program offerings differ for students from different disciplines? Competencies, coursework, and practicum experiences should clearly reflect the differing needs of these different types of students. Questions in relation to licensure are similar, and must be recognized and addressed by states and professional organizations developing standards for certification and for personnel preparation programs.

Many issues must be addressed by states, professional organizations, and personnel preparation programs.

It is clear that many issues must be addressed by states, professional organizations, and personnel preparation programs in terms of clarifying professional responsibility and disciplinary responsibility within the field of early intervention. Much of this clarification will come about as the boundaries and variations within early intervention service delivery systems become more clearly defined. Competencies needed by infant specialists in all disciplines, including early childhood special education, will become clarified as part of this process of growth.

REFERENCES

Als, H., Lester, B., Tronick, E., & Brazelton, T. B. (1982). Toward a research instrument for the assessment of preterm infants' behavior. In H. Fitzgerald, B. M. Lester, & M. W. Yogman (Eds.), *Theory and research in behavioral pediatrics* (Vol. 1, pp. 35-132). New York: Plenum.

Bailey, D., Farel, A., O'Donnell, K., Simeonsson, R., & Miller, C. (1986). Preparing infant interventionists: Interdepartmental training in special education and maternal child health. *Journal of the Division for Early Childhood, 11*(1), 67-77.

Bricker, D. (1976). Educational Synthesizer. In M. A. Thomas (Ed.), *Hey, don't forget about me* (pp. 84-92). Reston, VA: The Council for Exceptional Children.

Bricker, D., & Slentz, K. (in press). Personnel preparation: Handicapped infants. In M. C. Wang, M. C. Reynolds, & H. J. Walberg (Eds.), *Handbook of special education: Research and practice* (Vol. 3). Elmsford, NY: Pergamon Books.

Brown, C., & Thorp, E. (1986). *A resouce guide to infant personnel preparation programs.* (1986). Unpublished manuscript. The George Washington University, Department of Special Education, Washington, DC.

CEC session identifies issues in training personnel to work with handicapped/risk infants. (1984, May-June). *DEC Communicator, 10*(3).

Cohen, S., Givens, R., Guralnick, M., Hutinger, P. L., & Llewllyn, E. (1981). Service for young handicapped children: A position paper of the Division for Early Childhood, Council for Exceptional Children. *DEC Communicator, 7*(2), 21-25.

Dunst, C. (1983). Emerging trends and advances in early intervention programs. *New Jersey Journal of School Psychology, 2,* 26-40.

Dunst, C., & Trivette, C. (in press). Enabling and empowering families: Conceptual and intervention issues. *School Psychology Review.*

Ensher, G., & Clark, D. (1986). Physicians, educators, and the child care team. In G. Ensher & D. Clark (Eds.), *Newborns at risk: Medical care and psychoeducational intervention* (pp. 271-283). Rockville, MD: Aspen.

Farel, A., Bailey, D., & O'Donnell, K. (1987). A new approach for training infant intervention specialists. *Infant Mental Health Journal, 8*(1), 76-85.

Fewell, R. (1983). The team approach to infant education. In S. G. Garwood & R. Fewell (Eds.), *Educating handicapped infants* (pp. 299-322). Rockville, MD: Aspen.

Garland, C. (1978). *Skills inventory for teachers* (SIFT). Lightfoot, VA: Child Development Resources.

Geik, I., Gilkerson, L., & Sponseller, D. (1982, June). An early intervention training model. *Journal of the Division for Early Childhood, 5,* 42-52.

Guildelines for infant personnel training programs. (1984, September). Results of meeting held at The George Washington University, Washington, DC.

Healy, A., Keesee, P., Smith, B. (1985). *Early services for children with special needs: Transactions for family support.* Iowa City: University of Iowa.

Hutinger, P. (1984). *Infant and preschool handicapped personnel competencies: Results of a survey.* Paper presented at the international meeting of The Council for Exceptional Children, Washington, DC.

Illinois State Board of Education, Department of Specialized Educational Services. (1985, March). *A training curriculum for birth to six specialists.* Report of the Higher Education Advisory Committee. Springfield, IL: Author.

Mallory, B. (1983). The preparation of early childhood special educators: A model program. *Journal of the Division for Early Childhood, 7,* 32-40.

McCollum, J. (1987). *Early interventionists in infant and early childhood programs: A comparison of preservice training needs.* Unpublished manuscript.

Meisels, S. J., Harbin, G., Modigliani, K., & Olson, K. (1986). *Formulating optimal state early childhood intervention policies.* Unpublished manuscript.

National Association of State Directors of Special Education (NASDSE) (1987). *Results of Early Childhood Survey #4.* Washington, DC: Author.

National Center for Clinical Infant Programs (NCCIP). (1985, July). *Training and manpower issues in services to disabled and at-risk infants, toddlers and their families.* Unpublished report of a national meeting on training needs. Washington, DC: Author.

National Easter Seal Society. (1986). *Early intervention: Considerations for establishing programs.* Chicago, IL: Author.

Northcott, W. H. (1973). Competencies needed by teachers of hearing impaired infants, birth to three years, and their parents. *Volta Review, 75*(9), 532-544.

Ryan, S. B. (1982). *Competencies necessary for work with preschool handicapped children: Teachers' perceptions.* Unpublished doctoral dissertation, Temple University, Philadelphia.

Sweet, N. (1981). New faces and approaches in the ICN: The role of the educational specialist. In D. Gelderman, D. Taylor-Hershel, S. Prestridge, & J. Anderson (Eds.), *The health care/education relationship: Services for infants with special needs and their families.* Chapel Hill, NC: TADS.

Vanden Berg, K. A. (1985, June). *Infant stimulation versus developmental interventions: Practical suggestions for what really works.* Paper presented at Contemporary Forums, Developmental Interventions in Neonatal Care, Washington, DC.

Weiner, R., & Koppelman, J. (1987). *From birth to 5: Serving the youngest handicapped children.* Alexandria, VA: Capitol Publications.

Williamsburg Area Child Development Resources. (1985). *Virginia early intervention program guide.* Richmond, VA: Virginia Department of Education.

8.
Early Intervention Team Approaches: The Transdisciplinary Model

Geneva Woodruff and Mary J. McGonigel

❏ The team approach is becoming more widespread (Fewell, 1983) and is gaining support among early intervention professionals as the way to serve young children with special needs and their families. The 1975 passage of the Education for All Handicapped Children Act (Public Law 94-142) and its requirements that assessments and program plans be developed by professionals from multiple disciplines and by the parents made the team approach the standard for school-age special education programs. Public Law 99-457, the Education of the Handicapped Act Amendments of 1986, further endorsed this approach by extending the recommendations for team assessments and program planning to infants and toddlers and their families. As a result of the new legislation and the growing acceptance of the team approach to early intervention, professionals in the field are beginning to look systematically at team functioning.

This chapter defines the concept of team as it relates to the field of early intervention and describes three team approaches commonly used to organize services for infants with special needs and their families. These three approaches are the multidisciplinary, interdisciplinary, and transdisciplinary models. The transdisciplinary approach is explored in detail and recommended as a sound, logical, and valid system for offering coordinated and comprehensive services to infants and their families.

THE TEAM

❏ The growing acceptance and implementation of the team approach are not solely the results of federal mandates. They also reflect early intervention professionals' view of human development that regards a child as an integrated and interactive whole, rather than as a collection of separate parts (Golin & Duncanis, 1981). The team approach also recognizes that the multifaceted problems of very young children are too complex to be addressed by a single discipline (Holm & McCartin, 1978). The complexity of developmental problems in early life (Fewell, 1983) and the interrelated nature of an infant's developmental domains are prompting early intervention specialists to recognize the need for professionals to work together as a team.

Multifaceted problems of very young children are too complex to be addressed by a single discipline.

Holm and McCartin (1978) described a team as "an interacting group performing integrated and interdependent activities" (p. 121). To be effective, a team must be more than a collection of individuals, each pursuing his or her own tasks. Fewell (1983) identified a major problem encountered by early intervention programs that are attempting to use a team approach: "Unfortunately, teams are made, not born" (p. 304). Teams cannot function effectively unless every member shares common goals and purposes, and unless the team leader provides continuing inspiration, support, and a vision of the team's mission. This truth is self-evident to any fan of team sports. Coaches and athletes devote their time to team building and practicing so that they can give their best performance at each game. Early intervention teams can learn from their example.

Teams cannot function effectively unless every member shares common goals and purposes.

Although team building and group dynamics are relatively recent concerns in the field of early intervention, organizational behavior specialists have long investigated these issues. During the late 1920s, researchers in the now classic Hawthorne studies discovered that the essential elements in work productivity are group identity and cohesion among workers (Dyer, 1977). Since that time, organizational development research has recognized and acknowledged the need for team-building skills as a necessary prerequisite for successful teams:

> Everyone who works together needs to learn new, more effective ways of problem solving, planning, decision making, coordination, integrating resources, sharing information, and dealing with problem situations that arise. (Dyer, 1977, p. 24)

Only recently have early intervention professionals become aware of the need to examine the process of team functioning and prepare professionals to become team members and team leaders.

EARLY INTERVENTION TEAM MODELS

❑ Early intervention teams have several factors in common. Most are composed of professionals representing a variety of disciplines: special education; social work; psychology; medicine; child development; and physical, occupational, and speech and language therapy. Teams also involve the family in varying ways and degrees. Team members share common tasks including the assessment of a child's developmental status and the development and implementation of a program plan to meet the assessed needs of the child and, sometimes, of the family.

Teams are composed of professionals representing a variety of disciplines.

Teams involve the family.

What usually distinguishes early intervention teams from one another is neither composition nor task, but rather the structure for interaction among team members. Three service delivery models that structure interaction among team members have been identified and differentiated in the literature: multidisciplinary, interdisciplinary, and transdisciplinary (Fewell, 1983; Haynes, 1983; Linder, 1983; Peterson, 1987; United Cerebral Palsy National Collaborative Infant Project, 1976). Woodruff and Hanson (1987) have illustrated the similarities and differences in these team interaction models as they relate to early intervention program components. (See Figure 1.)

MULTIDISCIPLINARY TEAMS

❑ On multidisciplinary teams, professionals from several disciplines work independently of each other (Fewell, 1983). Peterson (1987) has compared the mode of interaction among members of multidisciplinary teams to parallel play in young children: "side by side, but separate" (p. 484). Although multidisciplinary team members may work together and share the same space and tools, they usually function quite separately.

Multidisciplinary team members usually function quite separately.

Early intervention teams using this approach usually conduct assessments in which the child is seen and evaluated separately by each team member only in his or her own area of specialization. For example, the educator uses an assessment instrument specifically designed to measure cognitive functioning, while the physical therapist uses a gross motor instrument to assess the level of motor functioning. Upon completion of the assessments, team members develop the part of the service plan related to their own disciplines, and then each member implements the resulting intervention activities. The structure for inter-

Early Childhood Special Education: Birth to Three

Figure 1. Three Models for Early Intervention.

	Multidisciplinary	Interdisciplinary	Transdisciplinary
Assessment	Separate assessments by team members	Separate assessments by team members	Team members and family conduct a comprehensive developmental assessment together
Parent Participation	Parents meet with individual team members	Parents meet with team or team representative	Parents are full, active, and participating members of the team
Service Plan Development	Team members develop separate plans for their discipline	Team members share their separate plans with one another	Team members and the parents develop a service plan based upon family priorities, needs, and resources
Service Plan Responsibility	Team members are responsible for implementing their section of the plan	Team members are responsible for sharing information with one another as well as for implementing their section of the plan	Team members are responsible and accountable for how the primary service provider implements the plan
Service Plan Implementation	Team members implement the part of the service plan related to their discipline	Team members implement their section of the plan and incorporate other sections where possible	A primary service provider is assigned to implement the plan with the family
Lines of Communication	Informal lines	Periodic case-specific team meetings	Regular team meeting where continuous transfer of information, knowledge, and skills are shared among team members
Guiding Philosophy	Team members recognize the importance of contributions from other disciplines	Team members are willing and able to develop, share, and be responsible for providing services that are a part of the total service plan	Team members make a commitment to teach, learn, and work together across discipline boundaries to implement unified service plan
Staff Development	Independent and within their discipline	Independent within as well as outside of their discipline	An integral component of team meetings for learning across disciplines and team building

Source: Woodruff, G. & Hanson, C. (1987). Project KAI, 77B Warren Street, Brighton, MA 02135. Funded by U.S. Department of Education, Special Education Programs, Handicapped Children's Early Education Program.

action among team members in the multidisciplinary approach does not foster services that reflect the view of the child as an integrated and interactive whole (Linder, 1983).

By design, professionals on multidisciplinary teams function as independent specialists. For the most part, professionals on these teams work independently and in isolation from one another (Bennett, 1982; Fewell, 1983). This in turn can lead to fragmented services for children and confusing or conflicting reports to parents.

Another concern about the multidisciplinary model is the lack of communication between team members that places the burden of coordination and case management on the family. In contrast, both the interdisciplinary and the transdisciplinary approaches avoid the pitfalls of multidisciplinary service fragmentation by having the team develop a case management plan that coordinates both their services and the information that is presented to the family.

INTERDISCIPLINARY TEAMS

❑ Interdisciplinary teams are composed of parents as well as professionals representing several disciplines. The difference between multidisciplinary and interdisciplinary teams lies in the interaction among team members. Interdisciplinary teams are characterized by formal channels of communication that encourage team members to share their information and discuss individual results (Fewell, 1983; Peterson, 1987). Regular meetings are usually scheduled to discuss shared cases.

Interdisciplinary teams are characterized by formal channels of communication.

Representatives of various professional disciplines separately assess children and families, but the team does come together at some point to discuss the results of their individual assessments and to develop plans for intervention. Generally, each specialist is responsible for the part of the service plan related to his or her professional discipline. The intervention plan is carried out by a single staff member with scheduled consultation or therapy from other specialists on the team.

Although this approach solves some of the problems associated with multidisciplinary teams, communication and interaction problems still exist within the interdisciplinary framework. Professional "turf" issues are a major problem (Fewell, 1983; Linder, 1983). Sometimes interdisciplinary team members do not fully understand the professional training and expertise of other team members who are from different disciplines. Many teams have discovered to their dismay that shared terminology does not always result in shared meaning (Howard, 1982).

Communication and interaction problems still exist.

Howard (1982) stated that in order for an interdisciplinary team to be successful, members must recognize and accept one another's differences:

> This requires an atmosphere of (a) acceptance of differences in skills; (b) acceptance of differences in approach; (c) willingness not to try to know everything; (d) an ability to call on others for assistance and ongoing knowledge; and (e) non-threatening opportunities for discussion in these areas. (p. 320)

Although Howard was addressing the highest goals of interdisciplinary team interaction, these principles serve as the foundation for a transdisciplinary team, too.

TRANSDISCIPLINARY TEAMS

❑ Transdisciplinary (TD) teams are also composed of professionals from several disciplines. The TD approach attempts to overcome the confines of individual disciplines in order to form a team that crosses and recrosses disciplinary boundaries and thereby maximizes communication, interaction, and cooperation among team members.

Fundamental to this model are two beliefs: (a) children's development must be viewed as integrated and interactive and (b) children must be served within the context of the family. Since families have the greatest influence on their children's development, families are seen as part of the TD team and are involved in setting goals and making programmatic decision for themselves and their children. All decisions in the areas of assessment and program planning, implementation, and evaluation are made by team consensus. Although all team members share responsibility for the development of the service plan, it is carried out by the family and one other team member who is designated as the primary service provider.

Continuum of Interaction

❑ Although these three forms of team interaction are frequently compared, another productive way of looking at them is to consider them as points on a continuum, moving from less to more interaction among disciplines. Figure 2 illustrates this view. The perspective of a continuum also acknowledges the progression of individual staff members (United Cerebral Palsy National Collaborative Infant Project, 1976) and of teams as they become more experienced and recognize the merits of transdisciplinary exchange. Seen in this light, the TD approach can be regarded as evolutionary for early intervention teams who, with experience and training, learn to increase interaction among members and among disciplines.

DESCRIPTION OF THE TRANSDISCIPLINARY APPROACH

❑ The TD approach was developed in the mid-1970s by the United Cerebral Palsy (UCP) National Collaborative Infant Project. Like many innovations in early education and special education, it was developed in response to budget constraints as a way for understaffed and underfunded infant teams to pool their knowledge and skills to provide better, more cost-effective services to infants and families.

TD team members plan and monitor services to all children and their families.

The need to make the best use of professional staff time led the UCP Project to formulate a model in which all team members are involved in planning and monitoring services for all children and their families, but all are not involved in providing these services directly. The team uses its time together to plan an integrated program that is then implemented by the family and the primary service provider. The UCP National Collaborative Infant Project (1978) called this innovative model *transdisciplinary service delivery*, which they defined as "of or relating to a transfer of information, knowledge, or skills across disciplinary boundaries" (p.1).

To become transdisciplinary, program administrators and other professionals must commit themselves to teaching, learning, and working across disciplinary boundaries. They must exchange information, knowledge, and skills so that one person, together with the family, accepts primary responsibility for carrying out the early intervention plan for the child and family.

The UCP National Collaborative Infant Project called the stages of TD team development "role release." Role release is the sum of several separate but related processes labeled role extension, role enrichment,

Figure 2. Team Interaction.

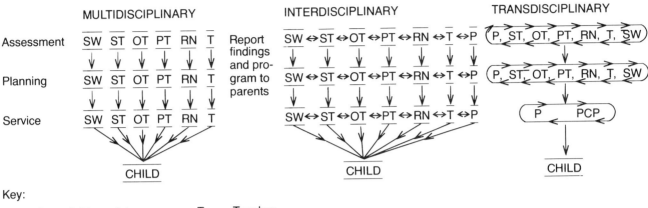

Key:

ST —Speech Therapist
OT —Occupational Therapist
PT —Physical Therapist
RN —Registered Nurse

T —Teacher
P —Parent
PCP—Primary Care Provider
SW —Social Worker or Psychologist

Source: Woodruff, G., & Hanson, C. (1987). Project KAI, 77B Warren Street, Brighton, MA 02135. Funded by U.S. Department of Education, Special Education Programs, Handicapped Children's Early Education Program.

role expansion, role exchange, role release, and role support. Role release allows individual team members to carry out an intervention plan for the child and family backed by the authorization and consultative support of team members from other disciplines (UCP National Collaborative Infant Project, 1978).

Early intervention administrators and program planners interested in establishing transdisciplinary services must become familiar with the entire role release process, for it is central to the functioning of a TD team. Successful implementation of this process requires almost constant attention to team building and team maintenance activities. Without the necessary commitment from administrative staff, the TD team cannot have adequate time and support for successful role release.

The role release process is central to the functioning of a TD team.

Role Extension

❏ Role extension is the first step team members take in the role release process as they move from an interdisciplinary to a transdisciplinary focus. In this phase of team development, professionals engage in self-directed study and other staff development efforts such as attending conferences, inservice training, and courses to increase their depth of understanding, theoretical knowledge, and clinical skills in their own disciplines. Role extension is a continuing process in which team members accept responsibility and use their resources to keep fully abreast of the latest developments in their fields. Competence in one's profession and self-confidence are necessary prerequisites for TD team members.

Professionals engage in self-directed study and other staff development efforts.

Role Enrichment

❏ Role enrichment follows role extension. TD team members who are well versed in their own disciplines are ready to begin learning more about other disciplines. Role enrichment allows team members to develop a general awareness and understanding of other disciplines through a process of defining terminology and sharing information about basic practices. Teams can engage in role enrichment during discussions at team meetings and after conferences. In addition, the team can create a reference library of conference notes and professional journals to share their resources, and can offer instruction to one another.

Role Expansion

❑ Role expansion is the third phase of development for TD teams. In this phase, team members continue the transdisciplinary teaching/learning process by pooling ideas and exchanging information on how to make observational and programmatic judgments outside their own disciplines.

Role Exchange

Role exchange is often misconstrued as role replacement.

❑ Role exchange occurs when TD team members have learned the theory, methods, and procedures of other disciplines and begin to implement techniques from these disciplines. Role exchange is often misconstrued as role replacement by critics of the model. A common criticism is that team members lose their professional identities on a TD team. This, however, is not the case. For example, the nurse on a TD team is not expected to become a speech therapist. Rather, what is expected on a properly functioning team is that team members expand their intervention skills. The nurse is expected to acquire some intervention skills that she is able to incorporate into her therapeutic repertoire. In this phase of the role release process, the nurse must first demonstrate these procedures to the speech therapist and later carry them out under the speech therapist's supervision. Role exchange is facilitated when team members work side by side or as buddies, and when they have sufficient indirect service time.

Role Release

❑ Perhaps the most challenging component is role release. In this phase of team development, a team member puts newly acquired techniques into practice under the supervision of the team member from the discipline that has accountability for those practices.

The team becomes transdisciplinary when team members begin to give up or "release" intervention strategies from their disciplines to one another. Because the team authorizes the primary service provider to carry out the plan that the entire team has developed, the child is handled by one staff person and the parents. The family also benefits by interacting chiefly with a primary service provider rather than with a number of specialists, thereby reducing the confusion that can result from working with a large number of staff to develop and implement the service plan. Many families of infants with special needs report that they are uncomfortable dealing with several professionals at a time, some of whom may have differing and contradictory perspectives. Having one service provider who represents the team is an aspect of the TD model that is particularly valued by families.

The family also benefits by interacting with a primary service provider.

Role Support

❑ Sometimes interventions are required by law to be provided by a specific discipline. At other times they are too complicated, too new, or simply beyond the skills of the best-trained TD primary service provider. In these cases, the team member from the identified discipline works directly with the primary service provider and the family to provide this intervention. Team members also receive role support through the continuing informal encouragement of other team members. Role support provides the necessary backup to the processes of role exchange and role release and is a critical component of the transdisciplinary approach.

Role support provides backup to role exchange and role release.

Sometimes, in the interests of saving professional time or increasing caseloads, transdisciplinary programs neglect to provide role support to team members. These programs deserve the criticism leveled at the TD approach—that the primary service provider attempts to become everything to every child and family. Holm and McCartin (1978) voiced this concern:

> There is a danger that the "transdisciplinary" idea could be used by solo practitioners (in whatever field) with a sprinkling of skills from a variety of child development fields to obliterate the distinction between solo practice and a team approach. ...the full array of knowledge and skills available in the child development field will never be offered by a single practitioner, however skilled. (p. 103)

In fact, the transdisciplinary approach, appropriately implemented, causes just the opposite to occur. Rather than replacing the skills of individual disciplines with one person who functions as an "unitherapist," the TD process allows individual members of the team to add to their own expertise by incorporating into their service repertoires the information and skills offered by the other members of the team.

The educator or child development specialist on the transdisciplinary team, for example, does not attempt to replace the physical therapist. Instead, the educator pools his or her information and skills with that of the physical therapist and the other team members to develop and implement an integrated service plan that takes advantage of the full range of skills that each discipline brings to the team. If the educator is the primary service provider, she or he is responsible, with the family, for carrying out the plan with role support from other team members whenever appropriate. If the child is in need of direct, "hands on" physical therapy, the physical therapist on the TD team provides this therapy as role support to the primary service provider.

The educator does not attempt to replace the physical therapist.

TRANSDISCIPLINARY PROGRAM COMPONENTS

❑ The transdisciplinary principles of viewing child development as an integrated and interactive process, requiring team accountability and including families as team members, govern all components of a TD program (Figure 3). In order for the TD approach to be effective, administrators and team members must be thoroughly aware of how the model affects program operation and must consistently implement TD procedures throughout each phase of service delivery. In Chapter 2,

Garland and Linder describe the administrative issues that must be addressed before a program can become transdisciplinary.

It is important to know how the TD model functions in each program component.

Adapting the TD model to the needs and resources of an individual program can be a necessary part of developing the program's philosophy and structure. In attempting to implement the transdisciplinary model without adequate forethought or technical assistance, many programs end up with a hodgepodge of bits and pieces from all three of the early intervention team models. Unfortunately, some of the resulting program models combine the least effective, most difficult aspects of each of the three team models. In order to avoid such confusion, it is important for administrators and program planners to know how the TD model functions in each program component, so that adaptations can be carefully made and supported by a consistent program philosophy.

The TD model is not for everyone, nor for every program. Becoming transdisciplinary is not an easy process. It requires a great deal of planning, effort, time, and initially, expense. Program administrators must provide the necessary inservice time and training for the development of a TD team and the necessary indirect service time for the team to implement TD procedures. In turn, the team must adequately prepare each family for their active role as team members in assessing their own and their child's needs and in implementing and evaluating the effectiveness of their service plan.

The team must adequately prepare each family for an active role as team members.

In the following section, team and family roles for implementing TD intake, assessment, program planning, program implementation, and reassessment are discussed and illustrated. Some of these procedures are common to all high-quality early intervention programs. Some are unique to the TD approach. All, however, should be carefully considered by programs wanting to become transdisciplinary.

Intake

❑ In many early intervention programs, one person or one discipline is responsible for bringing children and families into the program. In a TD program, however, responsibility for intake interviews or home visits may be rotated among team members or assigned as a continuing task to each team member. This shared responsibility allows all team members to participate.

Responsiblity for intake interviews may be rotated among team members.

Project Optimus, an Outreach project funded from 1978 to 1986 to provide transdisciplinary training, developed the following guidelines for TD team members to consider before the initial intake: (a) anticipate the family's need for information, (b) anticipate the team's need for information, and (c) plan for team feedback to each other (Woodruff, 1985). Intake procedures in a transdisciplinary program are aimed at accomplishing three goals: to establish a basis for rapport with the family and child, to gather information about the child and family, and to provide the family with information about participation in a TD program.

Establishing rapport with the family is the first task for all early intervention staff, regardless of their program's philosophical orientation. In a TD program, however, this task is critical because the family is considered a functioning member of the team.

Intake represents a family's first exposure to the early intervention program.

Intake represents a family's first exposure to the early intervention program and their first opportunity to be treated as decision-making members of the team. When meeting with the family during intake, the staff member's goal is to create a warm, understanding atmosphere that

Figure 3. Components of the Transdisciplinary Model.

INTAKE
Responsibility rotated among team members.
Rapport established with family.
Family information and child data gathered.
Transdisciplinary model explained.

PRE-ARENA PREPARATION
Facilitator and coach chosen for assessment.
Case presentation provided.
Team members coach facilitator.
Team members share information across disciplines.
Staff member chosen to lead post-arena feedback to parent.

ARENA ASSESSMENT
Arena facilitator works with child and parents.
Team members observe all aspects of child's behavior and parent-child interaction.
Team members observe and record across all developmental areas.
Arena facilitator works to reassure parent and gain involvement.

POST-ARENA FEEDBACK TO FAMILY
Child's strengths and needs are established.
Family's goals and priorities are discussed.
Activities are recommended for home implementation.

POST-ARENA DISCUSSION OF TEAM PROCESS
Primary service provider (PSP) assignment is made.
Team evaluates assessment process and provides feedback to one another.

IFSP DEVELOPMENT
Team develops goals, objectives, and activities.
Parents and PSP reach consensus on which IFSP goals, objectives, and activities
     will be initiated first.

ACTIVITY PLANNING
Team establishes regular meetings to monitor the implementation of the IFSP, to
     assign daily or weekly activities, and to make revisions in the plan.

PROGRAM IMPLEMENTATION
PSP implements the plan.
Team members monitor the implementation, maintain accountability for their
     discipline, provide role support, and when needed, supervision.

REASSESSMENT
Team follows pre-arena, arena, and post-arena procedures.

PROGRAM CONTINUES TO REPEAT CYCLE

Source: Woodruff, G. & Hanson, C. (1987). Project KAI, 77B Warren Street, Brighton, MA
02135. Funded by the U.S. Department of Education, Special Education Programs,
Handicapped Children's Early Education Program.

The challenge is to make sure that families are able to make informed decisions.

reduces parental anxiety by acknowledging the family's needs and their reasons for seeking services.

The relationship and roles established by the family and the team member during intake set the pattern for the family's future interactions with program staff. If the staff member in these initial contacts fails to convey respect for the family's ability to identify their needs and make choices for themselves and their child, it will be extremely difficult, if not impossible, for the family to later feel and act like team members. The challenge for the primary service provider is to make sure that families are able to make informed decisions based on a review of available options.

Another goal of the intake is to gather information on the child and family. Although most early intervention programs gather similar information, the method used in a TD program may more consciously involve the family in determining their needs and expectations.

Information to be gathered on the child during intake includes the presenting diagnosis, if any; a medical history; the family's perception of the child's level of functioning in each of the developmental areas, as well as of the child's learning style, temperament, motivators, and reinforcers; a developmental screening; a record of the child's involvement with other agencies or programs; and release forms for intervention.

Information to be gathered on the family includes a description of the family constellation, family support systems, family stresses and coping behaviors, the degree of family awareness of the child's condition and needs, and the family's expectations for the child's program and services. Because the TD approach requires that children be considered within the context of their families, this information is especially critical to the TD team. As the provisions of Public Law 99-457 become widely implemented in early intervention programs, such a family focus may become routine in all early intervention programs, regardless of their service delivery model.

Providing information to the family is as important as gathering information from the family. During these initial contacts, the staff member explains the TD philosophy to the family and describes how this philosophy affects all components of the child's and family's program. The role of the family on the TD team and the process of including parents as active decision makers is explained and emphasized during intake. The family's role in the assessment process, in the establishment of service priorities, and in the development of the individualized family service plan (IFSP) is presented by the staff member during intake. Program options for the family are also described.

Informed of what to expect and how to prepare, families are more likely to participate actively.

During intake, families are prepared for the next step in the TD intervention process—the arena assessment. Informed of what to expect and how to prepare for the assessment, families are more likely to participate actively. Parents are asked, for example, to choose the best time for the assessment, bring their child's favorite toys and snack, and suggest enjoyable activities for their child, as well as be prepared to play with the child during the assessment.

The team member doing the intake also makes it clear to families that their opinions and insights will be an important part of the assessment. Parents are asked to be prepared to talk after the assessment about their goals for their child and family and to comment on whether or not the child's behavior during the assessment represented his or her behavior in normal settings such as the home. Parents are also encouraged to bring one or more people of their choice to the assessment for moral support.

Assessment

❑ In a TD program, children are assessed using an "arena" approach. In an arena assessment the family and all other team members gather together in one room to evaluate the child. All team members on a TD team observe and record every aspect of the child's behavior. In most instances only the parent and one team member, who functions as the facilitator, handle the child. This limited handling reduces the potentially disruptive effect of having several strange adults present at one time.

All team members observe and record.

In a traditional assessment, a child is usually exposed to a series of professionals who touch, stimulate, and interact with him or her. In an arena assessment, the child is not expected to adjust to handling by many strangers. Thus, the child's ability to perform during the arena assessment is enhanced. Because the child is required to go through only one combined assessment and adjust to interacting with only one new adult, fatigue and resistance are minimized as well.

The child often does not adjust well to handling by many strangers.

Having all team members observe the child's reactions and responses in all developmental areas offers many behavioral and developmental perspectives. Team members have an opportunity for rich and varied observations because they are positioned around the child, parent, and assessment facilitator. Little is missed during a well-conducted arena assessment. With a variety of team members attending, varying impressions and observations can be shared, and a synthesis of ideas evolves.

Little is missed during a well-conducted arena assessment.

Every member of the TD team needs to believe in the assessment process and share a sense of equal participation in and responsibility for the outcome. Arena assessments are not easy to do. Orchestrating the arena requires meticulous planning and forethought. Like the performance of an opera, a play, or a team sports event, it requires a great deal of advance planning and coordination by the team members under the guidance of a skilled and committed leader.

Orchestrating the arena requires planning.

Programs implementing the TD model often lack adequate training and practice in arena assessment procedures. A necessary step for teams learning to do arena assessments is first to understand the importance of this component of the model and then to obtain the commitment of the entire team to its implementation. An issue for some members evolving toward a TD approach is their uneasiness about participating in an assessment in which they to not individually work with and handle the child, or in which they do not use their standardized assessment instruments with the child one on one.

For a team to become transdisciplinary, members must be able to openly discuss these individual issues and reservations. As teams ask themselves what they need to learn during a child's assessment, they will be able to weigh the relative merits of the arena and other assessment approaches.

In planning each arena assessment, the team meets to decide who will facilitate the assessment. For some programs, the assessment facilitator is the person who conducted the intake. In other programs, this responsibility is rotated among team members.

For some programs, the assessment facilitator is the person who conducted the intake.

In the pre-assessment meeting, information from intake is shared with the team. The assessment facilitator is advised by the other team members about what child behaviors to look for, what assessment instruments to use, how best to elicit specific information and behavior from the child, and how best to include the family. Team members share specific information from their own disciplines to help other team members observe child behaviors. For example, the psychologist helps other team members to be aware of emotional aspects of behavior, while the occupational therapist coaches the team to look for the interplay of sensory, motor, and cognitive skills.

The family's level of involvement in the assessment is dictated by how comfortable they feel with the process and how much they wish to involve themselves. Parents may be co-facilitators or observers, and may ask or answer questions. Families are encouraged to participate actively in the assessment by interpreting their child's responses and making suggestions about approaches the facilitator might use with the child. The following comments by parents illustrate the value of their observations during an arena assessment: "I don't think he understands that word"; "She calls it a choo-choo, not a train"; and "He could do that if he were sitting this way." The assessment facilitator must be sensitive to cues from the family and be aware of the family's concerns at all times.

The facilitator must be aware of the family's concerns.

As soon as the arena assessment is completed, the family and other team members share their preliminary impressions about the child's performance. This post-assessment discussion provides the family and the other team members with an opportunity to exchange their views and concerns. It also provides the family with a chance to discuss their child's strengths and needs and their priorities for services and to take home ideas for helping him.

The TD team also meets without the family after each arena assessment. At this meeting the team assesses the process, the performance of the facilitator, and each other's participation. This evaluation of team functioning is a critical component of TD staff and team development, but it can be accomplished only in an atmosphere of mutual trust and support. In the interests of saving time and increasing the number of assessments, some programs neglect this team maintenance activity. Yet a lack of attention to such team process issues as these is a frequent cause of failure for TD teams.

Evaluation of team function is a critical component of TD staff and team development.

A final step in a TD arena assessment is the written report. One member of the team, usually the primary service provider, organizes the information gathered from the team assessment discussions into a report that clearly summarizes the results and provides the family with a written record of the team's findings and recommendations.

The arena assessment is a major component of the TD model and is appropriate for use with most young children and their families. Rarely, however, the arena format may not be best for an individual child or family. Some children may be so sensitive or distractible that they cannot perform well in an arena. Some families may be so uneasy in the presence of more than one person at a time that they may not be willing to participate in an arena. Programs implementing the TD approach must be sensitive to these rare exceptions and be willing to alter their assessment practices accordingly.

Program Planning

An IFSP is the initial program planning step.

❏ The development of an individualized family service plan (IFSP) as mandated by Public Law 99-457 is the initial program planning step for TD and other early intervention teams. The TD team develops the IFSP by designing goals, objectives, and activities for the child and family in all areas of concern. These are based on the child's strengths and needs and the family's priorities and resources. Some TD programs develop the IFSP in a team meeting immediately following the assessment. Others meet again at a later time, after the assessment report has been written and shared with family and other team members.

Teams choosing to develop the IFSP at a later date may be tempted to formulate goals and objectives as they write the report. When this happens, the family members of the team are not really part of the goal development process. Instead, they may be in the position of approving goals already developed by the professional members of the team.

As members of the TD team, families determine their own level of involvement in the development of the IFSP. Some families feel most comfortable with a passive role, primarily answering the questions of other team members about their own goals for their child. Other families take a major role in IFSP development, seeking information from other team members, presenting the family's concerns and priorities, and insisting that these concerns be met. The goal of any TD program is to enable the family to choose its level of involvement. Programs can accomplish this goal by providing families with the information and support they need to make informed decisions about their participation.

The goal is to enable the family to choose its level of involvement.

The TD approach to program planning, which begins with the development of the IFSP, continues during regularly scheduled planning meetings. TD teams recognize that planning services for children and families is too complex a task to be accomplished entirely at the completion of an assessment or during any single meeting. Rather, the entire TD team meets regularly to monitor the implementation of the IFSP, to discuss the child and the family's response to the service plan activities, and to plan revisions as needed. These continuing team meetings in which each child and family is discussed are essential to the transdisciplinary approach. Although the team authorizes one person to carry out the IFSP along with the family, the primary service provider relies on regular consultation with and support from other team members to carry out the program successfully. At all times, the primary service provider is accountable to the team for family interventions.

Program Implementation

❑ Implementation of the program plan in the transdisciplinary approach depends on the process of role release. As discussed earlier in this chapter, the primary service provider uses the information and skills offered by other team members as well as the expertise of his or her own discipline to carry out the child's program. Careful and thoughtful selection of the primary service provider is important for the success of the TD approach.

Selection of the primary service provider is important.

Many variables are considered in the selection of the primary service provider, including personality factors and special skills and abilities that match the needs of the child and family. Other important considerations are caseload size and composition and logistics of scheduling and transportation. Use of a primary service provider enhances rapport between the family and the staff and avoids the interference with parent/child bonding that may be caused by excessive handling of the child in the clinical setting (Haynes, 1976).

The degree of family involvement in implementing the IFSP is determined by the family itself. Some parents are immediately able to function as co-facilitators for the IFSP. Others initially choose a less active role. Although TD program staff want families to be as fully involved as possible in implementing the IFSP, this is a choice that ultimately must be left to the family.

It is the intent of a TD program that the degree of the family's involvement results from a conscious, informed, and educated choice made from an array of possible options offered by the primary service provider. Included in this discussion with the family is the option that they may choose not to be fully involved in service delivery. Family participation in a TD program may be usefully regarded as a learning process that enables the family to move along a continuum from lesser to greater involvement as they become more familiar and comfortable with the program and the staff.

The primary service provider meets regularly with the TD team.

The primary service provider meets regularly with the entire TD team to discuss the implementation of the IFSP. These consultations ensure that each child and family have access to the full range of expertise of the whole team. Occasionally, however, the needs of some children and families are so complex in specific areas of disciplinary expertise that the primary service provider is not able to meet these needs, even with consultative support from other team members. In such cases, the team member from the discipline concerned provides direct therapy or intervention, together with the primary service provider and the family.

This role support is a vital component in implementing a TD service plan, yet many early intervention programs who consider themselves to be transdisciplinary do not provide for role support. In the interests of saving personnel costs, administrators sometimes eliminate the therapist positions from a program and appoint a staff member from a special or early education background to be the primary service provider. This staff member is then given some time in periodic consultation with therapists, and is expected to be responsible for single-handedly meeting the service needs of the child and family. This unfortunate arrangement does not allow individual children to receive direct therapy regardless of their needs.

Although these programs may call themselves transdisciplinary, such program practices are inimical to the TD approach. A program cannot be transdisciplinary without the presence of team members from several disciplines who share responsibility and accountability for meeting the needs of the child and family. Much misunderstanding of the TD model arises from the misapplication of the term "transdisciplinary" to describe such programs.

Implementing the IFSP requires that the professional members of the team meet regularly.

Another frequent problem for TD programs is that adequate team meeting time is not scheduled for case conferences. Implementing the IFSP in a TD program requires that the professional members of the team meet regularly to discuss child and family progress and problems. Individual members of the TD team cannot release the role of their disciplines unless they are assured that the primary service provider is able to implement the integrated plan developed and approved by the entire team. Primary service providers cannot use information from other disciplines well unless they receive regular advice, support, and authorization from team members in these disciplines.

Although administrators may be tempted to limit available team meeting time in order to serve more children and families, such a step is shortsighted. The quality of services provided by the TD team cannot be assured without the necessary team meeting time to reflect upon what is being offered. It should also be expected that a newly formed team or one with several relatively inexperienced members will need more meeting time than established teams or teams with more experienced members.

Reassessment

❑ When it is time for a child to be reassessed, the TD team conducts another arena assessment. The frequency of reassessments varies with the individual needs of the child and the success of the IFSP. Reassessments, especially for infants, are usually no further than 6 months apart. During reassessment, staff and parents again use an arena format to carefully examine the child's and family's accomplishment of program plan objectives.

Reassessments, especially for infants, are no further than 6 months apart.

Following the arena assessment, the IFSP is revised by the team. This is also a time for the staff team members to assess whether or not the services they provide meet the needs of the child and family as well as their own performance standards. The team then sets goals for improving interaction, consultation, and supervision.

IMPLICATIONS OF THE TRANSDISCIPLINARY MODEL FOR STAFF

❑ It is not enough for early intervention specialists to decide to form a transdisciplinary team and follow the framework just outlined. They must also be committed to the TD model and recognize the implications it has for their behavior and for the team. The TD model is most successfully accomplished when adequate care and forethought are given to the process of forming the team. Once team members are chosen, a system for continuing staff development must be designed and carried out.

A system for continuing staff development must be designed and carried out.

In some instances, forming the TD team means obtaining a commitment from existing staff to become transdisciplinary. In other circumstances, the program administrator will hire new staff to form the TD team. In either case, certain qualities contribute to the team's successful functioning.

Professionals who thrive on TD teams include those who enjoy working in highly interactive, fairly public group situations and who enjoy brainstorming, problem solving, and negotiating as a continuing part of their work. Most often, successful TD team members exhibit qualities of good sportsmanship. They also have the ability to tolerate a team decision that they may not completely support, but are willing to try for a time. All of these qualities are characteristic of people who are personally and professionally mature.

Successful TD team members exhibit qualities of good sportsmanship.

Because TD team members are interdependent, all must commit themselves to assist and support one another. This commitment is demonstrated by the following behaviors:

- Giving the time and energy necessary to teach, learn, and work across traditional disciplinary boundaries.
- Working toward making all decisions about the child and family by team consensus—that is, giving up disciplinary control.
- Supporting the family and one other team member as the child's primary service provider.
- Recognizing the family as the most important influence in the child's life and including them as equal team members who have a say in all decisions about the child's program.

The TD team must have a strong leader.

The TD team, like all other teams, must have a strong leader (Bennett, 1982; Holm & McCartin, 1978; Orlando, 1981). In addition to possessing all the qualities necessary for TD team members, the TD team leader must have the ability to foster a climate of mutual trust and support in which the team can thrive. The team leader must also have:

1. A belief in the transdisciplinary model and a strong commitment to making the model work.
2. The ability to listen carefully and review what is being said analytically.
3. The ability to participate in and manage a group.
4. The ability to organize and conduct meetings.
5. The ability to manage the team's time efficiently.
6. The ability to supervise staff, regardless of their disciplines.
7. The ability to facilitate decision making by consensus.
8. The ability to include families as equal team members.

Interpersonal dynamics is a strong factor influencing behavior in group settings.

Obviously, this list of attitudes and skills for TD team members and team leaders is not exhaustive. Interpersonal dynamics, too, is a strong factor influencing behavior in group settings. Never are two teams alike; every team has its own team issues, personality, and problems. The TD approach can only provide guidelines for forming teams and making them work well. It is up to the program administrator, team leader, and team members to have the desire and to create the atmosphere necessary for the TD approach to succeed.

ISSUES AND CONCLUSIONS

The TD approach sets high standards for communication and collaboration.

❑ The TD model is one reasonable, practical, and efficient method for providing services to infants and toddlers with special needs and their families. It is not the only high-quality model for early intervention programs. The TD team approach, however, does remedy many of the problems associated with multi- and interdisciplinary approaches and does set high standards for team communication and collaboration. The family focus of the TD model is also consistent with the newest federal early intervention legislation and best practices in the field.

The TD model has direct and immediate benefits for the child and family.

In addition to the benefits for the team already mentioned, the TD model also has direct and immediate benefits for the child and family. From the outset of their involvement with a transdisciplinary intervention team, the family are respected team members. They are informed that their knowledge of their child and their priorities for services for themselves and for the child are important and respected. These priorities form the basis of the individualized family service plan. The family is supported, not supplanted, by the TD team because the family carries out the service plan that they have helped design.

Parents have a great opportunity to feel invested in the program.

Relating primarily to one service provider over the course of their involvement with the program, the family has a good opportunity to develop an intense and lasting rapport with this person. In general, parents involved with a TD program have a great opportunity to feel invested in the program and become more effective advocates for themselves and their child.

Children enrolled in a TD program benefit from having their development viewed as an integrated and interactive process. Their intervention activities are designed to fit into their normal daily routines and to address their multiple developmental needs simultaneously. Children also benefit from having their families involved and from being required to interact primarily with only one person other than their parents. The end result of a child's participation in a TD program may be a more normal, responsive, and adaptable program plan because of the joint problem solving between the staff and family.

The TD approach recognizes that the greatest resources in any program are the families and the staff. The TD model offers early intervention professionals an opportunity to continuously evaluate the structure of their programs, their staffing patterns, and the quality of their direct services.

Vital to any high-quality program is this kind of continuing examination and refinement. The TD model offers a service delivery structure that forces a team to continually ask and seek credible answers to the question: "Are we making the most of our time and resources to best meet the needs of the children and families we serve?" But in the final analysis, the greatest joy and the pleasure of the transdisciplinary model is that it offers an ever growing and renewing positive experience for all involved—the children, the families, and the staff.

"Are we making the most of our time and resources to best meet the needs of the children and families we serve?"

REFERENCES

Bennett, F. C. (1982). The pediatrician and the interdisciplinary process. *Exceptional Children, 48*, 306-314.

Dyer, W. G. (1977). *Team building: Issues and alternatives.* Reading, MA: Addison-Wesley.

Fewell, R. R. (1983). The team approach to infant education. In S. G. Garwood & R. R. Fewell (Eds.),*Educating handicapped infants: Issues in development and intervention* (pp. 299-322). Rockville, MD: Aspen.

Golin, A. K. & Duncanis, A. J. (1981). *The interdisciplinary team.* Rockville, MD: Aspen.

Haynes, U. (1976). The National Collaborative Infant Project. In T. D. Tjossem (Ed.), *Intervention strategies for high risk infants and young children* (pp. 509-534). Baltimore, MD: University Park Press.

Haynes, U. (1983). *Holistic health care for children with developmental disabilities.* Baltimore, MD: University Park Press.

Holm, V. A. & McCartin, R. E. (1978). Interdisciplinary child development team: Team issues and training in interdisciplinariness. In K. E. Allen, V. A. Holm, & R. L. Schiefelbusch (Eds.), *Early intervention—A team approach* (pp. 97-122). Baltimore, MD: University Park Press.

Howard, J. (1982). The role of the pediatrician with young exceptional children and their families. *Exceptional Children, 48*, 316-322.

Linder, T. (1983). *Early childhood special education: Program development and administration.* Baltimore, MD: Brookes.

Orlando, C. (1981). Multidisciplinary team approaches in the assessment of handicapped preschool children. *Topics in Early Childhood Special Education, 1*(2), 23-30.

Peterson, N. (1987). *Early intervention for handicapped and at-risk children: An introduction to early childhood special education.* Denver, CO: Love.

United Cerebral Palsy National Collaborative Infant Project (1976). *Staff development handbook: A resource for the transdisciplinary process.* New York: United Cerebral Palsy Associations of America.

Woodruff, G. (1985). *Project Optimus training materials.* Unpublished manuscript.

Woodruff, G., & Hanson, C. (1987). *Project KAI training packet.* Unpublished manuscript.

9.
Program Evaluation:
The Key to Quality Programming

Lawrence J. Johnson

Need for evaluation has intensified.

❑ With the passage of P.L. 99-457, services for handicapped infants and toddlers, ages birth to 3 have reached a critical crossroad. Within the next 5 years we are likely to see a dramatic increase in services to these children. However, much still needs to be done before mandated services become a reality. Although states can receive financial support for providing services for handicapped infants and toddlers under the age of 3, they will not be mandated to do so. As a result, the need for systematic evaluation of programs serving these children has intensified. It is likely that policy makers will raise many questions about programming for these children. They will ask what programming options are available and what are the merits and drawbacks of each. They will wonder what impact these programs have on children, their families, and the community. Undoubtedly, they will eventually ask if the cost of establishing and operating such programs is justified. It is up to us to make use of comprehensive evaluation plans that can provide the answers to these and other questions that are sure to be raised. Legislatures must be provided with reliable and valid data when they consider alternatives for providing services to children from birth to age 3.

Legislatures must be provided with reliable and valid data.

Data can be beneficial.

Although providing valid information to policy makers is an important function of evaluation, it is not the only function. Data collected from good evaluation plans can be beneficial to early childhood special education programs at many different levels. From an interviewer's perspective, it can provide information by which to make instructional decisions, monitor child and family progress, and document accountability. From a parent's perspective, it can be used to examine child and family programs and as an indication of program effectiveness. Finally, policy makers can use evaluation data to make informed decisions about program management, using information about the costs, benefits, and drawbacks of various program alternatives.

Unfortunately, the development and implementation of good evaluation plans is one aspect of early childhood special education that has not always been adequate (see Dunst & Rheingrover, 1981; Odom & Fewell, 1983; Simeonsson, Cooper, & Schiener, 1982; White & Casto, 1984; White, Mastropieri, & Casto, 1984; Wolery, 1987; Wolery & Bailey, 1984). Several factors contribute to this situation. Administrators often lack the knowledge or resources to carry out a comprehensive evaluation and may also fear what such an examination might reveal. Interveners are sometimes resistant to participating in evaluation efforts, and they see program evaluation as an extra burden. They may believe that evaluation efforts interfere with what they are doing, but have no particular benefits for the program or them. At the same time, however, interveners have always evaluated what they were doing. They identify child needs, make plans to meet those needs, and monitor child progress, although the rigor with which this is done varies.

Interviewers are sometimes resistant to evaluation efforts.

One problem lies in the mistaken belief that evaluation is separate from intervention and essentially involves the collection of a series of pre/post measures. In actuality, current thinking on evaluation suggests that there should be a strong link between programming and evaluation. This notion was eloquently presented by Bricker and Littman (1982) in their article, "Intervention and Evaluation: The Inseparable Mix." They argued that evaluation data should provide the basis for intervention and help determine the value of the intervention for groups of children. The viewpoint presented in this chapter is congruent with Bricker and Littman and others who have stressed the link between evaluation and

There should be a strong link between programming and evaluation.

intervention (Goodwin & Driscoll, 1980; Isaac & Michael, 1981; Wolery, 1987; Wolery & Bailey, 1984). The evaluation process presented here has three phases—input, process, and outcome—and is based on the evaluation models of Tyler, Scriven, and Stufflebeam. The phases are interwoven into a single process that begins with program planning, continues through implementation, and then turns its attention to program impact. For clarity and efficiency, this evaluation process will be referred to as *triphase evaluation*; however, this author does not claim that this process represents a new model. Rather, it is a common-sense approach to conducting a comprehensive program evaluation.

Evaluation has three phases.

Evaluation models that form the basis of the triphase evaluation process are presented here; the triphase evaluation process is described in detail and examples are provided; and finally, critical components of a high-quality evaluation plan are discussed.

EVALUATION MODELS

❏ In this section, three evaluation models are summarized. They are but a small sample of the many models that have been proposed for program evaluation (see Morris & Fitz-Gibbon, 1978 for a more complete description of evaluation models), but they have made significant contributions to thinking about program evaluation, and they form the basis of the triphase evaluation process. Strengths and weaknesses of the models are highlighted to give the reader a sense of their contributions to the triphase evaluation process.

TYLER'S OBJECTIVE MODEL

❏ The Tylerian model focuses on the delineation of objectives and measurement of progress on these objectives (Tyler, 1942, 1958, 1971, 1974). Simply stated, a set of objectives is identified, procedures to assess their attainment are established, data are collected, and judgments are made as to the success of the program based on child and/or family performance on the identified objectives.

There are several advantages to this model. Its simplicity makes it easy to understand and interpret. Its focus on measurable objectives encourages accountability and provides teachers with a means to demonstrate progress to parents and administrators. Finally, it includes the intervener as an integral member of the evaluation process and employs more than just pre/post measures.

Simplicity makes it easy to understand and interpret.

Ironically, the simplicity of the model and reliance on behavioral objectives are also cited as weaknesses. Linking evaluation so closely to objectives prevents actions not easily measured by objectives from being included in the evaluation process. Many of the most important educational outcomes are not amenable to behavioral statements. The simplification of such outcomes into objectives can trivialize them, or worse, prevent them from being included in the program. Finally, outcomes not tied to objectives are not examined. This is a serious flaw, because a program can have a dramatic positive or negative impact that is not directly related to a specific objective.

Outcomes not tied to objectives are not examined.

SCRIVEN'S GOAL-FREE MODEL

❑ Concerned with the potential biasing and limiting impact of linking the evaluation process so closely to objectives, Scriven (1967, 1973, 1974) proposed goal-free evaluation. Unlike the objective-based model, interveners are not directly involved in the evaluation process; instead, an outside evaluator with little knowledge of the program is employed. This evaluator does not need to know what the objectives are, but is concerned with identifying the actual impact of the program, intended or unintended. Scriven (1974) believes that knowing the goals of the program encourages the evaluator to look for alleged effects instead of actual effects. The evaluator's role is to discover the actual effects of the program, which may differ markedly from the program's stated goals.

Interviewers are not directly involved.

A goal-free approach to evaluation has several advantages. First, the evaluator is placed in a discovery role and is not limited to determining whether or not goals were obtained. Second, the search for unintended effects is positive and prevents tunnel vision. Someone with a new perspective can notice things about the program that those within the program or those focusing on the objectives of the program have missed. Finally, because the evaluator is independent from the program, he or she is in a better position to evaluate it critically.

The evaluator is placed in a discovery role.

Despite these advantages, the lack of structure can be a liability in this approach. Without clear objectives, the evaluation has no standard against which the effectiveness of the program can be consistently applied. This process does not include interveners in evaluation and is conducted after the fact, rather than being integral to the program from the beginning.

Lack of structure can be a liability.

STUFFLEBEAM'S DECISION-MAKING MODEL

❑ In this model, evaluation is defined as a decision-making process involving three steps: (a) delineating the information to be collected, (b) obtaining the information, and (c) providing the information to decision makers (Stufflebeam, 1971, 1974). Information collected through this process can then be used by decision makers to judge the merit of options presented to them.

There are four kinds of evaluation.

Stufflebeam has stated that there are four kinds of evaluation: context, input, process, and product. Within each of these kinds of evaluation are four types of decisions that can be made in an educational setting. In context evaluation, the decisions to be made relate to planning. The primary purpose is to identify needs of individuals to be served by the program and identify objectives to meet those needs. The decisions of concern in input evaluation relate to the structuring of programs to meet the needs of the individuals to be served. Primary areas for examination are issues related to such areas as program management, staffing, and budgeting. In process evaluation, decisions relate to implementation of the program. Data are collected to determine any flaws in the program as it is being implemented. In product evaluation, decisions relate to what Stufflebeam has termed *recycling*, which refers to decisions being made to continue, terminate, modify, or refocus the program.

Comprehensiveness is one of its greatest strengths.

The comprehensiveness of this model is one of its greatest strengths. The interrelationship between the four types of evaluation encourages a focus beyond just pre/post measures. This model presents evaluation as a continuous cycle that builds on information collected in the other types of evaluation. Finally, it provides a vehicle to establish accountability in implementing the program as well as judging the impact of the program. However, the comprehensiveness of the model makes it complex, difficult to coordinate, and expensive.

TRIPHASE EVALUATION

❑ The basis of the Triphase evaluation process is Stufflebeam's decision-making model. As with Stufflebeam's model, the Triphase process is comprehensive and concerns itself with all aspects of the program. However, interrelationship between the phases is stressed more than in Stufflebeam's model. In Stufflebeam's model, evaluation is presented as the coordination of types of evaluation context—input, process, and product—that are used depending on the decision to be made. Evaluation from the Triphase perspective is seen as one process made up of three interwoven phases: input, process, and outcome. During each of these phases the evaluation plan focuses on a different aspect of the program. In the input phase, attention is directed at determining child, family, and community needs and developing a program to meet them. In the process phase, attention is directed at monitoring progress toward objectives and determining whether or not there are any discrepancies between what was proposed and what is being implemented. These phases build on each other, with the input and process phases being the most critical to the implementation of a good program. The influence of Tyler can be seen in the emphasis on behavioral objectives. The development of objectives and the monitoring of progress toward objectives is the backbone of the model. However, recognizing the concerns of Scriven's goal-free evaluation, efforts are not limited to performance on objectives.

Evaluation is made up of three interwoven phases.

The input and process phases are considered part of formative evaluation, which is the collection of evaluation data to aid in program planning and implementation. The outcome phase is part of summative evaluation in that the purpose of data collection is to provide information on the impact of the program. Unfortunately, people often think of evaluation as being equivalent to summative evaluation and do not consider the importance of formative evaluation. During formative phases, when problems are detected, changes can be made to the original plan to avoid potential disaster. However, in the summative phases, by the time problems are detected it is too late, and we must wait until next time to correct mistakes or change project orientation. On the other hand, it is not enough to document the proper implementation of a project; we must also determine whether or not it has a meaningful impact on the children, their families, and the community. Clearly all three phases are critical to the evaluation plan and the program. In the following sections, each of these phases is discussed in greater detail.

Outcome is part of summative evaluation.

All three phases are critical.

INPUT EVALUATION

❑ The focus of the input phase is on assessing the needs of children and their families and developing a plan to meet those needs. An important step in this phase is to examine services that currently exist and compare them to what is being proposed to meet identified needs. In other words, after needs are identified we must determine whether or not there are any discrepancies between what is, what ought to be, and what is being proposed. Based on information obtained in this step of the evaluation plan, recommendations can be made for revisions in the proposed plan to address any discrepancies that are uncovered. This phase of the evaluation plan is vital to the development of a high-quality program. If the needs of children and their families are not adequately identified, everything we do in an attempt to meet their needs will be flawed. Beyond this problem, it is equally important to ensure that the program has the resources to carry out the proposed plan and that the plan is not a duplication of already existing services. Duplication of services is particularly common with programs serving exceptional children ages birth to 3. Many different agencies serve these children and their families, and unfortunately the linkages between these programs are not always strong. As a result, valuable resources are wasted, possibly preventing needed services from being instituted.

Recommendations can be made for revisions in the plan.

Duplication of services is common.

From an intervener's viewpoint, input evaluation is a concern every time a new child and family enter the program. The intervener must assess child and family needs and then develop a plan to meet those needs. This information can be used at a program level to keep in touch with the needs of the broader community. Essentially, the intervener contributes to the evaluation plan by forging a strong link between assessment and programming.

The intervener contributes the link between assessment and programming.

From a program perspective, input evaluation is particularly important when a new program or a new component of an existing program is being developed. One of the first steps in program development is to conduct a needs assessment. Borg and Gall (1983) defined a need as being a discrepancy between an existing set of conditions and a desired set of conditions. Using this definition, conducting a needs assessment becomes more than providing parents or teachers a brief questionnaire to gather their perceptions of what is needed. Rather, it is a comprehensive plan by which data are collected from several sources. The steps outlined below can help ensure the systematic collection of needs assessment data. They are equally useful in collecting outcome evaluation data. They will be discussed in detail here and will be referred to in the section on outcome evaluation.

Data are collected from several sources.

Determine Key Elements

❑ The first step in the process is to determine the purpose of the needs assessment and the clients and audiences for the needs assessment. A helpful technique is to develop a set of goals or questions to be addressed and then prioritize the goals to ensure that the critical data are collected. In this way some of the less important goals can be sacrificed if the process becomes unduly complex or resources dwindle.

Develop a set of goals.

As an example, let us suppose that a small school decides to expand its preschool program to meet the needs of handicapped children from birth to age 3. Recognizing the importance of a good input evaluation, the administrators would probably decide to conduct a needs assessment. They might identify the *clients* as the handicapped children and their families within the community and the *consumers* of the needs assessment as parents of handicapped children, program administrators, and interveners. The following prioritized questions are examples of a set that the small school might use to guide their needs and assessment:

1. How many handicapped children ages birth to 3 need services?
2. What are the characteristics of these children and their families?
3. Who is providing services to these children and their families?
4. What alternatives within this community could meet the needs of these children and their families?

Identify Sources of Information

❑ The next step in conducting the needs assessment is to determine the sources of information from which to answer identified questions. In addition, a data collection method must be developed that will obtain the needed information efficiently and accurately. Usually we must collect information from a variety of sources and therefore need a variety of methods for collecting data. For example, in the sample questions presented in the previous section, no one data sources would be able to provide information to answer adequately all the questions generated. Therefore, we must use multiple sources of data to be sure that we collect all the information to determine child, family, and community needs. Typical data collection methods include unobtrusive measures, observation, interviews, questionnaires, and tests. These methods are equally useful in the outcome phase of the evaluation plan.

We need a variety of methods for collecting data.

Unobtrusive Measures. These sources are classified as nonreactive because children and their families are not required to change their daily routine and are, for the most part, not aware of the data gathering. As Casto (in press) pointed out, unobtrusive measures have been used infrequently as an evaluation tool by programs serving handicapped infants and toddlers but could provide valuable, inexpensive information. For example, if we were interested in determining parent concerns we might examine the books checked out of a parent-resource library or the toys checked out of a toy-lending library.

Unobtrusive measures could provide valuable information.

Another important source of information can be the records and documents of agencies that might come into contact with children from birth to age 3 and their families. For example, as Casto (in press) noted, many of the children who eventually receive services in programs for handicapped toddlers and infants are graduates of neonatal intensive care units (NICUs). Fortunately, most of these units have computerized data bases and routinely collect extensive information on NICU patients. This information can be useful in locating children, determining numbers of potential clients, and providing critical family information. Much of this information, however, is confidential, so releases need to be obtained. When such releases are not feasible, a protocol can be developed with someone in the agency who can summarize the information of interest across clients, without violating individuals' rights of privacy.

Observations. Observations to collect needs assessment information are generally made by interveners at a programming level to determine performance of children and families in relation to specific objectives. The essence of behavioral observations is the systematic recording of operationally defined behaviors. When operational definitions are properly done, ambiguity is reduced to a minimum. Definitions should be based

Definitions should be based on observable characteristics of behavior.

on observable characteristics of the behavior, clearly stated, with variations of the behavior defined so that rules can be established for their scoring. Alberto and Troutman (1982) delineated several dimensions of behavior that can be recorded, which depend upon the type of behavior targeted and the circumstances of the evaluation. For example:

1. *Frequency*: A count of how often the behavior occurs.
   Example: Susan had nine tantrums this week.
2. *Rate*: Frequency data expressed in a ratio with time.
   Example: On the average, Susan has six tantrums per week.
3. *Duration*: A measure of how long the behavior lasts.
   Example: Susan's last tantrum lasted 40 minutes.
4. *Latency*: A measure of how long it takes before a new behavior is started.
   Example: It took 20 minutes for Susan to stop her tantrum when she was removed from the other children.
5. *Topography*: A description of what the behavior looks like.
   Example: Susan shrieks, kicks her heels, and throws herself on the floor when she has a tantrum.
6. *Force*: A description of the intensity of the behavior.
   Example: Susan cries so hard during a tantrum that her veins stick out of her neck and her face turns bright red.
7. *Locus*: A description of where the behavior occurs.
   Example: Susan seems to have her tantrums in the bathroom or the hall.

The dimension of behavior recorded depends on the focus of the evaluation. The first four dimensions of behavior are useful when we want to quantify behavior, while the last three dimensions are of interest when we are interested in the quality of the behavior. The reader is referred to Alberto and Troutman (1982) for an excellent description of the issues and concerns of collecting observational data.

Conducting interviews is a powerful tool.

Interviews. Conducting interviews is an extremely powerful tool for the collection of needs assessment data. At its simplest level interviewing is simply asking questions and recording the responses. There are three basic interview structures: unstructured, semistructured, and structured (Patton, 1980).

In unstructured interviews, the interviewer may have a general objective but believes this objective is best met by allowing respondents to respond in their own words in their own time. This interview structure is very useful to help identify issues for further examination that were previously unknown or when information to be collected is potentially damaging.

Lack of structure makes interviewer vulnerable to bias.

However, the lack of structure makes such interviews vulnerable to bias and can often produce uninterpretable information.

Semistructured interviews are built around a core of questions that all respondents are asked, but they allow the interviewer to branch off and explore responses in greater depth. This structure helps ensure that information of interest is collected from all respondents and allows the opportunity to uncover issues or relationships that were unanticipataed or too complex to be identified by simple questions. Again, however, the unstructured component increases the chances of subjective biases. Because the interviewer follows up on responses to specific questions, there is the potential for the interviewer to lead the interviewee to a desired response.

Structured interviews are very similar to objective questionnaires. The interviewer reads a specific set of questions and might even provide the respondent with a set of responses from which to choose. Clarification of responses is not allowed or is restricted to very narrow limits. This structure reduces the potential of leading interviewees but precludes the uncovering of unexpected issues or complex relationships that are not easily represented in responses to simple objective questions.

Structured interviews are similar to objective questionnaires.

In most cases, the semistructured method has the best chance to provide the most useful information. To maximize this method's potential, steps should be taken to minimize biases and prevent the interviewer from leading the respondent. One helpful technique is to develop a set of acceptable probes that can be used to encourage the respondent to elaborate on responses. Also, the interview should be piloted. In this way a decision can be made as to whether questions in the interview elicit useful information and the interviewing technique of the interviewer can be examined. Based on the pilot test, questions can be modified, probes can be refined, and interviewers can receive feedback on their interviewing technique. By listening through an interview, good probes can be reinforced and leading probes can be identified and alternatives suggested. The following guidelines may be helpful in the development of good interview questions (adapted from Udinsky, Osterlind, & Lynch, 1981):

Develop a set of acceptable probes.

1. Word questions clearly and encourage effective communication between the interviewer and the respondent.

2. Make respondents aware of the purpose of each question they are asked.

3. Be sure that the population from which the respondents have been selected actually has the information being sought and that the interview questions permit the reasonable recovery of this information.

4. Avoid leading questions; that is, questions that suggest a desirable or preferred answer.

5. Ensure that a clear frame of reference is provided for each question, so that all respondents hear questions in the same way.

Another issue to be decided is how information obtained from the interview is to be recorded. Tape recording and writing summaries of each answer after the interview are methods generally used. Writing during the interview is discouraged because it tends to inhibit the interviewee. Tape recording is superior because it allows the interviewer and others to review the interview and prevents the possibility of bias that arises from having the interviewer summarize responses.

Writing is discouraged.

Although we generally think of interviews as being a one-on-one endeavor, a group interview can be extremely useful. Using this technique, the interviewer holds a meeting with the group from which information is being sought, such as parents, interveners, and administrators. The interviewer then explains the purpose of the meeting and breaks the group into a set of several small working groups, each one addressing a specific issue or question. The small groups present their responses to the larger group. Responses are then discussed and refined until there is a group consensus.

Problems are length and complexity of questions.

Questionnaires. One of the most commonly used data collection techniques for needs assessments is the questionnaire. Two of the greatest problems with questionnaires are length and complexity of questions. There is a tendency to keep adding questions to a questionnaire because the response on the question might be "interesting." It is important to keep the purpose of the questionnaire in mind and include only data specific to that purpose. It is equally important to state questions in unambiguous language. In other words, say it as simply as you can.

The majority of the questions on the questionnaire should be objective, with a set of alternatives. However, the inclusion of open-ended questions allows respondents to elaborate on answers and present concerns that were not reflected in the objective questions. Open-ended questions also help clarify ratings of respondents by providing a different source of data that reinforce interpretation of ratings or identify areas where caution should be exercised because of contradictions.

Often respondents are asked to rate specific statements along some kind of scale. In this case, one must decide to use an even-numbered or odd-numbered rating scale. For example, consider the following scale: SA = strongly agree, A = agree, U = undecided, D = disagree, and SD = strongly disagree, applied to the following statement using an odd and even response set:

I need information on appropriate feeding techniques.

Example 1	SA	A	U	D	SD
Example 2	SA	A	D	SD	

In the first example undecided responses can be confusing. Is the person truly undecided or does he or she choose the middle ground to avoid making an affirmative or negative decision? On the other hand, the second example forces the individual to make an affirmative or negative decision about the statement and increases the scorer's ability to interpret ratings of statements. In situations where a clear decision is wanted, an even-numbered scale is superior. Udinsky, Osterlind, and Lynch (1981) have provided detailed guidelines for the construction of questionnaires.

Importance of selecting instruments cannot be stressed enough.

Tests. Tests are another technique frequently used for collecting information in early childhood special education research. These can be particularly useful to interveners when they are attempting to assess child and family needs (see Chapter 3 for a complete discussion of this issue). Tests are usually easy to administer and score, and they have an aura of objectivity and rigor (Casto, in press). However, as many have pointed out (e.g., Garwood, 1982; Ramey, Campbell, & Wasik, 1982; Zigler & Balla, 1982), assessment devices used with handicapped toddlers and infants are unreliable, and they are often invalid for the purposes for which they are being used. Instruments that have the greatest potential are those that are developmentally based and can be used as a tool to help identify needs and then monitor progress throughout the intervention. The importance of selecting appropriate instruments cannot be stressed enough. The following questions can be useful in selecting appropriate tests:

1. Is this instrument appropriate for the population that it is to be used with?

2. What is the purpose of the instrument, and more importantly, is the purpose compatible with data collection needs?

3. Will this instrument provide the best set of information or is there a more appropriate instrument or data collection procedure?

Develop a Management Plan

❑ A critical step is the development of a plan for collecting data from the identified sources. A schedule that delineates data-gathering procedures, data synthesis and analysis, and reporting activities is the backbone of the plan. Without a plan data may be collected haphazardly and key data may be missed. Often a time line such as the one in Figure 1 is helpful in summarizing when activities will be initiated and completed. In addition, it is important to delineate individuals who will be responsible for collecting specific data. The staff loading chart contained in Table 1 is an example of a simple way to keep track of these individuals and the data for which they are responsible.

A schedule is the backbone.

Collect Data

❑ Data should be collected according to steps delineated in the management plan. The time line and staff-loading chart should be referred

Figure 1. *An Example of a Time Line for the Collection and Analysis of Needs Assessment Data.*

	July Aug Sept Oct Nov Dec Jan Feb Mar Apr May June
Hire project staff	├────┤
Train observers	├────┤
Train interviewers	├────┤
Collect teacher questionnaire data	├──┤
Collect principal questionnaire data	├──┤
Select subjects to be interviewed	├────┤
Select subjects to be observed	├────┤
Collect interview data	├────┤
Collect observation data	├──────┤
Collect referral data	├────┤
Analyze data	├──────┤
Prepare summary report	├────┤

Table 1. *Example of a Staff-Loading Chart for Collection of Evaluation Data.*

Source	What	When	Who Responsible
1. Individual teachers	1.1 Attitude survey	1.1 As recruited	1.1 Child care liaison
	1.2 Individual plan (teacher objectives)	1.2 Postconsultation (when individual plan completed)	1.2 Child care liaison
		1.3 As recruited	
2. Groups of teachers in centers	2.1 Checklist of workshops	2.1 Returned by 9/30/86	2.1 Child care liaison
3. Directors (in directors' group)	3.1 Checklist of workshops	3.1 Returned by 7/30/86	3.1 Child care liaison
4. Workshop attendees	4.1 Postworkshop evaluations	4.1 Are attending workshops	4.1 Child care liaison, presenters
5. Individual teachers	5.1 Critical inci- dence ques- tionnaires or multiple choice questions (satisfaction questions on posttest)	5.1 Recruited	5.1 Child care liaison
		5.2 Postconsultation	5.2 Child care liaison
6. Parents	6.1 Interviews	6.1 Midway through and after the intervention	6.2 Data collectors

to often to ensure that data are collected as planned. Changes in original plans should be thought out carefully. Once data collection is under way, there is a tendency to lose track of the original plan or to change the plan because of various data collection pressures. When this occurs, the quality of data invariably suffers, making interpretation impossible. Nothing is more frustrating than spending staff time and program resources collecting data and finding out after all the data have been collected that time and money have been wasted because key data are missing, or data collected are flawed, making interpretation impossible.

Analyze and Interpret Data

Analysis is bringing order to data.

❏ The purpose of this step is twofold: to analyze data and to interpret the analysis. Analysis is the process of bringing order to the data by grouping them into meaningful descriptive units, examining data trends within units, and making comparisons between units. Interpretation involves attaching meaning to data trends within and between descriptive units. Techniques or tools are available to aid in the analysis of data, whereas interpretation relies on the evaluator's ability to see and explain meaningful trends and relationships.

Two distinct types of data have been discussed thus far in this chapter. One type lends itself to being quantified and includes such things as frequency counts of behavior, ratings on a scale, or scores on a test. This type of data is categorized as *quantitative* data. The second type is not as easily quantified and includes such things as responses to open-ended questions, descriptions of behavior, and written records.

This type of data is called *qualitative* because these sources provide an indication of the quality of the behavior under study. Both types of data are useful in determining needs and program impact. The techniques used to analyze and interpret these data sources, however, are different. A complete discussion of analysis techniques available for qualitative and quantitative data is beyond the scope of this chapter, and the reader is referred to Borg and Gall (1983) for a more complete discussion of data analysis techniques. In the following section, brief descriptions of analysis techniques for qualitative and quantitative sources are presented and the rationale for their use is examined.

Quantitative Analysis. The analysis of quantitative data is generally performed through some type of statistical procedure. Statistics can be a useful tool for summarizing large data sets, comparing groups, establishing causal influences, and predicting future performance. Statistical procedures can be broken down into three basic types: descriptive, inferential, and nonparametric. Nonparametric procedures are less commonly used and will not be discussed here; the interested reader is referred to Siegel (1956).

Statistics can be useful for summarizing large data sets.

The purpose of *descriptive* procedures is to summarize data systematically to make them more manageable and understandable (Kirk, 1978). As the name suggests, descriptive statistics are used to describe the data that have been collected. They are used to describe average scores (mean, median, or mode), the degree that scores differ from one another (standard deviation), and the degree of association between two groups of subjects (correlations). The advantage of descriptive procedures is that they enable us to summarize large amounts of data in a few descriptive statistics, which greatly aids our ability to interpret findings (Borg & Gall, 1983). A caveat should be noted, however; descriptive statistics often oversimplify data. Rarely are the mean, standard deviation, or other descriptive statistics representative of any one subject from which the data were collected.

Descriptive statistics are used.

Descriptive statistics often oversimplify data.

Common to inferential procedures are such statistical tests as *t*-tests and *F*-tests. The purpose of inferential procedures is to draw conclusions about the whole population from a sample or samples of subjects drawn from the population. These statistical tests are used to determine the likelihood of an observed occurrence happening by mere chance. If the chances of the occurrence are slim, then it is concluded that something systematic has happened, that is, that there is something different about the group that received intervention compared to the group that did not receive intervention. If the research design is sound, a convincing case can be made that it is the intervention that accounts for this difference.

Before we move on to qualitative procedures, it is important to spend some time discussing the limitations of statistics. An understanding of these limitations is crucial if one is to make intelligent decisions regarding their use. First, statistics will not compensate for an evaluation that is poorly designed and conducted. If the data are ambiguous, the statistical analyses will provide answers of equal uncertainty. Second, the absence

Statistical significance tells little about practical significance.

of statistical confirmation does not "prove" that there was no relationship or impact. It is only through repeated analysis that confirmation of the lack of existence of a relationship is obtained. Finally, statistical significance tells very little about practical significance. With a large enough sample, small differences between groups can be statistically different but be of little practical significance.

This is not to say that statistical analyses should be discouraged in evaluations. Statistical procedures can have extraordinary power when properly applied. However, it is important to realize there are limitations to their use. For the field-based practitioner in the small class setting, practical significance should be the major consideration in evaluation of impact.

Qualitative Procedures. Qualitative procedures are used to analyze data collected from open-ended questions, interviews, observations, and other data collection methods that provide "softer" data. The procedures can provide a richness of information that is often difficult to achieve with quantitative methods. This richness, however, extracts a price. A qualitative data base typically consists of vast amounts of information from a variety of sources such as written notes on observations, interviews, written impressions, transcripts of electronic recordings, and anecdotal reports. Their management, reduction, and analysis represents a major challenge for the evaluator. The reader is referred to Miles and Huberman (1984) or Patton (1980) for specific guidelines for analyzing qualitative data.

Qualitative data consists of vast amounts of information.

Miles and Huberman (1984) described three components or activities for analysis of qualitative data: data reduction, data displays, and conclusion-drawing/verification. *Data reduction* refers to transforming the large body of written and verbal data collected during observations into clusters, themes, and summaries for the purpose of drawing conclusions. A common technique for the reduction or analysis of qualitative data is through a content analysis. Berelson (1952) described content analysis as a method by which the manifest content of communication can be described objectively and systematically. Typically, the manifest content of communication is clarified by a series of systematic procedures in which (a) the communication is divided into separate units or blocks for analysis; (b) coding categories are developed, defined, and refined; and (c) units of analysis are scored according to the previously developed categories.

Conclusion drawing is based on interpretation of data trends.

Reduction leads to *data displays*, using matrices to organize the categories that most accurately characterize the data as a whole. Miles and Huberman (1984) have suggested that graphic, matrix, or charted displays result in greater accessibility of data than do narrative explanations alone. *Conclusion drawing* follows the data display component and is based on the evaluators' interpretation of data trends.

Although the three data analysis stages occur one after the other, each phase impacts the other phases in a cyclical pattern. Thus, the ultimate interpretation of the data is achieved only after a number of cycles of interaction of data reduction/analysis, data display, and conclusions. The ongoing nature of a qualitative analysis is a critical feature of this approach. Interpretation is not a separate phase; rather, the evaluator attaches meanings and patterns to the data as they are being collected. (See Miles, 1979 for a more detailed discussion of problems associated with qualitative analysis.) Conclusions may be drawn, but they are subject to verification as observations proceed. Human beings are notoriously poor processors of information; judgment is readily flawed, and steps should be taken to prevent misinterpretations. Miles and Huberman (1984) have suggested some strategies, summarized here, that can be used to avoid such misinterpretations:

1. The evaluator should check for data representativeness, that is, assume the data base was derived from a nonrepresentative sample. For example, a check could involve the study of additional cases or the examination of contradictory cases. Similarly, the evaluator should check for reactivity effects of data collectors. In other words, are data representative of what actually occurs in the natural setting?

2. The evaluator should use multiple measurement techniques, referred to as *triangulation*. Since each form of data has its own special weakness, validity can be assessed by the convergence of different data types on the same observation. For example, the determination that an intervener is skilled would carry great weight if it were based on the evaluator's observations, comments from the intervener's peers, child progress, administrator reactions, and any number of other sources. Findings that cannot be substantiated by multiple sources might warrant further examination or be treated with caution.

3. The evaluator should weight items in the data base in terms of their "trustworthiness." A healthy attitude is to assume that data are questionable unless substantial evidence is provided to suggest otherwise.

4. Finally, there are a number of checks the evaluator can employ that are analogous to the considerations of an empirical study: (a) replicating a conclusion in other parts of the data, (b) checking out the plausibility of alternative explanations, (c) looking for negative evidence, and (d) ruling out spurious relationships.

The "fidelity" of qualitative data to reality will always be an issue. In the absence of a body of structured techniques and external checks, the method can very easily degenerate into meaningless, idiosyncratic observations. Qualitative evaluation techniques can be valid and systematic and can provide a rich source of information that is unlikely to be obtained from other sources. Moreover, they can enhance the meaning of quantitative findings and provide greater insight to statistically significant or nonsignificant findings (see Fujiura & Johnson, 1986, for a more complete discussion of this issue).

Qualitative evaluation techniques can be valid.

Develop the Program

❑ The final step in the input phase is to develop an intervention program that will meet the needs of the community. This is an ongoing process, in that plans are being developed throughout the collection of information. As tentative plans are developed, they are revised as new data are obtained and summarized. Eventually tentative plans are refined into goals. Goals are then subdivided into more specific objectives. As an example, Figure 2 contains a program goal, related objectives, and activities that were developed in Project APPLE (Gingold & Karnes, 1986) to meet identified community needs. As can be seen in this example, these are management objectives that will be of primary concern during the process evaluation phase of the evaluation plan. In addition, a set of

Tentative plans are refined into goals.

Figure 2. Sample of Goals and Related Objectives, Activities, and Process Evaluation Activities Used in Project APPLE at the Developmental Services Center of Champaign, Illinois.

GOAL 4 To demonstrate comprehensive training and support services for parents of high-risk infants.

Objective 4.1 To develop and maintain a system of ongoing assessment of the education, training, and support needs of parents whose children are receiving early intervention services.

Activities 4.1 (1) The Needs Assessment Inventory is currently administered to families upon entering the program. (2) In addition, after 6 months in the program, a questionnaire will be administered which assesses parent satisfaction and addresses parent's interests in additional training and support.

Process Evaluation 4.1 (1) The Needs Assessment Inventory will be in each child's file within 2 weeks of the child's team assessment. (2) The Family Involvement Checklist will be in each child's file within 7 months of initial team assessment.

Objective 4.2 To maintain and enhance the range of parent activities which will satisfy the assessed needs for training, education, or support.

Activities 4.2 (1) In order to be able to meet expressed interests and needs of parents, the staff must be able to develop groups with variable schedules, addressing a variety of topics. Consequently, an annual schedule of parent activities cannot be arranged in advance, but staff can anticipate several short series of information-based meetings for parents. In addition, several support groups will be anticipated. These may be organized according to specific problems (e.g., acting out behavior) or parental characteristics (e.g., single parents). Informal parent-baby play groups may also be organized. (2) Parent-to-parent linkages will continue to be made at the request of parents and of other social service agencies. (3) Parent groups will be coordinated by a program development specialist.

Process Evaluation 4.2 (1) During the first 9 months of the project, at least four information-based meetings will be held at times convenient to parents, with child care provided, on topics of expressed interest to parents. (2) Documentation of all Parent-to-parent linkages will be kept on file.

Objective 4.3 To develop and maintain an individualized service program for each parent.

Activities 4.3 In order to plan each parent's involvement in the program, an individualized plan will be drawn up for the parent(s) of each child. This will be a simplified IEP which specifies activities which each parent will participate in. It will be mutually agreed upon by the parent and by the case manager. This plan will include possible participation in group activities, participation in the child's program, any particular training the parents want or need, and potential referral and linkage to other services.

Process Evaluation 4.3 (1) Within 2 weeks of each child's staffing, the parent's program plan will be in each child's chart. (2) Parent program plans will be monitored at 6-month intervals, as are the children's plans, for progress toward achieving the objectives set forth.

Objective 4.4 To develop and maintain special training and support services for parents who are identified as delayed, disabled, or potentially abusive/neglectful.

(Continued)

Figure 2. Sample of Goals and Related Objectives, Activities,and Process Evaluation Activities Used in Project APPLE at the Developmental Services Center of Champaign, Illinois. (Continued)

Activities 4.4 (1) The proposed project director and associates of Children's Services are currently developing materials for use with low-functioning or developmentally disabled parents. These materials are being developed with the assistance of a grant from the Governor's Planning Council. They are directed at helping adults understand normal child development and parenting issues and are to be used with small groups of parents.

Process Evaluation 4.4 Copies of session outlines including agendas, attendance records, and parent evaluations of sessions will be on file. Similar documentation will be on file as subsequent training sessions occur.

objectives related to child and family outcomes would be developed that would be of primary concern in the outcome phase of the evaluation plan.

In closing, the purpose of the input phase of the evaluation plan is to assess the needs of handicapped young children and their families. In a sense it is like developing a navigation plan for an ocean voyage. If the navigation plan of a voyage is flawed, the ship will never reach its destination, no matter how competent or diligent the crew. In the same way, if a program does not conduct an adequate input evaluation, the plans developed to reach its destination (to meet the needs of handicapped infants, toddlers and their families) will be flawed, preventing the program from ever reaching its goals.

PROCESS EVALUATION

❏ In process evaluation the focus is on navigation toward the goals and objectives of the proposed plan. As information is obtained, adjustments can be made in the implementation process to keep the proposed plan on track. Furthermore, this process provides feedback to interveners on progress being made by specific children and their families as well as information on the overall progress of the program.

Adjustments can be made in the implementation process.

Program procedures and intervention methods or strategies that are employed to achieve program goals must be closely monitored. If the process is not monitored, the outcome evaluation of the program will be misleading. For example, suppose program objectives had not been met; we would probably conclude that the intervention used in the program was ineffective. The outcome, however, could also be attributed to inadequate implementation of procedures. For example, teachers might lack the time to complete interventions, materials might be insufficient, or a child's illness might preclude program completion. Negative findings may not be an indication of the program's "goodness"; rather, they may indicate the inadequacy of its implementation. One can see how evaluation of procedures supersedes the evaluation of objectives. If the procedures have not been monitored, then the evaluation of outcome is necessarily ambiguous.

Negative findings may indicate inadequacy of implementation.

Another concern in process evaluation is program management. Effective implementation of the program is intimately related to the adequate management of program resources. Again, the major concern

How do resources constrain or enhance implementation?

is the identification of the relationship of management practices to program effectiveness. Management systems must efficiently allocate program resources such as personnel, equipment, and space. The basic evaluation question is, How do these and other resources constrain or enhance the implementation of the program?

Related to program management is the recent concern over program costs and costs in relation to program benefits. Cost effectiveness techniques have been developed to address this concern (see Levin, 1983, for a detailed discussion of cost effectiveness). These techniques fall somewhere between the process and output phases of evaluation. At one level, cost effectiveness techniques provide information that provides direction as to inefficient program components. However, we also obtain information concerning program effectiveness relative to costs. Although cost effectiveness evaluation is very popular, some have questioned its worth in early childhood special education programs (Strain, 1984).

Most important is monitoring child or family progress.

Perhaps the most important aspect of the process evaluation phase is the monitoring of child or family progress toward objectives. This may be the first indication of faulty intervention plans that need modification. Furthermore, monitoring of progress creates a template that can be used to trace the effect of the program on children and families throughout the intervention.

The purpose of this phase of the evaluation plan is to monitor progress toward goals and objectives and to modify the original plan when data indicate a need for a change. In the same way that a captain navigates a ship to its destination by taking frequent measurements and adjusting the ship's course as needed, the evaluator navigates the program to its destination by taking frequent measurements and adjusting the plan as needed. As an example, Figure 2 contains a sample set of goals, objectives, planned activities to meet goals and objectives, and possible process evaluation activities to be used to monitor progress toward goals and objectives.

OUTCOME EVALUATION

❏ The focus of this phase is to determine the impact of the program on children, their families, and the community. Such a view equates this phase of the evaluation with educational research; interpretation means determining the causal effect of the program on outcomes. That is, we attempt to determine the impact of the program on children and their families. Research methods are used to establish that the program is the most likely explanation for family or child outcomes. In other words, the purpose of outcome evaluation procedures is the elimination of as many rival explanations for child and family changes as possible. For example, with a "strong" research design, if we were to observe improvement in test scores after an educational intervention, we would infer that test score improvement was caused by the intervention. However, to the extent that other explanations can account for this improvement, we lack what is termed *internal validity.* The "stronger" a design is, the greater the internal validity or the more readily other explanations for the findings can be dismissed. In essence, we attempt to design our research so that all other explanations except the intervention are ruled out as causing observed changes. Described below are the eight threats to internal validity outlined

We would infer that test score improvement was caused by intervention.

by Campbell and Stanley (1963). Each threat can be logically controlled by the elements of evaluation design.

1. *Historical* threats are events unrelated to the program that affect outcomes. For example, the introduction of a child into a program may stimulate greater home involvement by the child's parents. Therefore, changes at postprogram assessments may be equally attributable to the program or the parents.

2. *Maturation* threats refer to various forms of growth by the child over the course of the program. If maturation is unrelated to the program, then the effect of the program is indeterminate. This is problematic in programs for children under age 3, for whom rapid change is expected over very short time periods.

3. *Testing* threats relate to the concern that the act of testing (or observing) may affect in some manner the postprogram assessment. This is most often seen in subjects becoming more "test-wise" after having been administered the preprogram assessment.

4. *Instrumentation* threats are changes occurring in the measurement. For example, if we have one observer rating a child's performance on a set of skills prior to intervention and a second observer rate the child's performance after the intervention, we may not be able to determine whether differences in pre/post ratings are attributable to differences in the interpretations of observers or differences in the child's behavior.

5. *Regression* is a statistical tendency for subjects with extreme scores at one time to score closer to "average" the second time. This has important implications for the evaluation of programs designed to intervene with children who perform differently than the "average" child (e.g., handicapped infants and toddlers). For example, subjects selected on the basis of low test scores in a screening may perform significantly better at postprogram assessment. The change may be due to regression and not the program.

6. *Selection* is a major threat in evaluation, particularly when we must use intact groups and cannot randomly select who will receive intervention. Since program effects are frequently inferred when differences are observed between subjects in the program and a comparison group excluded from the program, we must take steps to ensure that preintervention differences do not explain the postintervention differences. In other words, the quality of mother-infant interactions in the intervention group may have been superior to the mother-infant interactions of the comparison group prior to intervention. As a result, it will be difficult to conclude that the program accounted for discrepancy in mother-infant interactions between the control and intervention groups.

7. *Mortality* represents the loss of subjects during the course of the program. The remaining subjects may bias the outcome since the pre- and postprogram comparisons are based on different sets of subjects. For example, uncooperative families may withdraw from a program because of differences with the program staff. As a result, only cooperative families remain in the program; their postprogram scores are then compared to the preprogram scores, or the scores of another group that contains scores from both cooperative and uncooperative families.

8. *Selection interactions* are the interactions of other threats with selection. Some threats may be manifested with certain types of children. For example, a program may be composed of children equally deficient in some skill area. Half the group is chosen to receive a remedial intervention and the other half comprises a control group for purposes of comparison. If the intervener were to select children on the basis of their "promise," then a threat of selection-maturation exists.

Design Considerations

Research designs systematically examine effectiveness of programs.

❑ Research designs are the structures by which the search for answers to questions about interventions are organized (Udinsky, Osterlind, & Lynch, 1981). In other words, they enable us to systematically examine the effectiveness of our programs and collect insights about how the programs might operate in other situations. The strength of a given design is determined by the design's potential to control for the threats to internal validity. A "strong design" is one that allows us to conclude that changes in children and their families are most likely a result of the intervention rather than some unrelated factor.

Three dimensions differentiate most evaluation designs: (a) presence or absence of a preprogram measure on the outcome measure, (b) presence or absence of a nontreatment comparison group, and (c) whether groups are intact or randomly composed. A complete discussion of experimental design is beyond the scope of this chapter. The reader is referred to Campbell and Stanley (1963) for more information on issues related to research design. The designs included in this section are limited to those with the greatest potential for controlling the threats to internal validity.

Qualitative ideal is an extensive description of events in the natural setting.

Absence of Preprogram Measures and a Nontreatment Group. Under these conditions quantitative procedures are useless. The only potential for useful information is the use of qualitative methods. These methods have stimulated recent interest in the educational evaluation literature. What had been heresy years ago has achieved respectability. The qualitative ideal is represented by an extensive description of events in the natural setting.

The observer is in stark contrast to experimental tradition.

The field work of anthropologists perhaps best exemplifies the qualitative methodology. Of primary importance to this method is the attempt to faithfully and continuously record all events. This requires detailed descriptions of the setting and of the involved individuals and their interactions; usually generous quantities of quotations are used. Values of the observer must be "suspended" so that interpretations of events are not distorted by observer values. The observer who considers the context of the events being recorded is in stark contrast to the experimental tradition, where control of variables is paramount to the research effort.

The strength of qualitative approaches is the degree of detail that can be brought to bear upon the evaluation question. Rich portrayals of the subject matter and its associated context can be a source of valuable insights into process and possible causal relations. Furthermore, the researcher is less susceptible to being blinded by structured methods and is therefore more likely to be sensitive to unanticipated findings.

A serious weakness in the qualitative strategy is the difficulty of establishing the validity of the data. It is impossible for observers to be passive recorders of events; rather, they are filters through which considerable amounts of information do not pass. There are several explanations for this situation. First, it is not possible to accurately record every event in a given situation. Every situation presents far too many pieces of information; this is compounded by the exploratory nature of most qualitative studies, where there is uncertainty about which events are relevant and which irrelevant. Second, there are no guarantees that attitudes and biases do not distort the observer's perception of events. If information is selectively attended to, then it will very likely be the information most congruent with the observer's frame of reference. Third, the intimate involvement typically required of the observer can invite reactivity effects. In addition, the involvement can be emotional, which necessarily reduces the observer's objectivity. Fourth, many data bases must be constructed from memory, which compounds the problems of attitudes and biases.

A weakness is establishing validity of the data.

Although these problems may be more pronounced in the qualitative method, they are not unique to the approach. An evaluator conducting a traditional empirical study is just as susceptible to biases in the determination of what variables to manipulate and outcomes to assess. Regardless of the method employed, reality must be reconstructed, and biases and values of the individual doing the reconstruction will impact the effort.

Absence of a Nontreatment Comparison Group. As with the previous design dimension, under these conditions traditional quantitative procedures are of little value. Single subject designs, however, can control the threats to internal validity and be extremely useful in attempts to determine program impact.

Single subject methodology was developed to create conditions closely approximating those in control group designs when control groups are not available. Basically, children receiving the intervention are assessed repeatedly throughout the treatment period. Essentially, they serve as their own controls. This is a powerful design, whose logical strength rivals that of the true experimental design. Kazdin (1982) outlined three characteristics of the single subject design: continuous assessment, baseline assessment, and analysis of trend.

Children are assessed repeatedly.

The single subject design has many variations, and a systematic review of them would require many more pages than are available here. This variability reflects the adaptability of the repeated measures design to many different contexts and needs. It is an extremely flexible design.

1. Continuous assessment is the fundamental characteristic of the repeated measures design. Since no control group is employed, the evaluation of effect is based on performance changes that coincide with the onset of the intervention. There is strong basis for inferring effect when a series of assessments begins to yield different results after implementation of an intervention. Use of continuous assessment provides a control for maturational threats since program effects can be seen against the backdrop of growth prior to the intervention.

2. Baselines provide (a) an estimate of existing levels of performance, and (b) a "prediction" of what the future performance should be if the

intervention has no effect. Prediction is central to this design, since inferring effect requires changes in predicted performance at the point of intervention. Baselines provide a control for selection threats since treatment and nontreatment comparisons are within the same subject. In addition, regression effects are improbable explanations when stable baselines are achieved.

3. The notion of trend is related to predicted performance. If program effectiveness is inferred from departures from baseline performance, then performance trends over the repeated assessments have important analytic value. *Trend* refers to stable increases or decreases in performance. In the ideal evaluation example, baseline performance is stable (no change in the preintervention period), and with the onset of intervention, performance shows a marked trend.

A number of design options can help the evaluator better assess the impact of an intervention when a comparison group cannot be constructed. Some of the more commonly employed single subject designs are (a) reversal designs, (b) multiple baseline designs, (c) changing criteria designs, and (d) multielement designs. The reader is referred to Kazdin (1982) or Kratochwill (1978) for detailed reviews of single subject designs.

Intact Groups Pretest and Posttest. This situation allows us to use traditional quantitative procedures to establish that the program had a significant impact. At the simplest level, one group is given the intervention and one group is not; both groups are tested on a pre/post basis. This is a reasonably strong design that depends on how plausible the selection bias is an alternative explanation for findings. By analyzing pretest, however, the evaluator can determine whether or not groups were equivalent prior to the intervention. If they are equivalent prior to intervention, selection bias is much less plausible. History, maturation, testing, and instrumentation are controlled by the presence of a comparison group since each of these effects should operate equally on both groups. The pretest accounts for selection and mortality effects. However, regression is a threat, as it is in all intact group designs.

One group is given the intervention, one is not.

Regression is a threat.

Many educational researchers and evaluators have resorted to *matching* as an additional methodological control when intact groups exist. In matching, the evaluator selects children for the nonintervention group on the basis of their similarity to the intervention group members. The matching process is systematic in that behavior scales, test scores, or other quantifiable measures (rather than subjective judgments) are used to determine similarity. Having matched the children, the implicit assumption is made that the two groups are equivalent. Any changes observed at the posttest are presumed to be due to the intervention. However, there may be an array of other relevant variables not considered, such as motivation and parental support, that may be equally as important as or more important than the variables used for matching. If we can be reasonably confident that no other variable is important to determining posttest skill, then the matching process adds to our confidence. It strengthens the inference only to the extent that the matching variable(s) represents the array of factors important to the outcome. Otherwise, selection-maturation interactions continue to be threats to this design.

Changes at posttest are presumed due to intervention.

Randomly Created Groups. Evaluations comparing groups are most conclusive when random assignment of subjects to groups is employed. Rather than employing an intact group for the intervention group, the evaluator would assign children to the treatment program and control group in some random fashion to control for a systematic bias. This is the most elegant and powerful design available. With the exception of mortality, the design effectively controls all threats to internal validity.

The design controls threats to internal validity.

However, random assignment guarantees only probabilistic equivalence, a notion many nonresearchers find less than compelling. Sampling variability can lead to initial group nonequivalence on critical variables (e.g., IQ, motivation, or any other key variable). In order to avoid this problem, many evaluators first match subjects and then randomly assign each member of a matched pair to either the intervention or nonintervention group. Again, what we have done by random assignment is eliminate any systematic bias in group membership.

A major impediment to the use of this design is the lack of control an evaluator typically has in the applied setting. This can be an ethical issue. Service delivery is dictated by chance rather than need. For this reason, we find relatively few true experiments in field situations. A situation that may allow us to use this design is when we have limited resources and are not able to serve all children or families who may need services. Random assignment of these individuals to a control or intervention group may be the most equitable distribution of limited resources.

A major impediment is lack of control in the applied setting.

Implementing the Outcome Evaluation Phase

❑ As previously discussed in the input evaluation section of this chapter, it is critical that this phase of the evaluation plan be carried out in a systematic and careful manner. A poorly conceived or implemented outcome evaluation will obscure interpretation of program impact, with a disastrous effect on the program. With some slight changes, the steps outlined in the input evaluation section for determining needs are equally useful for the implementation of a good outcome evaluation. To review, the steps are (a) determine key elements, (b) identify information sources, (c) develop a management plan, (d) collect data, (e) analyze and interpret data, and (f) develop the program (this step is not included in the output evaluation phase). The slight changes in these steps in the outcome evaluation phase are described below.

Determine Key Elements. As in the input phase, we must determine the purpose of and audience for the outcome evaluation. We must also develop a set of questions that should be answered. For example,

1. What impact did the support groups have on families that participated in the program?
2. Do children make significant progress as measured by the Bailey Scales?
3. Are parents satisfied with the program?

Identify Information Sources. As in the input phase, we must determine the sources of information needed to answer our evaluation questions. It is important that our data collection efforts go beyond just collecting child change data. Programs for handicapped infants, toddlers, and their

*Data collection efforts go
beyond change data.*

families have impact beyond those limited to children, and we must go beyond them as a data source so that we can assess these impacts.

An additional concern in this step is the selection of a research design. We must select the design that will give us the greatest control over the internal threats to validity and still be within the limitations of the situation (e.g., is there a comparison group or can we randomize?).

The methods available to collect data are essentially the same as those described in detail in the input evaluation section of this chapter.

Develop a Management Plan. The importance of a management plan as described in the input evaluation phase applies equally to outcome evaluation. Steps described to help manage data collection should also be employed.

Collect Data. Again, the issues and concerns discussed in regard to the input evaluation are equally applicable to the output evaluation.

Analyze and Interpret the Data. As with the previous phases, issues related to analysis and interpretation have been discussed in detail earlier in this chapter.

In closing, the purpose of this phase is to determine the impact of our program on children, their families, and the community. In the voyage analogy, the plan developed by the mayor was considered successful only if the health of the port improved. In the same vein, even the best-designed program, appropriately implemented, would be of little value if it didn't have the desired impact on children and their families.

A HIGH-QUALITY EVALUATION PLAN

❏ How do we define a high-quality evaluation plan? The Joint Committee on Standards for Educational Evaluation (1981) was formed, under the direction of Daniel Stufflebeam, to develop a set of standards to which a good evaluaution plan must conform. This group was made up of representatives from some of the most prominent educational organizations: National School Boards Association, National Educational Association, National Association of Elementary School Principals, Education Commission of the States, National Council on Measurement in Education, American Association of School Administrators, American Educational Research Association, American Federation of Teachers, American Personnel and Guidance Association, American Psychological Association, Association for Supervision and Curriculum Development, and Council for American Private Education.

RATIONALE FOR DEVELOPING STANDARDS

❏ Standards were developed for two basic reasons. First, it was felt that the technical quality of many evaluation studies was insufficient to provide adequate data. As previously discussed, this concern has also been raised with regard to evaluation studies in early childhood special education (Dunst & Rheingrover, 1981; Odom & Fewell, 1983; Simeonsson, et al., 1982; White & Casto, 1984; White, et al., 1984; Wolery, in press; Wolery & Bailey, 1984). Second, it was realized that program evaluation could be corrupted to produce results that reflect the program's bias and serve the needs of the program. Suchman (1967) grouped such manipulations into four categories: eyewash, whitewash, posture, and postponement.

"Eyewash" is a technique by which an ineffective program is made to look better by selecting those aspects of the program that will make the program look good and ignoring those aspects that will not. A common technique is to collect many pre/post measures and then report only those measures on which significant growth was shown. If enough measures are used, significant changes can be found by mere chance.

Significant changes can be found by mere chance.

"Whitewash" takes the deception a step further than eyewash by presenting misleading or inaccurate data. An often-used method is to present glowing testimonials on the impact of a program without presenting data to support the claims. Anyone who has watched more than an hour of television should be familiar with this technique. "Posture" is used by a program to give the impression of a rigorous evaluation design and quality program. One method frequently used is to report complex data collection or analysis procedures that are difficult to understand. The complexity of the analysis sounds good and makes it appear that the program is being rigorously evaluated.

"Postponement" is used to avoid or delay some action that the program administration does not want undertaken. By suggesting that an evaluation study be conducted before a decision can be made, the administration can stall until the storm blows over and they are no longer receiving pressure to implement the action.

PURPOSE OF EVALUATION STANDARDS

❏ The committee felt that a set of standards could help improve the professionalism of program evaluation by giving people benchmarks for developing and judging the quality evaluation plan. It was the hope of the committee that these standards would reduce the number of technically inadequate evaluation plans and help ferret out reports of evaluation plans that have been corrupted. The committee concluded that a high-quality evaluation plan has (a) utility, (b) feasibility, (c) propriety, and (d) accuracy. Each of these elements has a set of more specific features that the evaluation plan must have in order to be considered as meeting the requirements of that standard.

Standards would reduce technically inadequate evaluation plans.

Utility

❏ For an evaluation plan to have utility, data collected from the evaluation plan must have potential usefulness to the program and/or consumers of the program. Several steps should be taken to ensure the utility of the evaluation plan. The audience for the evaluation must be identified and steps should be taken to ensure that the plan is appropriate to meet their needs. Furthermore, information must be of a broad enough scope to answer all the pertinent evaluation questions. When the results of the plan are written, information must be clear and easily understood. Otherwise, the report will sit on a shelf and be of little use. Finally, it is critical that results of the evaluation plan be disseminated promptly. Nothing detracts more from the impact of a good evaluation plan than the presentation of the findings after people are no longer concerned with the outcomes.

Feasibility

❏ Feasibility refers to the plausibility of implementing the evaluation plan. A major concern is the practicality of components of the plan. For example, asking interveners to give a battery of tests in addition to their normal duties is probably not practical. They will feel pressured to collect the data and will probably hurry through their administration. As a result, the morale of the interveners will be hurt and the data collected will be of poor quality.

In a similar vein, it is important that the cost of the evaluation plan can be in tune with the benefits to be obtained from the plan. Not every program can afford to develop a rigorous evaluation that employs a solid experimental design to establish program impact. In fact, if a program does not have the resources to conduct an adequately controlled study, it should not be undertaken. Results from technically unsound investigations are bound to be specious and add to the confusion regarding the efficacy of early intervention (see Wolery & Bailey, 1984 for a complete discussion of this issue). Furthermore, it is far more important that the program document a high-quality implementation of intervention, rather than the impact of the intervention. If a program can establish that the intervention being used represents "best practice" and that the intervention is implemented properly, results are bound to occur. If they do not, however, this is not an indictment of the program. By documenting that what the interveners are doing represents "best practice" and that the program was adequately implemented, the program planners have established accountability. That is not to say that a question could not or should not be raised as to why there was little positive impact. This question may then be examined through an evaluation plan that uses good experimental (Campbell & Stanley, 1963) or at least good quasi-experimental design (Cook & Campbell, 1979). Furthermore, it is also important that when new innovations are proposed, they be based on solid data so that we are not in the business of creating new educational myths. For the typical program, however, efforts should be directed at identifying client needs, developing a plan to meet those needs, documenting the plan that represents "best practice," and monitoring progress on the plan.

Not every program can afford a rigorous evaluation.

New innovations should be based on solid data.

Propriety

❏ This standard relates to how equitable and ethical the evaluation plan is. Evaluators, like everyone else, have a responsibility to respect the rights of individuals connected with the program, and the evaluation plan should reflect this responsibility. Readers of evaluation reports should beware of reports that have nothing but positive findings. It is a rare educational endeavor that has all positive outcomes. Readers should also be concerned when a report does not seem to have a breadth of measures included in the evaluation plan. Sometimes we must ask what is not included in the report. We can have greater confidence in a report that includes both positive and negative findings and will be less likely to believe that damaging results were withheld.

It is a rare endeavor that has all positive outcomes.

Accuracy

❑ For an evaluation plan to have accuracy, steps must be taken to ensure that the data collected are correct and representative of the program.

Perhaps the most important consideration for an evaluation plan is the validity of information obtained. Validity can be thought of as the degree to which a test or procedure provides information relevant to the decision to be made. In other words, do the tests or procedures used in the identification plan measure what they purport to measure?

Validity...degree which a test provides relevant information.

Several steps should be taken to help ensure the development of a valid evaluation plan (see Goodwin & Driscoll, 1980, for a detailed discussion of validity).

1. It is imperative that multiple sources of information be used. Using multiple sources of information maximizes opportunities for children and their families to demonstrate their growth and thereby enhances the program's ability to monitor progress toward objectives and determine the impact of the program.

2. The selection of formal sources of data (e.g., standardized tests or published criterion-referenced tests) should be based on the degree of validity that has been established for these sources. Either they should be highly correlated with established tests that measure the same trait (concurrent validity), or they should be good predictors of the child's future behavior (predictive validity). Formal sources of data that only report face or content validity are suspect and should be avoided. Technical manuals of tests should include a discussion of the tests' validity.

3. Formal sources of data chosen should be used with the population for which they were intended as well as in the manner in which they were intended to be used.

4. Informal methods of data collection (e.g., intervener observations, intervener developed tests or checklists, interviews, etc.) should have good face validity. That is, the information obtained from the informal source should be relevant to the trait or traits being measured.

A second consideration, of equal importance, is reliability—the extent to which variations in data reflect actual variations in the phenomena under study rather than being a result of measurement error (see Goodwin & Driscoll, 1980, for detailed discussion of reliability). In other words, can we be assured that the test or procedure being used will consistently produce the same results given the same input? As with validity there are steps that can be taken to ensure the development of a reliable identification and plan. First, selection of formal sources of data should be based on the degree of reliability established for each source. Reliability coefficients should be found in the test's technical manual. Second, programs can take steps to examine the reliability of informal sources of data they are using. For example, both parents could be asked to fill out checklists, or it may be possible to have an intervener and an aide complete the intervener checklist independently. By examining the same informal source of data completed by two individuals regarding the same child, one can determine whether or not information obtained from this source is consistent across individuals.

Reliability coefficients should be found in the test's manual.

An often overlooked concern is *harmony*, or the degree to which the evaluation plan is associated with the goals of the program. Harmony depends on whether the tests and procedures chosen are appropriate for matching the child with the program. It is possible that specific tests or procedures within an evaluation plan are reliable and valid but are not compatible with the goals of the program. Although data collected through these procedures will provide what appear to be good data in the sense that they are derived from reliable and valid practices, the data are not useful in determining the impact of the program.

A concern related to harmony is the collection of defensible information sources. In other words, does the information source have the potential to provide good information about the activity being judged? For example, one program goal might be to improve parent-child interactions during play periods. The intervener who has worked on this goal all year may not be the best source of data to judge whether or not any growth has occurred. The intervener may be too invested to make an unbiased judgment. On the other hand, asking the program administrator who has limited contact with the parents would be even worse. This individual would not have adequate knowledge of parent-child interactions to make such a judgment.

When reading evaluation reports we should examine the methods section carefully and not just read the conclusions. We must look for a systematic data collection procedure that relates to the intentions of the program.

It is critical that we determine whether or not the conclusions are justified based on the data collected. Without examining how data were collected and analyzed we have no basis from which to make such a judgment. As a general rule, it is best to be guarded when interpreting the results of any evaluation study that does not adequately describe how data were collected and analyzed.

We must determine whether conclusions are justified.

CONCLUSION

❏ In this chapter, program evaluation has been presented as a comprehensive interwoven process comprising three phases: input, process, and output. In the input phase, evaluation efforts are directed at the identification of needs and the matching of program capabilities to identified needs. In the process phase, the focus of evaluation efforts is on the monitoring of progress toward objectives and program implementation. In the outcome phase, program impact is determined. The first two phases are critical to the development of a high-quality program. The emphasis of most programs for handicapped infants, toddlers, and their families should be placed on the input and process phases of evaluation. Without these phases a program is sure to have problems. Moreover, a program should not attempt to undertake an outcome evaluation for which it does not have the resources or expertise. The literature is full of confusing findings with regard to the impact of early intervention. A poorly conceived outcome evaluation produces confusing findings. On the other hand, a good comprehensive evaluation plan can greatly enhance our ability to meet the needs of handicapped infants, toddlers, and their parents; help us establish accountability; and provide us with the ammunition to convince policy makers of the need for and benefits from early intervention.

REFERENCES

Alberto, P. A., & Troutman, A. C. (1982). *Applied behavior analysis for teachers: Influencing student performance.* Columbus, OH: Merrill.

Berelson, B. (1952). *Content analysis in communication research.* Glencoe, IL: Free Press.

Borg, W. R., & Gall, M. D. (1983). *Educational research.* New York: Longman.

Bricker, D., & Littman, D. (1982). Intervention and evaluation: The inseparable mix. *Topics in Early Childhood Special Education, 1*(4), 23-33.

Campbell, D. T., & Stanley, J. C. (1963). *Experimental and quasi-experimental designs for research.* Boston: Houghton, Mifflin.

Casto, G. (in press). Research and program evaluation in early childhood special education. In S. L. Odom and M. B. Karnes (Eds.), *Research in early childhood special education.* Monterey, CA: Brooks Cole.

Cook, T. D., & Campbell, D. T. (1979). *Quasi-experimentation: Design and analysis issues for field settings.* Chicago: Rand McNally.

Dunst, C. J., & Rheingrover, R. M. (1981). An analysis of the efficacy of infant intervention programs with organically handicapped children. *Evaluation and Program Planning, 4,* 287-323.

Fujiura, G. T., & Johnson, L. J. (1986). Methods of microcomputer research in early childhood special education. *Journal for the Division for Early Childhood, 10*(3), 264-269.

Garwood, S. G. (1982). (Mis)use of developmental scales in program evaluation. *Topics in Early Childhood Special Education, 1*(4), 61-69.

Gingold, W., & Karnes, M. B. (1986). *Program progress report: Project APPLE.* Springfield, IL: Illinois Governor's Planning Council on Developmental Disabilities.

Goodwin, W. L., & Driscoll, L. A. (1980). *Handbook for measurement and evaluation in early childhood education.* San Francisco: Jossey-Bass.

Isaac, S., & Michael, W. B. (1981). *Handbook in research on evaluation: For education and the behavioral sciences* (2nd ed.). San Diego, CA: EdITS.

Joint Committee on Standards for Educational Evaluation. (1981). *Standards for evaluations of educational programs, projects, and materials.* New York: McGraw-Hill.

Kazdin, A. E. (1982). *Single-case research designs.* New York: Oxford Press.

Kirk, R. E. (1978). *Introductory statistics.* Monterey, CA: Brooks/Cole.

Kratochwill, T. R. (1978). *Single-subject research: Strategies for evaluating change.* New York: Academic Press.

Levin, H. M. (1983). *Cost-effectiveness: A prover.* Beverly Hills, CA: Sage.

Miles, M. B. (1979). Qualitative data as an attractive nuisance: The problem of analysis. *Administrative Science Quarterly, 24,* 590-601.

Miles, M. B., & Huberman, A. M. (1984). Drawing valid meaning from qualitative data: Toward shared craft. *Educational Researcher, 13,* 20-30.

Morris, L. L., & Fitz-Gibbon, C. T. (1978). Evaluator's handbook. In L. L. Morris (Ed.), *Program evaluation kit* (pp. 1-133). Beverly Hills, CA: Sage.

Odom, S. L., & Fewell, R. R. (1983). Program evaluation in early childhood special education: A meta-evaluation. *Educational Evaluation and Policy Analysis, 5,* 445-460.

Patton, M. Q. (1980). *Qualitative evaluation methods.* Beverly Hills, CA: Sage.

Ramey, C. T., Campbell, F. A., & Wasik, B. H. (1982). Use of standardized tests to evaluate early childhood special education programs. *Topics in Early Childhood Special Education, 1*(4), 51-60.

Scriven, M. (1967). The methodology of evaluation. In R. W. Tyler, R. M. Gragne, & M. Scriven (Eds.), *Perspectives on curriculum evaluation,* (pp. 39-83). AERA Monograph Series on Curriculum Evaluation No. 1. Skokie, IL: Rand McNally.

Scriven, M. (1973). Goal-free evaluation. In E. R. House (Ed.), *School evaluation: The politics and process.* Berkeley, CA: McCutchan.

Scriven, M. (1974). Evaluation perspectives and procedures. In W. J. Popham

(Ed.), *Evaluation in education: Current applications,* (pp. 1-93). Berkeley, CA: McCutchan.

Siegel, S. (1956). *Nonparametric statistics for the behavioral sciences.* New York: McGraw-Hill.

Simeonsson,, R. J., Cooper, D. H., & Schiener, A. P. (1982). A review and analysis of the effectiveness of early intervention programs. *Pediatrics, 69*(5), 635-641.

Strain, P. S. (1984). Efficacy research with young handicapped children: A critique of the status quo. *Journal of the Division for Early Childhood, 9,* 4-10.

Stufflebeam, D. L. (1971). The relevance of the CIPP evaluation model for educational accountability. *Journal of Research and Development in Education, 5*(1), 19-23.

Stufflebeam, D. L. (1974). Alternative approaches to educational evaluation: A self-study guide for educators. In W. J. Popham (Ed.), *Evaluation in education: Current applications,* (pp. 95-143). Berkeley, CA: McCutchan.

Suchman, E. (1967). *Evaluation research.* New York: Sage.

Tyler, R. W. (1942). General statement on evaluation. *Journal of Educational Research, 35*(7), 492-501.

Tyler, R. W. (1958). The evaluation of teaching. In R. M. Cooper (Ed.), *The two ends of the log: Learning and teaching in today's college,* (pp. 164-176). Minneapolis: University of Minnesota Press.

Tyler, R. W. (1971). Accountability in education: The shift in criteria. In L. M. Lesinger & R. W. Tyler (Eds.), *Accountability in education.* Worthington, OH: Charles A. Jones.

Tyler, R. W. (1974). Introduction: A perspective on the issues. In R. W. Tyler & R. M. Wolf (Eds.), *Crucial issues in testing,* (pp. 1-10). Berkeley, CA: McCutchan.

Udinsky, B. F. Osterlind, S. J., & Lynch, S. W. (1981). *Evaluation resource handbook: Gathering, analyzing, reporting data.* San Diego, CA: EdITS.

White, K. R., & Casto, G. (1984). An integrative review of early intervention efficacy studies with at-risk children: Implications for the handicapped. *Analysis and Intervention in Developmental Disabilities, 5,* 7-31.

White, K. R., Mastropieri, M., & Casto, G. (1984). An analysis of special education early childhood projects approved by the joint dissemination review panel. *Journal of the Division for Early Childhood, 9,* 11-26.

Wolery, M. (1987). Program evaluation at the local level: Recommendations for improving services. *Topics in Early Childhood Special Education, 7*(2), 111-123.

Wolery, M., & Bailey, D. B. (1984). Alternatives to impact evaluation: Suggestions for program evaluation in early intervention. *Journal of the Division for Early Childhood, 9,* 27-37.

Zigler, E., & Balla, D. (1982). Selecting outcome variables in evaluations of early childhood special education programs. *Topics in Early Childhood Special Education, 1*(4), 11-22.

10.
Early Intervention Public Policy:
Past, Present, and Future

Barbara J. Smith

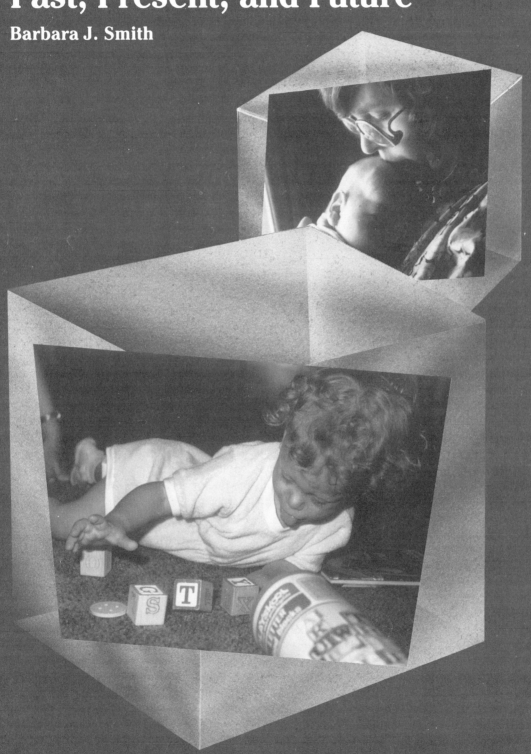

❏ Public policy commits the government to certain goals, determines whose interests and values will prevail, and regulates and distributes resources (Seekins & Fawcett, 1986). Public policies come in the form of laws, regulations, executive orders, guidelines, ordinances, and judicial rulings, and are found at all levels of government—local, state, and federal.

Policy has enjoyed a steady growth.

Early intervention public policy is a relatively recent phenomenon. Contrary to many social developments, early intervention policy has enjoyed a steady and almost meteoric growth, as compared to the pace of typical social policy developments. In 25 years, early intervention policy has progressed from being virtually nonexistent to the establishment of legal mandates for service in many states and an expanded federal commitment to provide high-quality early intervention services to handicapped and at-risk children and their families.

This chapter discusses the evolution of public policies related to early intervention services. It reviews the past—trends in federal and state policies that have provided for funding and programming for very young children and their families. It reviews the present—the state of the art, or status, of current federal and state policies for early intervention. And finally, future policy issues are proposed.

THE PAST

❏ Major milestones in early intervention and preschool policy at the federal level began in the 1960s (see Figure 1). Federal developments at that time focused on intervening early in order to promote optimal development. They included P.L. 88-156, which expanded maternal and child health services to expectant mothers from low-income areas in an effort to prevent mental retardation, and P.L. 89-313, which provided federal education money to state-operated schools and institutions for the handicapped and which has often been used by states to start experimental early intervention services (Allen, 1984).

Head Start was the first nationwide attempt to intervene.

Project Head Start was the first nationwide attempt to intervene directly with the young child with the goal of improving the child's development through a variety of services—educational, medical, nutritional, and parent training. Project Head Start was launched in 1965 as part of the War on Poverty. It was designed to help economically disadvantaged preschool-aged children achieve their full potential by attempting to remedy the damaging effects of poverty on their development through early intervention.

In the late 1960s, two major cornerstones of current services were laid. In 1967, P.L. 90-248 established the Early and Periodic Screening, Diagnosis and Treatment (EPSDT) program. EPSDT, a component of Medicaid, focuses on early identification and treatment as a method of preventing developmental and medical problems. In 1968, P.L. 90-538, the Handicapped Children's Early Education Assistance Act, was passed. This legislation established the landmark Handicapped Children's Early Education Program (HCEEP), which has provided federal support for 20 years for the development of effective model programs, methods, and state policies in early intervention and preschool services for handicapped children.

HCEEP has provided federal support for nearly 20 years.

Figure 1. *Evolution of Early Intervention Public Policy.*

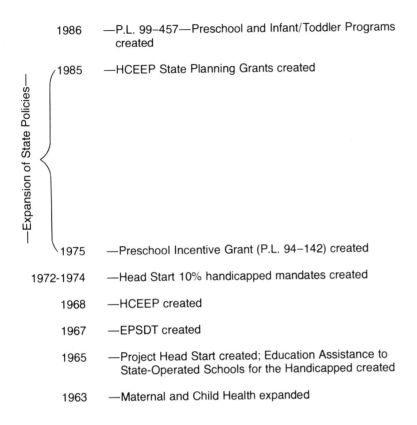

In 1968 few services existed, and the importance of early intervention was just emerging. Therefore, Congress passed P.L. 90-538 with the purpose of expanding the knowledge base of the potential impact of early intervention. Since 1968, HCEEP has funded over 500 projects that have demonstrated early intervention model practices, developed curricula and assessment instruments, and provided training to thousands of programs and practitioners nationwide. In addition to the development of effective models and practices, HCEEP has also provided support for research in early intervention, delivered technical assistance to projects, and encouraged state-level planning of universal services to young handicapped children (Garland, Black, & Jesien, 1986).

500 projects have demonstrated model practices.

In the early 1970s early intervention for handicapped children took a leap forward with the establishment of a new requirement that Head Start set aside 10% of its enrollment opportunities for handicapped children. P.L. 92-924 and P.L. 93-644 provided that 10% of the enrollment should be handicapped children and that these children should be provided services to meet their special needs within Head Start (Allen, 1984).

10% of the enrollment should be handicapped.

Consequently, Head Start has been the largest provider of "mainstreamed" services for preschool-aged handicapped children in the nation. In 1985, over 98% of Head Start programs enrolled at least one handicapped child. Over 60,000 handicapped children are enrolled in Head Start programs (U.S. Department of Health and Human Services, 1986).

Over 60,000 handicapped are enrolled in Head Start.

In 1975, Congress, while recognizing the importance of educational opportunities for all handicapped children, also recognized the importance

The Preschool Incentive Grant program was voluntary.

of *early* educational opportunities for preschool-aged handicapped children by passing P.L. 94-142—The Education for All Handicapped Children Act. While P.L. 94-142 fell short of mandating services for children below traditional school age, it did establish the Preschool Incentive Grant to encourage states to serve 3- through 5-year-old handicapped children. The Preschool Incentive Grant provided funds to states that elected to serve 3- through 5-year-olds. The Preschool Incentive Grant program was voluntary; however, once a state received these funds it was required to assure all the rights and services of P.L. 94-142 to the preschool child.

Concurrent with these federal initiatives, between 1970 and the early 1980s, state policies mandating early services increased dramatically. By 1984 over one half of the states required early services to some portion of the 3-through 5-year-old population and over 10 states began services at birth to some portion of the population (see Figure 2). However, to encourage further expansion of state policy, Congress passed P.L. 98-199 in 1984. P.L. 98-199 established a new state planning component within HCEEP—providing federal funds to states for the purpose of planning, developing, and implementing state-wide comprehensive services for handicapped and at-risk children from birth through 5 years of age and their families.

P.L. 98-199 established a new state planning component.

Then in 1986, Congress passed P.L. 99-457, The Education of the Handicapped Act Amendments of 1986—capping 20 years of evolution in early intervention policy. Prior to P.L. 99-457, federal policy was focused primarily on supporting effective models and technology, providing training for professionals, and encouraging the generation of new knowledge through research and development activities. However, with P.L. 99-457, the nation took one step closer to a national policy of access to services for all handicapped and at-risk children, birth through 5 years of age, and their families.

P.L. 99-457 took one step closer to services for children, birth-5.

THE PRESENT

❑ While P.L. 99-457 dominates the present early childhood policy arena, there are other important related trends and activities. This section reviews the trends in federal education funding for infant-related projects to the present, as well as an update of state early intervention policy. However, a description of the landmark legislation, P.L. 99-457, is the primary focus of this section.

Federal Education Funding Trends

Funds have increased dramatically since 1980.

❑ Federal education funds—particularly those from the U.S. Office of Special Education Programs (OSEP)—have been increasingly targeted to the birth through 2-year-old population. Funds for research, model and outreach projects, and personnel training have increased dramatically since 1980.

HCEEP model demonstration projects that focus on infant services, for example, have increased significantly since the first projects were funded in 1969. In 1969, 23 HCEEP projects were funded; five (22%) included infants. From 1982 to 1986, approximately 83% of the 131 HCEEP projects included services for infants (Suarez, Hurth, & Prestridge, 1987).

Figure 2. Age At Which States Mandate Services.

State	Birth–2	3–5
Alabama		
Alaska		Yes
American Samoa	Yes	
Arizona		
Arkansas		
California		Yes
Colorado		
Connecticut		Yes
Delaware	Yes (partial)	
D.C.		Yes
Florida		
Georgia		
Guam	Yes	
Hawaii		Yes
Idaho		
Illinois		Yes
Indiana		
Iowa	Yes	
Kansas		
Kentucky		
Louisiana		Yes
Maine		
Maryland	Yes	
Massachusetts		Yes
Michigan	Yes	
Minnesota		Yes
Mississippi		
Missouri		
Montana		
Nebraska	Yes	
Nevada		
New Hampshire		Yes
New Jersey	Yes	
New Mexico		Yes
New York		
North Carolina		
North Dakota		Yes
Ohio		
Oklahoma	Yes (partial)	
Oregon	Yes	
Pennsylvania		
Puerto Rico		
Rhode Island		Yes
South Carolina		Yes
South Dakota	Yes	

(Continued)

Figure 2. Age At Which States Mandate Services (Continued)

State	Birth–2	3–5
Tennessee		Yes
Texas	Yes	
Mariana Islands		
Utah		
Vermont		
Virgin Islands		
Virginia	Yes (from 2)	
Washington		Yes
West Virginia		Yes
Wisconsin		Yes
Wyoming	Yes	

Note: From U.S. Department of Education, Ninth Annual Report to Congress on the Implementation of the Education of the Handicapped Act (1987).

Funding for training of personnel has increased.

Similarly, funding for the training of personnel to work with infants and their families has increased dramatically. Until 1987, OSEP was not required to set aside personnel preparation funds specifically for early intervention personnel training. However, under P.L. 99-457, Congress instructed OSEP to make the training and preparation of personnel to work with handicapped infants and their families a priority for the Education of the Handicapped Act (EHA) Personnel Preparation program funding.

P.L. 99-457 contains many provisions relating to handicapped children of all ages. However, the most far-reaching initiatives pertain to children in the birth through 5-year age group. The law establishes two new programs—one for birth through 2-year-olds and, one for 3- through 5-year-olds. For purposes of this chapter, emphasis is placed on the birth through 2 provisions. Briefly, however, P.L. 99-457 extends the provisions of P.L. 94-142 to all children 3 years of age by 1990-1991, and significantly increases funding for this age group.

Handicapped Infants and Toddlers Program (B-2)

❑ The landmark early intervention program established by P.L. 99-457 is the Handicapped Infants and Toddlers Program, Part H of the Education of the Handicapped Act. This section of the law creates a new federal program for handicapped and at-risk children from birth to age 3 years and their families. The purpose of this program as described by Congress is to provide financial assistance to states to:

1. Develop and implement a statewide, comprehensive, coordinated, multidisciplinary, interagency program of early intervention services.

2. Facilitate the coordination of early intervention resources from federal, state, local, and private sources (including private insurers).

3. Enhance states' capacities to provide high-quality early intervention services.

While the Infant/Toddler Program is voluntary for states—that is, they may elect not to participate—if a state does choose to participate, or apply for funding under this law, it must meet the requirements of the law. In addition, to be eligible for a grant in the 5th year, the state must ensure that services are available to all eligible children.

If a state does participate, it must meet the requirements of the law.

Who Is Eligible for Services?

❑ The new Infant/Toddler Program is directed to the needs of children, birth to their 3rd birthday, who need early intervention because they:

1. Are experiencing developmental delays in one or more of the following areas: cognitive, physical, language and speech, psychosocial, or self-help skills.
2. Have a physical or mental condition that has a high probability of resulting in delay (e.g., Down syndrome, cerebral palsy, etc.).
3. At state discretion, are at-risk medically or environmentally for substantial developmental delays if early intervention is not provided.

Also, under this program the infant or toddler's family may receive services that are needed to facilitate their capacity to assist in the development of their child.

What Must States Provide?

❑ If a state applies for funds under this program, it must meet the following requirements. For the first 2 years:

1. The governor has established an Interagency Coordinating Council made up of parents, state agency representatives, personnel trainers, state legislature representatives, and others.
2. The governor has designated a lead agency (which may be the Interagency Coordinating Council).
3. The state ensures that the funds will be used to plan, develop, and implement statewide services.

The 3rd and 4th years:

1. In addition to the requirements of the first 2 years, the state must ensure that it has adopted a policy that contains the required components of a statewide system, which are as follows:
   (a) A definition of the term "developmentally delayed."
   (b) Timetables for ensuring services to all eligible children by the 5th year of participation.
   (c) Multidisciplinary evaluations of the functioning of all eligible children and the needs of their families to assist in the development of their child.
   (d) Provision of a written individualized family service plan (IFSP) for all eligible children.
   (e) Comprehensive Child Find system including a system for making referrals to providers. "Primary referral sources" must be included, including hospitals, physicians, other health care providers and agencies, and day-care facilities.
   (f) A public awareness program focusing on early identification.

(g) A central directory containing state resources, services, experts, and research and demonstration projects.

(h) A comprehensive system of personnel development, including training of public and private service providers and primary referral sources, as well as preservice training.

(i) A single line of authority in a *lead agency* designated or established by the governor to carry out the general administration, supervision, and monitoring of programs and activities; the identification and coordination of all available resources within the state from federal, state, local, and private sources and the assignment of financial responsibility to the appropriate state agency; the resolution of state interagency disputes and procedures for ensuring the provision of services pending the resolution of such disputes; and the entering into formal state interagency agreements that define the financial responsibility of each state agency for early intervention services (consistent with state law) and include, among other things, procedures for resolving disputes.

(j) A policy pertaining to the contracting or making of other arrangements with local providers.

(k) A procedure for securing timely reimbursement of funds between state and local agencies.

(l) Procedural safeguards with respect to the settlement of disagreements between parents and providers, the right to appeal, the right to confidentiality of information, the opportunity to examine records, assignment of surrogate parents, written prior notices to parents in their native language, and procedures to ensure the provision of services pending the resolution of complaints.

(m) Policies and procedures relating to the establishment and maintenance of personnel training, hiring, and certification/licensing standards.

(n) A system for compiling data on the early intervention programs (may include sampling).

2. The statewide system must be in effect no later than the beginning of the 4th year, except for the assurance of full service to all eligible children.

The 5th and succeeding years, the state must ensure that the system is in effect and full services are available to all eligible children.

Early intervention services must include, for each eligible child, a multidisciplinary assessment and a written individualized family service plan (IFSP) developed by a multidisciplinary team and the parents. Services provided must be designed to meet the developmental needs of the child and be in accordance with an IFSP. They may include special education, speech and language pathology and audiology, occupational therapy, physical therapy, psychological services, parent and family training and counseling services, transition services, medical services for diagnostic purposes, and health services necessary to enable the child to benefit from other early intervention services. Case management services must be provided for every eligible child and his or her parents.

Services must include multidisciplinary assessment and a written IFSP.

All early intervention services must be provided at no cost to parents except where federal or state law provides for a system of payments by parents, including provision for a schedule of sliding fees.

What Are the Individualized Family Service Plan (IFSP) Requirements?

❏ The IFSP must be developed by a multidisciplinary team and must contain: (a) a statement of the child's present levels of development (cognitive, speech/language, psychosocial, motor, and self-help); (b) a statement of the family's strengths and needs relating to enhancing the child's development; (c) a statement of major outcomes expected to be achieved for the child and family; (d) the criteria, procedures, and time lines for determining progress; (e) the specific early intervention services necessary to meet the unique needs of the child and family including the method, frequency, and intensity of service; (f) the projected dates for the initiation of services and expected duration; (g) the name of the case manager; and (h) procedures for transition from early intervention into the preschool program. The IFSP must be evaluated at least once a year, and must be reviewed every 6 months or more often where appropriate.

The IFSP must be evaluated at least once a year.

State Policy

❏ P.L. 99-457 does not require states to serve infants and toddlers. It does, however, provide significantly increased financial incentives as well as federal guidance and encouragement. All states are already implementing some of the provisions of P.L. 99-457.

All states are already implementing P.L. 99-457.

In a recent study of state early intervention and preschool policies, Meisels, Harbin, Modigliani, and Olson, (1987) provided the following national "profile":

- Very few states (*N* = 7) have entitlements for services to birth-3 year olds. Nevertheless, more than 80% of the states have some form of entitlement prior to school age.
- State Educational Agencies (SEAs) play an important role in administering programs for birth-6-year-olds. But Public Health and Social Services are more actively involved in overseeing birth-3 services than are SEAs.
- Funding emerges from more than 12 major public and private sources. P.L. 94-142 is a major funding mechanism, but state and local taxes are most frequently cited as fiscal support for birth-3 services. Medicaid, which is utilized by 2 of every 3 states, is the only non-education source widely used besides taxes.
- There is no single intervention service component that is universally mandated nationally. At best, two-thirds of the states mandate Public Awareness and Diagnosis/Assessment for 3-6 year olds, but only slightly more than half of the states require intervention services for 3-6 year olds. Fewer than 2 of every 5 states mandate such services for birth-3 year olds.
- All program components are in need of significant improvement in the area of interagency coordination. Case management, staff training, and diagnosis/assessment are the highest on the list of intervention components in greatest need of interagency coordination.
- Coordination among agencies faces numerous obstacles, stemming principally from low funding, inconsistent eligibility criteria, and inconsistent regulations. These problems are significantly reduced, but not eliminated, in states with mandates.

• Major problems remain to be solved in the areas of state regulations, teacher certification, and supply and demand of trained professionals. An alarming shortage of trained early childhood special educators, and physical, occupational, and speech therapists was identified—this shortage projected to continue until the end of the decade. (p. 15)

In an effort to track the early effects of P.L. 99-457 on state policy, the National Association of State Directors of Special Education (NASDSE) initiated periodic surveys of state special education directors requesting information on their states' initial responses to P.L. 99-457. Two of the issues surveyed were: (a) whether the state decided to participate; and (b) the designation of the "lead agency" for the Part H or Infant/Toddler Program. All states have entered the program and have designated a "lead agency." Figure 3 is a listing of the "lead agencies" in each state.

We have a wide variety of state policies and programs.

Thus, at present, we have a wide variety of state policies and state programs for young handicapped and at-risk children. We also have the advent of the first national initiative to provide full services to all eligible children—P.L. 99-457. Perhaps this federal guidance and incentive can help provide a unifying lead for state and local policy. The effect of P.L. 99-457 on state policy is only one of the possible challenges that lies ahead.

THE FUTURE

❑ The increased sociopolitical attention to the needs of infants and their families is probably a result of research-based advocacy that built upon the logic that if intervention at age 3 had significant, positive effects, earlier intervention was even better. Indeed, the data and the logic have been around a lot longer than the programs or the policies and had a laboratory research, clinical research, *and* conceptual basis (Strain & Smith, 1986). However, even in the face of decades of research, early intervention policy development has typically been a "trickle-down" phenomenon, that is, state and federal funds have been phased in from preschool-aged services downward toward services beginning at birth. This "phase-in" is, obviously, still with us. Until the "phase-in" is complete, with *all* states providing appropriate services to *all* eligible children from birth, there will continue to be significant and emerging policy developments. These developments, hopefully, will be based on research and "best practice" and will move us forward.

Data and logic have been around longer than programs.

Four obvious policy challenges lie ahead for early intervention: (a) full participation by all states in P.L. 99-457; (b) effective implementation of the intent of P.L. 99-457 at state and local levels; (c) evaluation of the effects of P.L. 99-457 and state and local policies on young children and their families; and (d) revision of P.L. 99-457 based on the evaluation data.

Policy challenges lie ahead.

Full Participation

❑ Just as P.L. 94-142 is a voluntary program, so too is the Infant/Toddler Program of P.L. 99-457 (Part H). States do not have to participate. However, if a state applies for Part H funds it must comply with the requirements of the law. Therefore, the first challenge ahead is to convince governors and agency administrators of the importance of participation.

Figure 3. Participation and Lead Agency Designation.

State	State Participation	Lead Agency
Alabama	Yes	Education
Alaska	Yes	Health and Social Services
American Samoa	Yes	Health
Arizona	Yes	Econ. Security—DD
Arkansas	Yes	Human Services
California	Yes	Developmental Services
Colorado	Yes	Education
Connecticut	Yes	Education
Delaware	Yes	Public Instruction
D.C.	Yes	Human Services
Florida	Yes	Education
Georgia	Yes	Human Resources
Guam	Yes	Education
Hawaii	Yes	Health (Crippled Services)
Idaho	Yes	Health and Welfare—DD
Illinois	Yes	Education
Indiana	Yes	Mental Health
Iowa	Yes	Education
Kansas	Yes	Health and Environment
Kentucky	Yes	Cabinet for Human Resources
Louisiana	Yes	Education
Maine	Yes	Interdepartmental Committee
Maryland	Yes	Office of Children and Youth
Massachusetts	Yes	Public Health
Michigan	Yes	Education
Minnesota	Yes	Education
Mississippi	Yes	Health
Missouri	Yes	Education
Montana	Yes	Developmental Disabilities
Nebraska	Yes	Education
Nevada	Yes	Human Resources
New Hampshire	Yes	Education
New Jersey	Yes	Education
New Mexico	Yes	Health and Environment
New York	Yes	Health
North Carolina	Yes	Human Resources
North Dakota	Yes	Human Services
Ohio	Yes	Health Department
Oklahoma	Yes	State Dept. of Education
Oregon	Yes	M.H. Program for D.D.
Pennsylvania	Yes	Public Welfare
Puerto Rico	Yes	Education
Rhode Island	Yes	Interagency Coord. Council
South Carolina	Yes	Health and Env. Control
South Dakota	Yes	Education and Cultural Affairs

(Continued)

Figure 3. Participation and Lead Agency Designation. (Continued)

State	State Participation	Lead Agency
Tennessee	Yes	Education
Texas	Yes	Inter Council on EC Intervention
Mariana Islands	Yes	Education
Utah	Yes	Health
Vermont	Yes	Education
Virgin Islands	Yes	Health
Virginia	Yes	Mental Health/Mental Retardation
Washington	Yes	Social and Health Services
West Virginia	Yes	Health
Wisconsin	Yes	Health and Social Services
Wyoming	Yes	Health and Human Services

Note: From National Association of State Directors of Special Education, September 4, 1987.

Research and evaluation studies will help shape challenges.

Once a state participates it faces the three remaining challenges. All three of these challenges have one fact in common—they should be driven by research efforts.

Effective Implementation

❏ One unique feature of early intervention social policy is the role that research and development activities have played in its development. One of the possible reasons for this is the fact that early intervention policy has developed concurrently with a tightening of the national economy. Over the past 20 years, policy makers have gradually lost the luxury of frivolous decisions. Each policy decision has had to be weighed against all other competing interests and values. Thus, early intervention advocates have learned to present convincing arguments based on research data and practice. Therefore, the use of research in the future challenges of selecting effective program and policy options and evaluating and refining policies does not present an unfamiliar task to early intervention advocates. The important factor will be *how* research is used to advance high-quality services to children and families.

Advocates have learned to present arguments based on research and practice.

There are four stages of policy making.

Seekins and Fawcett (1986) suggest that there are four stages of policy making: agenda formation (deciding which issues to act upon), policy adoption(making the policy itself), policy implementation (translating the policy into action), and policy review (evaluating the value and satisfaction of the consequences of the policy). Each stage dictates a particular use of research.

When one reads the House Report (99-860) (1986) accompanying P.L. 99-457, it is evident that research data played an important role in the development and adoption of the legislation. For instance, the report contains the following excerpt as the rationale for the new federal initiative:

> Because of advances in research methodology, instrumentation, and theory, educators and behavioral scientists have come to view even very young infants as capable of participating in complex interactions with the world. For example, we now believe that newborns have a functioning perceptual system capable of intersensory coordination,

that they are capable of making multiple categorizations, that they possess both central and peripheral vision at birth, can coordinate visual and auditory input by age 2-1/2 months, show evidence of recognition memory by 4 months, and are able to recognize relatively abstract two-dimensional stimuli by 5 months. . . .

Thus, the infant's developing physical, cognitive, and social competencies are very important. Because of our recognition of the early appearance of these and other competencies, infants increasingly are being viewed as active organizers of their experience and not as passive and helpless creatures. Likewise, such recognition has also made it more feasible and tenable to develop early successful intervention approaches for handicapped infants and toddlers.

Infants are being viewed as active organizers of their experience.

The Committee therefore concludes that an overwhelming case exists for expanding and improving the provision of early intervention and preschool programs. The Committee's conclusions comport with the Department's findings in its Seventh Annual Report to the Congress:

Studies of the effectiveness of preschool education for the handicapped have demonstrated beyond doubt the economic and educational benefits of programs for young handicapped children. In addition, the studies have shown that the earlier intervention is started, the greater is the ultimate dollar savings and the higher is the rate of educational attainment by these handicapped children.

More specifically, testimony and research indicate that early intervention and preschool services accomplish the following:

- Help enhance intelligence in some children;
- Produce substantial gains in physical development, cognitive development, language and speech development, psychosocial development and self-help skills;
- Help prevent the development of secondary handicapping conditions;
- Reduce family stress;
- Reduce societal dependency and institutionalization;
- Reduce the need for special class placement in special education programs once the children reach school age; and,
- Save substantial costs to society and our nation's schools. (pp. 4-5).

Research and evaluation activities will continue to play an important role. Using Seekins and Fawcett's (1986) model, early intervention policy under P.L. 99-457 is entering the latter two stages—implementation and review.

There are many provisions in P.L. 99-457 that are subject to interpretation. Some of these dimensions already have a research base that points the way to the most effective implementation. Therefore, the challenge is the dissemination and adoption of these research and model development findings. Until recently, research findings have not been readily available to or used by practitioners. Indeed, B. F. Skinner (1956) summarized the state of the art at that time when he wrote: "We are more concerned with the discovery of knowledge than with its dissemination" (p. 221). More recently there has been an increase in the attempts to have research findings accessible to and adopted by practitioners and "lay" public (Couch, Miller, Johnson & Welsh, 1986). In fact, this interest

The challenge is the dissemination and adoption of findings.

has facilitated a growth in "technical assistance" efforts aimed at translating research and development findings into practice, as well as a growing body of literature regarding factors that enhance or impede the field adoption of research findings. After reviewing the literature, Kohler (1985) developed a synopsis of 12 criteria for the effective dissemination of educational findings. According to Kohler, in order to be readily adopted, research should be

Applied: Study behaviors that society has some interest in.

Behavioral: Increase peoples' ability to do something effectively.

Compatible: Consistent with the values, past experiences, and current needs of its consumers.

Decentralized: Suitable for small-scale application.

Effective: Produce large enough effects for practical value.

Flexible: Invite consumers to create their own procedures based on original models.

Generalizable: Improvements should endure across settings, responses, and over time.

Inexpensive: Economic profitability, low initial cost, low perceived risk, and a savings in time and effort.

Simple: Comprehensible and usable.

Socially Valid: Select goals that society really wants. Use procedures that are acceptable to consumers. Produce effects that are satisfying to society.

Sustainable: Maintained by local individuals and resources.

Technological: A typically trained consumer can replicate a procedure with effective results.

Loucks (1983) proposed seven tasks that must be undertaken in order to achieve successful implementation of a model program or procedure. According to her, the researcher or model developer must

- Create awareness of the model.
- Establish a commitment from the adopting site.
- Provide and explain materials.
- Train site personnel in the model program and procedures, including follow-up training.
- Help the adopting site to plan for the implementation of the model.
- Solve implementation problems and "trouble shoot" solutions.
- Monitor and evaluate the implementation.

Using dissemination guidelines such as those just described may increase the adoption of research findings. Because of the time factor involved in studying certain program and implementation options of P.L. 99-457, attention to the "adoptability" of related studies may prove to be a critical factor in the success of this legislation.

Many dimensions or provisions, however, are not so clear. Instead, they lend themselves to the study of the most effective options. For instance, dimensions such as interagency funding and reimbursement options, effective inservice training and credentialing models, and the most effective options for implementing the case management system, because of their innovative nature, demonstrate the need to evaluate the effects of various options or services to children and families. At this stage, research is used to answer the question "how to intervene" rather than "whether to intervene." Or as Weiss (1977) put it, there are two primary uses of research in policy making—to set the agenda (whether to intervene) or to suggest alternative policy actions (how to intervene). Indeed, Bulmer (1981) suggested that information on the effects of various options may be the most powerful type of research information for decision makers.

Research is used to answer "how to intervene."

Currently, one policy dimension presented by P.L. 99-457 that necessitates the assessment of the effects of various options is the frequency and intensity of services to be provided. Decision makers need information on the effectiveness of varying levels of service intensity and frequency on various populations of children. Information on the consequences of various models can help shape policy decisions at all levels—school/community, state, and federal. In other words, studies of the effectiveness of services delivered for a variety of days per week and hours per day, and percentage of instructional time versus program hours for groups of children of varying conditions and severity of delay are needed. Comparative results will help decision makers to provide the most effective and yet efficient quantities of service.

Information on models can help shape policy decisions.

Comparative results will help decision makers.

Policy Evaluation and Revision

❑ Evaluative data, as described above, could prove to be invaluable to policy makers and program developers. Policy evaluation or analysis provides an important, systematic way of measuring whether or not the intent of the policy has been met and of determining how the policy needs to be changed to increase the success rate (Gallagher, 1984). However, a word of caution is needed. A high level of research validity and integrity is imperative. As stated earlier, data on the effects of program options form a powerful policy tool. Poor data can be as powerful as high-quality data. For an example of the potential negative impact data may have on program and policy, one need not look far. Brown (1985) reviewed the impact that the 1969 "Westinghouse Report" nearly had on Head Start. In his paper, Brown pointed out that although the study was flawed and the conclusions questionable at best, policy wheels were set in motion. The report concluded that the summer Head Start program was ineffective and even had a negative effect, and the full-year program had only marginal effects. Even though the report was questioned immediately and other researchers demonstrated the problems with the study, in 1971 a plan was developed to phase out Head Start. While the phase-out was eventually prevented, the negative impact of the Westinghouse report lingered for many years.

A high level of research validity is imperative.

It was not until another study was completed, according to Brown, that the negative impact was in fact, reversed. The Consortium for Longitudinal Studies (1979) conducted a "meticulous" study of the effects of early intervention and reported significantly different findings from the West-inghouse study. Since them, Head Start funding has increased dramatically and was one of few domestic programs to be placed in the Reagan budget "safety net" in 1981 (Brown, 1985).

While research and evaluation activities can facilitate the development of effective programs and implementation policies, they can also help to review the effectiveness of the policy itself. Over the next several years, systematic policy research and collection of data on the effect of P.L. 99-457 on children and families could assist in any future review and revision of state and national early intervention policies. Periodically, the

Policy research on P.L. 99-457 could assist in future intervention policies.

Congress reviews its policies. In a few years, it will review P.L. 99-457—whether the intent of the law has been met and whether there is need to revise it. High-quality evaluative data at that time will help to shape national early intervention policy for years to come.

REFERENCES

Allen, K. E. (1984). Federal legislation and young handicapped children. *Topics in Early Childhood Special Education, 4,* 9-18.

Brown, B. (1985). HEAD START: How research changed public policy. *Young Children, 40,* 9-13.

Bulmer, M. (1981). Applied social research: A reformation of "applied" and "enlightenment" models. *Knowledge: Creation, Diffusion, Utilization, 3,* 187-210.

Consortium for Longitudinal Studies. (1979). *Lasting effects after preschool, summary report.* Washington, DC: Department of Health and Human Services, Administration for Children, Youth and Families.

Couch, R., Miller, L. K., Johnson, M., & Welsh, T. (1986). Some considerations for behavior analysts developing social change interventions. *Behavior Analysis and Social Action, 5,* 9-13.

Gallagher, J. (1984). Policy analysis and program implementation (P.L. 94-142). *Topics in Early Childhood Special Education, 4,* 43-53.

Garland, C., Black, T., & Jesien, G. (1986). *The future of outreach: A DEC position paper.* Unpublished manuscript. The Division for Early Childhood.

House Report, 99-860. (1986). Education of the handicapped act amendments of 1986. U.S. Congress, 4-5.

Kohler, F. (1985). Unpublished review paper. University of Kansas, Lawrence, KS.

Loucks, S. F. (1983). *Planning for dissemination.* Chapel Hill, NC: TADS.

Meisels, S. J., Harbin, G., Modigliani, K., & Olson, K. (in press). Formulating optimal state early childhood intervention policies. *Exceptional Children.*

National Association of State Directors of Special Education. (1987). Washington, DC.

Seekins, T., & Fawcett, S. (1986). Public policy making and research information. *The Behavior Analyst, 9,* 35-45.

Skinner, B. F. (1956). A case history in scientific method. *American Psychologist, 11,* 221-233.

Strain, P. S., & Smith, B. J. (1986). A counter-interpretation of early intervention effects: A response to Casto and Mastropieri. *Exceptional Children, 53*(3), 260-265.

Suarez, T. M., Hurth, J. L., & Prestridge, S. (1987). *Innovation in early childhood special education: An analysis of the Handicapped Children's Early Education Program projects funded from 1982-1986.* Paper delivered at the Annual Meeting of the American Education Research Association, Washington, DC.

U.S. Department of Education. (1987). *Ninth annual report to Congress on the implementation of the education of the handicapped act.* Washington, DC: U.S. Government Printing Office.

U.S. Department of Health and Human Services (1986). *The status of handicapped children in Head Start programs.* Washington, DC: U.S. Government Printing Office.

Weiss, C. H. (1977). Introduction. In C. H. Weiss (Ed.), *Using social research in public policy making* (pp. 1-22). Lexington, MA: Lexington Books.

11.
Preparing for Change: The Implementation of Public Law 99–457

Pascal L. Trohanis

There is nothing permanent except change. (Heraclitus, 560 B.C.)

❏ Congress expects concrete benefits and improvements over the next 5 years, resulting from the handicapped infant and toddler portion of P.L. 99-457. For example:

1. America's eligible children with special needs and their families and society will reap positive outcomes from the implementation of this law, which includes reduced institutionalization, optimal child development, and family participation.
2. All states will have implemented and routinized comprehensive, coordinated, interdisciplinary service systems and accompanying state policies and standards.
3. Appropriate funds, technologies, knowledge, and personnel will be available to ensure the efficient and effective implementation of the early intervention initiative.

In reality, over the next 60 months, will these goals be accomplished in our nation?

For most states fulfilling these goals represents an enormous implementation challenge, grounded in bringing about substantive changes in people and organizations. Plans for these changes must be developed and channeled into positive action rather than allowed to succumb to barriers of inaction and the status quo. State agents of change, such as the state interagency coordinating council and the lead agency, must provide leadership and vision for this action planning.

This chapter will acquaint the reader with ideas and perspectives on the process of change in relation to policy implementation. As agents of change, parents, professionals, and others must be able to adapt to and provide leadership for change—the betterment of young children with special needs and their families. Also, implementers must build upon the best of the past and recognize that change and improvement take time, persistence, and patience. Finally, sound implementation calls for a team of people to plan and work together, for no one discipline, profession, advocate or parent group, setting, or agency can provide everything all alone.

This chapter begins with a description of the process of change in relation to policy implementation. Next, a planning approach is introduced to help develop a thoughtful action plan for the implementation of an early intervention policy. Suggested guidelines are also included.

Plans for changes must be channeled into positive action.

Parents, professionals others must provide leadership to change.

PROCESS OF CHANGE IN RELATION TO POLICY IMPLEMENTATION

❏ As described in earlier chapters of this book, a public policy provides a vision, a particular strategy to solve a problem, a sanction of behaviors and attitudes, and a distribution of resources. A national policy for early intervention has been conceptualized, formulated, and enacted. Also, catalytic monies have been appropriated and disbursed by the federal administering agency, the U.S. Department of Education.

A national policy has been enacted.

P.L. 99-457 represents a new policy that must be translated into action by all states, territories, the District of Columbia, and the Bureau of Indian Affairs. To do so effectively and efficiently, agents of change in all jurisdictions must plan an implementation process that takes into account four sets of intertwined elements of change—context, PIPPS (policies, ideas, programs, products, and systems), user decision making, and techniques.

Context and Change

❑ Context refers to a cluster of characteristics that represent the impetus and expectations for change, authority for involvement, and climate in terms of support for implementation of the early intervention policy. The following three dimensions can be defined:

1. Congressional dimension

   (a) Encourage optimal child and family development.

   (b) Minimize likelihood of institutionalization.

   (c) Reduce need for special and more costly class placements.

   (d) Reaffirm dignity and self-esteem of each individual.

   (e) Seek concurrence, cooperation, and teamwork among federal, state, and local organizations and parents.

2. Federal government dimension

   (a) Designate an administering agency of the U.S. Department of Education (OSERS and OSEP) for day-to-day management, monitoring, and technical assistance to the program.

   (b) Compose regulations based on P.L. 99-457 and make them available to help guide the implementation process.

   (c) Implement funding levels (uncertain beyond the current one-year appropriation of $50 million).

   (d) Sponsor other discretionary assistance projects, such as technical assistance and training, research, and demonstration, to provide support to states.

3. State dimension

   (a) Make interpretations of P.L. 99-457 and its early intervention provisions.

   (b) Make known current status of and support for changes and improvements in community-based early intervention services across the state.

   (c) Provide major leadership in state change efforts by members of lead agency and state interagency coordinating council.

   (d) Make available status of and needs for resources, personnel, and know-how to conduct implementation.

   (e) Support collaborative comprehensive service system planning and implementation activities among public and private state and local agencies and parents.

These three dimensions will serve as contextual building blocks used by the states' agents of change for the implementation process. They will influence views toward the substance of change, decision-making models, and various techniques.

PIPPS and Change

❏ *Change* is seen here as a complex and dynamic communication process of ensuring that early intervention policies, ideas, programs, products, or systems (PIPPS) are put into practice within local communities and states. Agents of change and users (targets of change) will interact mutually with one another about PIPPS and their value and contributions to comprehensive service systems. As the substance of change efforts in states, PIPPS pertinent to early intervention may consist of the following:

Agents of change and users interact with one another.

1. Some of the minimum components of early intervention system such as

    (a) definition of developmental delay

    (b) multidisciplinary evaluation

    (c) IFSP (individualized family service plan)

    (d) case management

    (e) child find

    (f) public awareness

    (g) central directory

    (h) single line of responsibility

    (i) procedural safeguards.

2. Funding and matters such as payor of last resort, private sector finance, and no reduction of other benefits.

3. State interagency coordinating council and lead agency—new roles, responsibilities, and relationships.

Agents of change must be able to resolve questions that users in states and communities may have about PIPPS such as: What is the content of the PIPPS? What makes our PIPPS worthwhile and effective? How does it benefit children, families, professionals? What are the costs? Is it compatible with local values? Does it meet the intent of the law? Are there issues and challenges of PIPPS still unresolved? (See Figure 1.)

Early intervention PIPPS such as those tied to P.L. 99-457 will provoke changes. The introduction of PIPPS will spark mental/attitudinal processing by people involved in the implementation process. These affected users (e.g., parents, therapists, teachers, social workers, bureaucrats) will go through a series of reorganizations in their behaviors, skills, knowledge bases, and attitudes as they accept or reject PIPPS. Assuming that a posture of acceptance can be nurtured, positive action should follow, along with the eventual installation and routinization of the early intervention PIPPS, that is, case management, IFSP, and procedural safeguards. In essence, the implementation of P.L. 99-457 and its early intervention provisions involves the transfer of knowledge (PIPPS) from one agency or person (e.g., "According to lead agency policy, this is what case management is.") to another (e.g., "I as a parent can accept and implement this procedure."). This transfer represents an instance of change including innovation, diffusion, and adoption. As Zaltman (1979) observed, "As knowledge and its use may diffuse through a population, social change may occur. Thus, many instances of intended knowledge utilization are instances of planned change" (p. 84).

Users go through reorganizations in behaviors as they accept or reject PIPPS.

Transfer represents innovation, diffusion, adoption.

Figure 1. Sample of PIPPS and Unresolved Issues/Challenges for Implementation.

1. IFSP
   a. Should IFSP indicate who is fiscally responsible?
   b. What constitutes family?
   c. Should assessment include family's perception of the child?
   d. What is the best way to ensure that services are provided in a manner least disruptive to child and family?

2. Child Find and Evaluation
   a. What constitutes comprehensive and timely?
   b. What about confidentiality of information about total family functioning?
   c. Should there be a single portal of entry into the service system?
   d. Who should do the testing?

3. Procedural Safeguards
   a. Are complaint procedures limited to parent initiatives?
   b. What is the difference between a complaint and a dispute?
   c. What about specified time frames to resolve disputes?

4. Lead Agency and State Interagency Coordinating Council
   a. What are the roles and authority of each?
   b. How can infant/toddler and preschool initiatives be closely related since P.L. 99-457 separates them into two titles?
   c. How should physicians be involved?

5. Case Management
   a. What does this term mean for implementation?
   b. Who is being case managed?
   c. Is there a better term that can be used?

6. Personnel Preparation
   a. Are the numbers of professionals sufficient or insufficient to meet needs over the next 5 years?
   b. What core competencies, if any, are necessary?
   c. How will credentials and licensure be addressed?

User Decision Making and Change

❏ Agents of change must see to it that the users (targets of change) are kept in mind. This notion is vital, since apparently people go through a decision process in considering, accepting, and/or rejecting the PIPPS that are being introduced. Rogers (1983) outlined the following decision process:

Agents of change must see to it that the users are kept in mind.

1. Knowledge stage: User acquires general information about PIPPS.

2. Persuasion stage: User develops a leaning toward PIPPS.

3. Decision stage: User decides to adopt PIPPS.

4. Implementation stage: User puts PIPPS into use.

5. Confirmation stage: User seeks further information to support choice of PIPPS.

Loucks (1983) provided a view similar to Rogers'. She described change as a process and not an event—a personal process that individuals experience differently. Further, Loucks suggested that as people get involved with the new PIPPS, individuals experience similar growth patterns. These views are summarized best in what is known as CBAM—concerns-based adoption model. Following is an example of the stages of concern and some typical expressions of concern about the PIPPS:

Stages of Concern	Typical Expressions of Concern by Users
0. Awareness:	"I am not concerned about the PIPPS."
1. Informational:	"I would like to know more about the PIPPS."
2. Personal:	"How will using the PIPPS affect me?"
3. Management:	"I seem to be spending all my time shuffling paperwork and getting ready."
4. Consequence:	"How is my use of the PIPPS affecting children and families?"
5. Collaboration:	"I am concerned about relating what I am doing with what others are doing."
6. Refocusing:	"I have some ideas about something that would work even better."

Framework starts with an awareness of PIPPS.

A third view of change and decision making was offered by Trohanis (1982). See Figure 2 for an overview of user decision making that deals with the considerations users are likely to weigh as they make decisions concerning PIPPS. The framework starts with developing an *awareness* of the PIPPS and moves through phases of showing *interest*, weighing or *evaluating* its value, seeking wider *support* for the PIPPS, identifying and securing *resources*, and deciding to *try out* the PIPPS; the framework concludes with finalizing the *preoperations* necessary for adoption, adaption, or installation. Of course, the agent of change hopes the user accepts the PIPPS and then works toward its installation and routine use. However, the user may choose to accept or reject the PIPPS depending upon a host of factors. A decision-making framework can help point to factors that can cause a potential user to reject PIPPS; awareness of these factors allows the agent of change to correct or minimize their impact.

Any oversight can lead to rejection. Any oversight can lead to rejection. For example, if potential benefits of PIPPS are unclear, the user may reject the practice from the outset. Factors outside the agent's control (resources, for example) may also lead to rejection.

Thus, people react to and get involved in new early intervention PIPPS through information-gathering activities—awareness of and wanting to know more about PIPPS such as IFSP, evaluation, and case management; through learning more about PIPPS by trying it out mentally or setting up small-scale trials or pilot projects; and through decision-making activities—accepting, implementing, installing, and routinizing the PIPPS until a better one comes along.

Techniques and Change

❑ In order to bring about positive change and effective implementation of an early intervention policy, some different techniques must be considered and used by the agents of change:

● *Rational* calls for the unbiased presentation of facts, appropriate knowledge, and data to help people change through such strategies as reports, concept papers, research studies, and information presentations at forums. This technique seems most useful for developing awareness of and information about PIPPS.

Figure 2. *User Decision Making by Phases.*

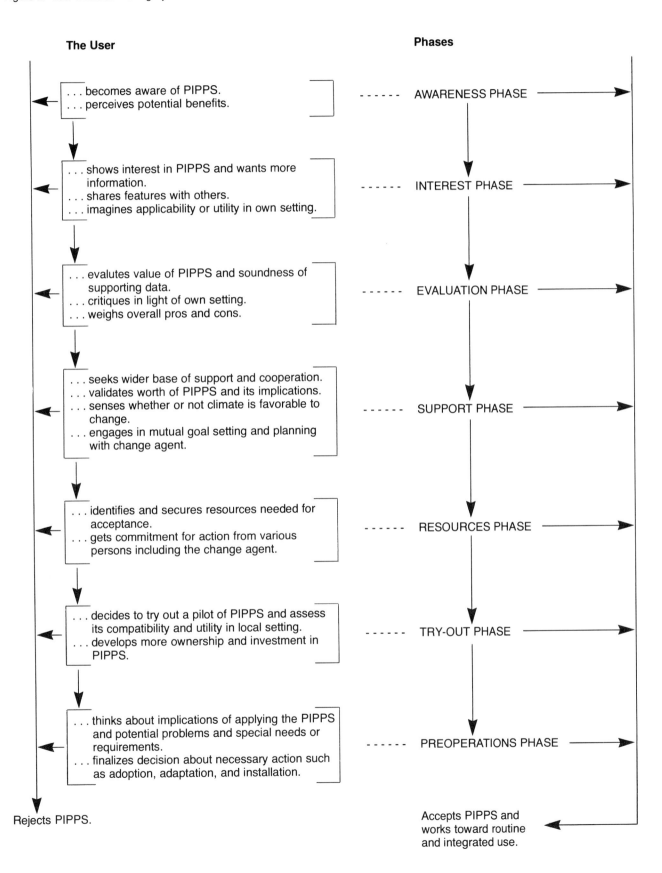

The User

Phases

. . . becomes aware of PIPPS.
. . . perceives potential benefits.
------ AWARENESS PHASE ----→

. . . shows interest in PIPPS and wants more
information.
. . . shares features with others.
. . . imagines applicability or utility in own setting.
------ INTEREST PHASE ----→

. . . evalutes value of PIPPS and soundness of
supporting data.
. . . critiques in light of own setting.
. . . weighs overall pros and cons.
------ EVALUATION PHASE ----→

. . . seeks wider base of support and cooperation.
. . . validates worth of PIPPS and its implications.
. . . senses whether or not climate is favorable to
change.
. . . engages in mutual goal setting and planning
with change agent.
------ SUPPORT PHASE ----→

. . . identifies and secures resources needed for
acceptance.
. . . gets commitment for action from various
persons including the change agent.
------ RESOURCES PHASE ----→

. . . decides to try out a pilot of PIPPS and assess
its compatibility and utility in local setting.
. . . develops more ownership and investment in
PIPPS.
------ TRY-OUT PHASE ----→

. . . thinks about implications of applying the PIPPS
and potential problems and special needs or
requirements.
. . . finalizes decision about necessary action such
as adoption, adaptation, and installation.
------ PREOPERATIONS PHASE ----→

Rejects PIPPS.

Accepts PIPPS and
works toward routine
and integrated use.

- *Training* stresses the provision of preservice and inservice training to upgrade knowledge and skills and help people face changes through such strategies as workshops, courses, seminars, and visiting other programs. This technique appears most suitable for management and try-out stages.

- *Persuasion* represents the selling of PIPPS to help change peoples' attitudes and predispositions through such strategies as public relations, lobbying, public service announcements, news releases, and audiovisual presentations. The technique seems best with building interest in PIPPS, weighing its value, and seeking wider support.

- *Consultation* focuses on a personal and collaborative problem-solving approach with strategies such as one-to-one (face-to-face) contact, technical assistance, and group processes to facilitate and nurture change and acceptance. This technique seems best with personal, management, and user concerns.

- *Power* mandates change by an authority through strategies such as sanctions, coercion, licensure, and compliance monitoring. This technique appears to work well with the decision and resources stages.

Agents of change must consider context, PIPPS, user decision making, techniques.

Agents of change must consider these four major ingredients of change—context, PIPPS, user decision making, and techniques—prior to engaging in more specific action planning. As Bowman (1981) said, "Change has a tendency to make us anxious and pessimistic, but it is frequently from change that our most innovative and effective programs arise" (p. 49).

A PLANNING APPROACH TO GUIDE IMPLEMENTATION

❑ A planning approach incorporating these major ingredients of change is depicted in Figure 3. This approach outlines 13 related tasks that must be considered and addressed to foster success. It is intended for use by agents of change who may be part of the state interagency coordinating council or lead agency to spark discussion and consensus, generate purposes, explore alternative techniques and strategies in relation to resources and constraints, and implement and evaluate efforts for change and improvement.

To further assist with planning endeavors, several implementation guidelines are offered for consideration (Bozeman and Fellows, 1987; Eliot & Dowling, 1982; House, 1976; Loucks, 1983; Parish & Arends, 1983; Rogers, 1983; Trohanis, 1982):

1. Implement a mix of top-down (forward mapping) planning strategies which start at the state-level and move to the community and bottom-up (backward mapping) strategies which begin at the community and work upward to the state. This mix promotes and sanctions formation of partnerships to conduct this type of planning.

2. Know the people and organizational milieu that are being asked to change. For example, who are supporters who can help with the implementation effort? Who are nonsupporters and who are "persuadables" who can be accounted for in planning.

3. Identify and work with peer/support networks that will make the implementation more efficient and effective.

Figure 3. Planning Approach to Guide Policy Implementation.

1. Pinpoint impetus and source of change for early intervention policy (note whether source is external, internal, or both).

2. Check status of current early intervention system of services and activities in state and communities and chart needs.
   a. Values and philosophy
   b. History
   c. Extant services and providers
   d. Manpower availability

3. Identify and specify content of early intervention (PIPPS) pertinent to a state's comprehensive coordinated, multidisciplinary interagency system.
   a. Policies
   b. Ideas
   c. Programs
   d. Products
   e. Systems

4. Define scope of change in relation to PIPPS.
   a. Simple—little modification of early intervention service system is intended; less time-consuming effort will be required
   b. In-between—some adaptations and time are required
   c. Complex—major changes are required including personnel, procedures, and organizational protocols; a time-consuming effort will be required

5. Describe agents of change at state and local levels.
   a. Governor and staff
   b. Lead agency
   c. State interagency coordinating council
   d. Parents
   e. Local administrators
   f. Others

6. Define targets (users) and beneficiaries of change and identify their readiness for and commitment to implementation.
   a. Target = social worker . . . beneficiary = family
   b. Target = university professor . . . beneficiary = graduate student in early intervention
   c. Others

7. Examine barriers.
   a. Who might hinder your efforts?
   b. Who are the persuadables?
   c. What occasions are particularly sensitive?
   d. What about factors such as bureaucracies, social systems, economics, transportation, politics?

8. Set implementation parameters.
   a. Finance
   b. Manpower, staff, coalitions
   c. Quality control and compliance
   d. Pilot project or widespread implementation
   e. Timelines

9. Study setting(s) for change including culture, geography, and locale.

10. Establish goals or intended outcomes and garner support for these.

11. Conceptualize, develop, and implement techniques (and strategies) to facilitate support and acceptance.

(Continued)

Figure 3. Planning Approach to Guide Policy Implementation (Continued)

    a. Rational
    b. Training
    c. Persuasion
    d. Consultation
    e. Power

12. Design an evaluation.

13. Determine amount and type of follow-along support necessary to help users (targets of change) adjust to new circumstances and use of PIPPS.

4. Address unintended and unexpected outcomes or consequences that emerge as policy is implemented.

5. Build long-term and short-term plans that include incentives to ensure that the PIPPS are accepted, installed, and routinized as intended.

6. Encourage and support accessing sound information from research and "best practices" (bridging theory with practice) to get high-quality, practical, and useful PIPPS.

7. If necessary, given the nature and scope of change and setting, plan a sequence of events to implement the PIPPS and be aware of particular "transportation routes" that must be used to get the message across to the intended users.

8. Facilitate implementation by person-to-person contact and transactions. This must be a primary strategy that is carefully planned and used.

9. Depending on the scope of the intended policy change, weigh the implementation strategy carefully. For example, if the scope of change is complex, it may be best to start out with a small-scale pilot effort before going statewide.

Ohme (1977) provided this observation about planning and implementing a strategy for change: "The success of a plan does not depend necessarily upon its merit, but rather upon the right combination of leadership plus client and practitioner involvement" (p. 263).

CONCLUSION

Formal organizations and members will promote change.

❑ P.L. 99-457 and its early intervention initiatives identify, among others, the lead agency and the state interagency coordinating council as primary leaders of the implementation effort. It will be these formal organizations and their members who will promote change to and through many other individuals and organizations so as to implement high-quality, comprehensive, coordinated, multidisciplinary interagency services for very young children with special needs and their families.

Lead agency and council personnel establish mission, oversee development, installation.

As primary agents of change, the lead agency and council personnel will engage in long-term (visionary) and short-term (operational) planning; they will establish a mission for early intervention and oversee development and installation of policies, ideas, programs, products, or systems (PIPPS) in their states. Their work will be to plan and carry out integration with other early childhood efforts in their states, a challenging and exciting effort.

It will be these people who must provide the direction, the energy, the communication, and the mobilization for positive change. Additionally, they must overcome resistance and synchronize a course that brings together the hopes of Congress, the administrative needs of the federal government, and the dreams and wishes of states for improved services to all of our nation's eligible infants, toddlers, and their families. While changes may alter the established order, cause stress, and create pain, people and their organizations are resilient. As Mack (1981) stated: "Social change asks you to alter the way you behave—to rethink what you can expect from others and what they can expect from you" (p. 5). He concluded by reminding us that human beings are able to learn to anticipate coping with new situations, ideas, circumstances, and practices. Human beings "can mentally practice coping with change before it happens; they can plan ahead" (p. 5).

Change agents must provide direction, energy, communication, mobilization for positive change.

REFERENCES

Bowman, B. (1981). Change and commitment. *Young Children, 36,* 49-50.

Bozeman, B., & Fellows, M. (1987). *Technology transfer at the U.S. National Laboratories.* Syracuse: Maxwell School for Public Affairs.

Eliot, P., & Dowling, M. (1982). A framework for technology transfer and brokering in human services. *Sharing, 7*(1), 1-5.

House, E. (1976). The micropolitics of innovation: Nine propositions. Phi Delta Kappan, 57(5), 337-340.

Loucks, S. (1983). *The concerns-based adoption model (CBAM).* Chapel Hill: Technical Assistance Development System at UNC.

Mack, R. (1981, November). Human resistance to technological revolution. Excerpts from October 1, 1981 address delivered at Northwestern University, Evanston, IL. *Northwestern Alumni News,* 4-5.

Ohme, H. (1977). Ohme's law of institutional change, *Phi Delta Kappan, 59*(4), 263-265.

Parish, R., & Arends, R. (1983). Why innovation programs are discontinued. *Educational Leadership, 40*(4), 62-65.

Rogers, E. (1983). *Diffusion of innovations.* New York: The Free Press.

Trohanis, P. (Ed.) (1982). *Strategies for change.* Chapel Hill: Technical Assistance Development System at UNC.

Zaltman, G. (1979). Knowledge utilization as planned social change. *Knowledge, 1*(1), 82-105.

12.
Where Do We Go From Here?
An Attempt at Synthesis

James J. Gallagher

❏ What have we learned from this volume about our own strengths and weaknesses and what steps are to be taken next to improve our professional performance with infants and toddlers who have handicaps? One conclusion that the reader is likely to reach after reading the various chapters in this volume is that we approach this major issue of implementing the new legislation for infants and toddlers with handicapping conditions with some major professional strengths.

The 20 years of experience in the Handicapped Children's Early Education Program (HCEEP) as well as programs such as Head Start have taught us a great deal about how to design multidisciplinary service programs for young children and their families. As is clear from Chapter 4 by Karnes and Stayton, we have the developed expertise of professionals from many different disciplines to draw upon. Part of our future planning must take into consideration how we can best use this range of experience to help a new generation of professionals and paraprofessionals who will shortly be entering the challenging area of infants and toddlers.

We have the expertise from different disciplines to draw upon.

At the same time, we need to come to grips with some obvious gaps in our existing program efforts if we are to avoid serious implementation pitfalls. For example, in all of the fine chapters that preceded this one, there is little or no mention made of *cost*, yet this may be the most important public policy issue that confronts the overall program. How much will it cost to deliver these treatment programs, and who will provide the funds? What proportion of the funds will be provided by the federal government, and how much by the state and the local community?

There is little or no mention of cost.

This one factor of cost can change all our plans for personnel preparation or the formation of transdisciplinary teams or program evaluation or for any program elements. The track record of the federal government relating to promises to fund P.L. 94-142, the Education for All Handicapped Children Act, is visible for all to see. In the mid-1970s when that legislation was passed, Congress estimated that the federal government would increase the proportion of funds that they would spend to implement the Act over the next decade until it reached a figure of 40% contribution. Well, that decade has now passed and the federal government is currently contributing only about 10% to 11% of the funds while the state and local communities make up the rest (Martin, 1987).

It is little wonder that states and local communities view this latest venture into public policy by the federal government (P.L. 99-457) with some degree of budget apprehension. Thus, one of the essential steps in policy implementation, as Trohanis suggests in Chapter 11, is an estimate of what costs will be incurred if the full purpose of the act, to serve all children who are handicapped in the infant and toddler age group, is to be achieved. Then, as is rarely done before big administrative trouble presents itself, we should consider what kind of program changes or modifications would have to be made if the funds come up short.

One essential step is an estimate of cost.

Would we write off the "at-risk" group as a luxury that limited funding cannot afford, for example? Would we place a hold on the development of the individualized family service plan (IFSP)? Would we limit services in the infant area? It is no good for us to state that we would prefer not to do any of those things. We know that, but some kind of contingency planning would be wise before we are up against fiscal pressure that demands an instant answer.

Would we write off the "at-risk" group as a luxury?

PROFESSIONAL ROLES

❏ One obvious consequence of the new legislation and the programs that it will spawn is the development of a great many new roles to be played by professionals from a wide variety of disciplines. Woodruff and McGonigel (Chapter 8), McCollum and Hughes (Chapter 6), Robinson, Rosenberg, and Beckman (Chapter 5), and Thorp and McCollum (Chapter 7), discuss how we must change our patterns of professional practice vis-a-vis each other and in interacting with families.

But it is more than that—we seem to be ready to invent a truly different role to be played in this service delivery model. That is the role of the *case manager* or *developmental specialist* or *coordinator* or whatever we choose to call it. However the person is labeled, the new responsibilities seem to be clear. Someone must be in charge of the coordination of all these various services from many different disciplines, and someone must be a single point of contact for the family.

We seem ready to invent a truly different role.

The point is well made in these chapters that we cannot have a large group of professionals each interacting with the family and probably confusing them. Someone must be the consistent contact person so that the family can feel that there is one point of intersection between them and the professional team. But once this assumption is accepted, then further questions arise. Where are these case managers going to come from, and how will they be prepared for their new role? Undoubtedly, many persons have already been playing this role in programs for young handicapped children, by necessity rather than by formal training.

It is tempting to try and develop lists of the ideal characteristics of the *case manager* or *developmental specialist*, both professional and personal, but there is a danger in that process as well. One often concludes such an exercise with a portrait of an ideal human being rather than human beings equipped with faults of jealousy, resentment, and pride that drive us all, from time to time. It is useful to remind ourselves that we are asking for an extraordinary set of professional skills and personal characteristics, especially for someone who will be asked to take an outrageously low salary, given their possession of these many positive features. This is only one more element in our natural attempt to picture an ideal service program—a useful task, as long as we remember that we all have had to compromise in the past, both in terms of professional skills and personal characteristics.

We are asking for an extraordinary set of professional skills and personal characteristics.

The transdisciplinary model spelled out in Chapter 8 by Woodruff and McGonigel discusses multiple role shifts and changes from role extension to role enrichment, expansion, exchange, release, and support. These are very real changes that we have to face, and they will be stressful as change always is, but they create some advantages and opportunities to improve our practices as well.

Two of the chapters mention *arena assessment*, for example. In this procedure all the involved professionals watch the entire assessment process rather than each taking the child or family off into a separate cubicle and then reporting back to a later case conference some shorthand version of what they learned. This arena assessment approach makes great sense, and if the professionals can learn to be comfortable with their colleagues watching them interact with the child, it can greatly increase the efficiency and even the accuracy of the assessment. Yet it

This arena assessment approach makes great sense.

Design of effective learning environments may be one of the most important skills we can employ.

often takes major policy changes such as P.L. 99-457 to stimulate constructive change in this fashion.

Another change that many professionals must make is a shift from the direct treatment approach to the construction of environments that will help the child explore or build sensorimotor skills. The design of effective learning environments may be one of the most important skills we can employ ourselves and pass along to parents.

THE PROFESSIONAL TEAM

Nature and membership may be different from setting to setting.

❑ One major point of universal agreement among those thinking about service delivery is that much of it is going to be done by a professional team. The nature and membership of that team may be different from setting to setting, and community to community, and just how it will operate is, of course, a major concern. The range of knowledge and skills necessary to bring good service to the child and family is too far beyond any individual's capacity to think in any other terms but a service team (Garland & Linder, Chapter 2).

The membership of the transdisciplinary service team has developed some identifiable characteristics, as shown in Chapter 6 by McCollum and Hughes, who perform a service in actually looking at the existing patterns in a number of demonstration programs. The early childhood specialists, the speech-language specialist, the physical therapists, and so forth would be expected members of such a team. But there was an absent member of those teams—the medical specialist. Despite the fact that medical problems loom large in many infants and toddlers with handicaps, particularly medically fragile infants, we are not likely to have the physician as a regular member of the team in many settings; therefore, patterns of adaptation need to be planned for, such as, at least, having medical consultation available on a continuing basis.

Almost certainly one of the issues for the professional team is the potential struggle over "professional turf." Who is going to be in charge? If there is a difference of opinion within the team as to what the service priority should be, or even what should be told to the family, then how will such disagreements be resolved? We can anticipate that psychologists will not take kindly to questions about their assessment of the child's intellectual capabilities or pediatricians feel warmly about questions about their medical diagnosis or suggestions for treatment.

It is easier to let loose of roles when working with infants and their families.

Fortunately, experience has apparently taught us that it is somehow easier for professionals to practice *role release* when working with infants and their families. Perhaps it is the obvious vulnerability of the child and family, or the absence of rigidly established turf. Whatever it is, we do have some success stories about cross-discipline cooperation, and if we can draw some general guidelines from these stories we will be in a position to guide future teams and case managers.

PERSONNEL PREPARATION

❑ Along with the new roles, we face the interesting question of how to prepare professionals, or perhaps paraprofessionals, for these roles. If we have cross-disciplinary or transdisciplinary responsibilities, then surely the training of such personnel should be transdisciplinary as well. This would seem to mean more than merely taking half of one's courses in the department of special education and half in the department of maternal and child health. It requires some type of general core discipline planning of that program for *developmental specialists*, a key part of which will be some type of practicum experience (Bailey et al., 1987).

A key part will be some type of practicum experience.

Perhaps our first task in designing such a program might be to interview, in depth, some of those who have been playing this *case manager* role in some of the existing demonstration programs to find out what special advantages and special problems exist for the appropriate execution of this role.

Universities have not often done well with programs that cut across departments or schools; that demon "professional turf," this time at the university level, is the major suspected culprit. A continuing issue is whether some general cross-discipline training ought not be a part of any professional preparation. Shouldn't school psychologists know what the pediatricians do and what their areas of special expertise are, for example? A seminar or course made up of modules describing each of these associated professions would be a desirable outcome, whether or not students taking the course intended to work with young children.

Nor should we forget the importance of on-site or inservice training. Many people who are currently providing services for young children need additional preparation on team operations, on the latest measures of assessment, or on work with families; such upgrading of talent cannot be ignored in favor of preprofessional training. A wholesome combination of both efforts needs to be embarked upon.

Nor should we forget on-site or inservice training.

THE FAMILY

❏ Interest in the young child with handicapping conditions has certainly spurred our interest in the family and its operation, since it clearly has such a powerful effect on the child (Robinson, Rosenberg, & Beckman, Chapter 5). For many years the family, in essence, really meant the mother, and the mother-child dyad was all that was considered, even in relatively sophisticated programs. During the past 5 years we have rediscovered the father and realized what an important direct and indirect role he plays in the total family system (Gallagher, Beckman, & Cross, 1983; Parke, 1986). We have also discovered that many fathers do not take increased interest in or responsibility for their handicapped child as we might have expected (Gallagher, Scharfman, & Bristol, 1984). So the exploration of appropriate ways of meeting family needs goes on, aided by a recent research emphasis on the topic (Gallagher, 1983; Strain, 1984).

Since the initiation of Project Head Start, there has been a deliberate effort made at the policy level to empower the parents, to give them some meaningful say in how their child is to be treated. In Head Start this was done with mandated advisory committees which had to have a certain proportion of members who were parents (Zigler, Kagan, & Klugman, 1983). In recent policy initiatives dealing with handicapped children, it took the form of the parents participating in the development of the individualized education program (IEP) for their child and signing off on the IEP itself. Provisions for due process were also included in much of

There has been a deliberate effort to empower parents.

The IFSP creates another challenge

the legislation, allowing parents to make effective protests if they felt that the massive bureaucracy of the public school was unfairly pressuring them to do things they did not want to do regarding their child (McNulty, 1987).

The individualized family service plan (IFSP) creates another challenge for professionals and parents. The underlying objective of the legislation that mandates such IFSPs is clear. The family is almost always a key component in the success of programs for children with handicaps, and such a mandate guarantees that the family will not be forgotten or ignored when the professionals devise their service plan.

On the other hand, such a mandate raises the potential problem of professionals trying to give treatment or services to parents whether they want them or not. This may be a problem particularly when the families are of one cultural background or social class and the professionals are of another, and a full understanding of the different cultural mores cannot be easily reached.

There is a fine line between helping families and interfering with family integrity and privacy.

In short, there is a fine line between helping the families of children with handicaps and interfering with family integrity and privacy. The mandate for an IFSP carries with it the prospect that more will be done with some families than the families themselves might wish and that they would trade off their privacy for treatment benefits for their children. Dokecki and Heflinger (1987) have pointed out that it seems self evident that family participation in either assessment or service delivery must remain optional, at the discretion of the family.

Turnbull and Turnbull (1986) presented the assumptions underlying parent participation in programs for handicapped children that (a) parents can and will want to participate, (b) parents can function as advocates to ensure the rights of their children, and (c) parents need and want training and counseling in order to continue the educational process at home. The Turnbulls pointed out that not all parents need or want to participate in this way and that there should be a range of parent involvement choices that recognizes the diversity of family interests and capabilities.

The message is diversity.

Again, the message is *diversity*: diversity of children, diversity of families, diversity of professionals, and diversity of settings. The regulations for such a program must be flexible to allow that diversity to express itself.

CHILD AND FAMILY ASSESSMENT

Legislation calls for evaluation.

As Hutinger covers well in Chapter 3, there are a variety of issues revolving around identification, screening, and assessment. As she points out, the legislation calls for "timely, comprehensive, and multidisciplinary evaluation"; each one of those adjectives requires attention.

Timely means that you have assigned sufficient staff to the effort and that you do not have a battery of instruments so extensive that you will spend the better part of a week trying to get them administered. *Comprehensive* means that you are trying to draw a total portrait of the child's development across sensory, motor, language, social, and cognitive avenues. But more than that, you must also provide "a statement of the family's strengths and needs relating to the enhancing of the child's development," so this requirement also must be factored into the total pattern of assessment.

The requirement for a Child Find program is another reminder of how comfortable it is, when the child is of school age, to work within the public school system. The public school requirements for compulsory schooling guarantee that the vast majority of the children you are interested in are where you can easily find and test them. In the case of infants and toddlers, community awareness needs to be aroused, and a number of professional disciplines need to be alerted.

The distinction between diagnosis and assessment is one worth making and defining. In a discipline such as medicine, diagnosis (the discovery of the cause of the condition) is often closely linked to the choice of treatment. Once you know the cause, you know what to do. In the area of developmental disorders that is not often the case. You need more than a diagnosis, you need an assessment. For example, the diagnosis may be deafness, but the assessment of the child must go on to find the strengths of the child and the status of his or her development so that a rational treatment program can be adopted. Fortunately, a number of instruments and procedures have been developed over the past few years, providing a rich source of assessment options, although the technical properties of such instruments often leave a good deal to be desired (Fewell, 1983; Simeonsson, 1986).

The distinction between diagnosis and assessment is worth making and defining.

The purpose of the assessment, then, is to provide information that can be incorporated into the goals and objectives of the treatment program. Bricker (1987) calls for a continuous assessment which would be done at periodic intervals to check on child progress. Depending upon the staff available, a periodic arena assessment, as noted earlier, would be highly desirable as an assessment strategy.

A periodic arena assessment would be highly desirable.

AT-RISK CHILDREN

❏ One of the more innovative concepts in the new legislation for infants and toddlers is the willingness of the sponsors to consider the concept of "at-risk" children. It recognizes the potentially constructive role that this legislation could play in *prevention* as well as in the amelioration of handicapping conditions and that many children are not necessarily destined to be identified as handicapped at birth or immediately following some disorganizing disease or disorder. The interaction of the environment and the child in influencing the future state of the child was noted by Sameroff and Chandler (1975); rigid definitions that insisted that services could go only to clearly diagnosed handicapped children often meant that children who could have profited immensely by professional services given early in their development were denied eligibility for such services.

What is left to individual states and communities, however, is the task of defining what is a "high-risk" child, and there are sure to be an interesting variety of answers to that question, unless there is some prior meeting of the minds by agency staff and professional groups. A highly significant question is whether "high risk" refers only to those infants and toddlers who have some biomedical problems that might develop into handicapping conditions or, on the other hand, high risk includes socioeconomic conditions. If so, then many if not most of the children growing up in poverty (and that represents an astonishingly high number of children in the United States) could be considered at high risk. Will the limited resources be watered down to try and deal with the prevention issue? Or will the at-risk group be put on the back burner until sufficient

Left to states and communities is the task of defining a "high-risk" child.

funds are forthcoming? This represents another major policy issue, with a negative consequence no matter which option is chosen, and is far from being resolved at this writing.

PROGRAM ADMINISTRATION

❏ Of the challenges and issues mandated by the new legislation, the area of program administration surely has at least its share, as is amply pointed out in Chapter 2 by Garland and Linder. The state agency that wins the responsibility of being the lead agency in this program has a plethora of challenging tasks including defining financial responsibility for it and other agencies, playing broker to local providers of services, and establishing local safeguards of confidentiality. At the same time, it must set up effective tracking systems, oversee the assignment of surrogate parents when necessary, establish the procedures of due process, settle disagreements between families and professionals, establish policies on personnel training including certification and licensing standards, and oversee the development of standards for IFSPs. By the fifth year of the program, the state must assure that the system is in effect and that full services are available to all eligible children. The leadership personnel of the lead agency might be forgiven for feeling that they have been handed a sack full of angry cats.

The lead agency has challenging tasks.

Fortunately, precedents exist in all of these dimensions, from personnel training to due process to establishing financial responsibility. The hard lessons learned through the implementation of P.L. 94-142 can now be put to use in dealing with this call for new standards and regulations. In each instance, a slightly new twist or adaption will have to be made; the IFSP is not the same as the IEP, and certification of personnel in this multidisciplinary realm is not the same as certification in a clearly defined area such as public education. Nevertheless, we have a right to expect that resolutions of these problems can be achieved because similar resolutions have been attained before.

Lessons learned in implementing P.L. 94-142 can be put to use.

PROGRAM EVALUATION

❏ The investment of large sums of federal money almost inevitably brings calls for accountability, which, in turn, brings up the topic of program evaluation. Public decision makers are basically interested in the answers to two major questions. First, did the resources that were allocated to the purpose of the legislation get delivered to the proper parties in a timely and effective way? This question calls for careful record keeping in order that the number of children served, the types of children served, who served them, and how much it cost can be tracked. In short, *did the money and resources get delivered*?

Did the money and resources get delivered?

The second question poses a much more serious set of technical problems for the various professions to solve. Given that the services were delivered, *did they do the clients any good*? Are there demonstrable improvements in the child or in the family as a result of this investment? The insistence on an answer to that question has spawned the development of program evaluation methodology and tools in a number of relevant professions.

Did they do the clients any good?

Program evaluation has been referred to as the "spinach of education." It is nutritious and good for you, but no one really likes it, and many will try to avoid it whenever possible. Thus, even though its value is manifest, evaluation almost has to be mandated before it will be implemented on a large scale.

Many evaluations have been done with insufficient attention to what actually happened in the program; often, inappropriate tools are used, giving a wrong or incomplete picture of program impact. One common fault is to administer a measure of cognitive development to a child at one time and then repeat the administration at a later time during the program. The pattern of development of cognitive abilities has proved to be resistant to change under the best of circumstances, and a severely handicapped child is not the best client for such change (Gallagher & Ramey, 1987).

Inappropriate tools are used.

Chapter 9, by Larry Johnson, makes it clear that there are many developing procedures and complex measurement issues that accompany a good evaluation program. Furthermore, the data collected from the evaluation should not only be useful for some outside person to judge the effectiveness of the program (summative evaluation), but should also provide information so that the professionals directly involved in the program can see their own strengths and weaknesses and so be able to improve their own performances (formative evaluation).

Perhaps the most outstanding need in this area is to develop better methods and more sensitive tools to measure change. It is not uncommon to find that clients are effusive in their praise of a program and will state in some detail how it has been helpful, only to find that the tests or instruments used to measure this change "objectively" show that no major difference has occurred. When this has happened in the past, one common interpretation has been that the clients have misperceived the situation. However, there is a growing suspicion that the explanation may be just the reverse. That is, real change has taken place and is being faithfully reported by the client, but our instruments have not been sensitive enough to report it accurately.

Develop better methods and more sensitive tools to measure change.

In the end we *must* answer that second question, did we do anybody any good? It does not matter if we throw the entire resources of our medical school or university behind the program if, in the end, we are not able to show that somebody, somewhere, has changed their understanding, social skills, motor abilities, emotional status, in a positive direction as a result of our efforts.

SUMMARY

❑ This major exercise in public policy, the passage of P.L. 99-457, the Education of the Handicapped Act Amendments of 1986, provides the professional community with a striking opportunity. Essentially, public policy determines the priorities for the allocation of scarce resources in our society and is a testimony to the beginning of a commitment of the federal government to provide resources for young children with handicapping conditions and their families. Chapter 10 by Barbara Smith, makes it clear that this initiative is not a brand new idea but has a history of over 20 years in the making. This mandate for service to all handicapped children from birth up was preceded by more limited initiatives such as the "set-aside" for young handicapped children in the

This initiative is not a brand new idea.

Head Start program, by preschool incentive grants in P.L. 94-142, and by various pieces of legislation that provided authority for demonstration and model programs, professional preparation, and research.

This law, then, is the final step in the long road to achieving what professionals have dreamed about for many years, the provision of services to children with handicaps at a developmental age where treatment might have its maximum effect in helping the child and family adapt to the handicap or even prevent the handicap from developing in more serious form.

Paradoxically, it also provides us with an unparalleled opportunity to fall flat on our collective faces, demonstrating for all the world to see that we cannot work together without invoking our professional pride, and that we cannot solve the laundry list of issues that is presented to us. Certainly there are enough problems and issues to satisfy anyone looking for a challenge. In each major dimension of this proposed service delivery system there are major obstacles to deal with, from assessment, to tracking, to developing a family plan, to confidentiality, to the concept of case manager, to the effective use of professional teams, to effective evaluation, and finally, to adequate financing.

There are enough problems and issues to satisfy anyone looking for a challenge.

We are going to need a large supply of patience, tolerance for ambiguity, and trust in the good will and intentions of our colleagues and of the many players who have a role in the development of these programs. The journals, national conferences, and special topical conferences will be major vehicles for trying out new ideas about professional teamwork and service delivery to this population. It may well be that we will need to keep a mental picture in front of us of a young girl with cerebral palsy curled up in a spastic semicircle in her crib, or an autistic boy staring at something only he can see, or an infant with sensory avenues impaired and motor skills uncertain, so that when the implementation of this effort becomes frustrating and difficult, as it surely will at times, we will remember why we are doing what we are doing, and for whom we are doing it.

We need patience, tolerance for ambiguity, and trust.

REFERENCES

Bailey, D., Simeonsson, R., Isbell, P., Huntington, G., Winton, P., Comfort, M., & Helin, J. (in press). Inservice training in family assessment and goal setting for early interventionists: Outcomes and issues. *Journal of the Division for Early Childhood.*

Bricker, D. (1987). Impact of research on social policy for handicapped infants and children. *Journal of the Division for Early Childhood, 11*(2), 98-105.

Dokecki, P., & Heflenger, C. (1987, April). *Strengthening families of young children with handicapping conditions: Mapping backward from the "street level" pursuant to effective implementation of Public Law 99-457.* Paper presented at Bush Institute for Child and Family Policy Conference, Chapel Hill, NC.

Fewell, R. (1983). Assessing handicapped infants. In S. Garwood & R. Fewell (Eds.), *Education of handicapped infants: Issues in development and interventions.* Rockville, MD: Aspen.

Gallagher, J. (1983). The Carolina Institute for Research: Early education for the handicapped. *Journal of the Division for Early Childhood, 7,* 18-24.

Gallagher, J., Beckman, P., & Cross, A. (1983). Families of handicapped children: Sources of stress and its amelioration. *Exceptional Children, 50*(1), 10-19.

Gallagher, J., Cross, A., & Scharfman, W. (1981). Parental adaptation to a young handicapped child: The father's role. *Journal of the Division for Early Childhood, 3,* 3-14.

Gallagher, J., & Ramey, C. (Eds.). (1987). *The malleability of children.* Baltimore, MD: Paul Brookes Co.

Gallagher, J., Scharfman, W., & Bristol, M. (1984). The division of responsibilities in families with preschool handicapped and nonhandicapped children. *Journal of the Division for Early Childhood, 8*(1), 3-11.

Martin, E. (1987, April). *Lessons from implementing public law 94-142.* Paper presented at Bush Institute for Child and Family Policy Conference, Chapel Hill, NC.

McNulty, B. (1987, April). *Leadership policy strategies for interagency planning: Meeting the early childhood mandate.* Paper presented at Bush Institute for Child and Family Policy Conference, Chapel Hill, NC.

Parke, R. (1986). Fathers, families, and support systems: Their role in the development of at-risk and retarded infants and children. In J. Gallagher & P. Vietze (Eds.), *Families of handicapped persons* (pp. 101-113). Baltimore, MD: Paul Brookes Co.

Sameroff, A., & Chandler, M. (1975). Reproductive risk and the continuum of caretaking casualty. In F. Horowitz, E. Heatherington, S. Scarr-Salapatek, & G. Segal (Eds.), *Review of child development research* (pp. 187-244). Chicago: University of Chicago Press.

Simeonsson, R. (1986). *Psychological and developmental assessment of special children.* Boston, MA: Allyn & Bacon.

Strain, P. (1984). Efficacy research with young handicapped children: A critique of the status quo. *Journal of the Division for Early Childhood, 9*(1), 11-26.

Turnbull, A., & Turnbull, H. (1986). *Families, professionals and exceptionality: A special partnership.* Columbus, OH: Merrill Publishing Company.

Zigler, E., Kagan, S., & Klugman, E. (Eds.). (1983). *Children, families, & government.* Cambridge: Cambridge University Press.

Contributors

Paula J. Beckman is Associate Professor of Special Education at the University of Maryland, College Park. She has worked with at-risk and handicapped infants and their families for over 10 years. Beckman is currently involved in longitudinal research concerned wtih families of at-risk, handicapped, and chronically ill infants. She also directs personnel preparation activities for students interested in intervention with handicapped infants and preschoolers at the University of Maryland.

James J. Gallagher is Kenan Professor of Education and Psychology at the University of North Carolina at Chapel Hill and a senior investigator at the Frank Porter Graham Child Development Center at the same university. Prior to that he directed the Bureau of Education for the Handicapped in the U.S. Office of Education and was Professor of Education at the Institute for Research on Exceptional Children at the University of Illinois. For 17 years he directed the Frank Porter Graham Child Development Center, a major research center that has focused on early development of young children and their relationships within the family unit. For the past 10 years he has directed the Carolina Institute for Research on Early Education for the Handicapped (CIREEH) which studied the effects of having a handicapped child on the family unit and studied various efforts to modify and improve the relationships between professionals and families. He also established TADS (Technical Assistance Development Center) which has provided major technical assistance to the Handicapped Children Early Education Program for 15 years. Gallagher has authored or edited several books and numerous articles relevant to the early childhood area as well as books on public policy, education of gifted children, and education of exceptional children.

Corinne W. Garland has been an administrator of early intervention programs in the public and private sectors. She currently serves as Executive Director of Child Development Resources (CDR) in Lightfoot, Virginia. CDR is a private, nonprofit agency providing services for young children with special needs and their families, and training and technical assistance for the professionals who serve them. CDR's transdisciplinary early intervention model has been widely replicated. Garland directs CDR's Early Intervention Institutes and CDR's federally funded projects which assist states in the collaborative planning process and provide individualized training and technical assistance to local early intervention programs. She is President of the International Division for Early Childhood of The Council for Exceptional Children and is a member of Virginia's Interagency Coordinating Council.

Mary-alayne Hughes is a speech/language pathologist whose experience has included working with children in both elementary school (K-5) and early childhood special education preschool settings. She is currently a doctoral candidate in the Department of Special Education at the University of Illinois, Champaign. Her research interests include the team process as well as family involvement in early intervention.

Patricia L. Hutinger is Professor of Early Childhood at Western Illinois University, Macomb. She directs the Macomb Projects, a group of projects which since 1975 have focused on improving the quality of services to young handicapped children and their families through personnel training; preparation of training materials, including videotapes; and dissemination of intervention modules. The projects focus on the birth-through-3-year-old special needs population and the use of microcomputer technology with the handicapped. Projects include Outreach: Macomb 0-3 Rural Project; Project ACTT (Activating Children Through Technology) Outreach; the WIU 0-3 Personnel Project; and a special project, Microcomputer Applications Training Modules. Hutinger has also been closely involved with birth-to-three planning groups in Illinois and other states. She conducted a study of the state of the art of programs for handicapped infants in addition to the state of the art of programs for 3- to 5-year-olds in Illinois.

Lawrence J. Johnson is Associate Professor and Chairperson of Early Childhood Education of the Handicapped at The University of Alabama, Tuscaloosa. In the past, he has served as a project evaluator or codirector, with project evaluation responsibilities, of over 10 externally funded projects. He is currently directing or codirecting the following externally funded projects: two training projects, one to train supervisors of early childhood special education programs, and one offering field-based opportunities for teachers in early childhood special education programs to become appropriately certified; two research projects, one to examine methods to facilitate the ability of general educators to accommodate the needs of students with mild learning and behavior problems, and one to evaluate the provision of services to children and their families with special needs under the age of 5 within Alabama; and an early childhood special education technical assistance center. He has been an evaluation consultant to the states of Alabama and Illinois and currently serves on the Research Committee of the Division for Early Childhood and the Research Task Force of the Teacher Education Division of The Council for Exceptional Children.

Merle B. Karnes is Professor in the Departments of Special Education and Elementary Education/Early Childhood, University of Illinois, Champaign. She directs a number of federal, state, and locally funded projects addressing the needs of young children (0 through 6) who are handicapped, from low income homes, at-risk for academic failure, and/or gifted. A strong component of these projects is a systems approach to family involvement. Since 1976, Karnes has directed one of the 10 federally funded Resource Access Projects (RAPs) whose charge it is to provide resources and training to Head Start personnel in effectively mainstreaming handicapped children. Since 1970, she has developed several model programs for handicapped children and their parents. One such model, PEECH (Precise Early Education for Children with Handicaps), is being replicated in over 175 sites in 36 states. Currently she is involved in developing a demonstration model entitled ALLIANCE which focuses on helping parents become more effective in utilizing resources and advocating for their young handicapped children. Her major curriculum publication for infants is *Small Wonder* which includes two parent manuals and addresses the needs of infants through 24 months. She has done ground-breaking work in identifying and programming more appropriately for young gifted children, especially the gifted/talented handicapped and those from low income homes.

Toni W. Linder is Associate Professor and Coordinator of Early Childhood Special Education at the University of Denver, Colorado. She has been the director of a program serving handicapped children, birth through 18 years of age. She is the author of *Early Childhood Special Education: Program Development and Administration* and is currently writing a book on transdisciplinary play-based assessment of young children.

Jeanette A. McCollum is Associate Professor of Special Education at the University of Illinois, Champaign. She coordinates the personnel preparation program in Early Childhood Special Education, which prepares teachers for public school settings serving 3- to 5-year-olds as well as personnel from a variety of disciplines interested in the birth-through-3-year-old population. McCollum's primary research interests are related to personnel preparation and to interactions between infants and their caregivers. She is active in the development of state and federal policy related to Early Childhood Special Education, particularly that having to do with personnel preparation.

Mary J. McGonigel is Family-Centered Care Project Coordinator at the Association for the Care of Children's Health in Washington, D.C. Her work since 1979 has focused on models and practices to enable and empower families of children with special needs in their interactions with the professionals who serve them. Among her experiences have been coordinating federal transition and transdisciplinary training projects. She has also been a technical assistance coordinator with the former Technical Assistance Development Systems (TADS) at the Frank Porter Graham Child Development Center, University of North Carolina at Chapel Hill. She has been on the executive board of INTERACT for several years and is currently President. INTERACT is a national organization for professionals who work with special needs young children and their families.

Eva K. Thorp is Assistant Professor of Special Education at the University of Illinois, Champaign. She is a faculty member in the Early Childhood Special Education program, where she has been involved in developing a practicum model for acquiring interdisciplinary parent-infant intervention skills. Thorp's other personnel preparation activities have included developing videotapes and training materials for infant service providers as a part of Project Year One, and directing a university-based parent-professional training program. Her research interests relate to parents' adaptations to caring for chronically ill and handicapped young children and to interdisciplinary teams.

Cordelia C. Robinson is Professor of Special Education and Director of the Human Development Center at Winthrop College, Rock Hill, South Carolina. For the previous 15 years she was Associate Professor of Nursing, University of Nebraska College of Nursing, and Director of Special Education at Meyer Children's Rehabilitation Institute, University of Nebraska Medical Center, Omaha. At the Meyer Children's Rehabilitation Institute she directed a number of federal and state funded demonstration and research projects serving young handicapped children and their parents. Research in collaboration with Steven Rosenberg has involved the development of a tool to examine parent-child interaction in the context of parent-mediated intervention. She has also written extensively on assessment of young handicapped children with particular emphasis upon use of Piagetian sensorimotor scales for assessment and design of intervention strategies. She is currently on the National Advisory Committee for the National Early Childhood Technical Assistance System and the Infant Personnel Preparation Institute, both projects at the University of North Carolina at Chapel Hill.

Steven A. Rosenberg is Associate Professor of Psychology and Director of Project Participate, a Handicapped Children's Early Education Program (HCEEP), at the University of Nebraska at Omaha. In addition he maintains a private practice serving families and children. For the past 12 years he has directed a number of demonstration and research projects addressing the needs of young handicapped children and their families. This work has focused on the prediction of parent involvement in parent-mediated instruction and the development of the Teaching Skills Inventory. Most recently his work has addressed the uses of technology to facilitate participation by young physically disabled children in their educational programs.

Barbara J. Smith is a national consultant in state and federal early childhood public policy development. She received her master's degree in early childhood special education and her doctorate in special education with an emphasis in public policy at the University of North Carolina at Chapel Hill. She worked with the Governmental Relations Department of The Council for Exceptional Children's (CEC) national headquarters for 6 years where she was involved in federal and state special education legislative activities. Smith has written many articles and monographs on early childhood policy and made over 100 presentations. Recently, she played an active role in developing the early childhood provision of P.L. 99-457, the Education of the Handicapped Act Amendments of 1986, and has provided consultation to many states in their efforts to develop effective early childhood state policies.

Vicki D. Stayton is Associate Professor in Early Childhood Special Education at Eastern Illinois University, Charleston. Her research and writing interests include family involvement, parent-infant interaction, and personnel preparation. She has served as a consultant to HCEEP Outreach projects and direct service programs in the areas of family assessment and family services. Stayton has also previously directed/ coordinated an HCEEP Outreach project and a state-funded birth-to-three project.

Pascal L. Trohanis is Director of the National Early Childhood Technical Assistance System (NEC*TAS) at the Frank Porter Graham Child Development Center, University of North Carolina at Chapel Hill. This project supports the planning, development, and implementation of the early childhood initiatives of P.L. 99-457 for all states, the District of Columbia, the Bureau of Indian Affairs, and eight territorial jurisdictions. Additionally, NEC*TAS provides assistance to the Handicapped Children's Early Education Program and other parent and professional groups. Trohanis has written articles on technical assistance, state planning, and public awareness. Also, he has provided consultation and workshops for state and local program personnel involved with services to young children with special needs and their families.

Geneva Woodruff is Director of Project KAI and Project WIN, two HCEEP programs federally funded under the auspices of the U.S. Department of Education, Office of Special Education and Rehabilitation. Project KAI is a national training program which provides training and technical assistance in the transdisciplinary and transagency service delivery model to early intervention and early childhood teams. Project WIN is a Boston-based direct service program for children under the age of 6 who are at risk or diagnosed with AIDS and their IV drug-using families. Woodruff is the founder of the Children with AIDS Network, which is an organization for medical, social service, allied health, and education professionals working in research and direct service with HIV infected children and their families. Advocates and family members are also members of the Children with AIDS Network.